THE UNCANNY AVENGERS

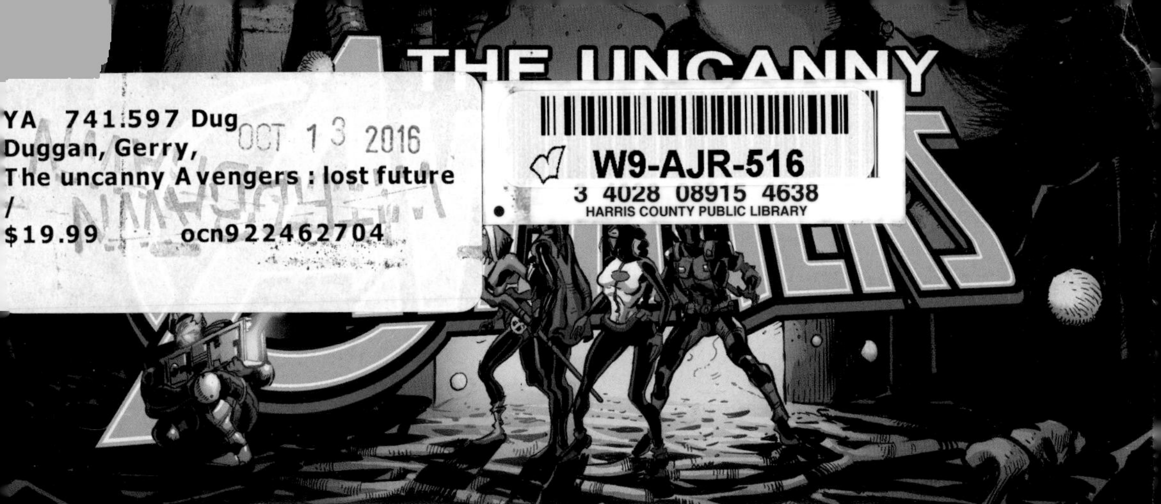

LOST FUTURE

GERRY DUGGAN
WRITER

DEADPOOL IN
"THE NIGHT THAT HELL FROZE OVER"
(FROM AVENGERS #0)

ARTIST: **RYAN STEGMAN**
COLOR ARTIST: **RICHARD ISANOVE**

UNCANNY AVENGERS #1-4

ARTIST: **RYAN STEGMAN**
COLOR ARTIST: **RICHARD ISANOVE**
COVER ART: **RYAN STEGMAN & RICHARD ISANOVE**

UNCANNY AVENGERS #5-6

PENCILER: **CARLOS PACHECO**

INKER: **MARIANO TAIBO** (#5-6),
DAVE MEIKIS (#5-6) & **SCOTT HANNA** (#6)

COLOR ARTIST: **RICHARD ISANOVE** (#5-6)
& ANTONIO FABELA (#6)

COVER ART: **YASMIN PUTRI** (#5) AND **CARLOS PACHECO,
MARIANO TAIBO & SONIA OBACK** (#6)

VC'S CLAYTON COWLES
LETTERER

ALANNA SMITH
ASSISTANT EDITOR

TOM BREVOORT WITH **DANIEL KETCHUM**
EDITORS

AVENGERS CREATED BY **STAN LEE & JACK KIRBY**

COLLECTION EDITOR: **JENNIFER GRÜNWALD**
ASSOCIATE EDITOR: **SARAH BRUNSTAD**
ASSOCIATE MANAGING EDITOR: **ALEX STARBUCK**
EDITOR, SPECIAL PROJECTS: **MARK D. BEAZLEY**

VP, PRODUCTION & SPECIAL PROJECTS: **JEFF YOUNGQUIST**
SVP PRINT, SALES & MARKETING: **DAVID GABRIEL**
BOOK DESIGNER: **JAY BOWEN**

EDITOR IN CHIEF: **AXEL ALONSO**
CHIEF CREATIVE OFFICER: **JOE QUESADA**
PUBLISHER: **DAN BUCKLEY**
EXECUTIVE PRODUCER: **ALAN FINE**

NY AVENGERS: UNITY VOL. 1 — LOST FUTURE. Contains material originally published in magazine form as UNCANNY AVENGERS #1-6 and AVENGERS #0. First printing 2016. ISBN# 978-0-7851-9615-0. Published by MARVEL WIDE, INC., a subsidiary of MARVEL ENTERTAINMENT, LLC. OFFICE OF PUBLICATION: 135 West 50th Street, New York, NY 10020. Copyright © 2016 MARVEL No similarity between any of the names, characters, persons, and/or ions in this magazine with those of any living or dead person or institution is intended, and any such similarity which may exist is purely coincidental. **Printed in the U.S.A.** ALAN FINE, President, Marvel Entertainment; DAN BUCKLEY, nt, TV, Publishing & Brand Management; JOE QUESADA, Chief Creative Officer; TOM BREVOORT, SVP of Publishing; DAVID BOGART, SVP of Business Affairs & Operations, Publishing & Partnership; C.B. CEBULSKI, VP of Brand Management opment, Asia; DAVID GABRIEL, SVP of Sales & Marketing, Publishing; JEFF YOUNGQUIST, VP of Production & Special Projects; DAN CARR, Executive Director of Publishing Technology; ALEX MORALES, Director of Publishing Operations; CRESPI, Production Manager; STAN LEE, Chairman Emeritus. For information regarding advertising in Marvel Comics or on Marvel.com, please contact Vit DeBellis, Integrated Sales Manager, at vdebellis@marvel.com. For Marvel otion inquiries, please call 888-511-5480. **Manufactured between 2/19/2016 and 3/28/2016 by R.R. Donnelley, INC., SALEM, VA, USA.**

654321

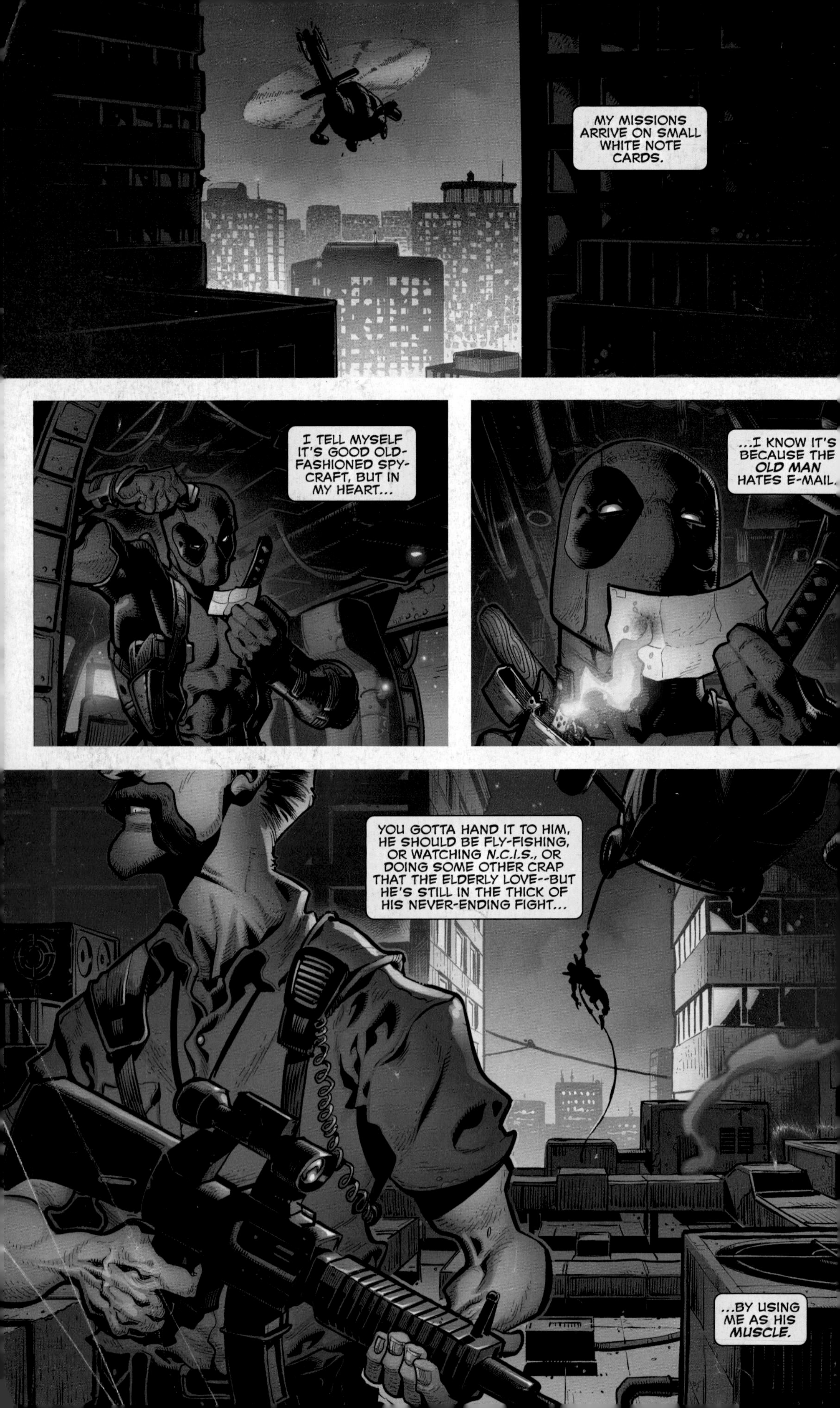
MY MISSIONS ARRIVE ON SMALL WHITE NOTE CARDS.
I TELL MYSELF IT'S GOOD OLD-FASHIONED SPY-CRAFT, BUT IN MY HEART...
...I KNOW IT'S BECAUSE THE *OLD MAN* HATES E-MAIL.
YOU GOTTA HAND IT TO HIM, HE SHOULD BE FLY-FISHING, OR WATCHING *N.C.I.S.*, OR DOING SOME OTHER CRAP THAT THE ELDERLY LOVE--BUT HE'S STILL IN THE THICK OF HIS NEVER-ENDING FIGHT...
...BY USING ME AS HIS *MUSCLE*.

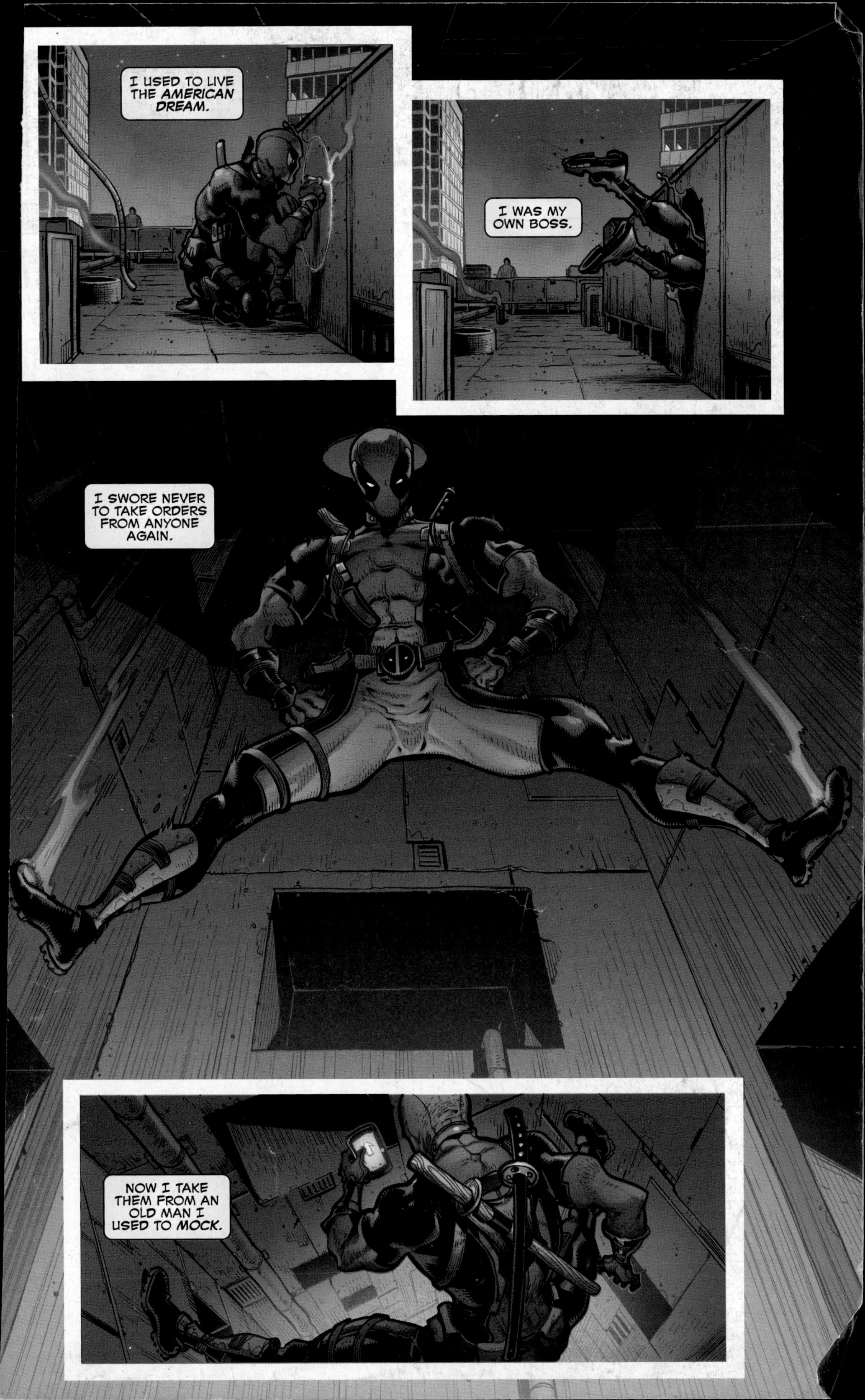
I USED TO LIVE THE AMERICAN DREAM.
I WAS MY OWN BOSS.
I SWORE NEVER TO TAKE ORDERS FROM ANYONE AGAIN.
NOW I TAKE THEM FROM AN OLD MAN I USED TO MOCK.

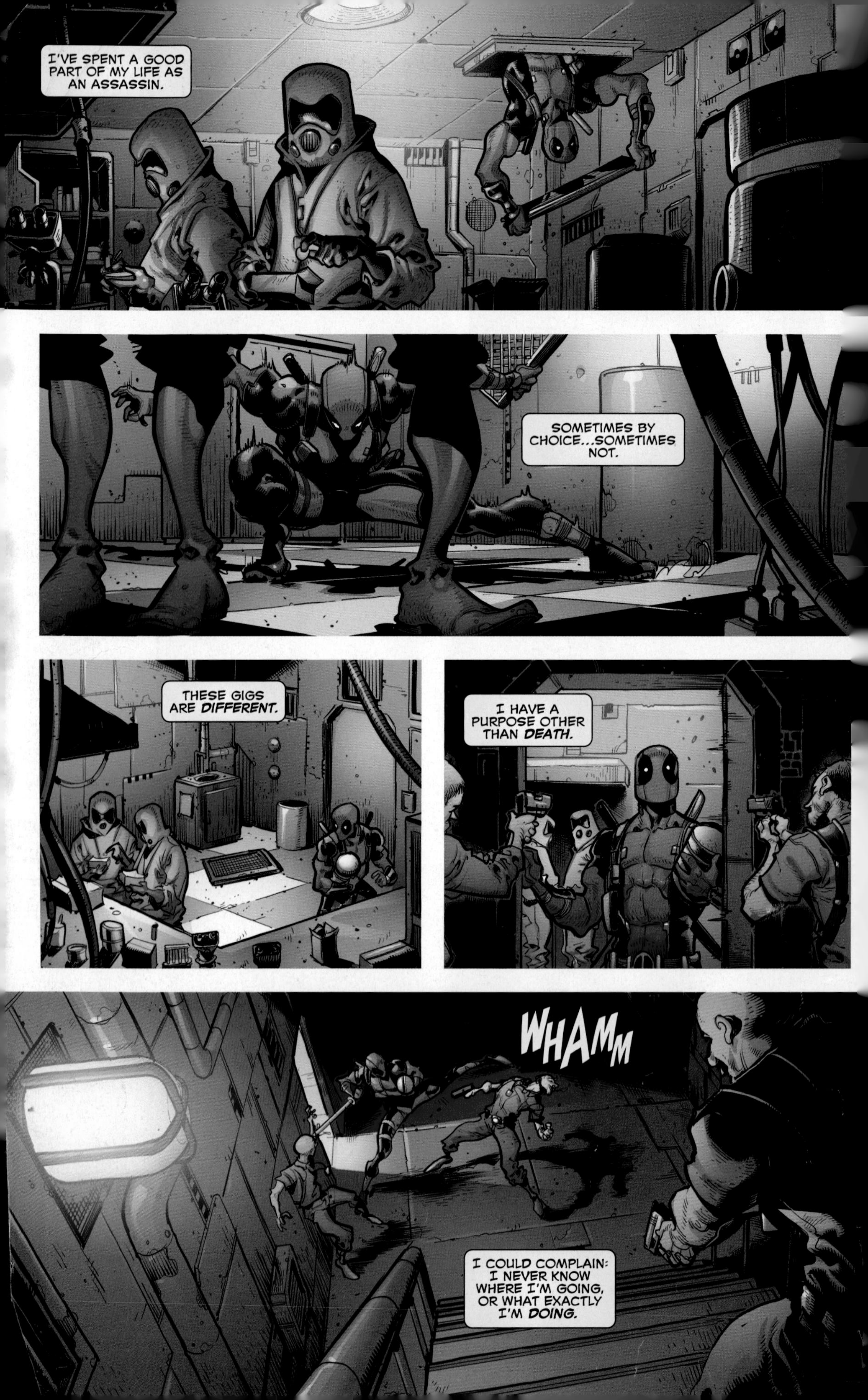
I'VE SPENT A GOOD PART OF MY LIFE AS AN ASSASSIN.
SOMETIMES BY CHOICE...SOMETIMES NOT.
THESE GIGS ARE *DIFFERENT.*
I HAVE A PURPOSE OTHER THAN *DEATH.*
WHAMM
I COULD COMPLAIN: I NEVER KNOW WHERE I'M GOING, OR WHAT EXACTLY I'M *DOING.*

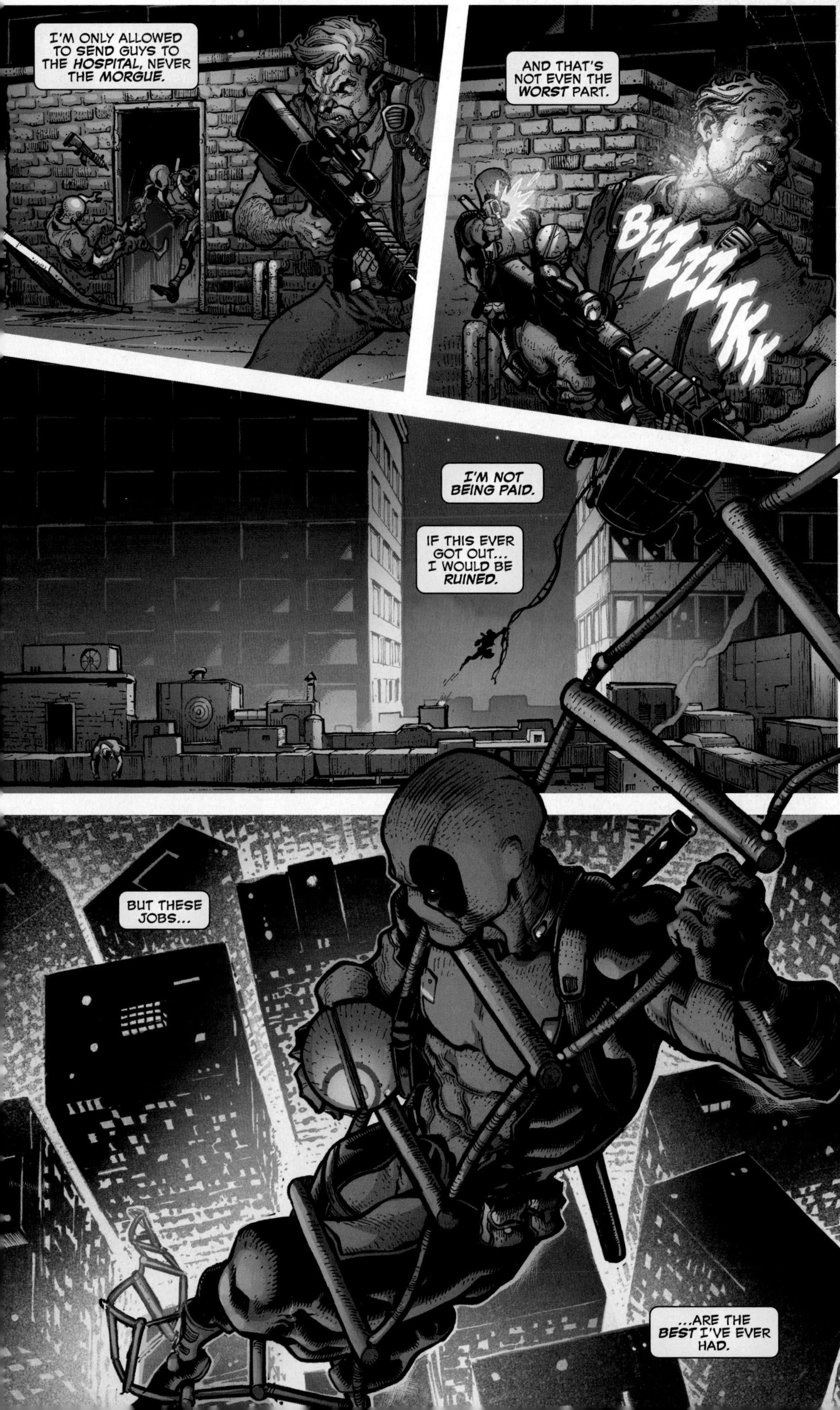
I'M ONLY ALLOWED TO SEND GUYS TO THE *HOSPITAL*, NEVER THE *MORGUE*.
AND THAT'S NOT EVEN THE *WORST* PART.
BZZZZZTKK
I'M NOT BEING PAID.
IF THIS EVER GOT OUT... I WOULD BE *RUINED*.
BUT THESE JOBS...
...ARE THE *BEST* I'VE EVER HAD.

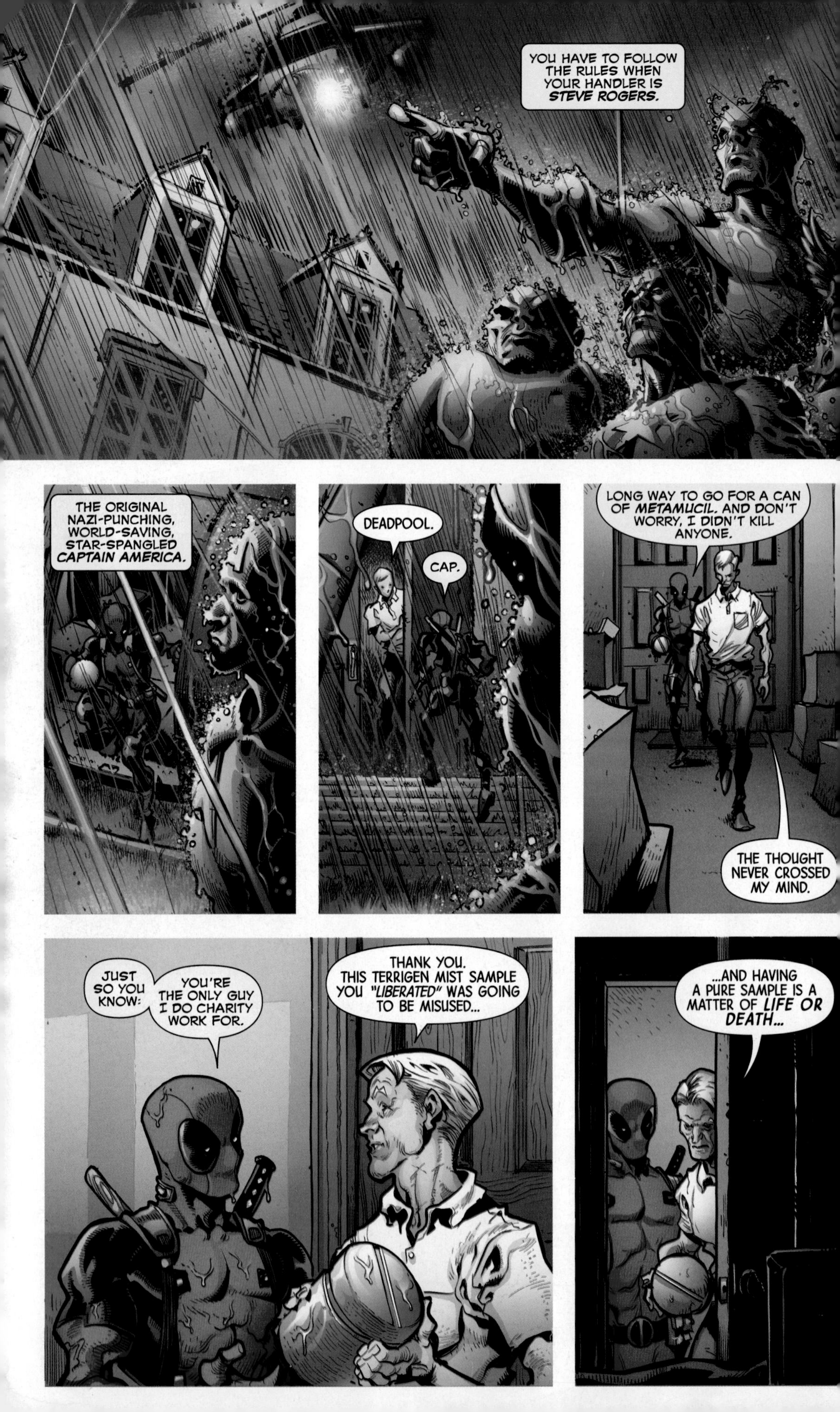
YOU HAVE TO FOLLOW THE RULES WHEN YOUR HANDLER IS STEVE ROGERS.
THE ORIGINAL NAZI-PUNCHING, WORLD-SAVING, STAR-SPANGLED CAPTAIN AMERICA.
DEADPOOL.
CAP.
LONG WAY TO GO FOR A CAN OF METAMUCIL. AND DON'T WORRY, I DIDN'T KILL ANYONE.
THE THOUGHT NEVER CROSSED MY MIND.
JUST SO YOU KNOW:
YOU'RE THE ONLY GUY I DO CHARITY WORK FOR.
THANK YOU. THIS TERRIGEN MIST SAMPLE YOU "LIBERATED" WAS GOING TO BE MISUSED...
...AND HAVING A PURE SAMPLE IS A MATTER OF LIFE OR DEATH...

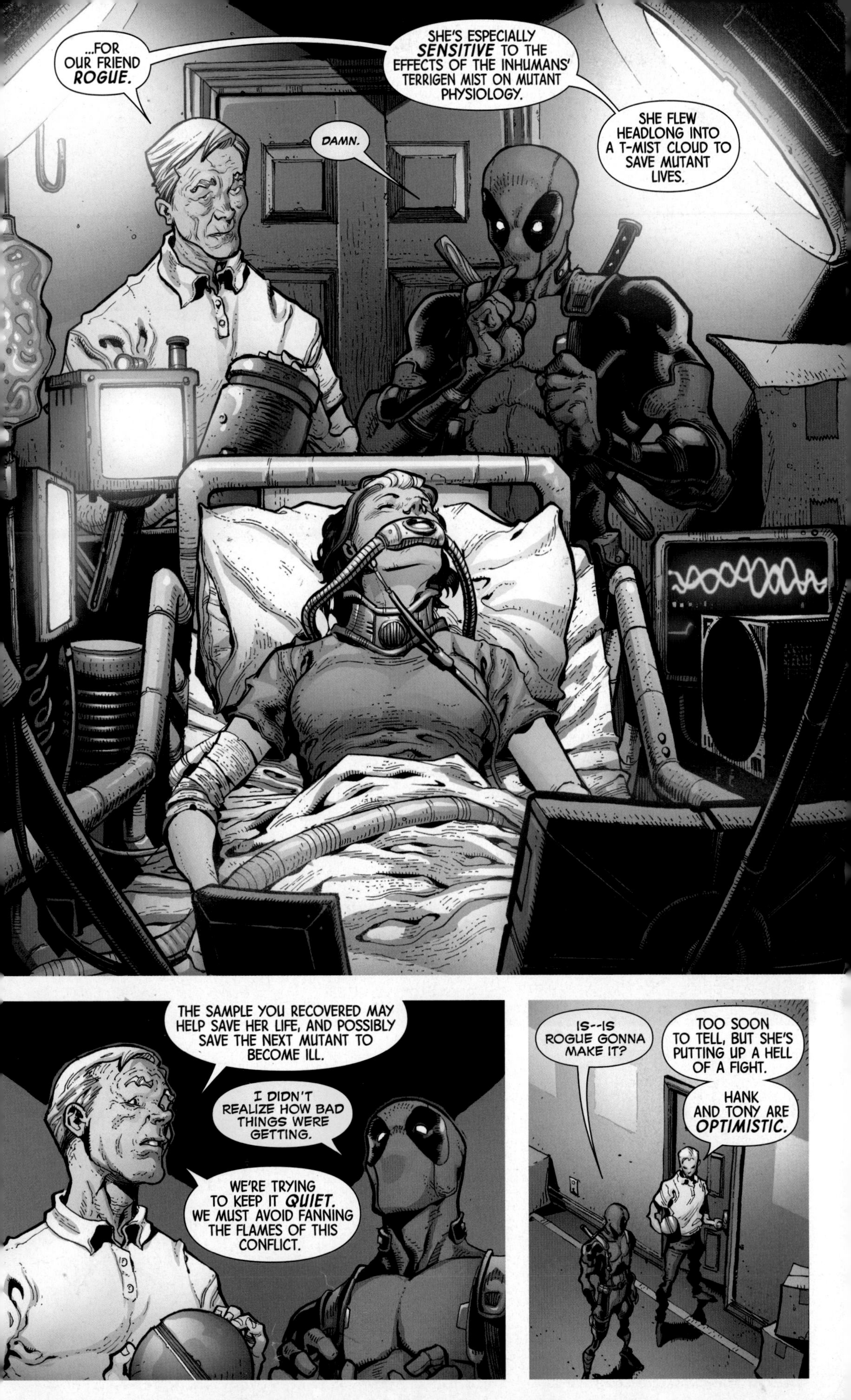
...FOR OUR FRIEND ROGUE.
SHE'S ESPECIALLY SENSITIVE TO THE EFFECTS OF THE INHUMANS' TERRIGEN MIST ON MUTANT PHYSIOLOGY.
DAMN.
SHE FLEW HEADLONG INTO A T-MIST CLOUD TO SAVE MUTANT LIVES.
THE SAMPLE YOU RECOVERED MAY HELP SAVE HER LIFE, AND POSSIBLY SAVE THE NEXT MUTANT TO BECOME ILL.
I DIDN'T REALIZE HOW BAD THINGS WERE GETTING.
WE'RE TRYING TO KEEP IT QUIET. WE MUST AVOID FANNING THE FLAMES OF THIS CONFLICT.
IS--IS ROGUE GONNA MAKE IT?
TOO SOON TO TELL, BUT SHE'S PUTTING UP A HELL OF A FIGHT.
HANK AND TONY ARE OPTIMISTIC.

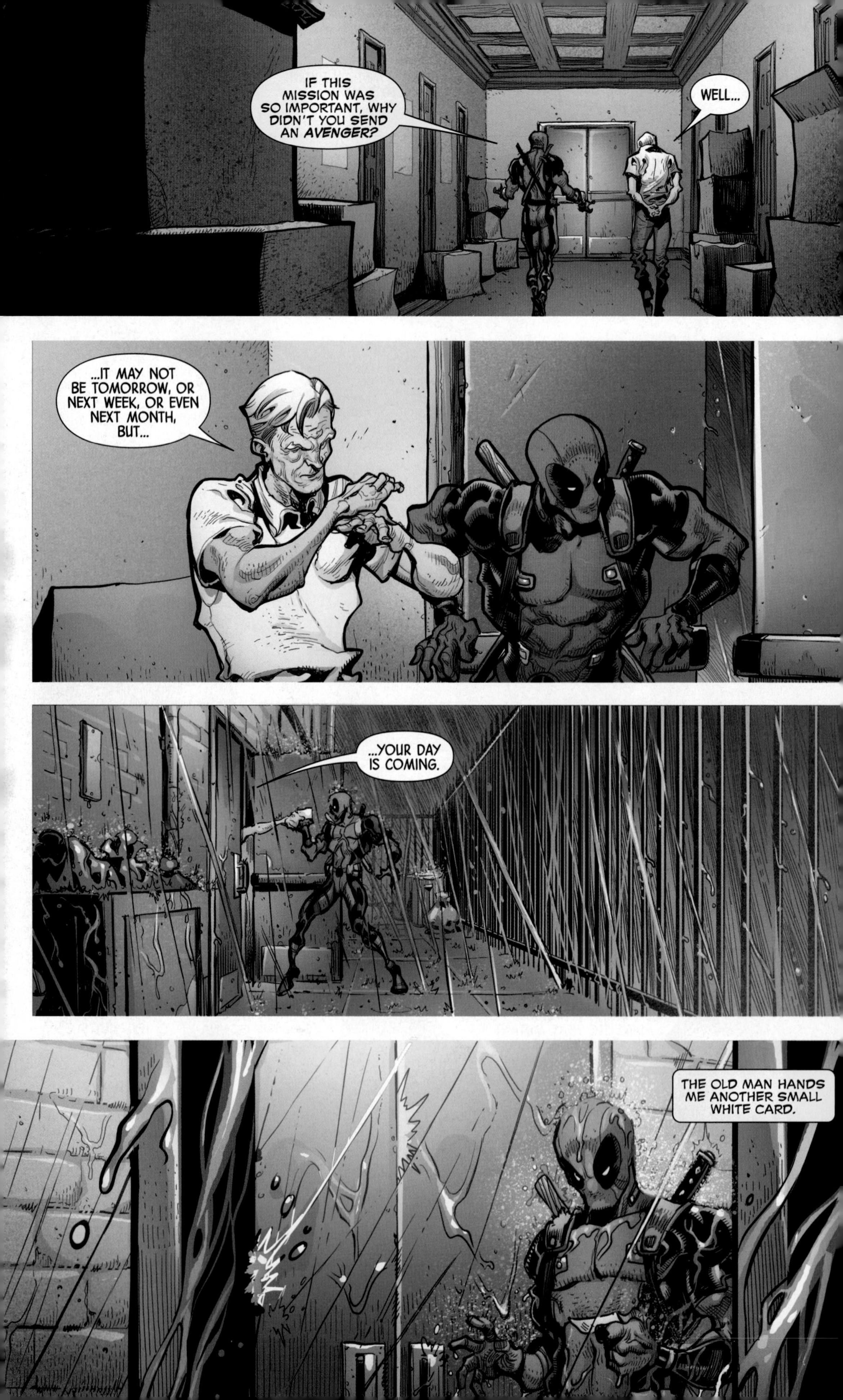
IF THIS MISSION WAS SO IMPORTANT, WHY DIDN'T YOU SEND AN *AVENGER?*
WELL...
...IT MAY NOT BE TOMORROW, OR NEXT WEEK, OR EVEN NEXT MONTH, BUT...
...YOUR DAY IS COMING.
THE OLD MAN HANDS ME ANOTHER SMALL WHITE CARD.

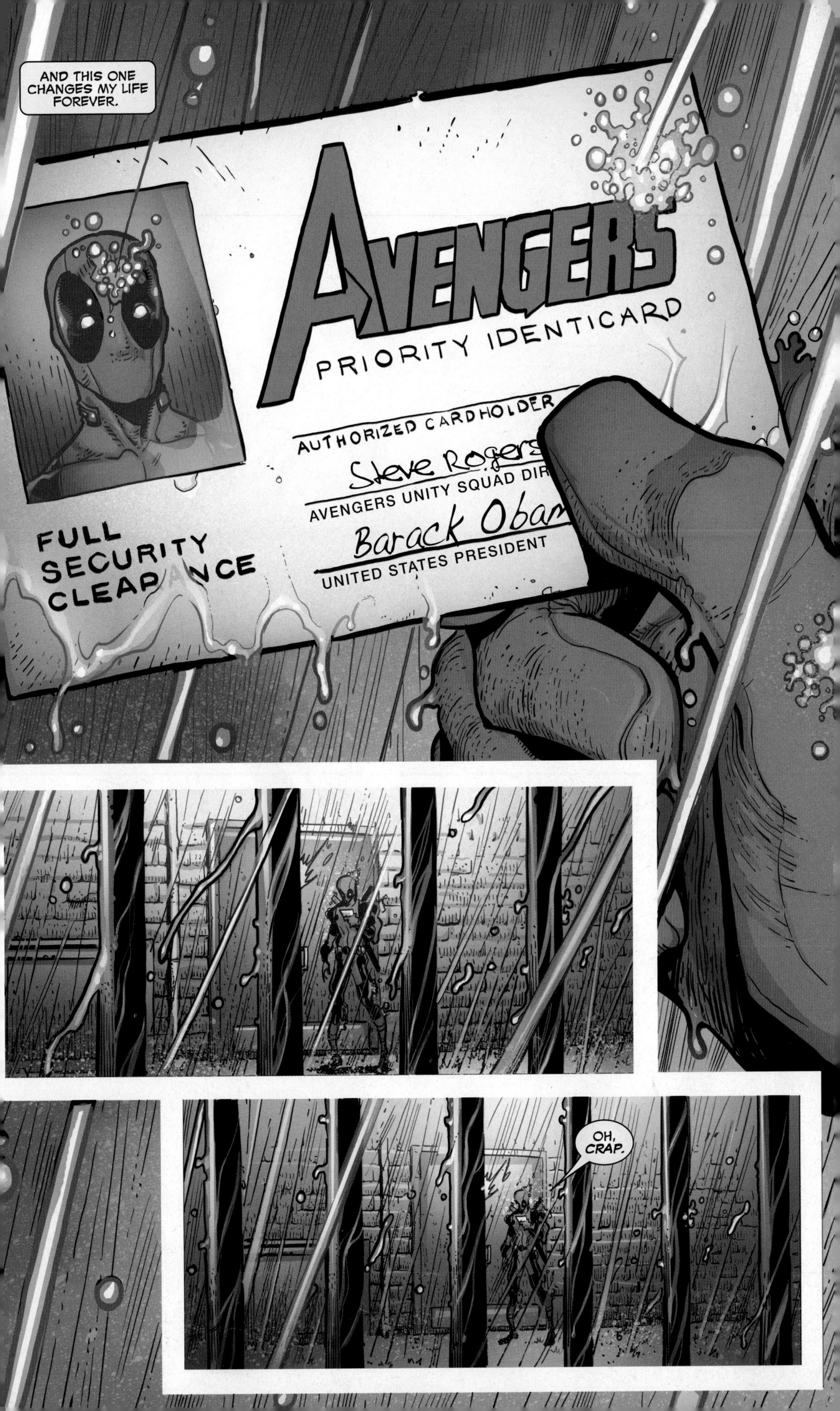
AND THIS ONE CHANGES MY LIFE FOREVER.
AVENGERS
PRIORITY IDENTICARD
AUTHORIZED CARDHOLDER
Steve Rogers
AVENGERS UNITY SQUAD DIR
Barack Obam
UNITED STATES PRESIDENT
FULL SECURITY CLEARANCE
OH, CRAP.

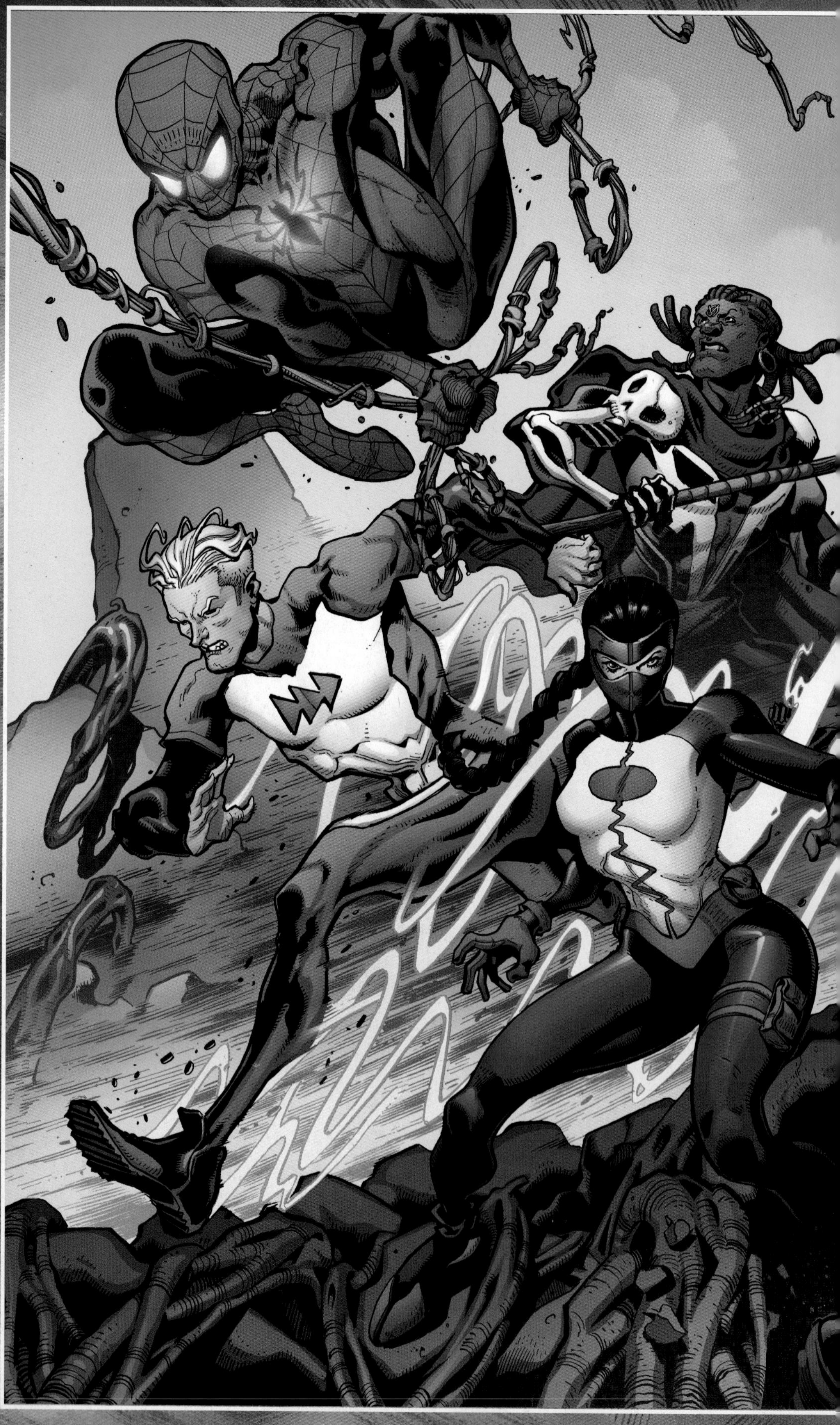

1

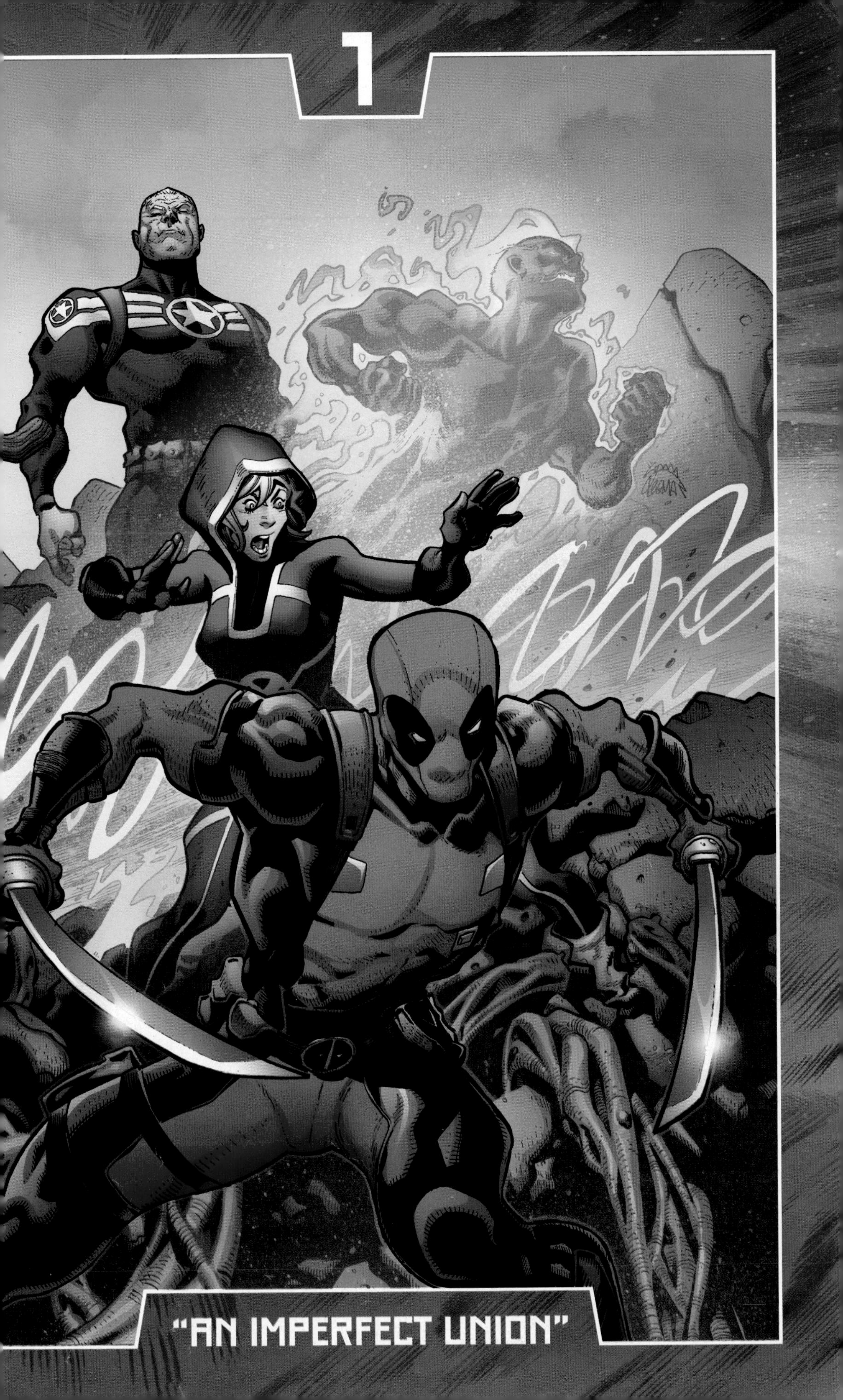

“AN IMPERFECT UNION”

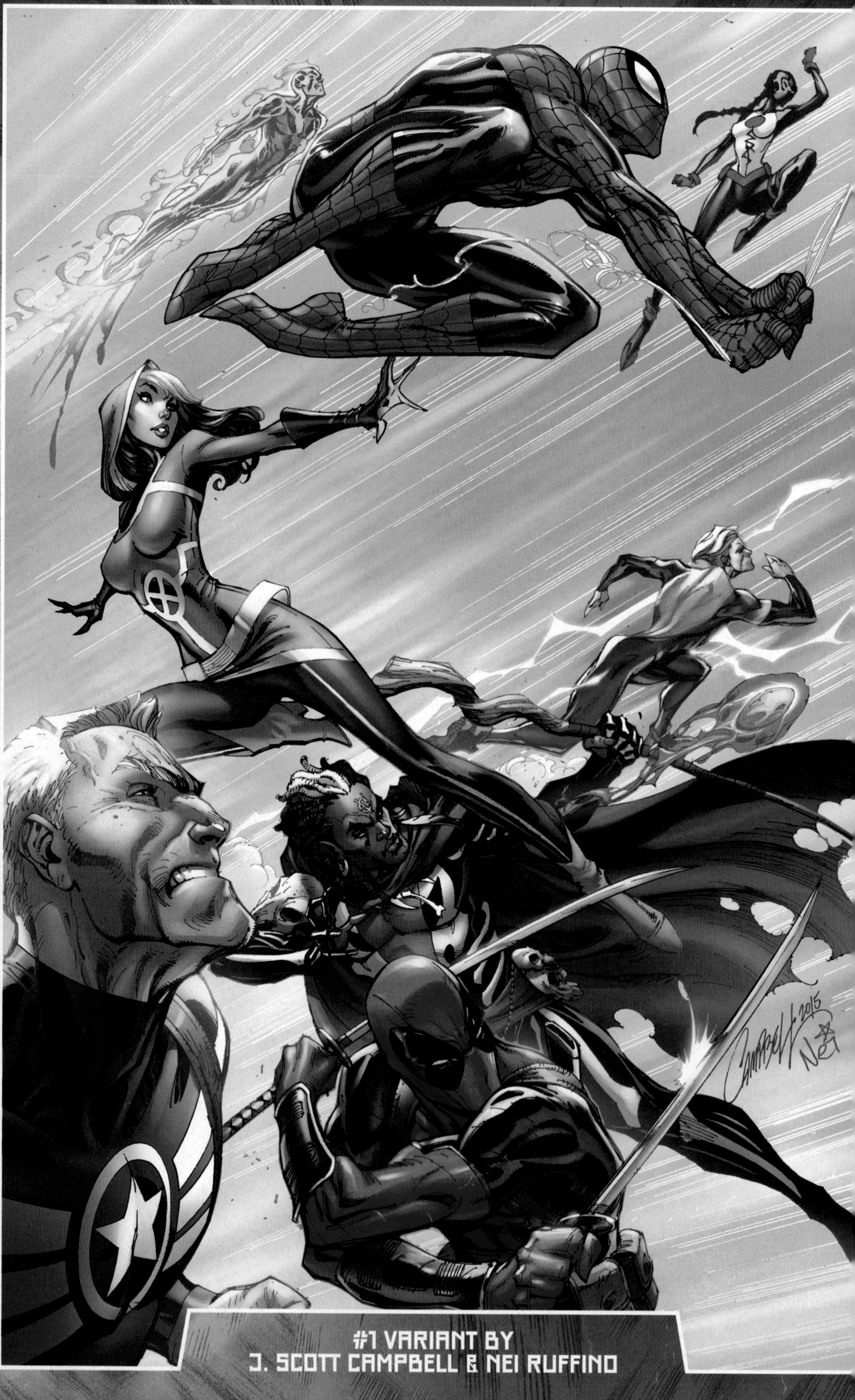
CAMPBELL 2015
Nei

#1 VARIANT BY
J. SCOTT CAMPBELL & NEI RUFFINO

THE LAST FEW MONTHS HAD BEEN HARD...

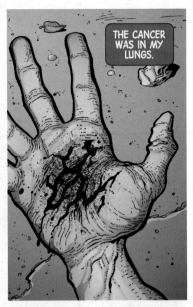

THE CANCER WAS IN MY LUNGS.

LOOKED LIKE I WASN'T GOING OUT ALONE, THOUGH.

I HAD TO LAUGH... THE PLANET'S DYING, TOO.

THE DARK SKIES CAME RUMBLING IN.

BUT NOT ALL STORM CLOUDS ARE THE SAME.

I COULD HEAR DEATH POUNDING DOWN MY DOOR...

...AS *SOMETHING ELSE* WAS SEEPING THROUGH MY WINDOW.

THAT'S HOW I *DIED*.

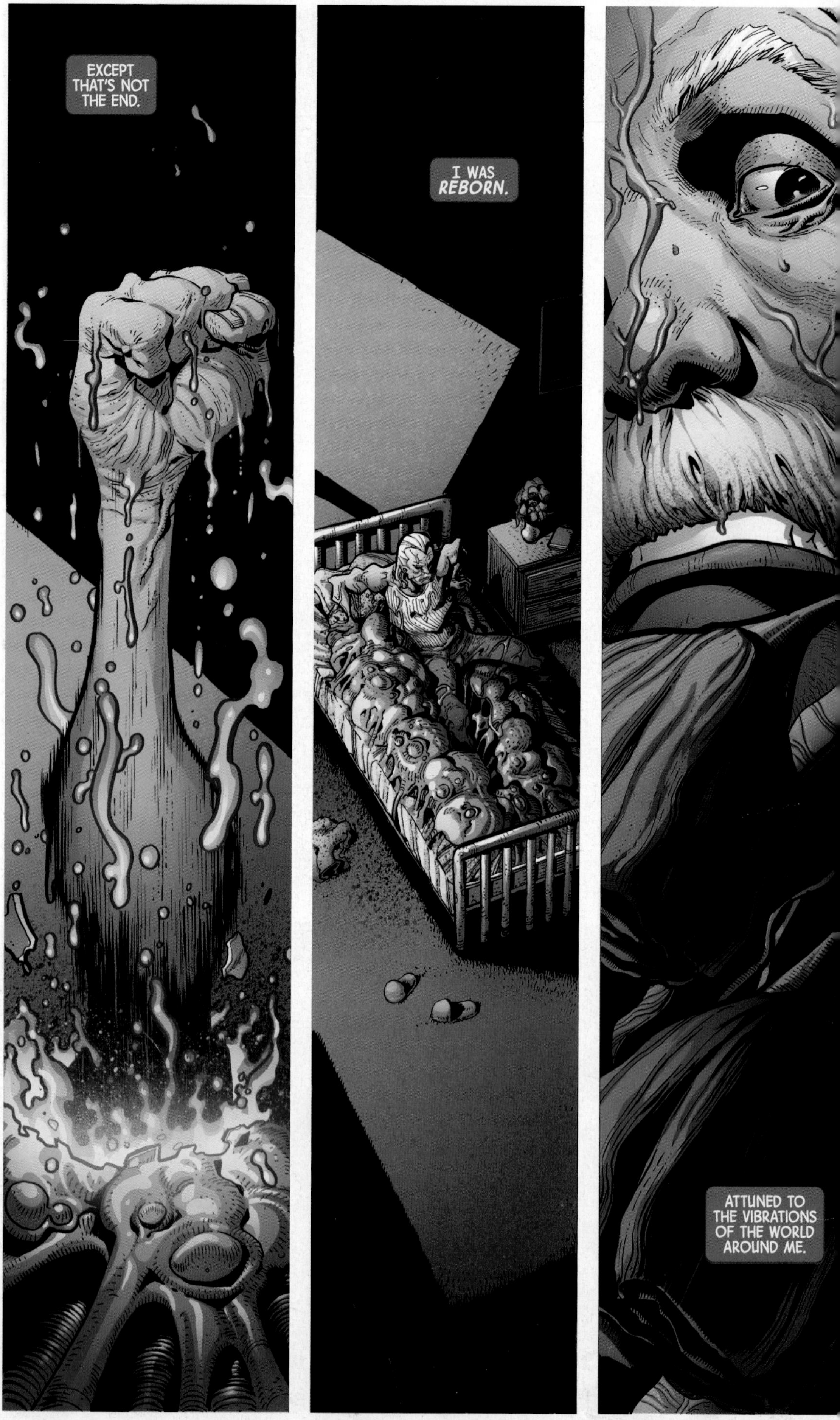
EXCEPT THAT'S NOT THE END.
I WAS *REBORN.*
ATTUNED TO THE VIBRATIONS OF THE WORLD AROUND ME.

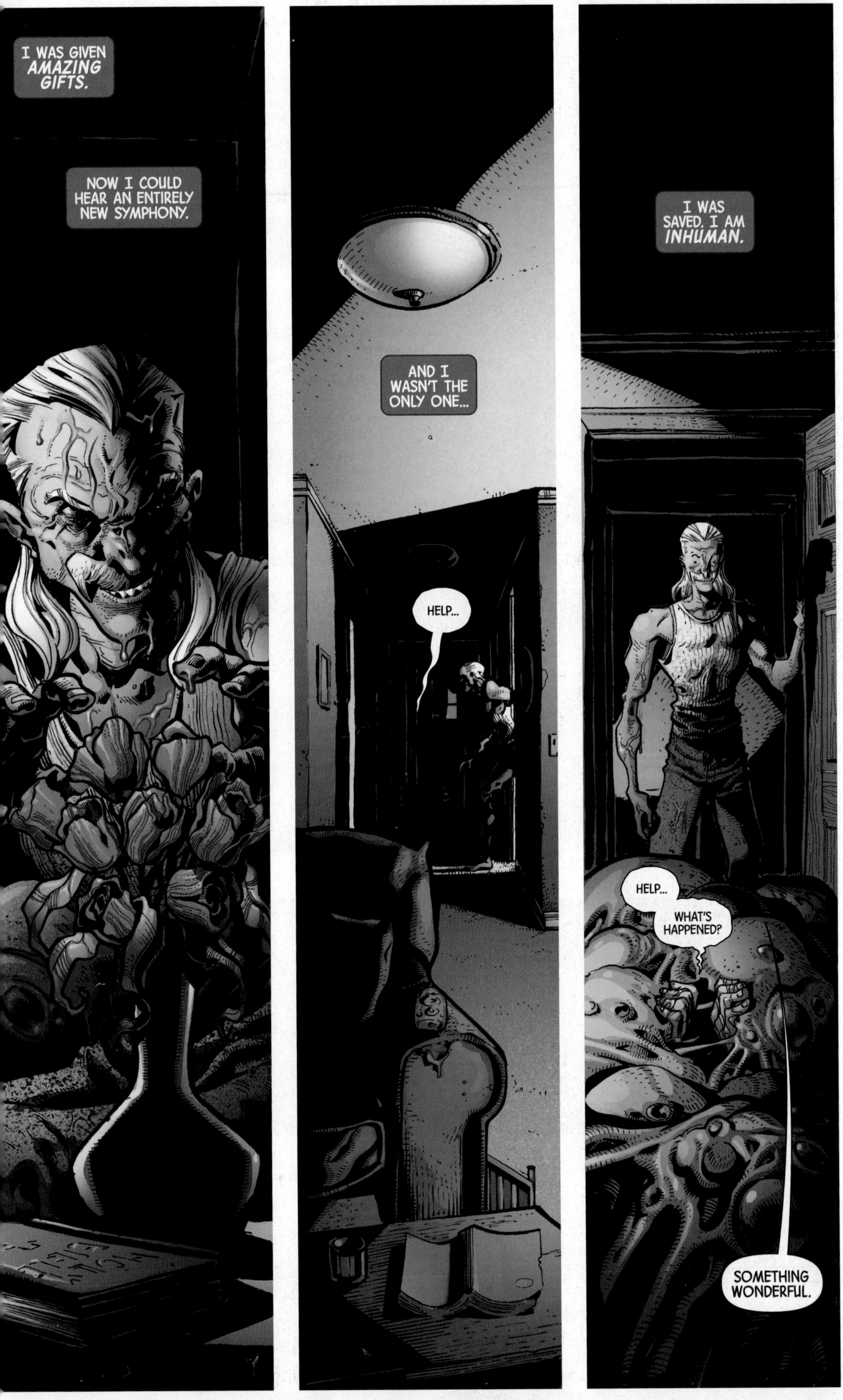

I WAS GIVEN *AMAZING GIFTS.*
NOW I COULD HEAR AN ENTIRELY NEW SYMPHONY.
AND I WASN'T THE ONLY ONE...
HELP...
I WAS SAVED. I AM *INHUMAN.*
HELP...
WHAT'S HAPPENED?
SOMETHING WONDERFUL.

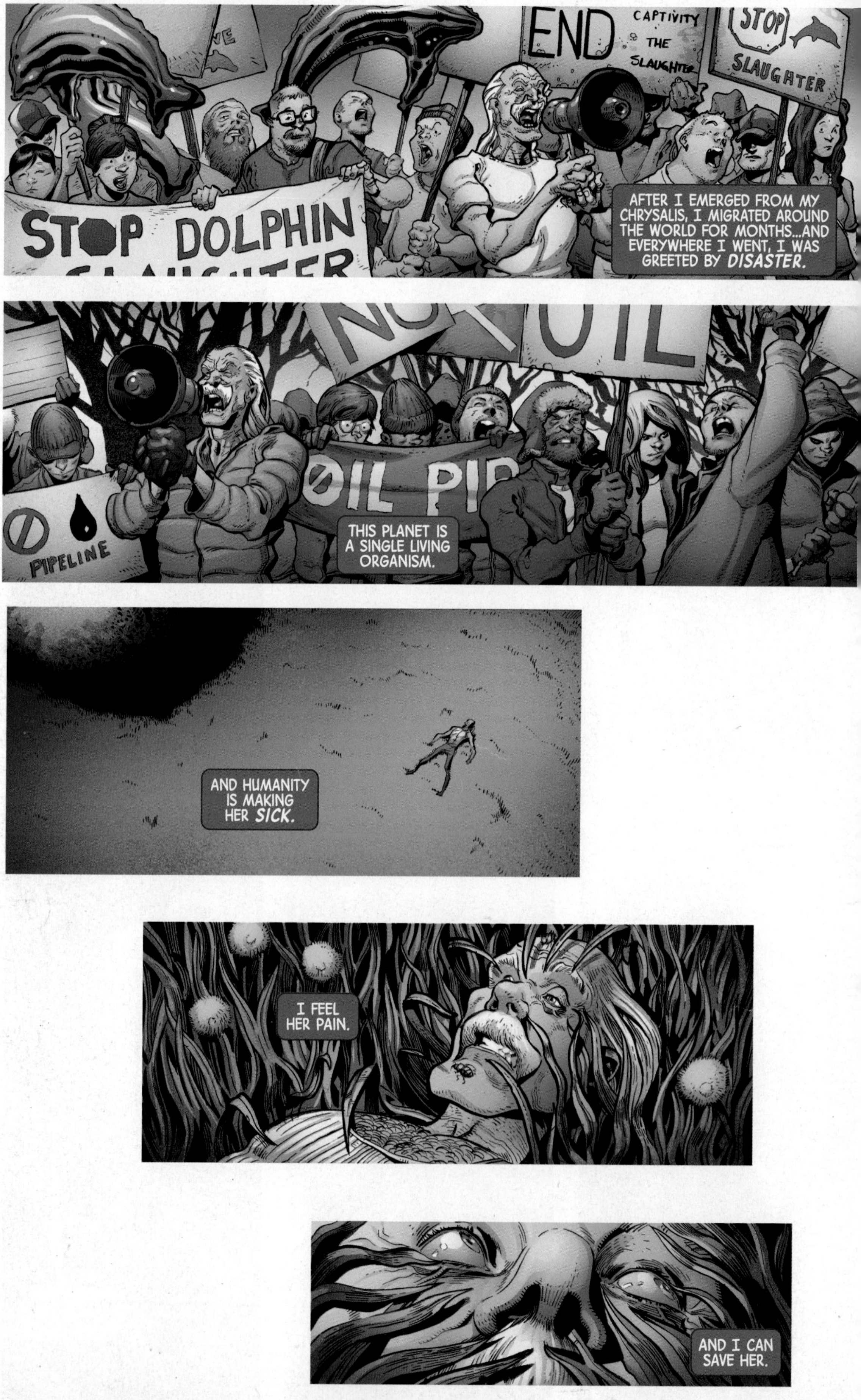
STOP DOLPHIN
END
CAPTIVITY THE SLAUGHTER
STOP SLAUGHTER
AFTER I EMERGED FROM MY CHRYSALIS, I MIGRATED AROUND THE WORLD FOR MONTHS...AND EVERYWHERE I WENT, I WAS GREETED BY ***DISASTER.***
OIL
PIPELINE
THIS PLANET IS A SINGLE LIVING ORGANISM.
AND HUMANITY IS MAKING HER ***SICK.***
I FEEL HER PAIN.
AND I CAN SAVE HER.

AFTER THE WAR BETWEEN THE AVENGERS AND THE X-MEN, THE ORIGINAL CAPTAIN AMERICA, STEVE ROGERS, BROUGHT TOGETHER MEMBERS OF BOTH TEAMS TO FORM THE AVENGERS UNITY SQUAD.

THE TEAM WAS DESIGNED TO SHOW THE WORLD THAT MUTANTS AND HUMANS COULD WORK TOGETHER.

(IT DIDN'T ALWAYS WORK THE WAY IT WAS SUPPOSED TO.)

NOW, TO PROMOTE COOPERATION IN THE FACE OF RISING TENSIONS, THE UNITY SQUAD HAS EXPANDED TO INCLUDE A NEW FACTION...

THE UNCANNY AVENGERS

EIGHT
MONTHS
LATER...

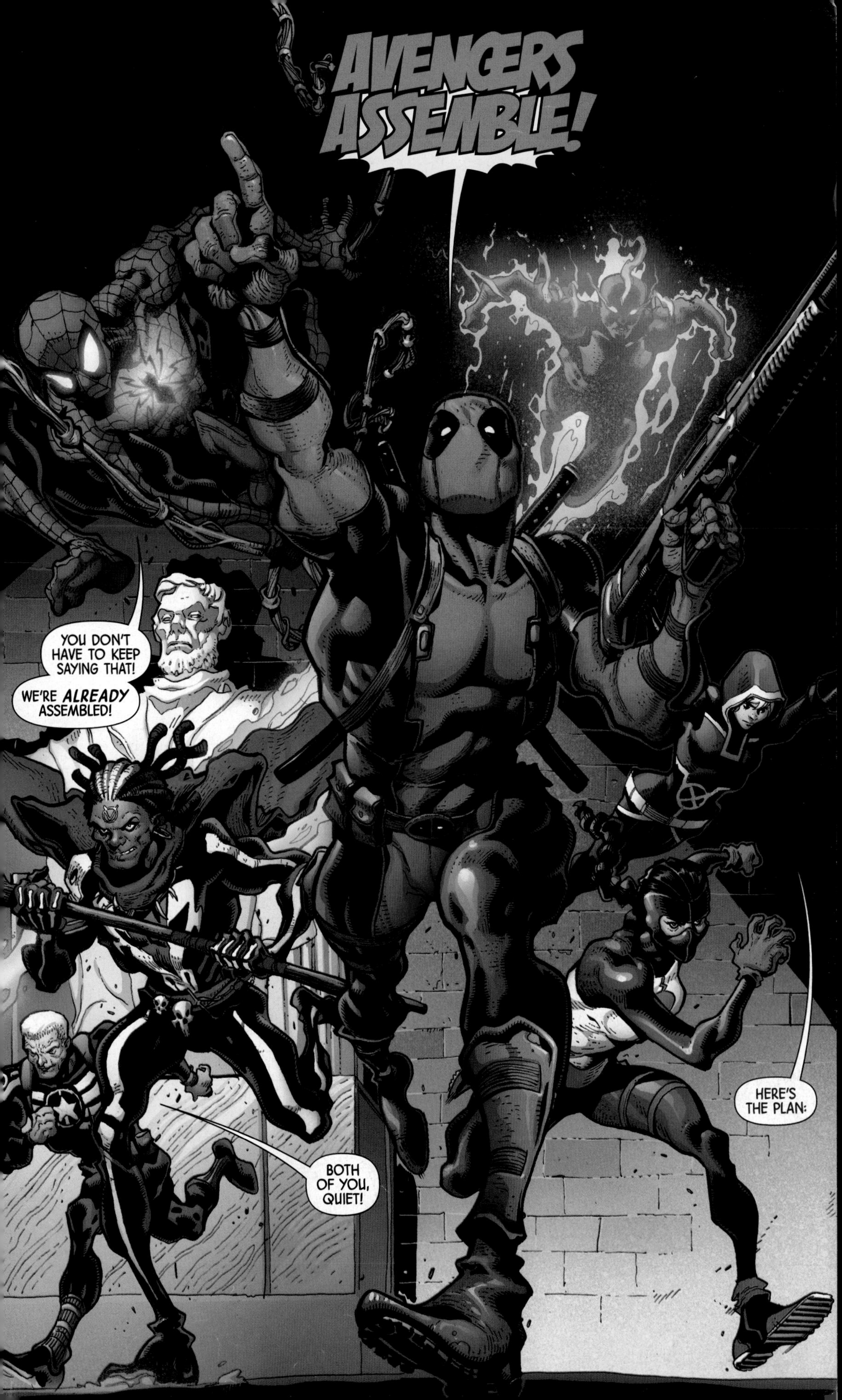
AVENGERS ASSEMBLE!
YOU DON'T HAVE TO KEEP SAYING THAT!
WE'RE *ALREADY* ASSEMBLED!
BOTH OF YOU, QUIET!
HERE'S THE PLAN:

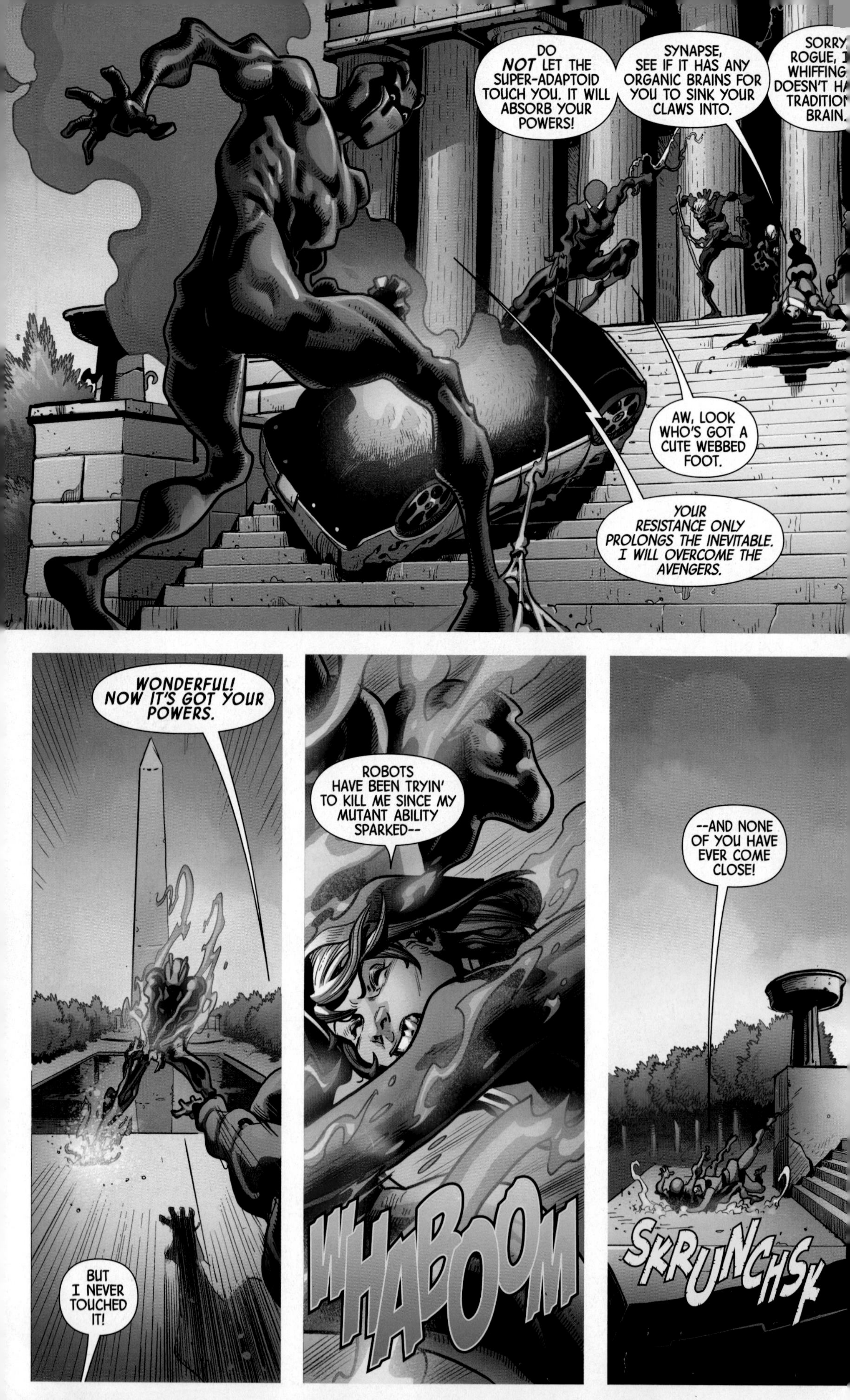

DO NOT LET THE SUPER-ADAPTOID TOUCH YOU. IT WILL ABSORB YOUR POWERS!
SYNAPSE, SEE IF IT HAS ANY ORGANIC BRAINS FOR YOU TO SINK YOUR CLAWS INTO.
SORRY ROGUE, I WHIFFING DOESN'T H TRADITION BRAIN.
AW, LOOK WHO'S GOT A CUTE WEBBED FOOT.
YOUR RESISTANCE ONLY PROLONGS THE INEVITABLE. I WILL OVERCOME THE AVENGERS.
WONDERFUL! NOW IT'S GOT YOUR POWERS.
BUT I NEVER TOUCHED IT!
ROBOTS HAVE BEEN TRYIN' TO KILL ME SINCE MY MUTANT ABILITY SPARKED--
WHABOOM
--AND NONE OF YOU HAVE EVER COME CLOSE!
SKRUNCHSK

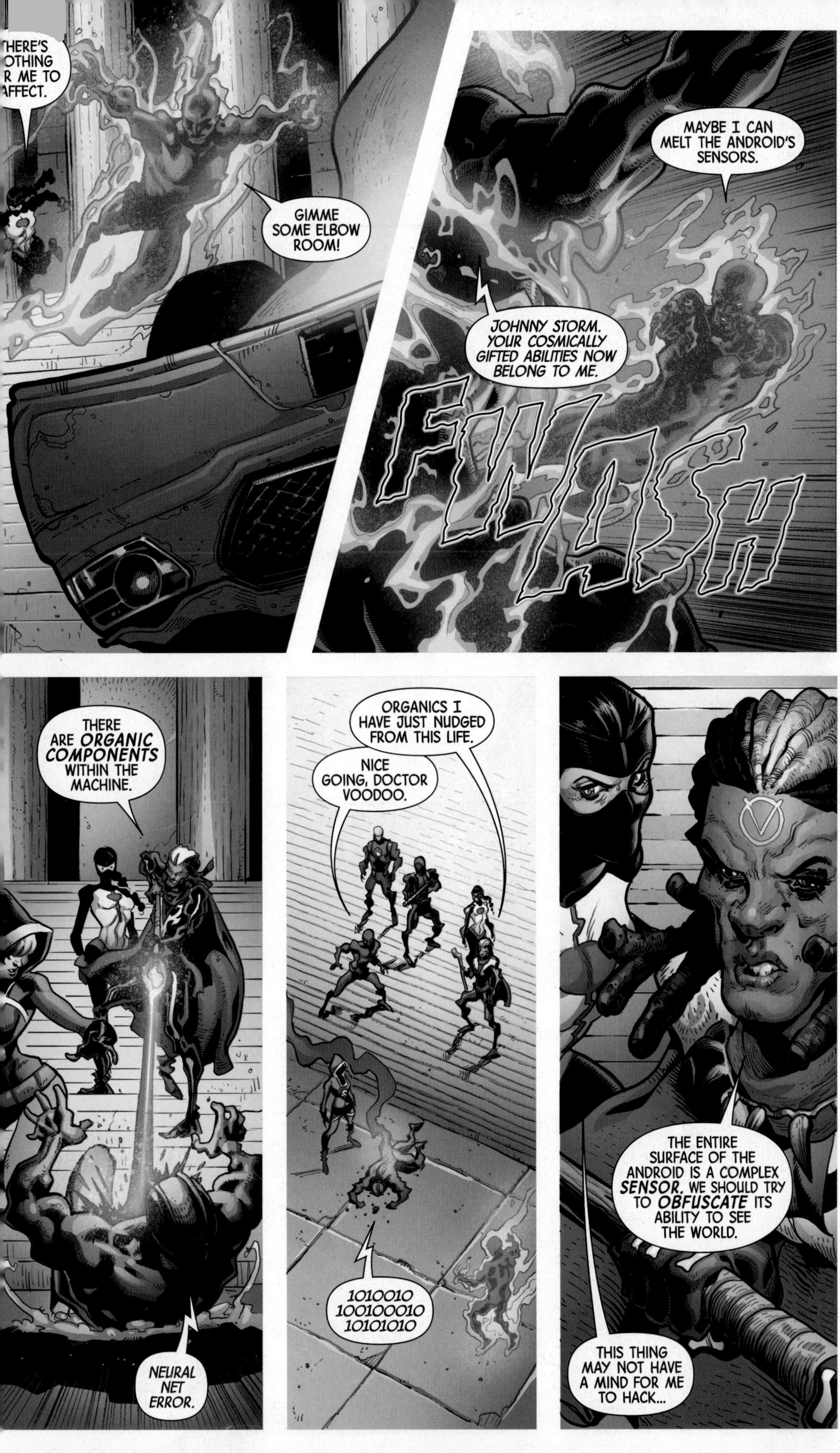
THERE'S
OTHING
R ME TO
AFFECT.
GIMME SOME ELBOW ROOM!
MAYBE I CAN MELT THE ANDROID'S SENSORS.
JOHNNY STORM. YOUR COSMICALLY GIFTED ABILITIES NOW BELONG TO ME.
FWOOSH
THERE ARE ORGANIC COMPONENTS WITHIN THE MACHINE.
NEURAL NET ERROR.
ORGANICS I HAVE JUST NUDGED FROM THIS LIFE.
NICE GOING, DOCTOR VOODOO.
1010010 100100010 10101010
THE ENTIRE SURFACE OF THE ANDROID IS A COMPLEX SENSOR. WE SHOULD TRY TO OBFUSCATE ITS ABILITY TO SEE THE WORLD.
THIS THING MAY NOT HAVE A MIND FOR ME TO HACK...

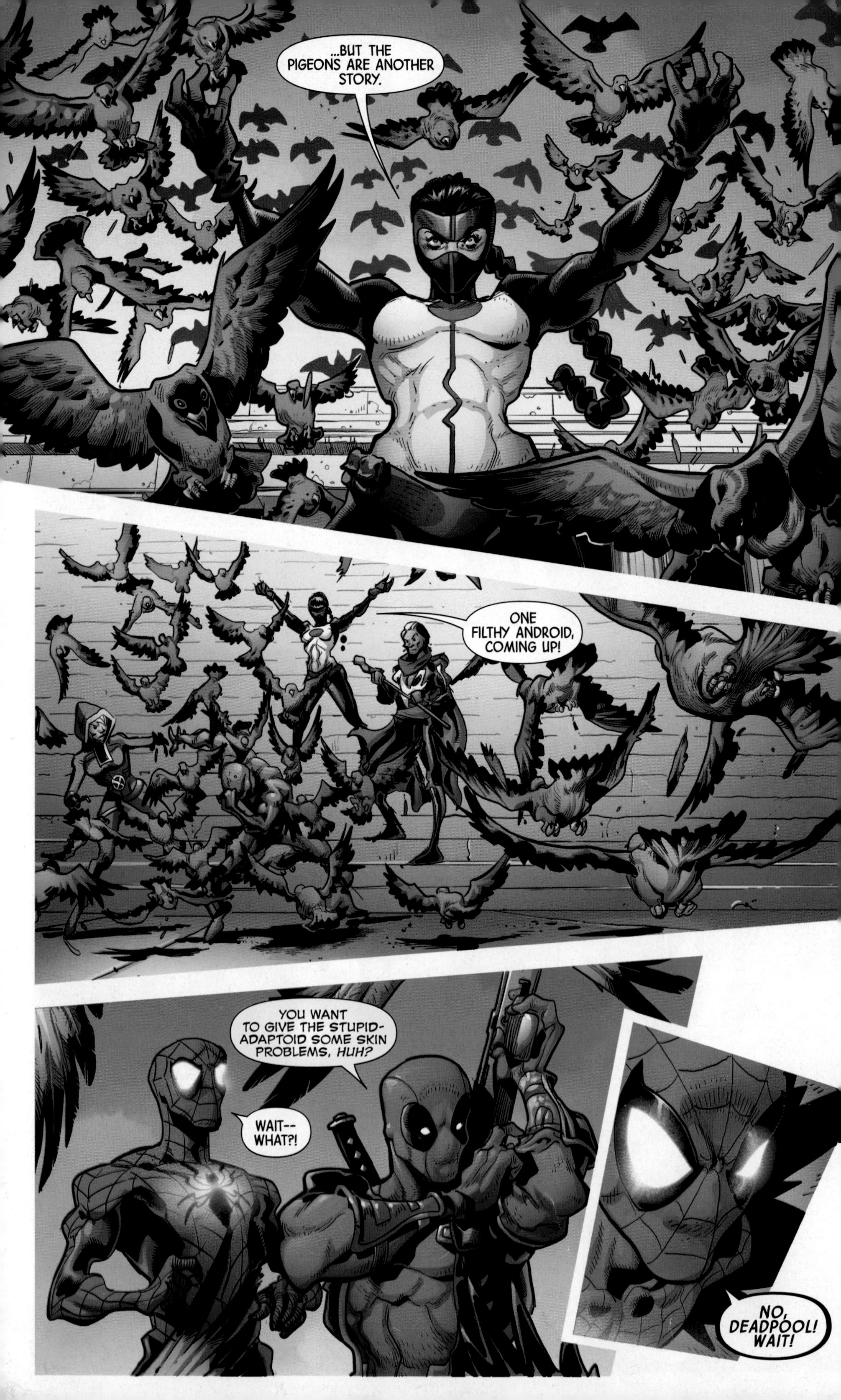
...BUT THE PIGEONS ARE ANOTHER STORY.
ONE FILTHY ANDROID, COMING UP!
YOU WANT TO GIVE THE STUPID-ADAPTOID SOME SKIN PROBLEMS, HUH?
WAIT-- WHAT?!
NO, DEADPOOL! WAIT!

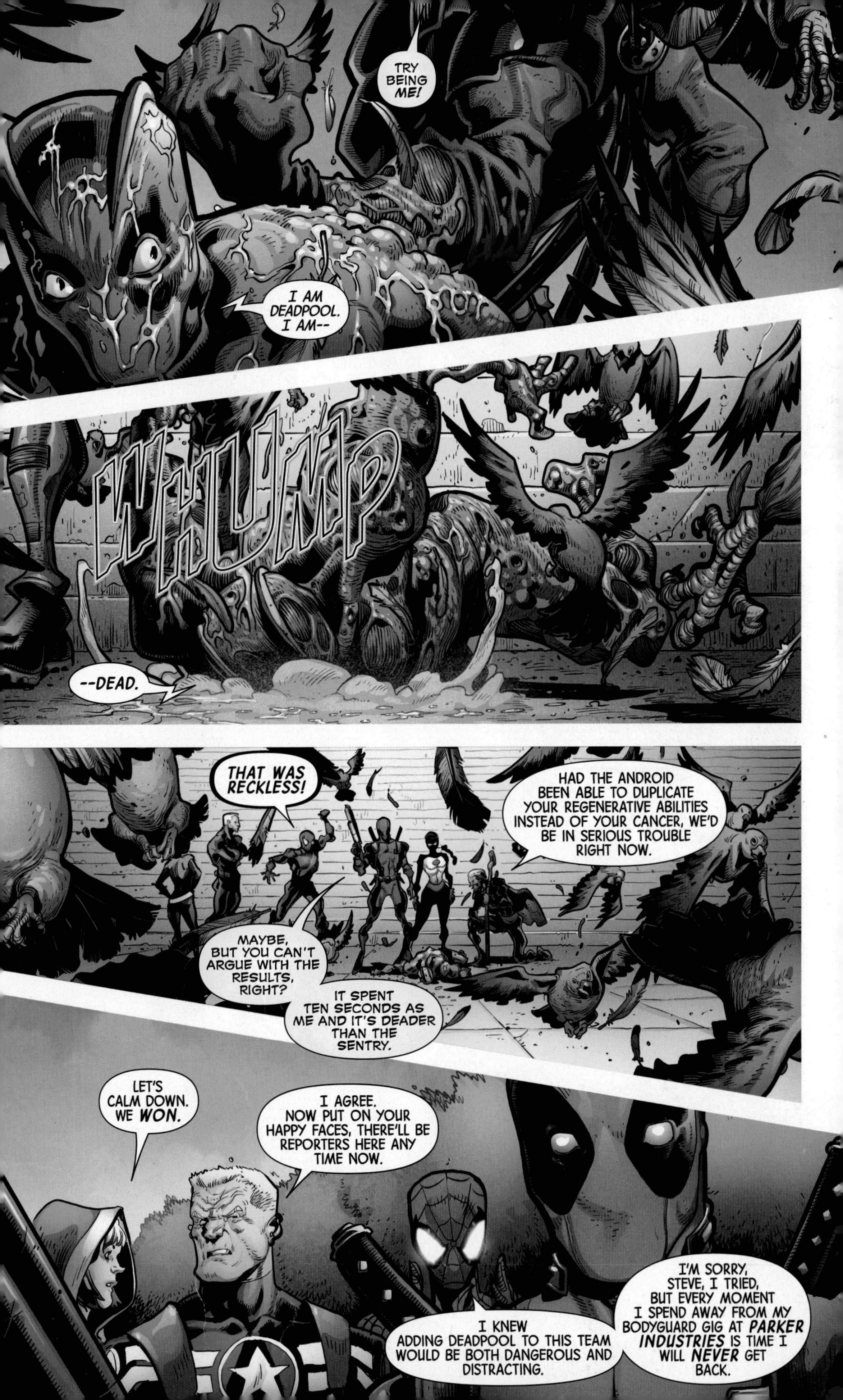
TRY BEING ME!
I AM DEADPOOL. I AM--
WHUMP
--DEAD.
THAT WAS RECKLESS!
HAD THE ANDROID BEEN ABLE TO DUPLICATE YOUR REGENERATIVE ABILITIES INSTEAD OF YOUR CANCER, WE'D BE IN SERIOUS TROUBLE RIGHT NOW.
MAYBE, BUT YOU CAN'T ARGUE WITH THE RESULTS, RIGHT?
IT SPENT TEN SECONDS AS ME AND IT'S DEADER THAN THE SENTRY.
LET'S CALM DOWN. WE WON.
I AGREE. NOW PUT ON YOUR HAPPY FACES, THERE'LL BE REPORTERS HERE ANY TIME NOW.
I KNEW ADDING DEADPOOL TO THIS TEAM WOULD BE BOTH DANGEROUS AND DISTRACTING.
I'M SORRY, STEVE, I TRIED, BUT EVERY MOMENT I SPEND AWAY FROM MY BODYGUARD GIG AT PARKER INDUSTRIES IS TIME I WILL NEVER GET BACK.

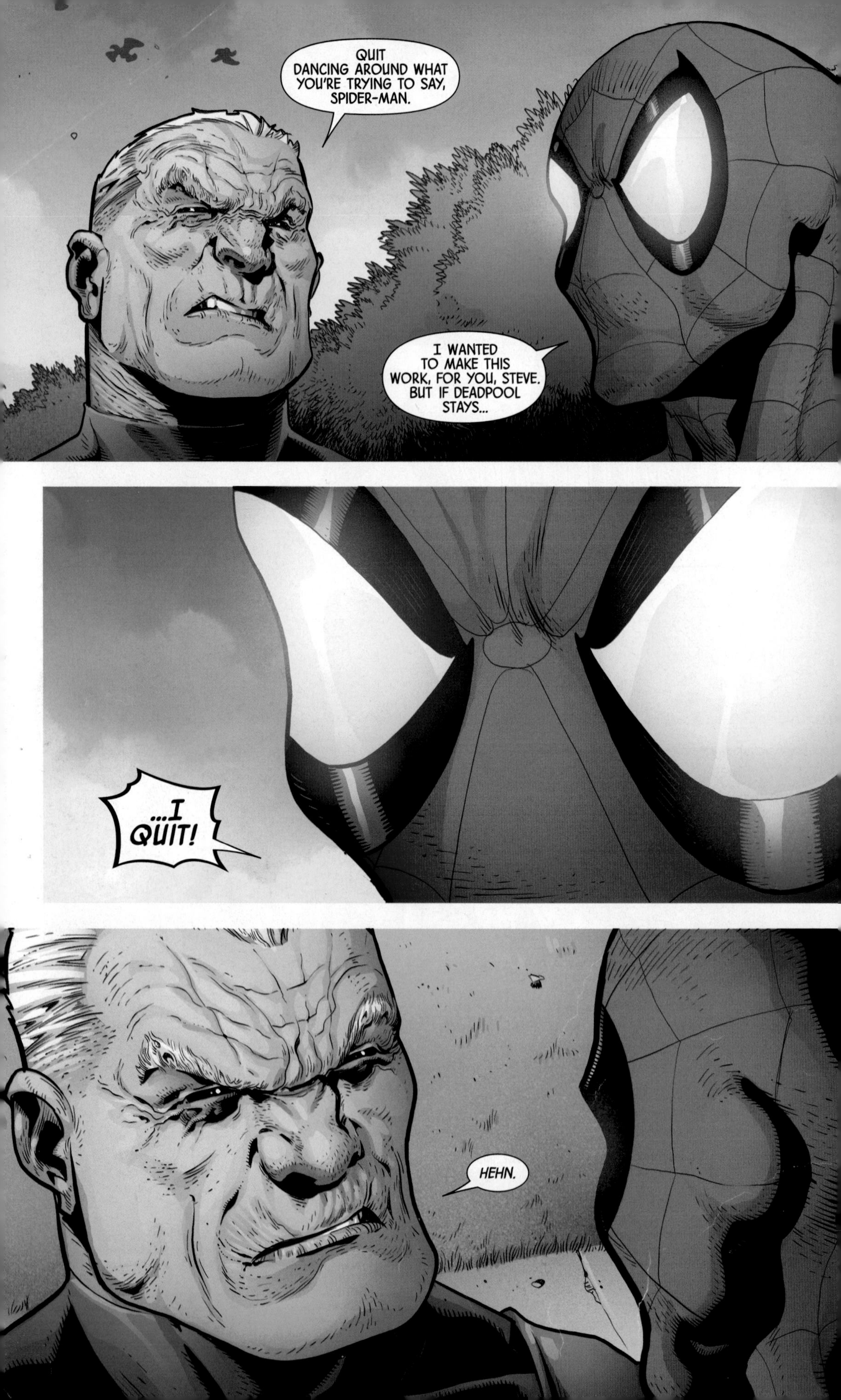
QUIT DANCING AROUND WHAT YOU'RE TRYING TO SAY, SPIDER-MAN.
I WANTED TO MAKE THIS WORK, FOR YOU, STEVE. BUT IF DEADPOOL STAYS...
...I QUIT!
HEHN.

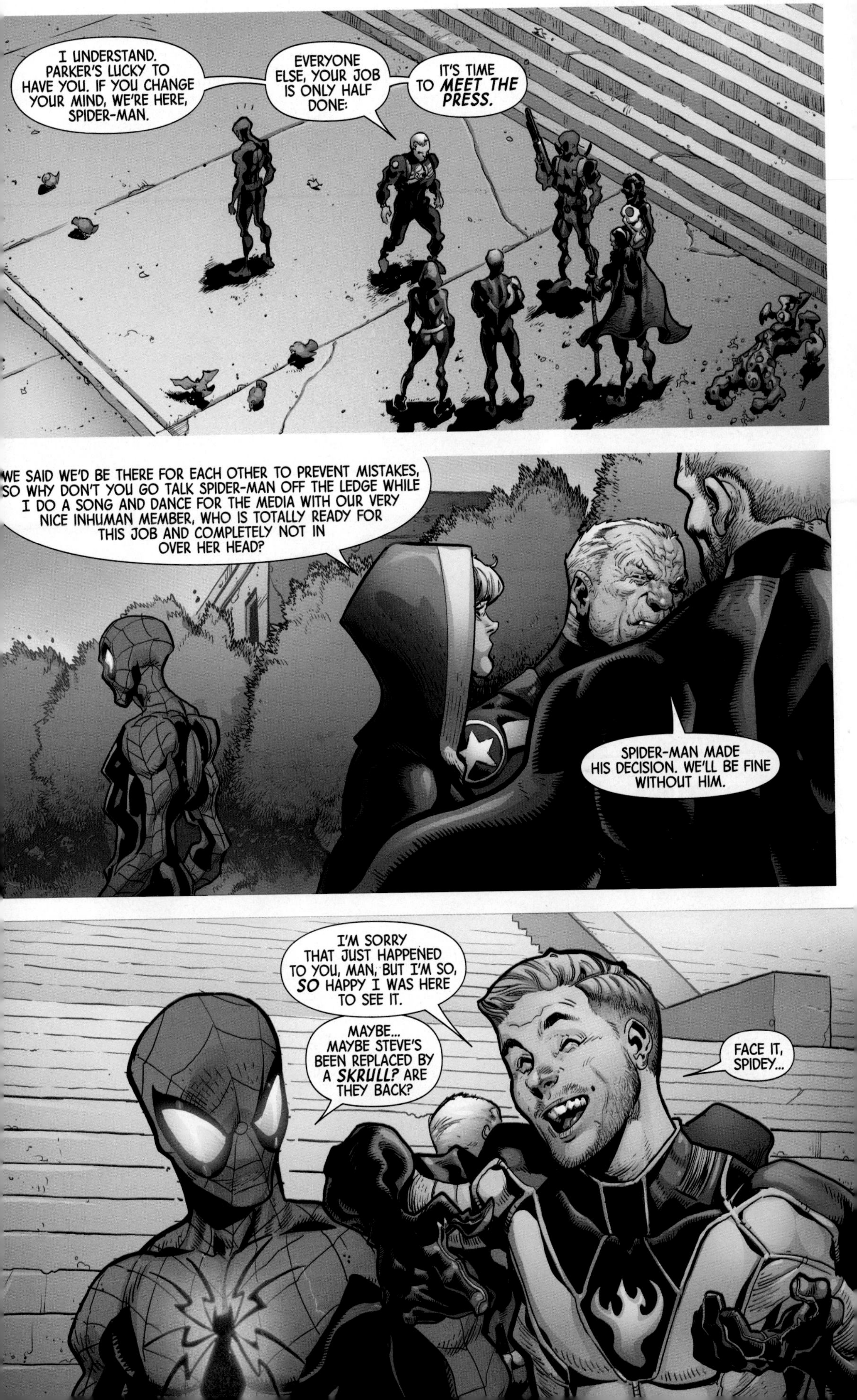

I UNDERSTAND. PARKER'S LUCKY TO HAVE YOU. IF YOU CHANGE YOUR MIND, WE'RE HERE, SPIDER-MAN.
EVERYONE ELSE, YOUR JOB IS ONLY HALF DONE:
IT'S TIME TO *MEET THE PRESS.*
WE SAID WE'D BE THERE FOR EACH OTHER TO PREVENT MISTAKES, SO WHY DON'T YOU GO TALK SPIDER-MAN OFF THE LEDGE WHILE I DO A SONG AND DANCE FOR THE MEDIA WITH OUR VERY NICE INHUMAN MEMBER, WHO IS TOTALLY READY FOR THIS JOB AND COMPLETELY NOT IN OVER HER HEAD?
SPIDER-MAN MADE HIS DECISION. WE'LL BE FINE WITHOUT HIM.
I'M SORRY THAT JUST HAPPENED TO YOU, MAN, BUT I'M SO, *SO* HAPPY I WAS HERE TO SEE IT.
MAYBE... MAYBE STEVE'S BEEN REPLACED BY A *SKRULL?* ARE THEY BACK?
FACE IT, SPIDEY...

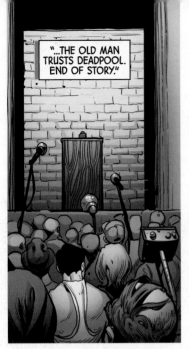

"...THE OLD MAN TRUSTS DEADPOOL. END OF STORY."

STEVE, ARE YOU SURE--

I'VE VOUCHED FOR BOTH *DEADPOOL* AND *SYNAPSE*. THAT SHOULD BE GOOD ENOUGH.

THIS IS THE MOST IMPORTANT PART OF THE DAY: LET'S APPEAR *UNIFIED* IN FRONT OF THESE REPORTERS.

I'M UNIFIED.

ROGUE'S RIGHT ABOUT ONE THING: I'M NOT READY FOR THE PUBLICITY PART OF THE AVENGERS BUSINESS.

LADIES AND GENTLEMEN...

MEET THE HEROES OF THE DAY. HUMANS, MUTANTS AND INHUMANS, WORKING TOGETHER TO MAKE THE WORLD A BETTER PLACE.

IMPORTANT TO NOTE BECAUSE OF ALL THE *RECENT TROUBLES.*

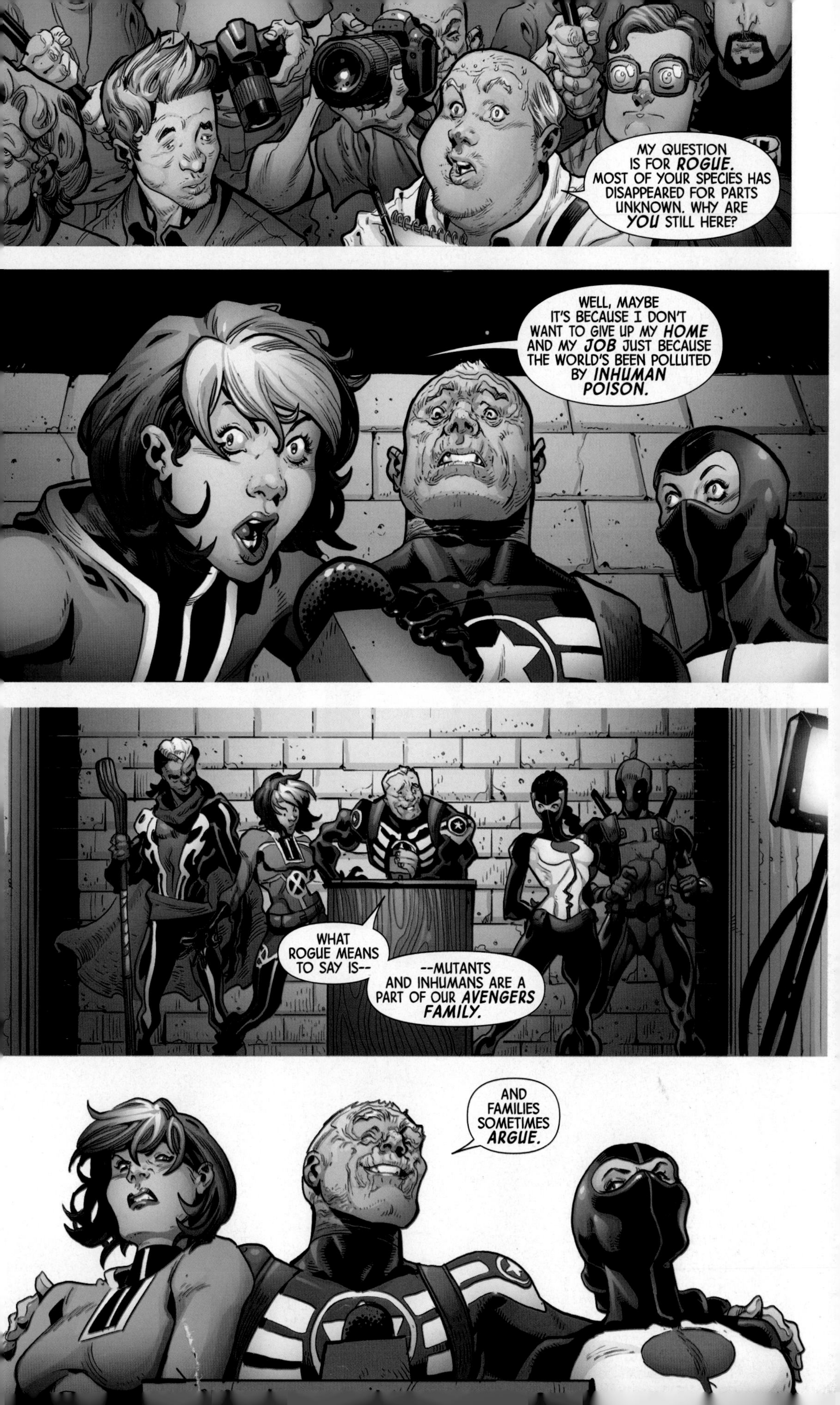
MY QUESTION IS FOR ROGUE. MOST OF YOUR SPECIES HAS DISAPPEARED FOR PARTS UNKNOWN. WHY ARE YOU STILL HERE?
WELL, MAYBE IT'S BECAUSE I DON'T WANT TO GIVE UP MY HOME AND MY JOB JUST BECAUSE THE WORLD'S BEEN POLLUTED BY INHUMAN POISON.
WHAT ROGUE MEANS TO SAY IS--
--MUTANTS AND INHUMANS ARE A PART OF OUR AVENGERS FAMILY.
AND FAMILIES SOMETIMES ARGUE.

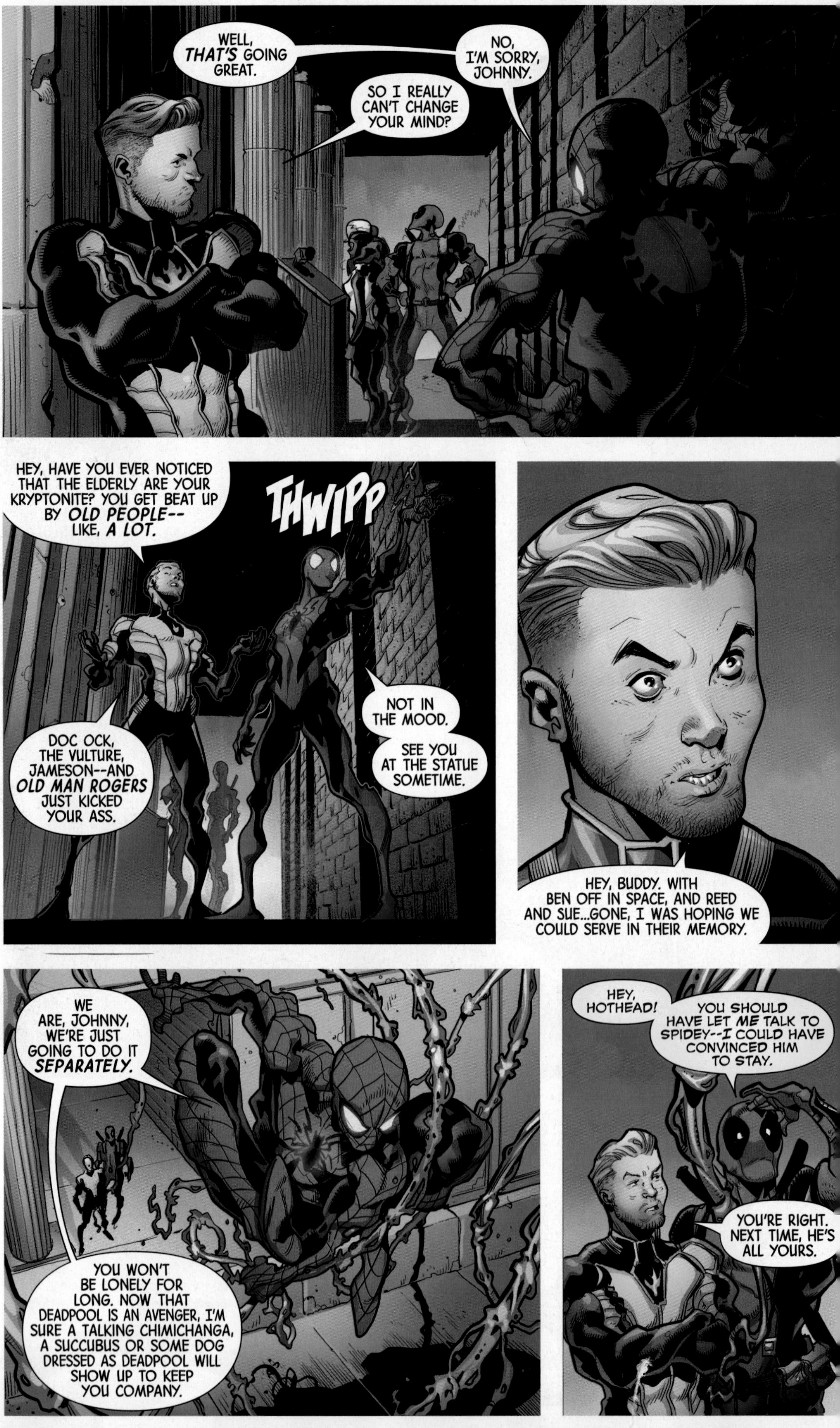
WELL, THAT'S GOING GREAT.
NO, I'M SORRY, JOHNNY.
SO I REALLY CAN'T CHANGE YOUR MIND?
HEY, HAVE YOU EVER NOTICED THAT THE ELDERLY ARE YOUR KRYPTONITE? YOU GET BEAT UP BY OLD PEOPLE-- LIKE, A LOT.
THWIPP
DOC OCK, THE VULTURE, JAMESON--AND OLD MAN ROGERS JUST KICKED YOUR ASS.
NOT IN THE MOOD.
SEE YOU AT THE STATUE SOMETIME.
HEY, BUDDY. WITH BEN OFF IN SPACE, AND REED AND SUE...GONE, I WAS HOPING WE COULD SERVE IN THEIR MEMORY.
WE ARE, JOHNNY, WE'RE JUST GOING TO DO IT SEPARATELY.
YOU WON'T BE LONELY FOR LONG. NOW THAT DEADPOOL IS AN AVENGER, I'M SURE A TALKING CHIMICHANGA, A SUCCUBUS OR SOME DOG DRESSED AS DEADPOOL WILL SHOW UP TO KEEP YOU COMPANY.
HEY, HOTHEAD!
YOU SHOULD HAVE LET ME TALK TO SPIDEY--I COULD HAVE CONVINCED HIM TO STAY.
YOU'RE RIGHT. NEXT TIME, HE'S ALL YOURS.

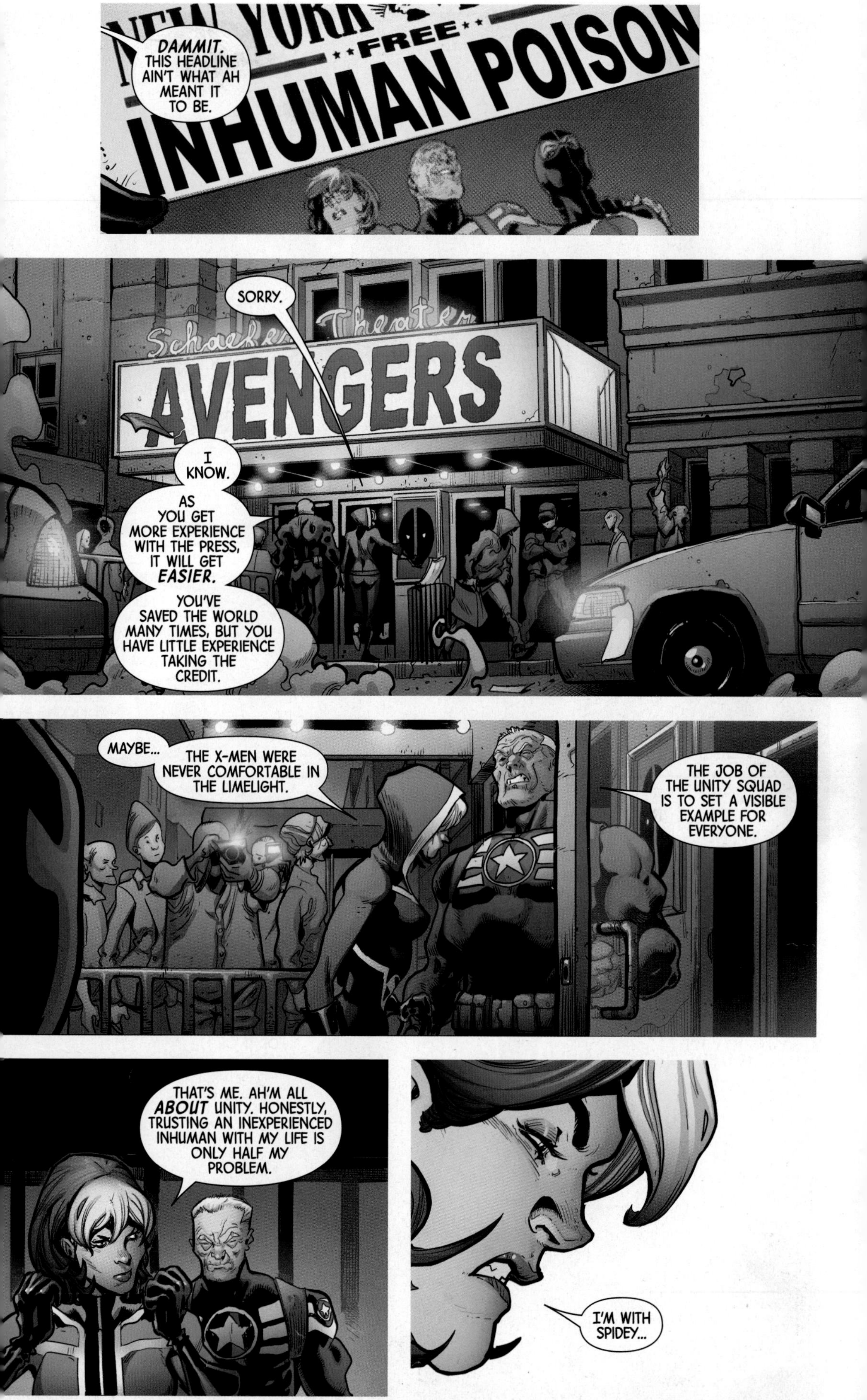
NEW YORK
FREE
INHUMAN POISON
DAMMIT. THIS HEADLINE AIN'T WHAT AH MEANT IT TO BE.
SORRY.
Schaefer Theater
AVENGERS
I KNOW.
AS YOU GET MORE EXPERIENCE WITH THE PRESS, IT WILL GET EASIER.
YOU'VE SAVED THE WORLD MANY TIMES, BUT YOU HAVE LITTLE EXPERIENCE TAKING THE CREDIT.
MAYBE...
THE X-MEN WERE NEVER COMFORTABLE IN THE LIMELIGHT.
THE JOB OF THE UNITY SQUAD IS TO SET A VISIBLE EXAMPLE FOR EVERYONE.
THAT'S ME. AH'M ALL ABOUT UNITY. HONESTLY, TRUSTING AN INEXPERIENCED INHUMAN WITH MY LIFE IS ONLY HALF MY PROBLEM.
I'M WITH SPIDEY...

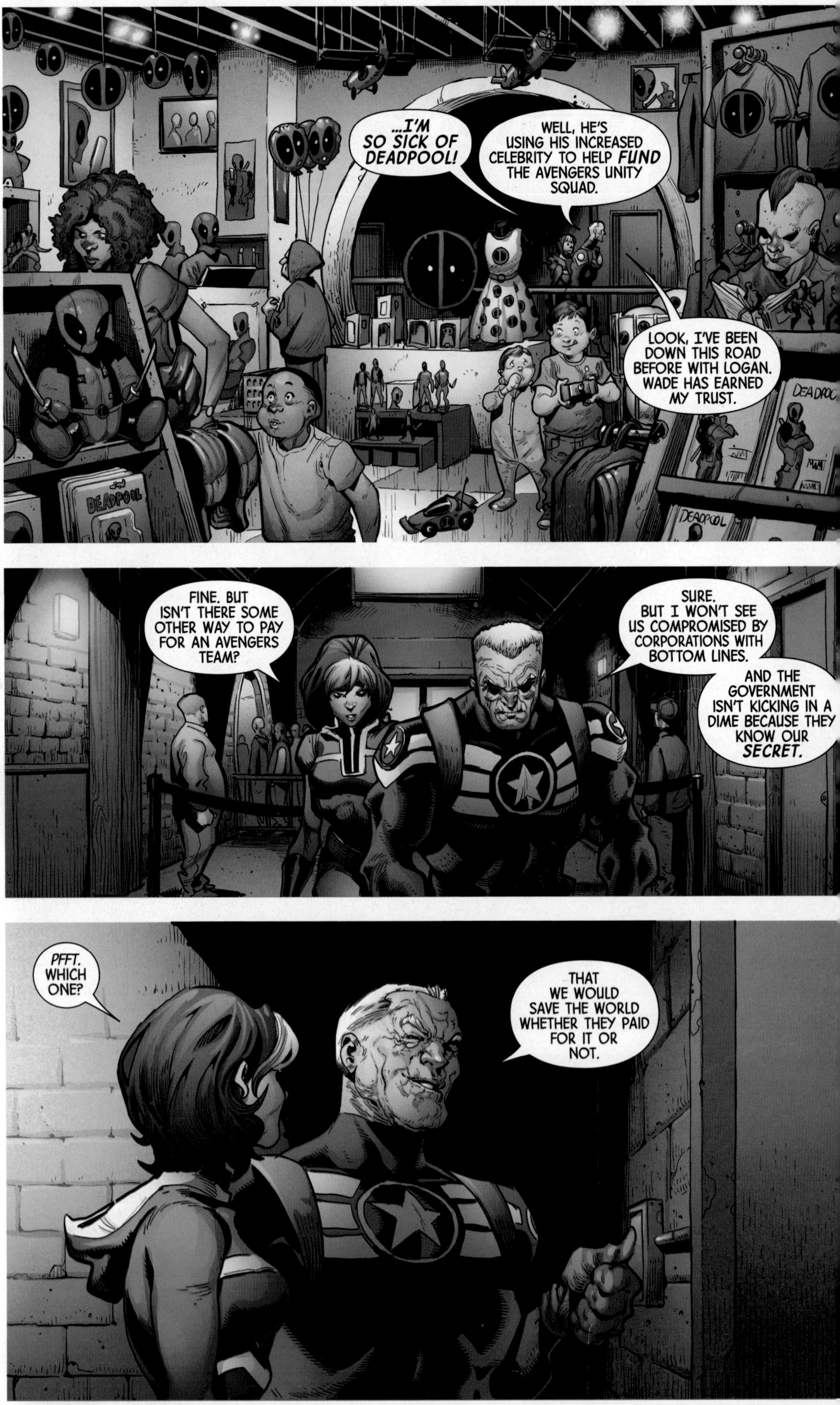
...I'M SO SICK OF DEADPOOL!
WELL, HE'S USING HIS INCREASED CELEBRITY TO HELP FUND THE AVENGERS UNITY SQUAD.
LOOK, I'VE BEEN DOWN THIS ROAD BEFORE WITH LOGAN. WADE HAS EARNED MY TRUST.
DEADPOOL
DEADPOOL
FINE. BUT ISN'T THERE SOME OTHER WAY TO PAY FOR AN AVENGERS TEAM?
SURE. BUT I WON'T SEE US COMPROMISED BY CORPORATIONS WITH BOTTOM LINES.
AND THE GOVERNMENT ISN'T KICKING IN A DIME BECAUSE THEY KNOW OUR SECRET.
PFFT. WHICH ONE?
THAT WE WOULD SAVE THE WORLD WHETHER THEY PAID FOR IT OR NOT.

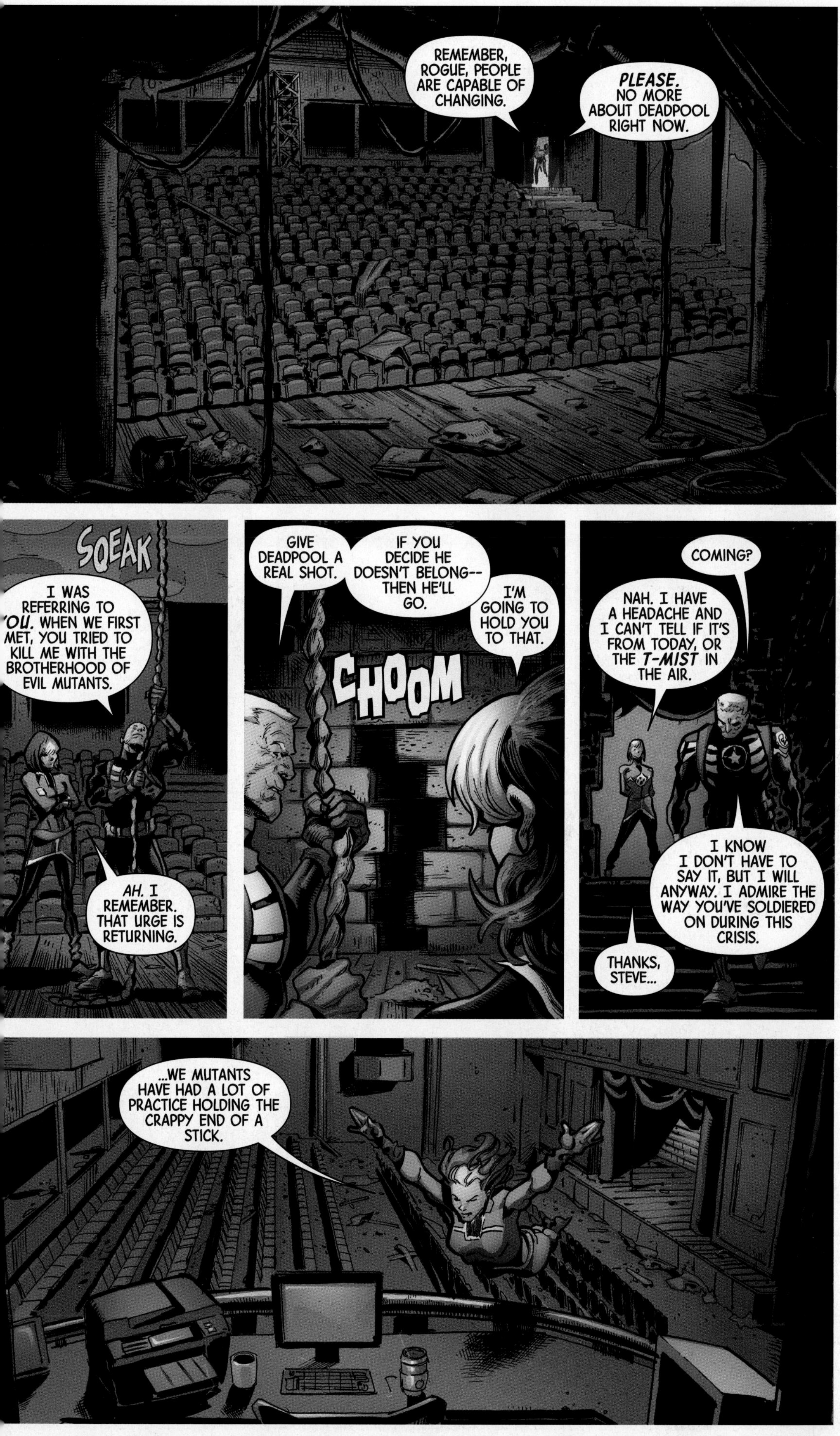

REMEMBER, ROGUE, PEOPLE ARE CAPABLE OF CHANGING.
PLEASE. NO MORE ABOUT DEADPOOL RIGHT NOW.
SQEAK
I WAS REFERRING TO OU. WHEN WE FIRST MET, YOU TRIED TO KILL ME WITH THE BROTHERHOOD OF EVIL MUTANTS.
AH. I REMEMBER. THAT URGE IS RETURNING.
GIVE DEADPOOL A REAL SHOT.
IF YOU DECIDE HE DOESN'T BELONG-- THEN HE'LL GO.
I'M GOING TO HOLD YOU TO THAT.
CHOOM
COMING?
NAH. I HAVE A HEADACHE AND I CAN'T TELL IF IT'S FROM TODAY, OR THE T-MIST IN THE AIR.
I KNOW I DON'T HAVE TO SAY IT, BUT I WILL ANYWAY. I ADMIRE THE WAY YOU'VE SOLDIERED ON DURING THIS CRISIS.
THANKS, STEVE...
...WE MUTANTS HAVE HAD A LOT OF PRACTICE HOLDING THE CRAPPY END OF A STICK.

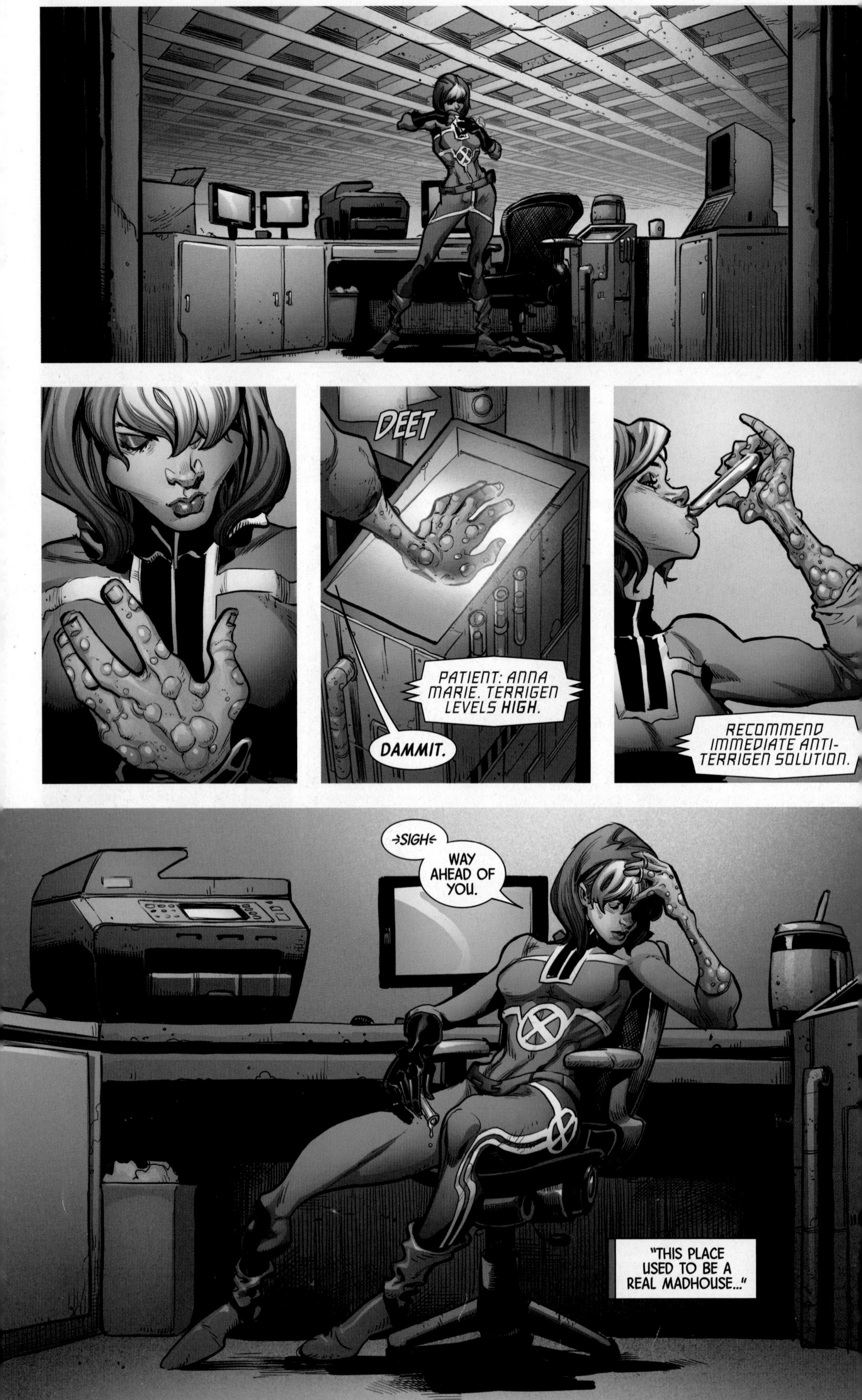
DEET
PATIENT: ANNA MARIE. TERRIGEN LEVELS HIGH.
DAMMIT.
RECOMMEND IMMEDIATE ANTI-TERRIGEN SOLUTION.
→SIGH←
WAY AHEAD OF YOU.
"THIS PLACE USED TO BE A REAL MADHOUSE..."

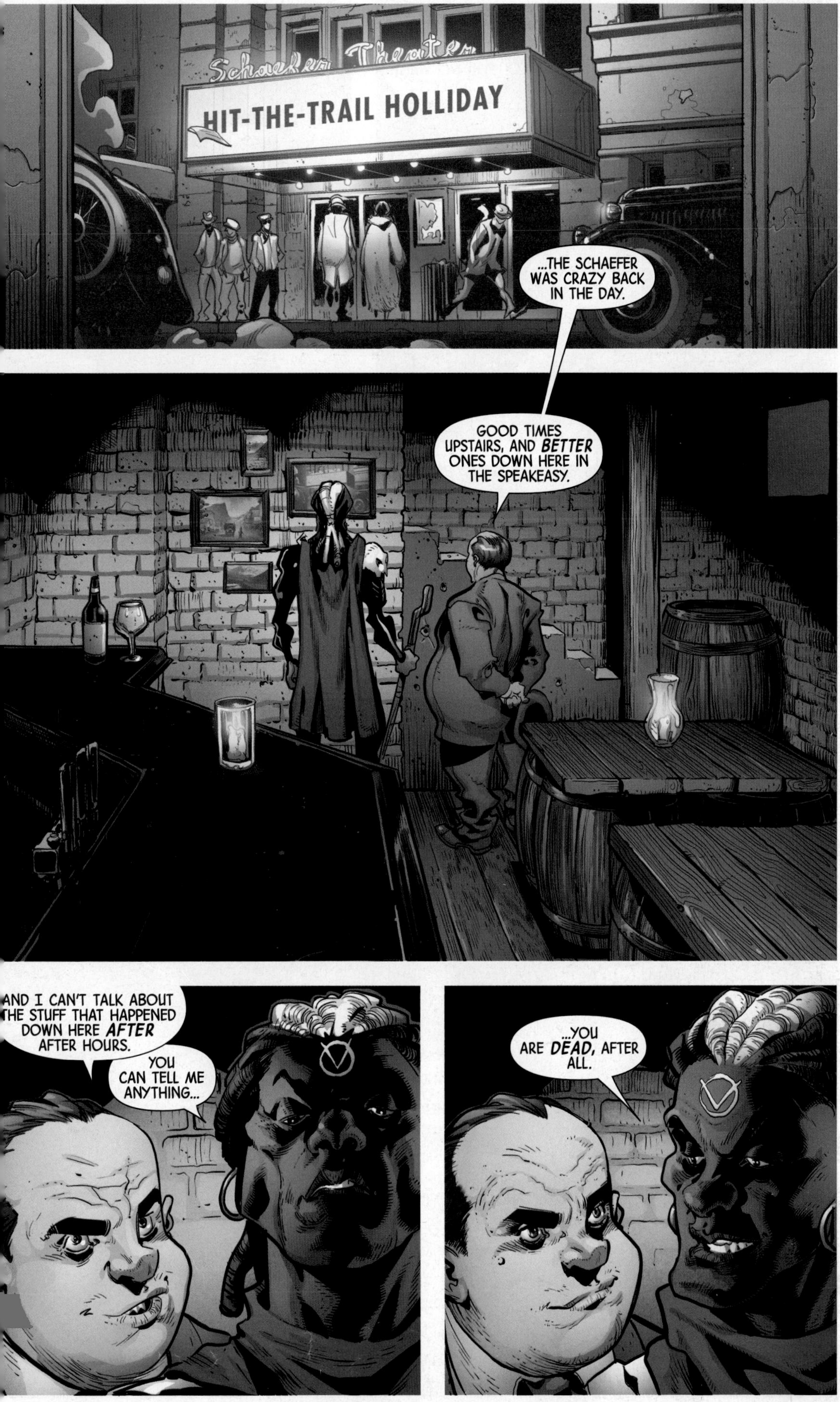
Schaefer Theater
HIT-THE-TRAIL HOLLIDAY
...THE SCHAEFER WAS CRAZY BACK IN THE DAY.
GOOD TIMES UPSTAIRS, AND *BETTER* ONES DOWN HERE IN THE SPEAKEASY.
AND I CAN'T TALK ABOUT THE STUFF THAT HAPPENED DOWN HERE *AFTER* AFTER HOURS.
YOU CAN TELL ME ANYTHING...
...YOU ARE *DEAD,* AFTER ALL.

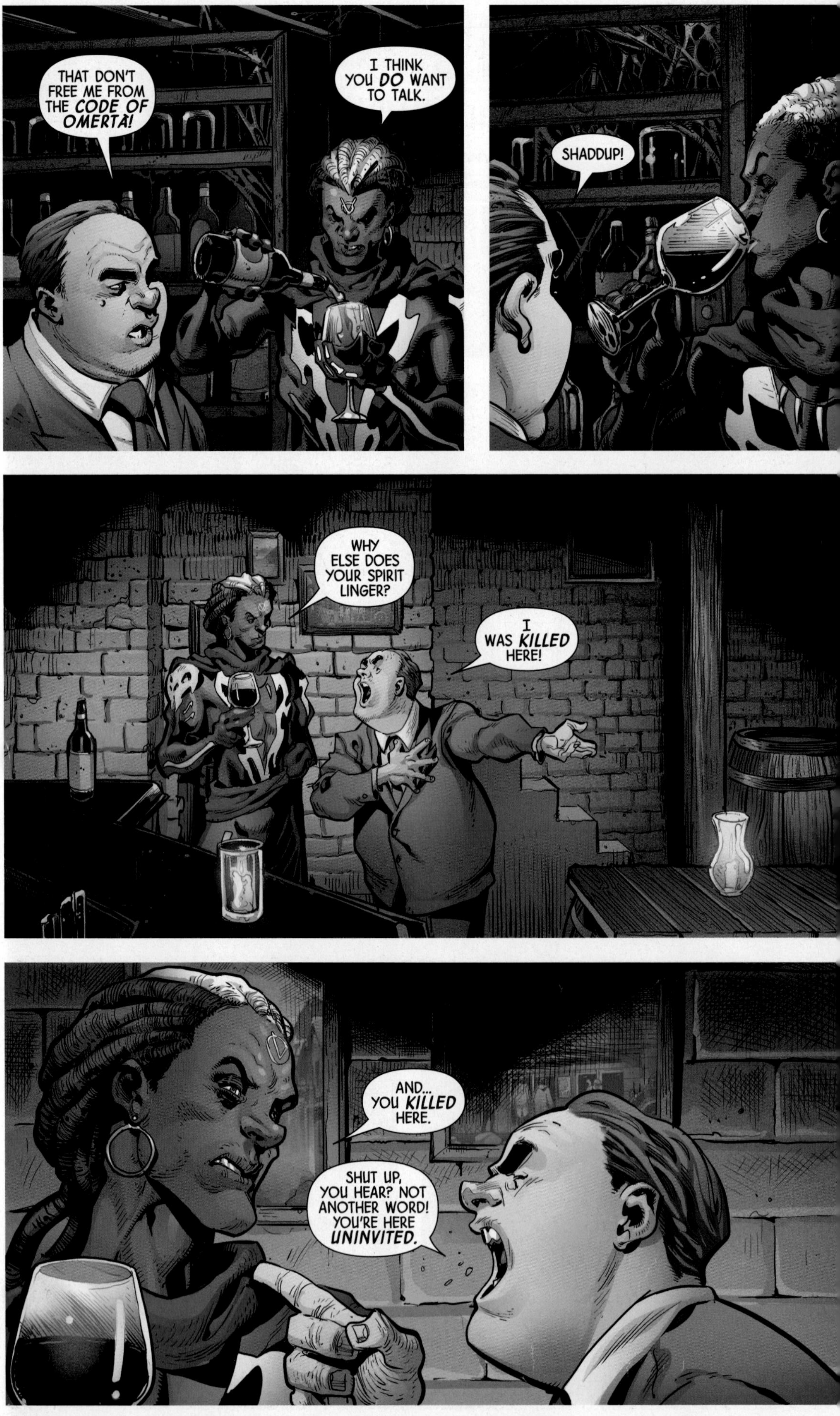

THAT DON'T FREE ME FROM THE CODE OF OMERTA!
I THINK YOU DO WANT TO TALK.
SHADDUP!
WHY ELSE DOES YOUR SPIRIT LINGER?
I WAS KILLED HERE!
AND... YOU KILLED HERE.
SHUT UP, YOU HEAR? NOT ANOTHER WORD! YOU'RE HERE UNINVITED.

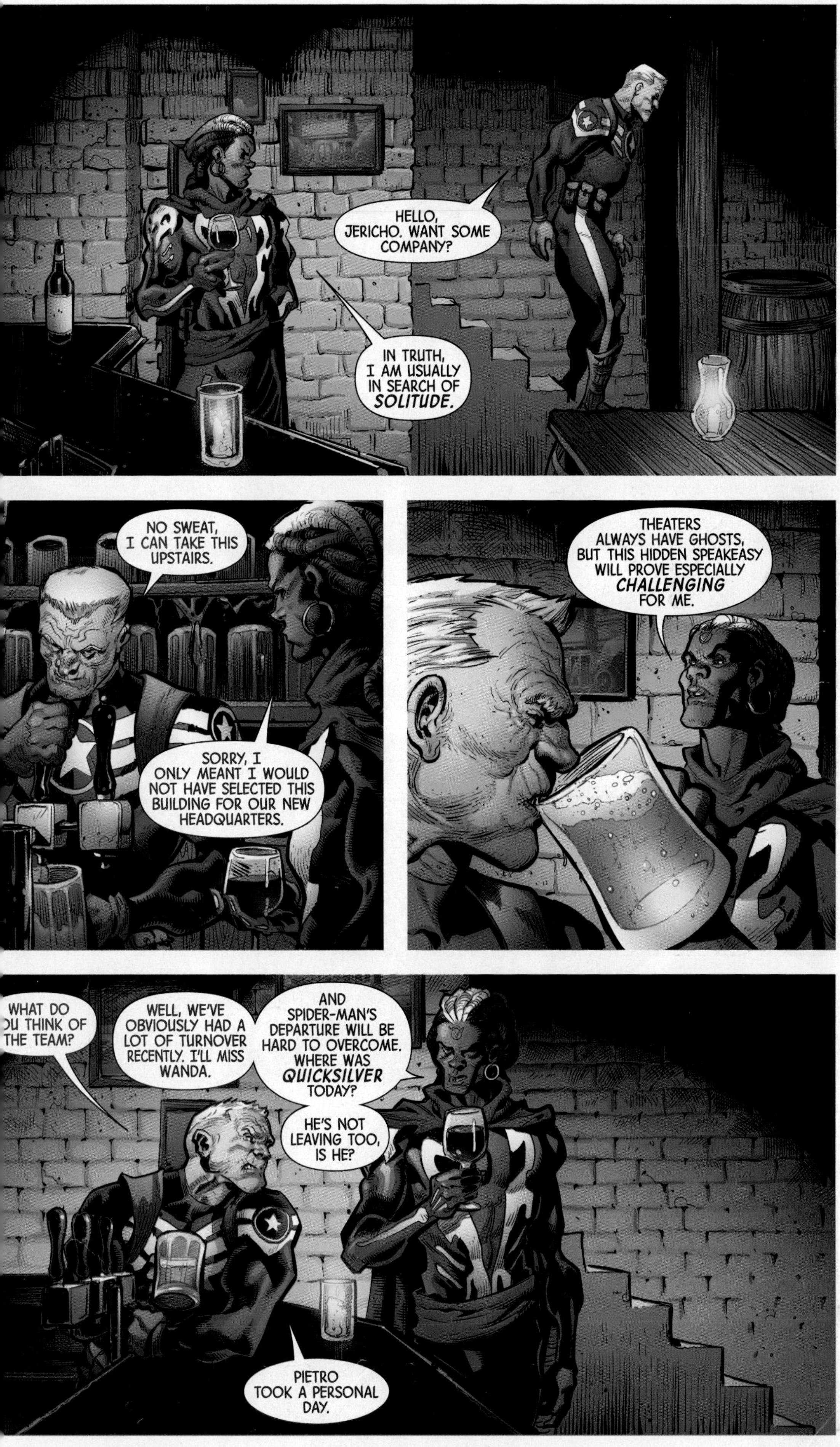
HELLO, JERICHO. WANT SOME COMPANY?
IN TRUTH, I AM USUALLY IN SEARCH OF SOLITUDE.
NO SWEAT, I CAN TAKE THIS UPSTAIRS.
SORRY, I ONLY MEANT I WOULD NOT HAVE SELECTED THIS BUILDING FOR OUR NEW HEADQUARTERS.
THEATERS ALWAYS HAVE GHOSTS, BUT THIS HIDDEN SPEAKEASY WILL PROVE ESPECIALLY CHALLENGING FOR ME.
WHAT DO OU THINK OF THE TEAM?
WELL, WE'VE OBVIOUSLY HAD A LOT OF TURNOVER RECENTLY. I'LL MISS WANDA.
AND SPIDER-MAN'S DEPARTURE WILL BE HARD TO OVERCOME. WHERE WAS QUICKSILVER TODAY?
HE'S NOT LEAVING TOO, IS HE?
PIETRO TOOK A PERSONAL DAY.

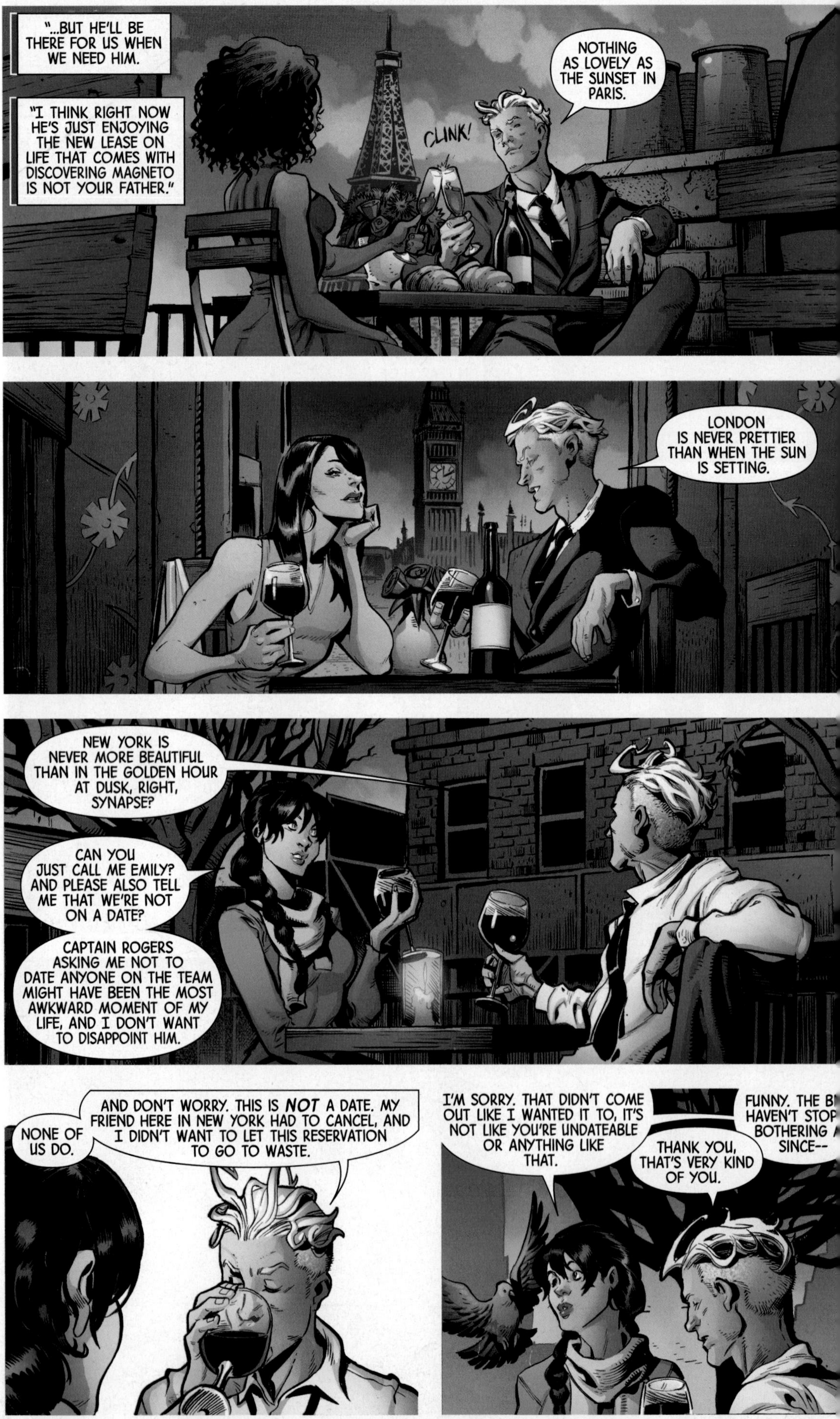
"...BUT HE'LL BE THERE FOR US WHEN WE NEED HIM.
"I THINK RIGHT NOW HE'S JUST ENJOYING THE NEW LEASE ON LIFE THAT COMES WITH DISCOVERING MAGNETO IS NOT YOUR FATHER."
CLINK!
NOTHING AS LOVELY AS THE SUNSET IN PARIS.
LONDON IS NEVER PRETTIER THAN WHEN THE SUN IS SETTING.
NEW YORK IS NEVER MORE BEAUTIFUL THAN IN THE GOLDEN HOUR AT DUSK, RIGHT, SYNAPSE?
CAN YOU JUST CALL ME EMILY? AND PLEASE ALSO TELL ME THAT WE'RE NOT ON A DATE?
CAPTAIN ROGERS ASKING ME NOT TO DATE ANYONE ON THE TEAM MIGHT HAVE BEEN THE MOST AWKWARD MOMENT OF MY LIFE, AND I DON'T WANT TO DISAPPOINT HIM.
NONE OF US DO.
AND DON'T WORRY. THIS IS *NOT* A DATE. MY FRIEND HERE IN NEW YORK HAD TO CANCEL, AND I DIDN'T WANT TO LET THIS RESERVATION TO GO TO WASTE.
I'M SORRY. THAT DIDN'T COME OUT LIKE I WANTED IT TO, IT'S NOT LIKE YOU'RE UNDATEABLE OR ANYTHING LIKE THAT.
THANK YOU, THAT'S VERY KIND OF YOU.
FUNNY. THE B HAVEN'T STOP BOTHERING SINCE--

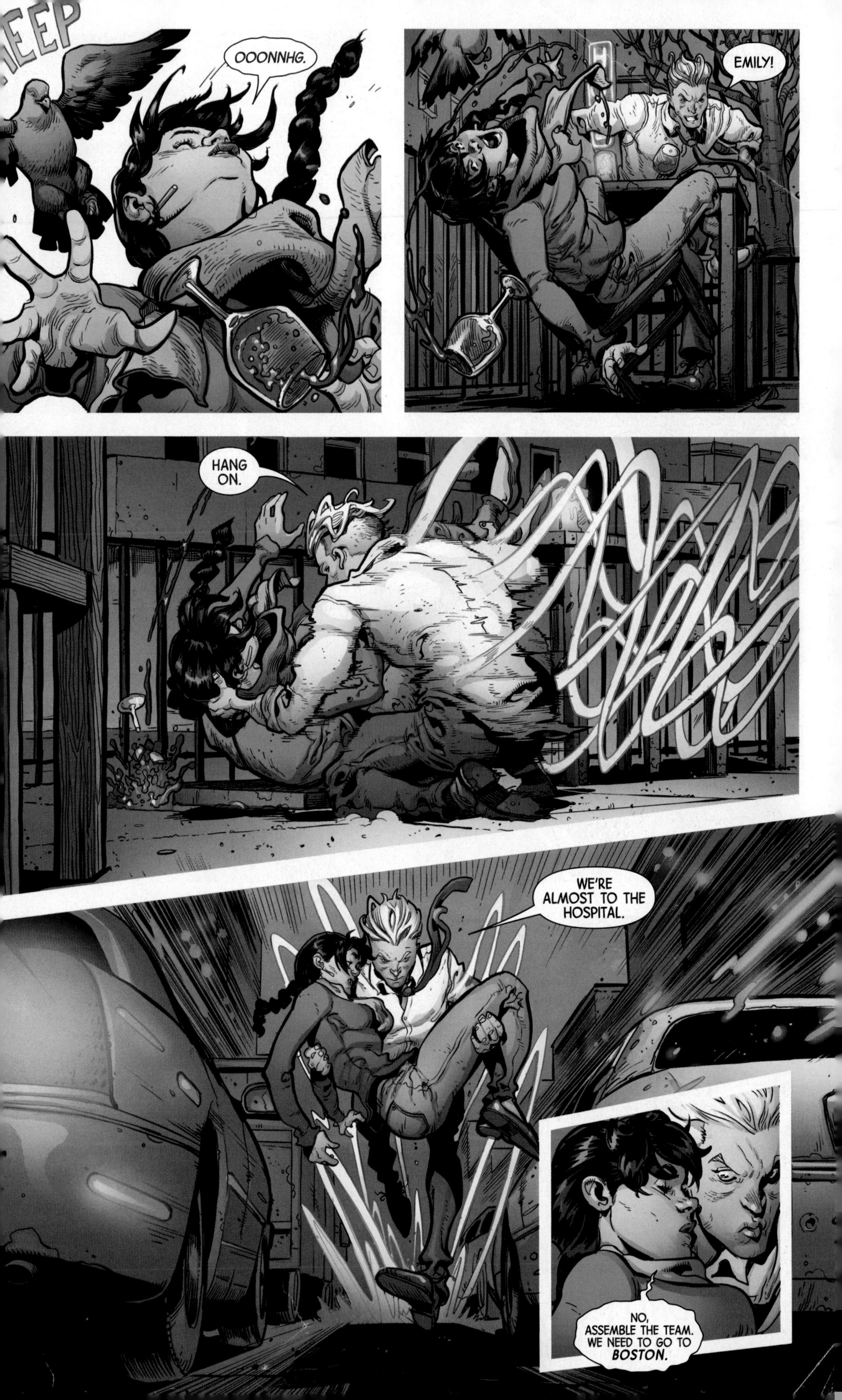

EEP
OOONNHG.
EMILY!
HANG ON.
WE'RE ALMOST TO THE HOSPITAL.
NO, ASSEMBLE THE TEAM. WE NEED TO GO TO *BOSTON*.

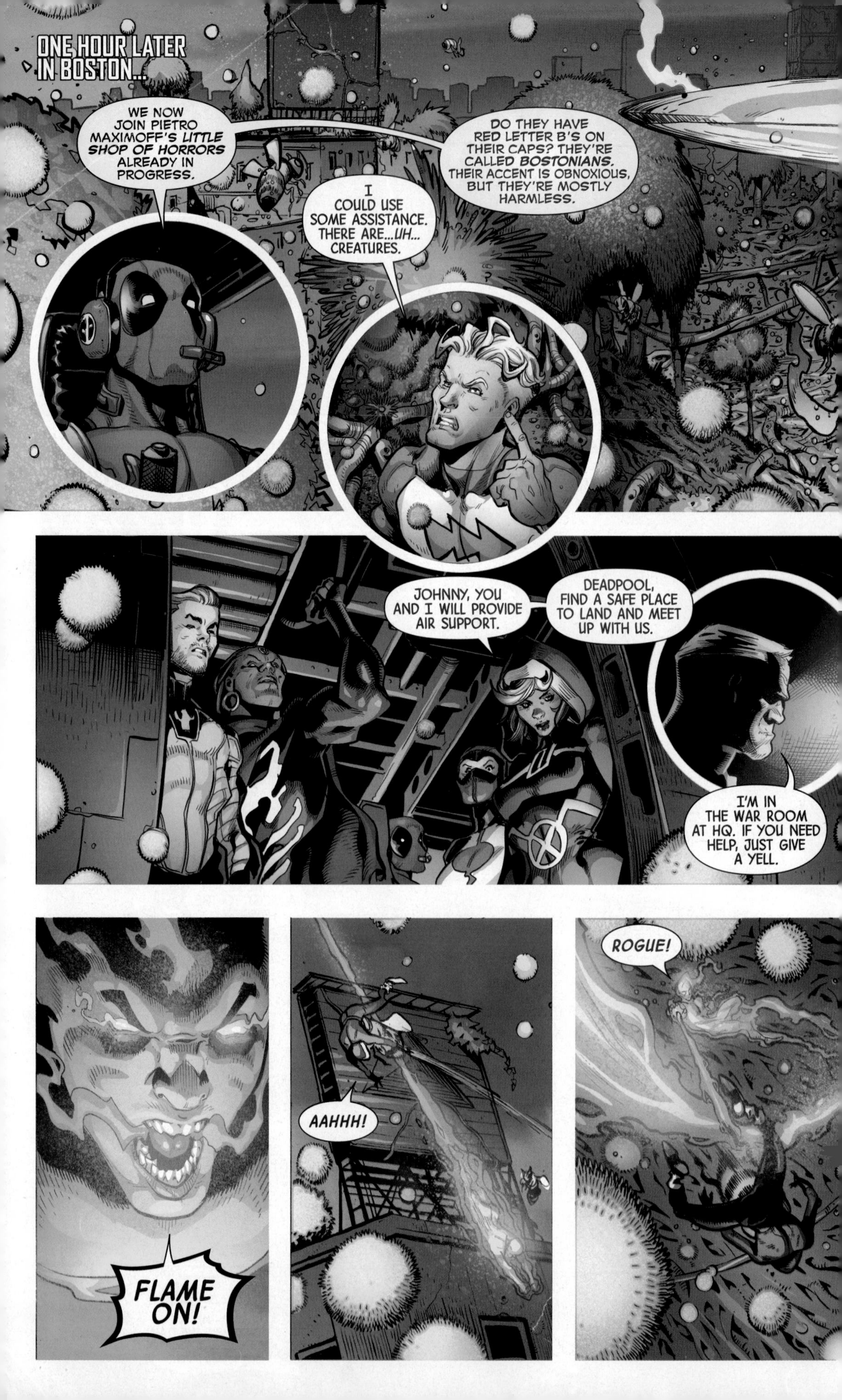
ONE HOUR LATER IN BOSTON...
WE NOW JOIN PIETRO MAXIMOFF'S *LITTLE SHOP OF HORRORS* ALREADY IN PROGRESS.
I COULD USE SOME ASSISTANCE. THERE ARE...*UH*... CREATURES.
DO THEY HAVE RED LETTER B'S ON THEIR CAPS? THEY'RE CALLED *BOSTONIANS.* THEIR ACCENT IS OBNOXIOUS, BUT THEY'RE MOSTLY HARMLESS.
JOHNNY, YOU AND I WILL PROVIDE AIR SUPPORT.
DEADPOOL, FIND A SAFE PLACE TO LAND AND MEET UP WITH US.
I'M IN THE WAR ROOM AT HQ. IF YOU NEED HELP, JUST GIVE A YELL.
FLAME ON!
AAHHH!
ROGUE!

SO--HOW'S MEDUSA?

DON'T BE LIKE THAT.

I WASN'T BUSTING YOUR CHOPS. JUST ASKING.

I'M FINE. JUST CAUGHT ME OFF GUARD.

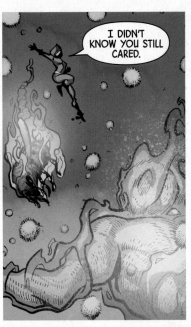

I DIDN'T KNOW YOU STILL CARED.

SERIOUSLY? IT'S BEEN, LIKE, MONTHS.

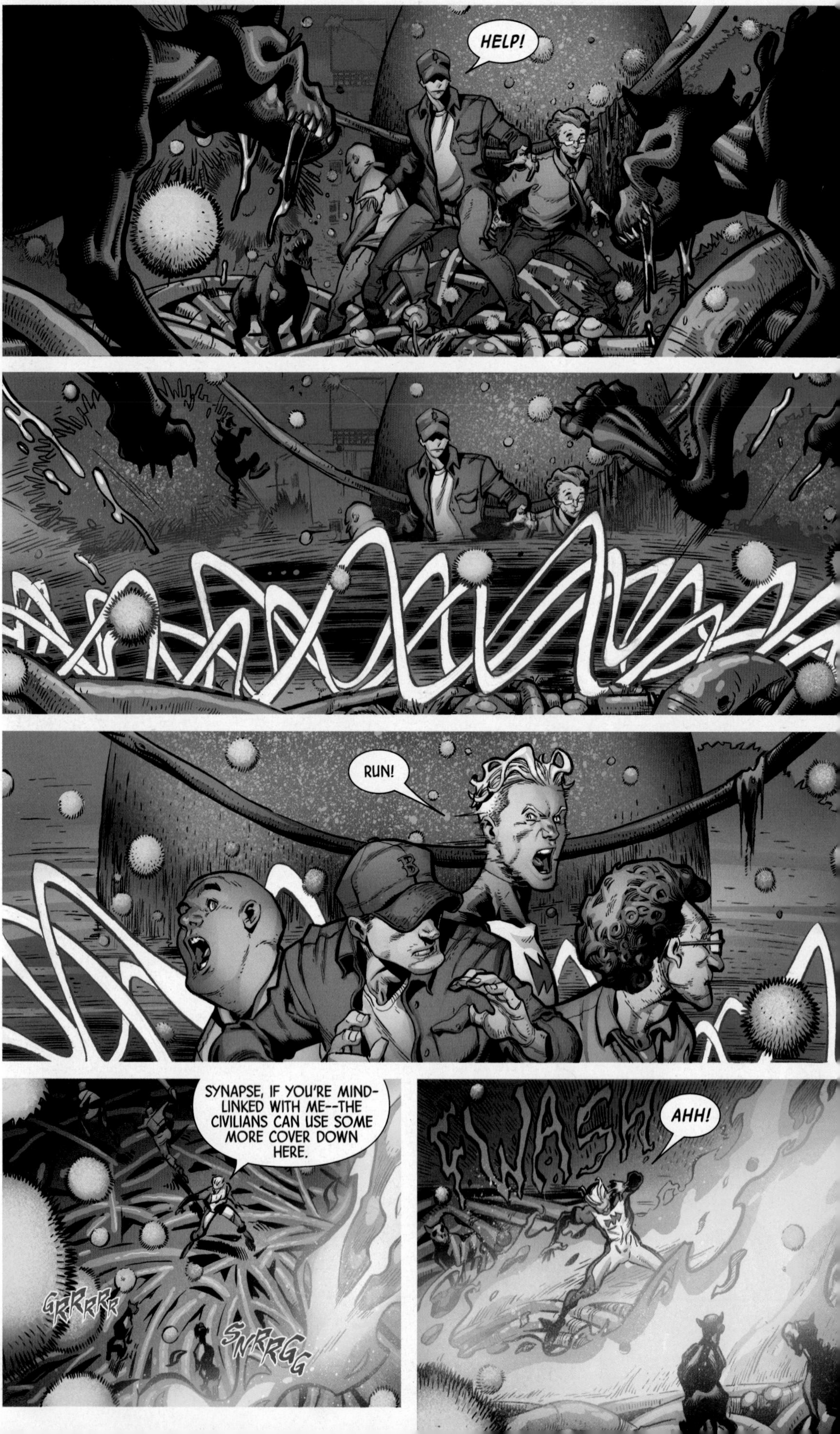
HELP!
RUN!
SYNAPSE, IF YOU'RE MIND-LINKED WITH ME--THE CIVILIANS CAN USE SOME MORE COVER DOWN HERE.
GRRRRR
SNRRGG
SWASH
AHH!

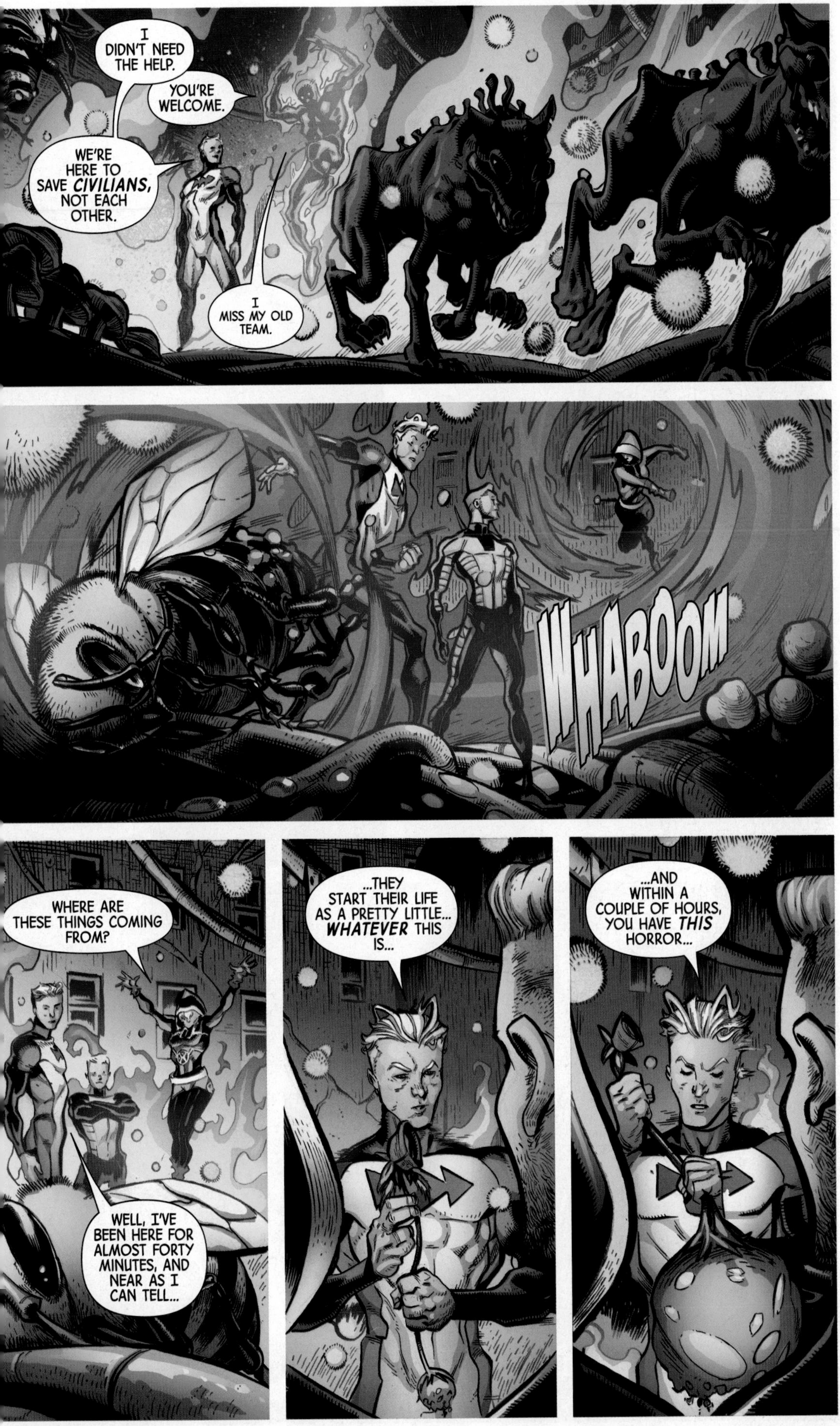
I DIDN'T NEED THE HELP.
YOU'RE WELCOME.
WE'RE HERE TO SAVE *CIVILIANS,* NOT EACH OTHER.
I MISS MY OLD TEAM.
WHABOOM
WHERE ARE THESE THINGS COMING FROM?
WELL, I'VE BEEN HERE FOR ALMOST FORTY MINUTES, AND NEAR AS I CAN TELL...
...THEY START THEIR LIFE AS A PRETTY LITTLE... *WHATEVER* THIS IS...
...AND WITHIN A COUPLE OF HOURS, YOU HAVE *THIS* HORROR...

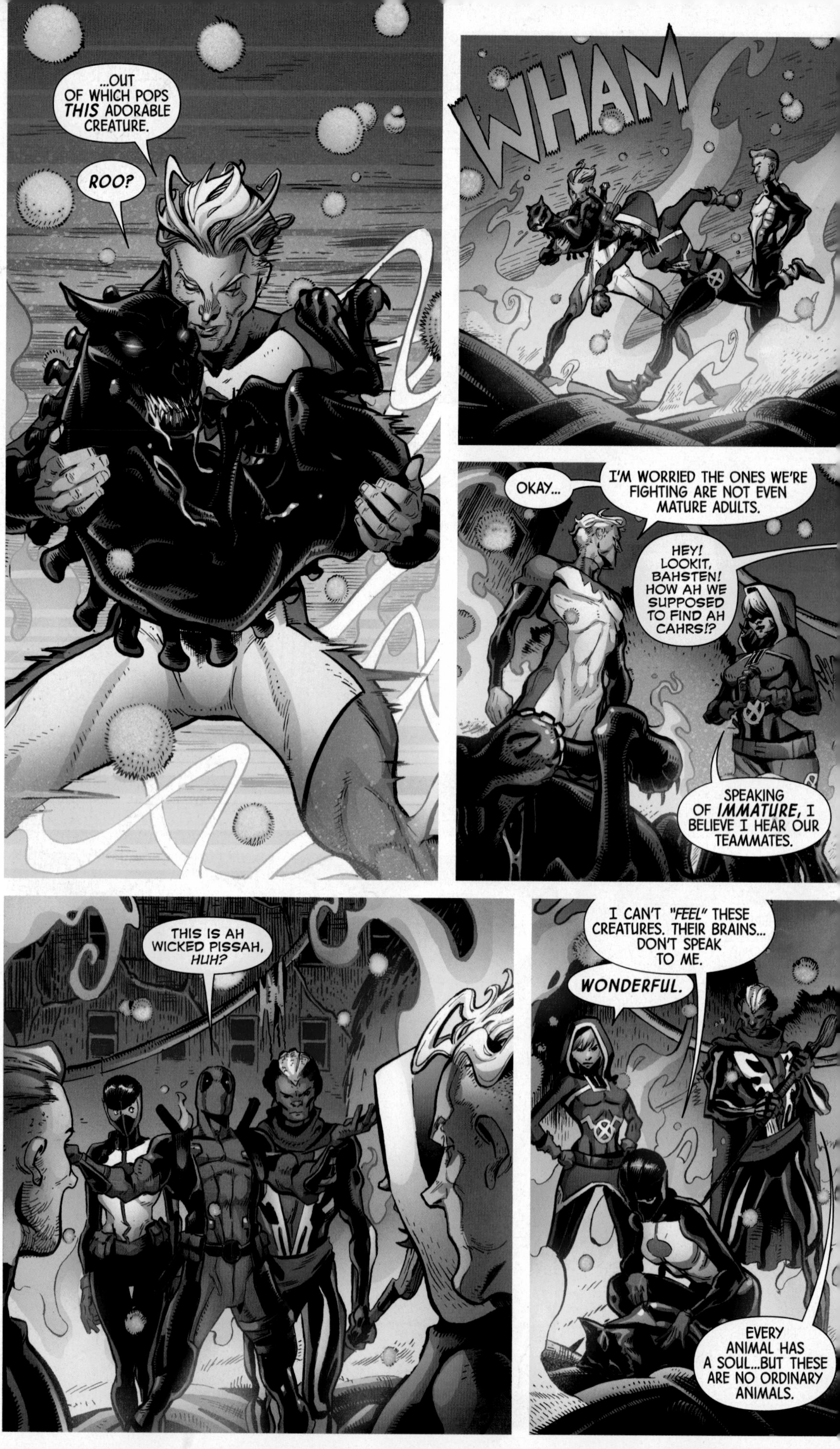

...OUT OF WHICH POPS THIS ADORABLE CREATURE.
ROO?
WHAM
OKAY...
I'M WORRIED THE ONES WE'RE FIGHTING ARE NOT EVEN MATURE ADULTS.
HEY! LOOKIT, BAHSTEN! HOW AH WE SUPPOSED TO FIND AH CAHRS!?
SPEAKING OF IMMATURE, I BELIEVE I HEAR OUR TEAMMATES.
THIS IS AH WICKED PISSAH, HUH?
I CAN'T "FEEL" THESE CREATURES. THEIR BRAINS... DON'T SPEAK TO ME.
WONDERFUL.
EVERY ANIMAL HAS A SOUL...BUT THESE ARE NO ORDINARY ANIMALS.

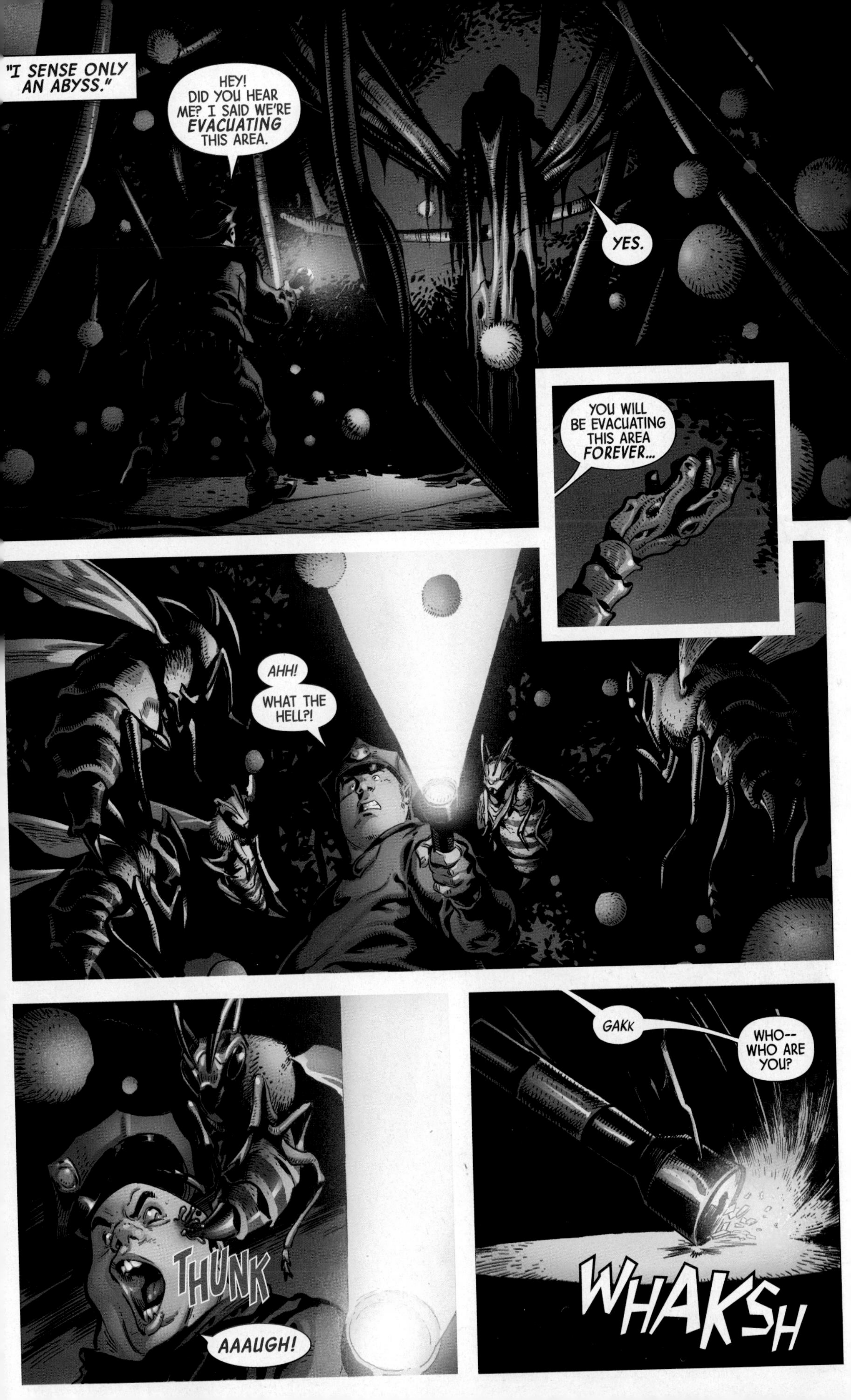
"I SENSE ONLY AN ABYSS."
HEY! DID YOU HEAR ME? I SAID WE'RE EVACUATING THIS AREA.
YES.
YOU WILL BE EVACUATING THIS AREA FOREVER...
AHH!
WHAT THE HELL?!
THUNK
AAAUGH!
GAKK
WHO-- WHO ARE YOU?
WHAKSH

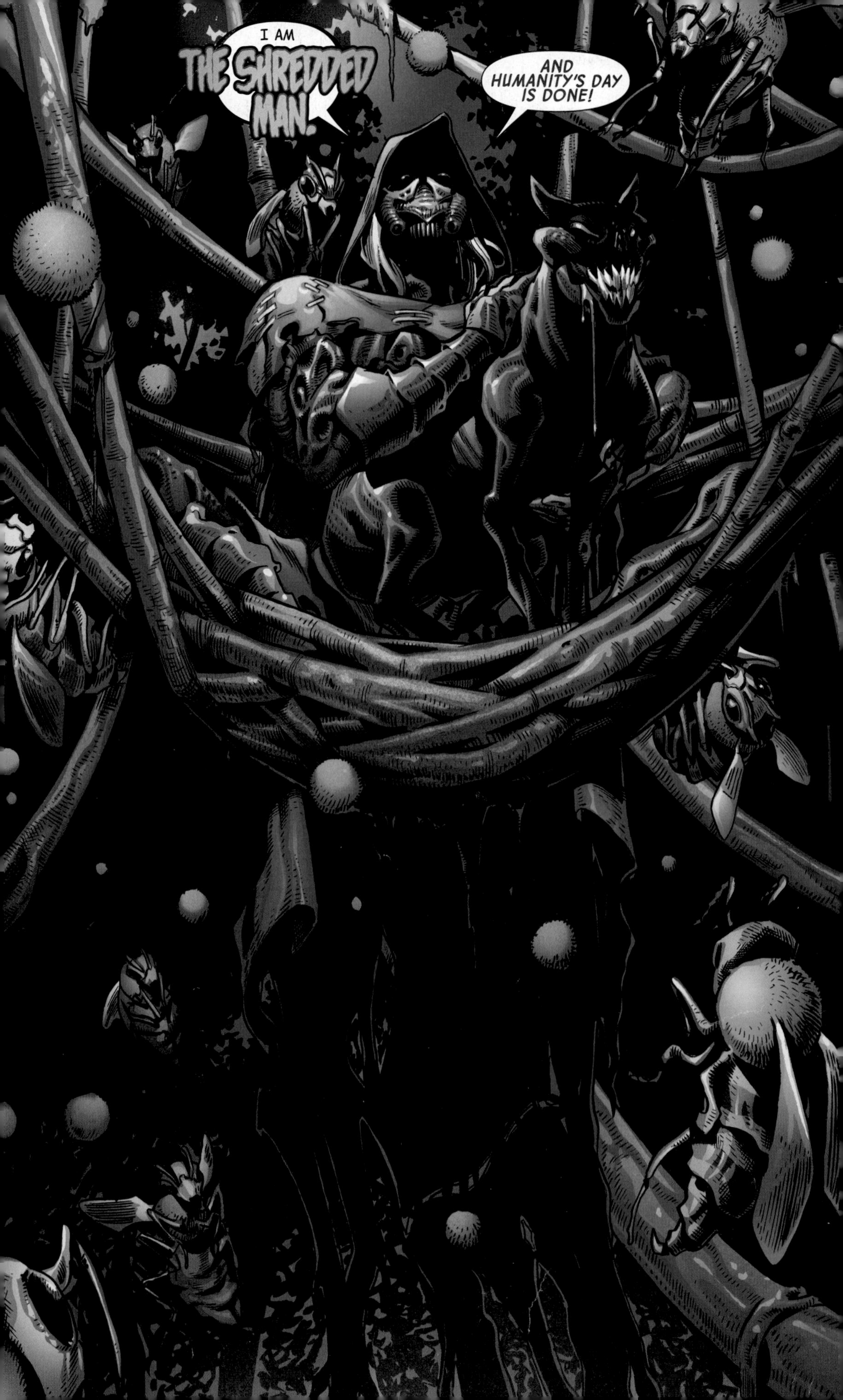

I AM THE SHREDDED MAN.
AND HUMANITY'S DAY IS DONE!

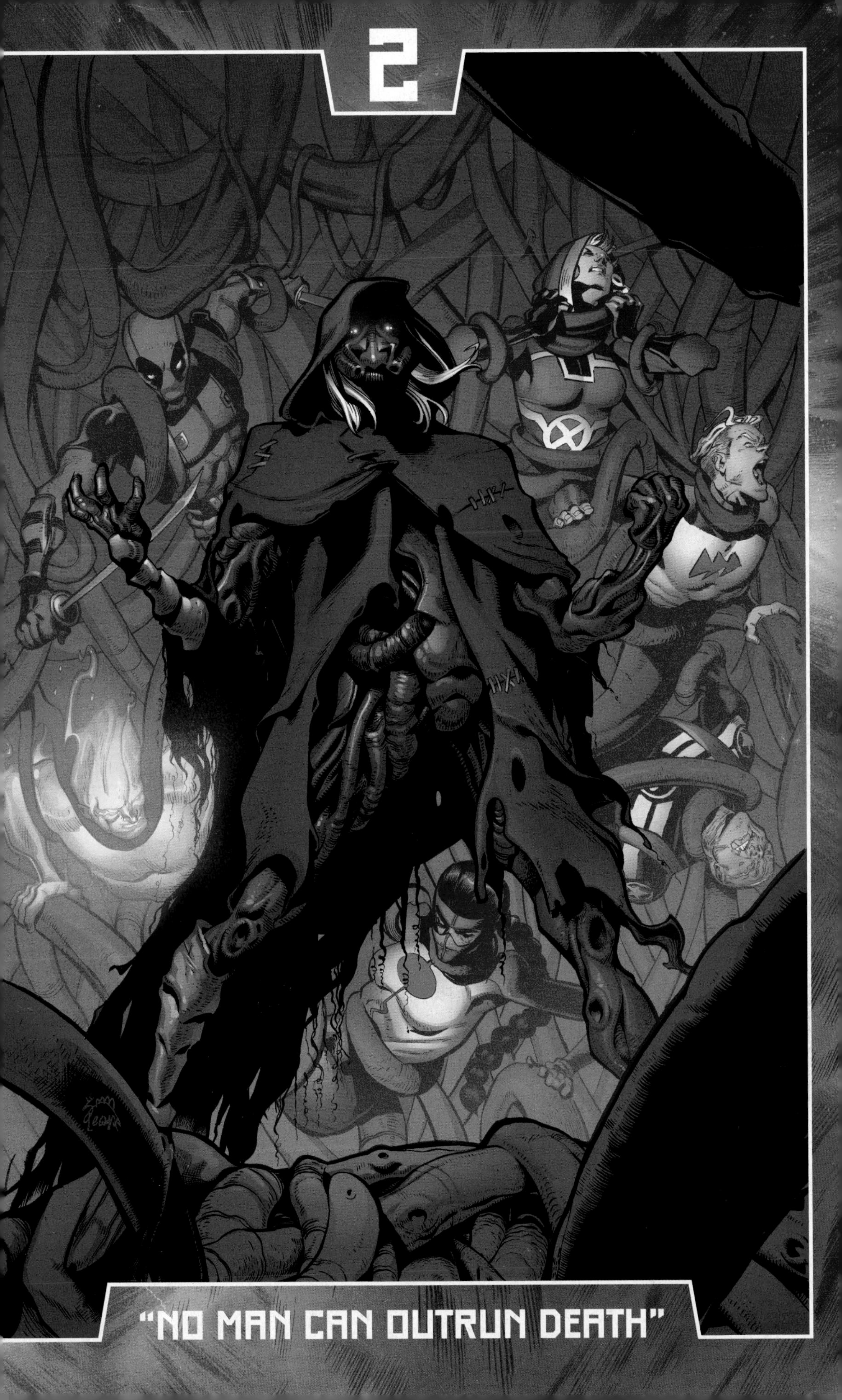
2
"NO MAN CAN OUTRUN DEATH"

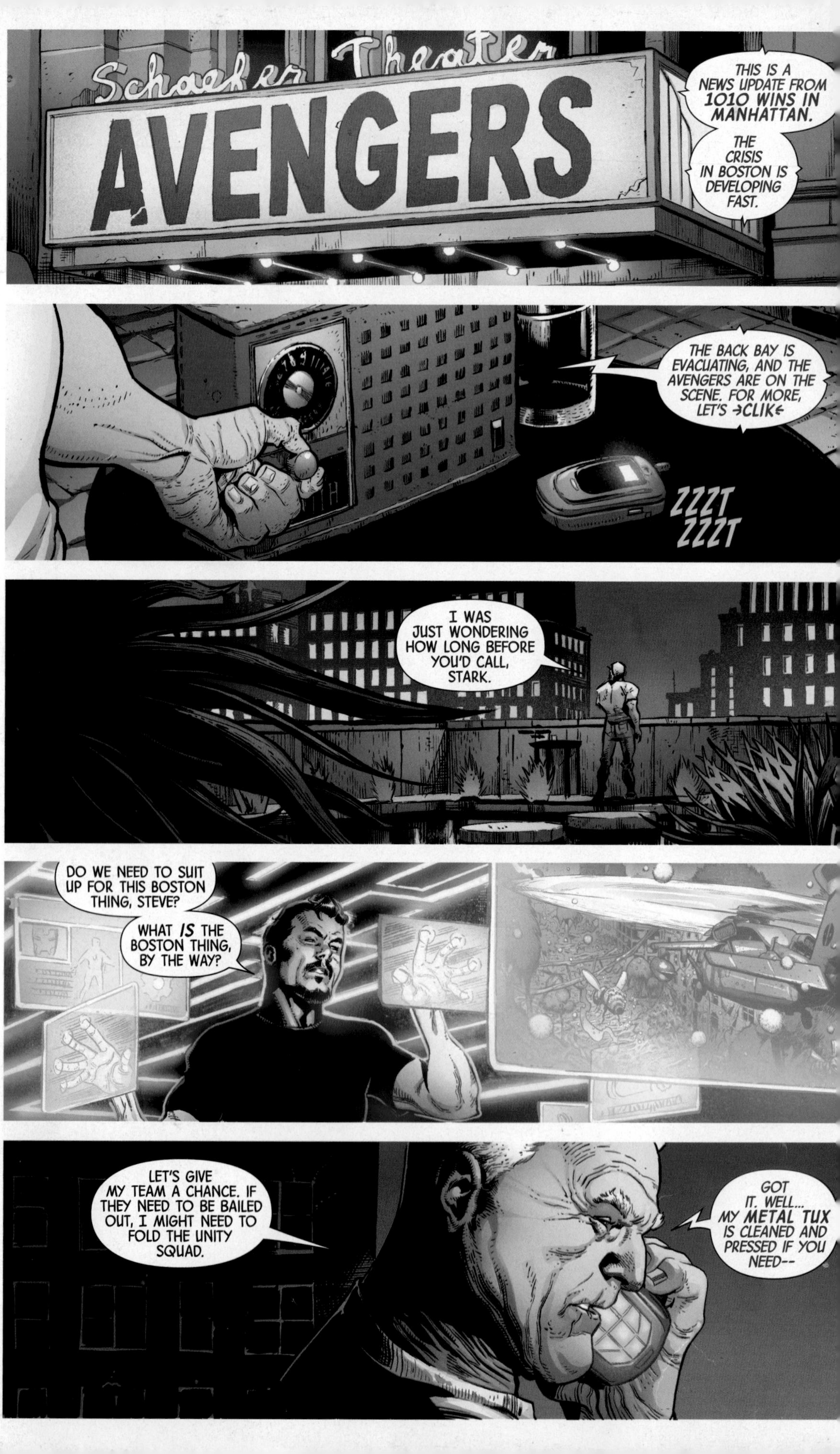
Schaefer Theater
AVENGERS
THIS IS A NEWS UPDATE FROM 1010 WINS IN MANHATTAN.
THE CRISIS IN BOSTON IS DEVELOPING FAST.
THE BACK BAY IS EVACUATING, AND THE AVENGERS ARE ON THE SCENE. FOR MORE, LET'S →CLIK←
ZZZT ZZZT
I WAS JUST WONDERING HOW LONG BEFORE YOU'D CALL, STARK.
DO WE NEED TO SUIT UP FOR THIS BOSTON THING, STEVE?
WHAT *IS* THE BOSTON THING, BY THE WAY?
LET'S GIVE MY TEAM A CHANCE. IF THEY NEED TO BE BAILED OUT, I MIGHT NEED TO FOLD THE UNITY SQUAD.
GOT IT. WELL... MY *METAL TUX* IS CLEANED AND PRESSED IF YOU NEED--

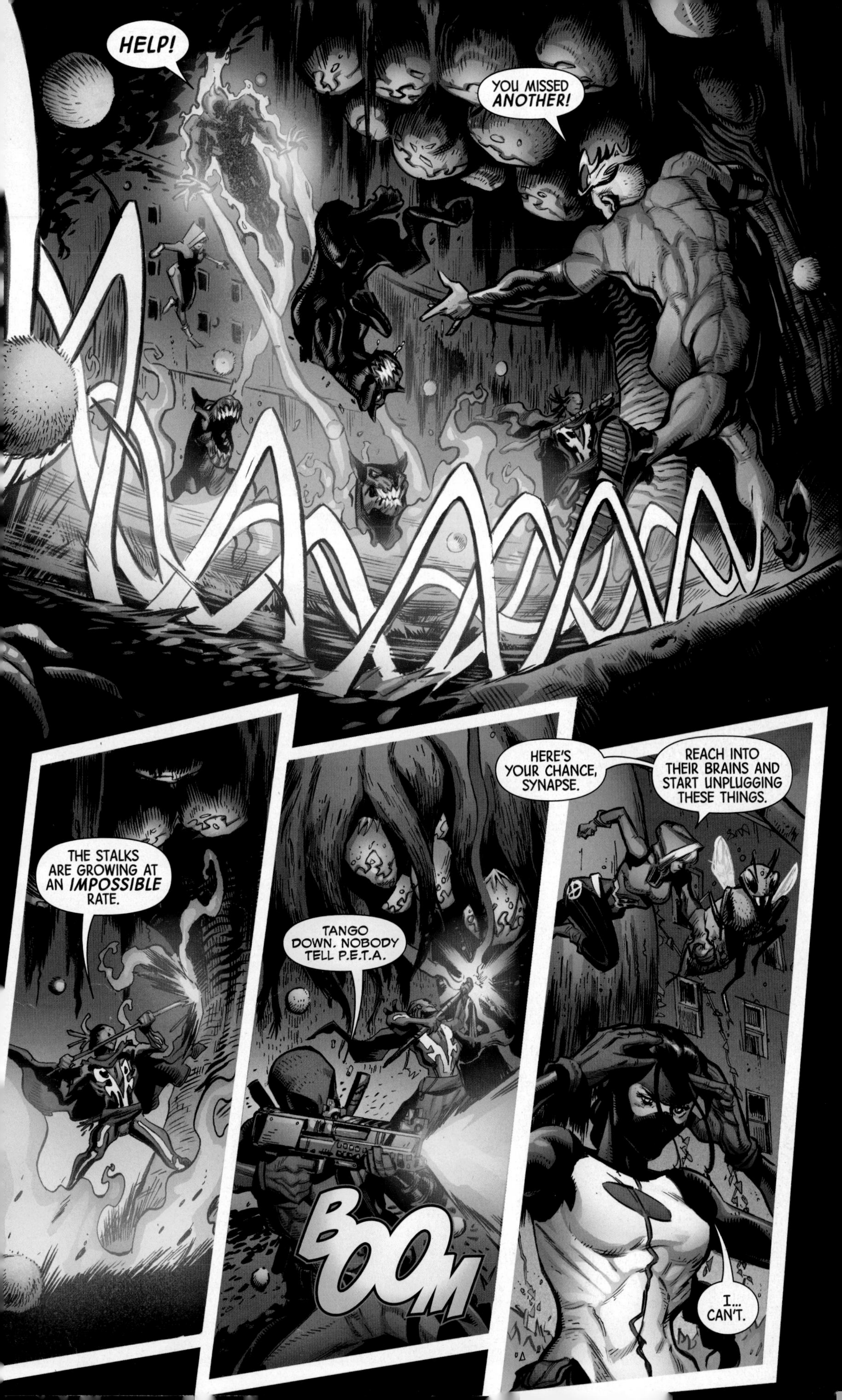
HELP!
YOU MISSED ANOTHER!
THE STALKS ARE GROWING AT AN IMPOSSIBLE RATE.
TANGO DOWN. NOBODY TELL P.E.T.A.
BOOM
HERE'S YOUR CHANCE, SYNAPSE.
REACH INTO THEIR BRAINS AND START UNPLUGGING THESE THINGS.
I... CAN'T.

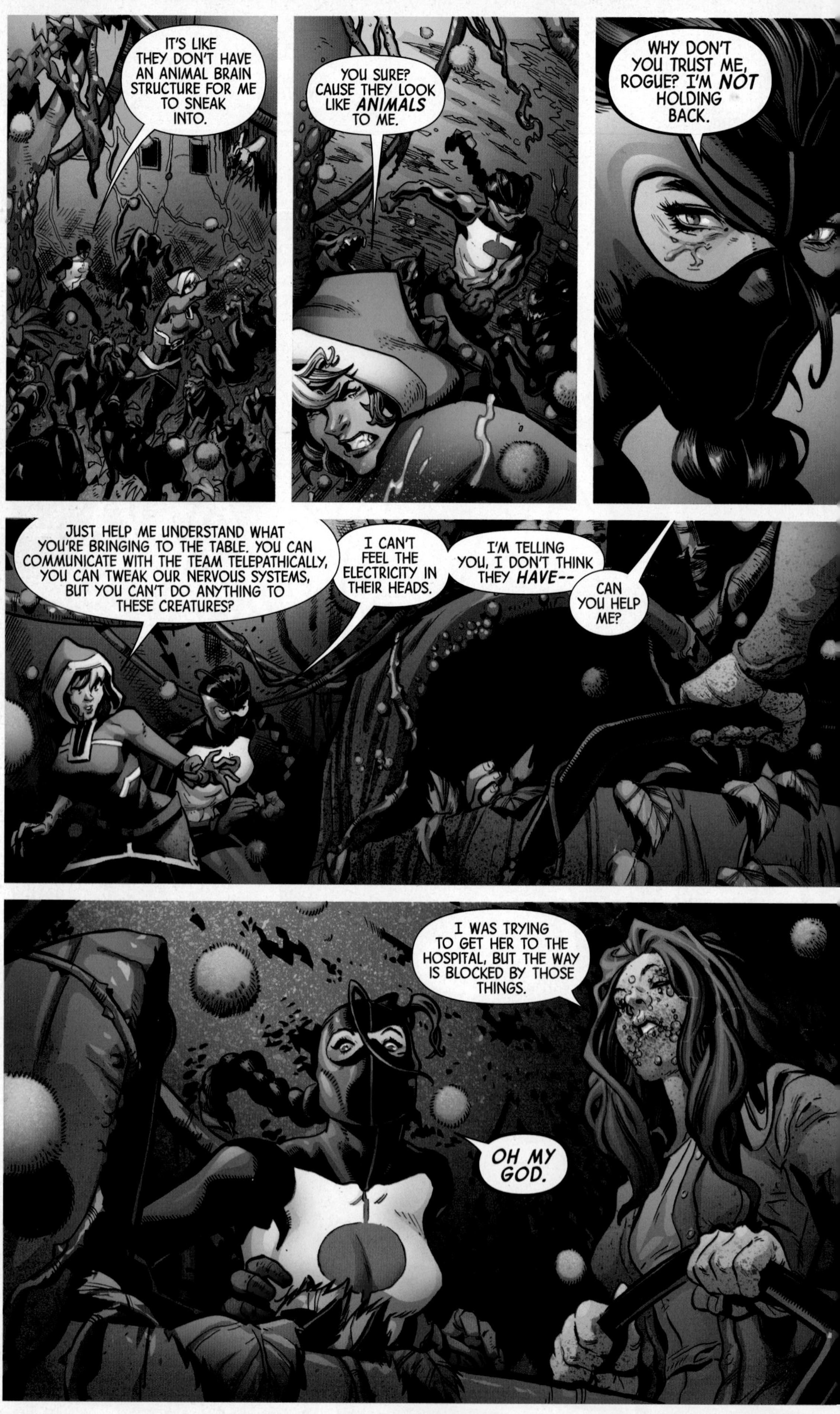
IT'S LIKE THEY DON'T HAVE AN ANIMAL BRAIN STRUCTURE FOR ME TO SNEAK INTO.
YOU SURE? CAUSE THEY LOOK LIKE *ANIMALS* TO ME.
WHY DON'T YOU TRUST ME, ROGUE? I'M *NOT* HOLDING BACK.
JUST HELP ME UNDERSTAND WHAT YOU'RE BRINGING TO THE TABLE. YOU CAN COMMUNICATE WITH THE TEAM TELEPATHICALLY, YOU CAN TWEAK OUR NERVOUS SYSTEMS, BUT YOU CAN'T DO ANYTHING TO THESE CREATURES?
I CAN'T FEEL THE ELECTRICITY IN THEIR HEADS.
I'M TELLING YOU, I DON'T THINK THEY *HAVE--*
CAN YOU HELP ME?
I WAS TRYING TO GET HER TO THE HOSPITAL, BUT THE WAY IS BLOCKED BY THOSE THINGS.
OH MY GOD.

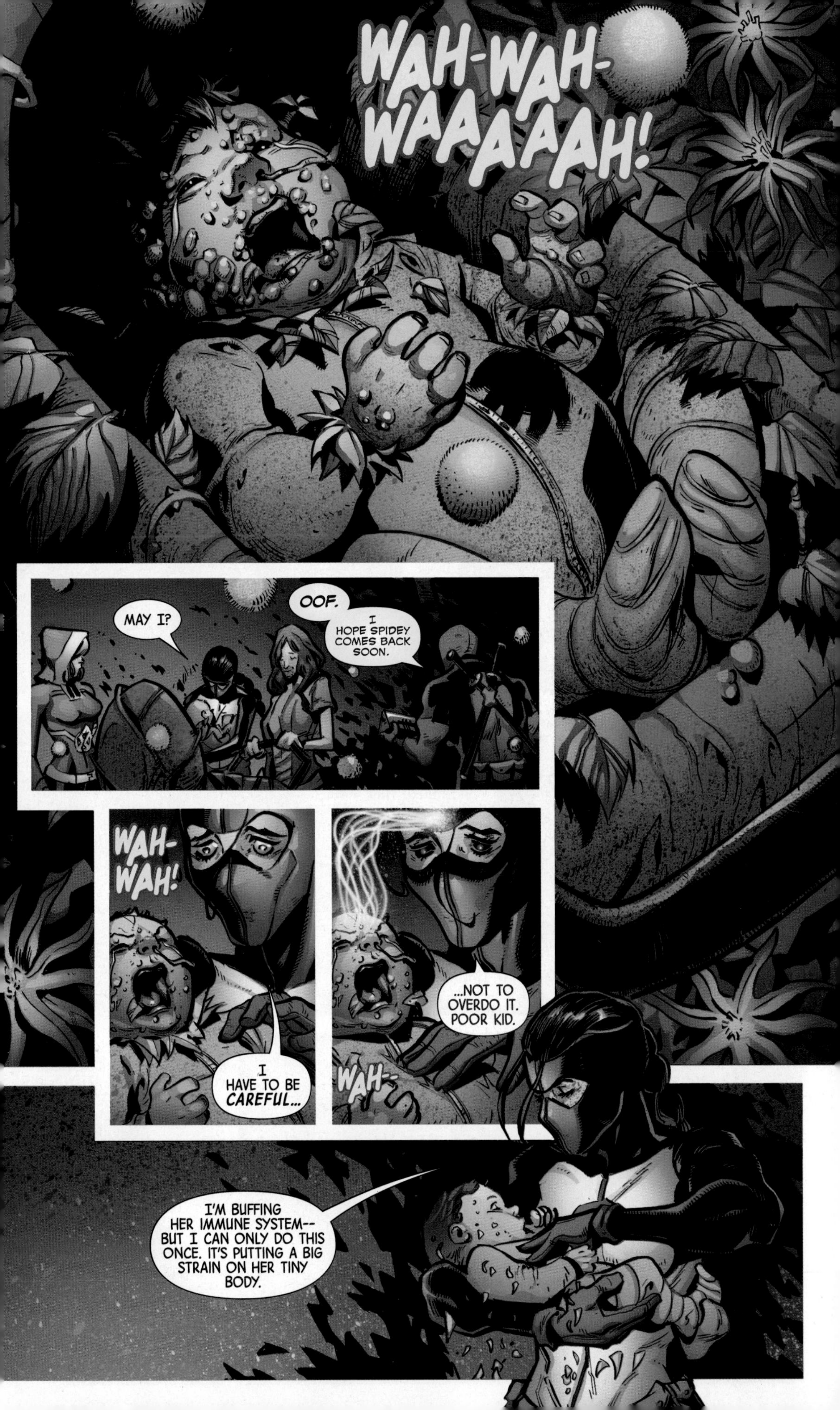
WAH-WAH-WAAAAAAH!
MAY I?
OOF.
I HOPE SPIDEY COMES BACK SOON.
WAH-WAH!
I HAVE TO BE *CAREFUL*...
...NOT TO OVERDO IT. POOR KID.
WAH-
I'M BUFFING HER IMMUNE SYSTEM-- BUT I CAN ONLY DO THIS ONCE. IT'S PUTTING A BIG STRAIN ON HER TINY BODY.

THANK YOU.

BEACON HILL SEEMS TO BE THE EPICENTER, AND IT'S SPREADING--

--FAST.

QUICKSILVER, GET THESE TWO TO A HOSPITAL.

DONE.

BLAM

WHAT ABOUT HAVING TORCH NUKE THIS PLACE FROM ABOVE?

NOT A GOOD IDEA.

STILL TOO MANY CIVILIANS AROUND.

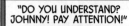

IT IS TOO LATE FOR THIS MAN.

THE ROOTS DUG INTO HIM AS THOUGH HE WERE SOIL.

WE NEED TO UNDERSTAND THE MECHANICS OF THIS ATTACK.

"DO YOU UNDERSTAND? JOHNNY! PAY ATTENTION!"

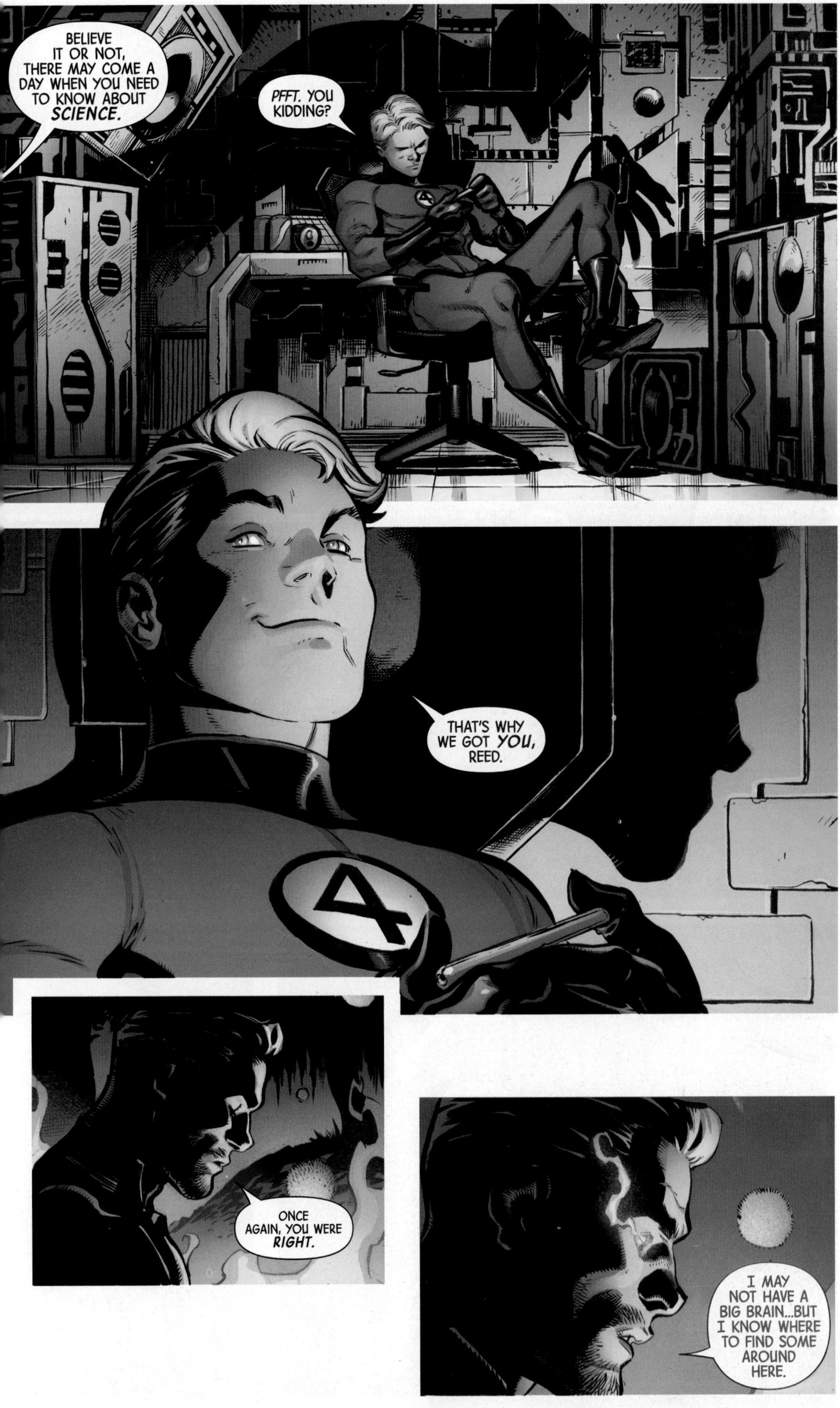
BELIEVE IT OR NOT, THERE MAY COME A DAY WHEN YOU NEED TO KNOW ABOUT SCIENCE.
PFFT. YOU KIDDING?
THAT'S WHY WE GOT YOU, REED.
ONCE AGAIN, YOU WERE RIGHT.
I MAY NOT HAVE A BIG BRAIN...BUT I KNOW WHERE TO FIND SOME AROUND HERE.

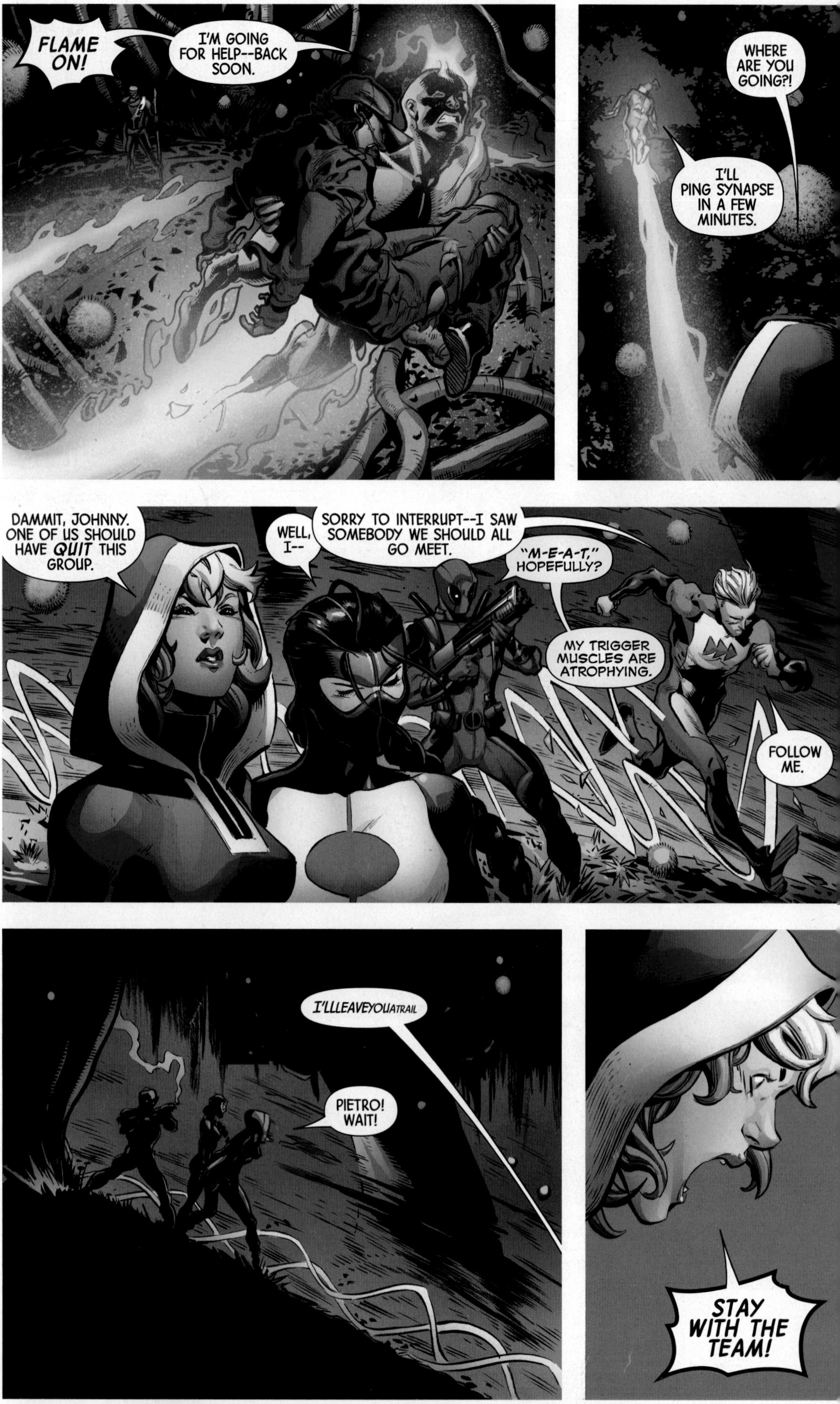
FLAME ON!
I'M GOING FOR HELP--BACK SOON.
WHERE ARE YOU GOING?!
I'LL PING SYNAPSE IN A FEW MINUTES.
DAMMIT, JOHNNY. ONE OF US SHOULD HAVE QUIT THIS GROUP.
WELL, I--
SORRY TO INTERRUPT--I SAW SOMEBODY WE SHOULD ALL GO MEET.
"M-E-A-T," HOPEFULLY?
MY TRIGGER MUSCLES ARE ATROPHYING.
FOLLOW ME.
I'LLLEAVEYOUATRAIL
PIETRO! WAIT!
STAY WITH THE TEAM!

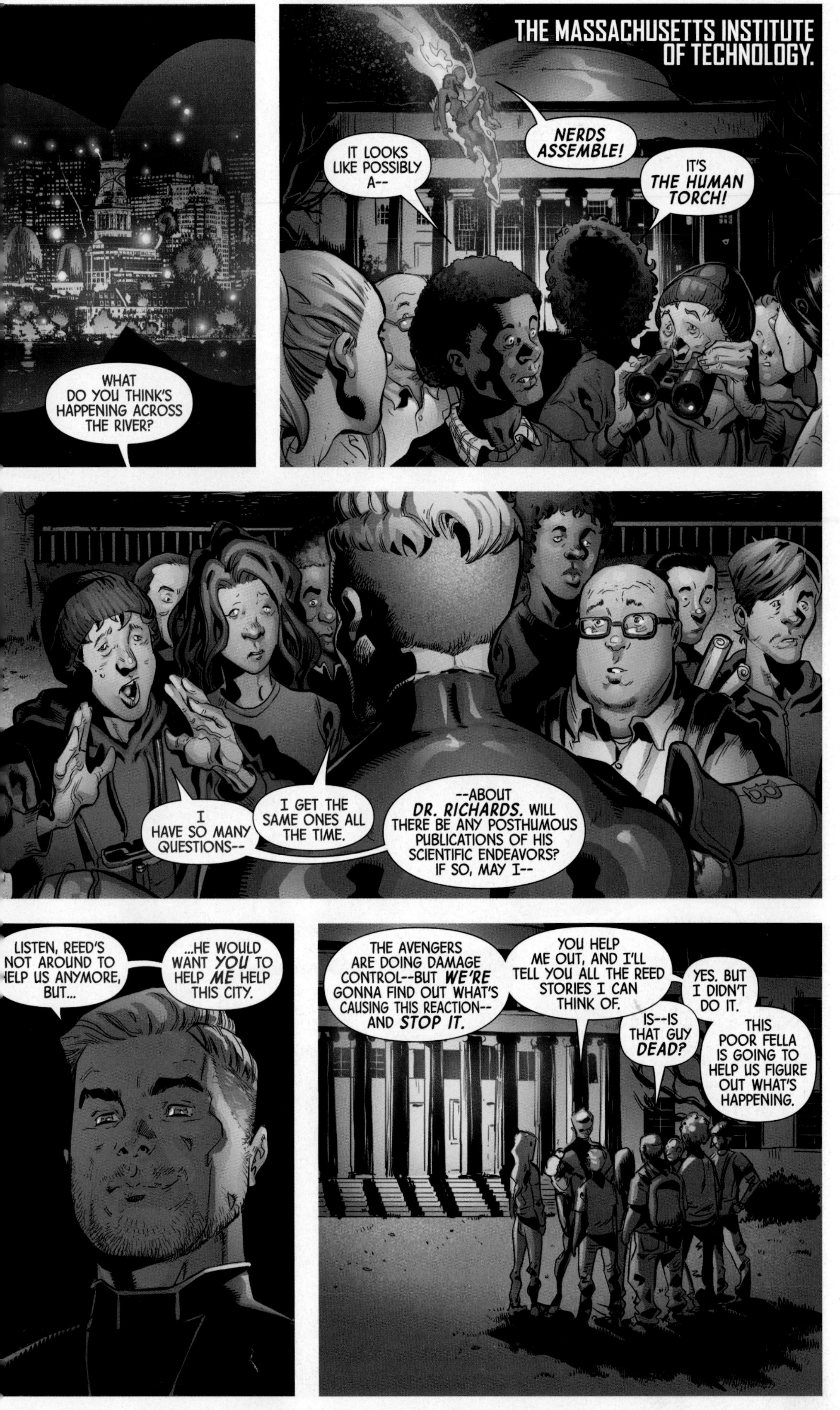

WHAT DO YOU THINK'S HAPPENING ACROSS THE RIVER?
THE MASSACHUSETTS INSTITUTE OF TECHNOLOGY.
IT LOOKS LIKE POSSIBLY A--
NERDS ASSEMBLE!
IT'S THE HUMAN TORCH!
I HAVE SO MANY QUESTIONS--
I GET THE SAME ONES ALL THE TIME.
--ABOUT DR. RICHARDS. WILL THERE BE ANY POSTHUMOUS PUBLICATIONS OF HIS SCIENTIFIC ENDEAVORS? IF SO, MAY I--
LISTEN, REED'S NOT AROUND TO HELP US ANYMORE, BUT...
...HE WOULD WANT YOU TO HELP ME HELP THIS CITY.
THE AVENGERS ARE DOING DAMAGE CONTROL--BUT WE'RE GONNA FIND OUT WHAT'S CAUSING THIS REACTION--AND STOP IT.
YOU HELP ME OUT, AND I'LL TELL YOU ALL THE REED STORIES I CAN THINK OF.
IS--IS THAT GUY DEAD?
YES. BUT I DIDN'T DO IT.
THIS POOR FELLA IS GOING TO HELP US FIGURE OUT WHAT'S HAPPENING.

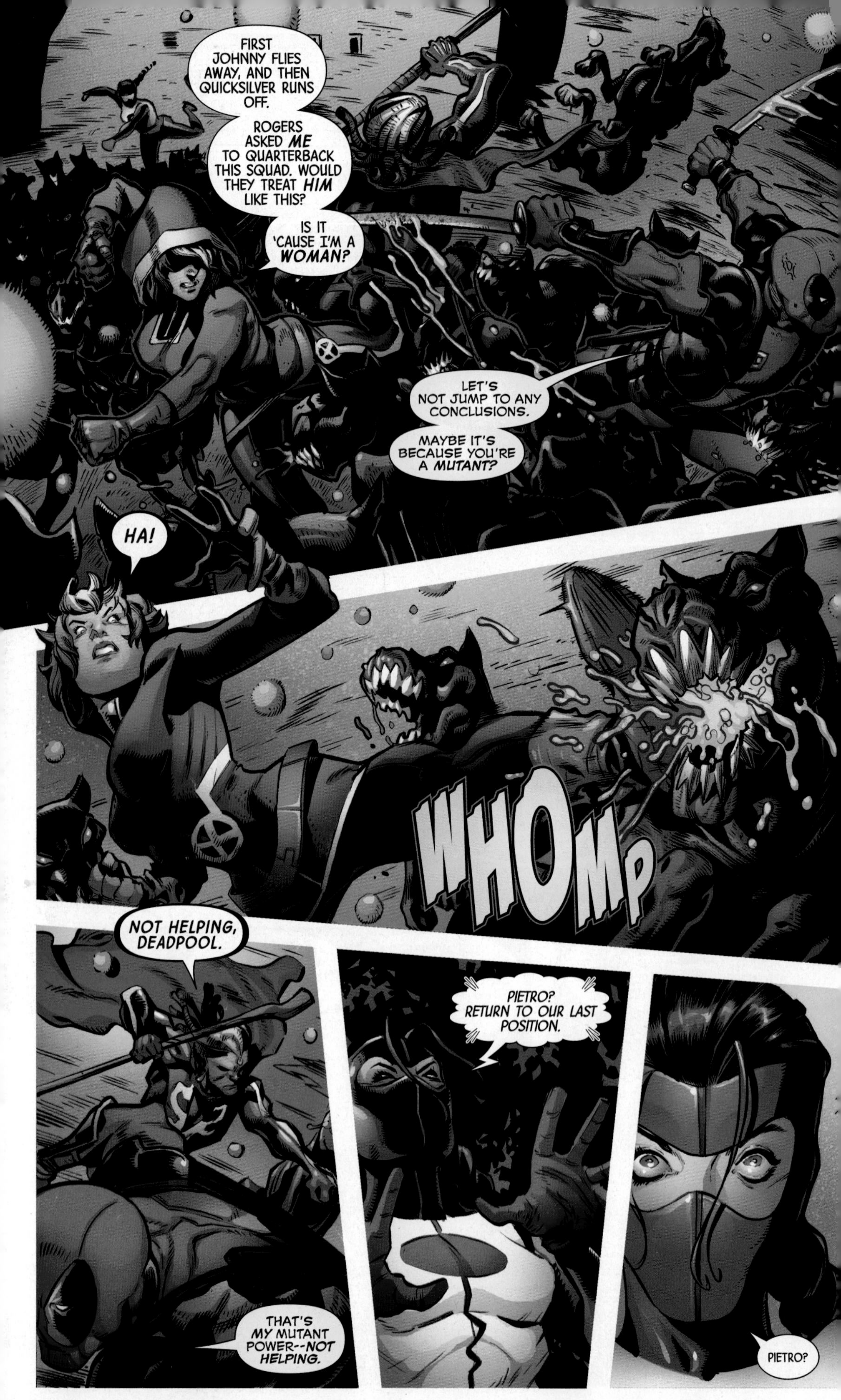
FIRST JOHNNY FLIES AWAY, AND THEN QUICKSILVER RUNS OFF.
ROGERS ASKED ME TO QUARTERBACK THIS SQUAD. WOULD THEY TREAT HIM LIKE THIS?
IS IT 'CAUSE I'M A WOMAN?
LET'S NOT JUMP TO ANY CONCLUSIONS.
MAYBE IT'S BECAUSE YOU'RE A MUTANT?
HA!
WHOMP
NOT HELPING, DEADPOOL.
THAT'S MY MUTANT POWER--NOT HELPING.
PIETRO? RETURN TO OUR LAST POSITION.
PIETRO?

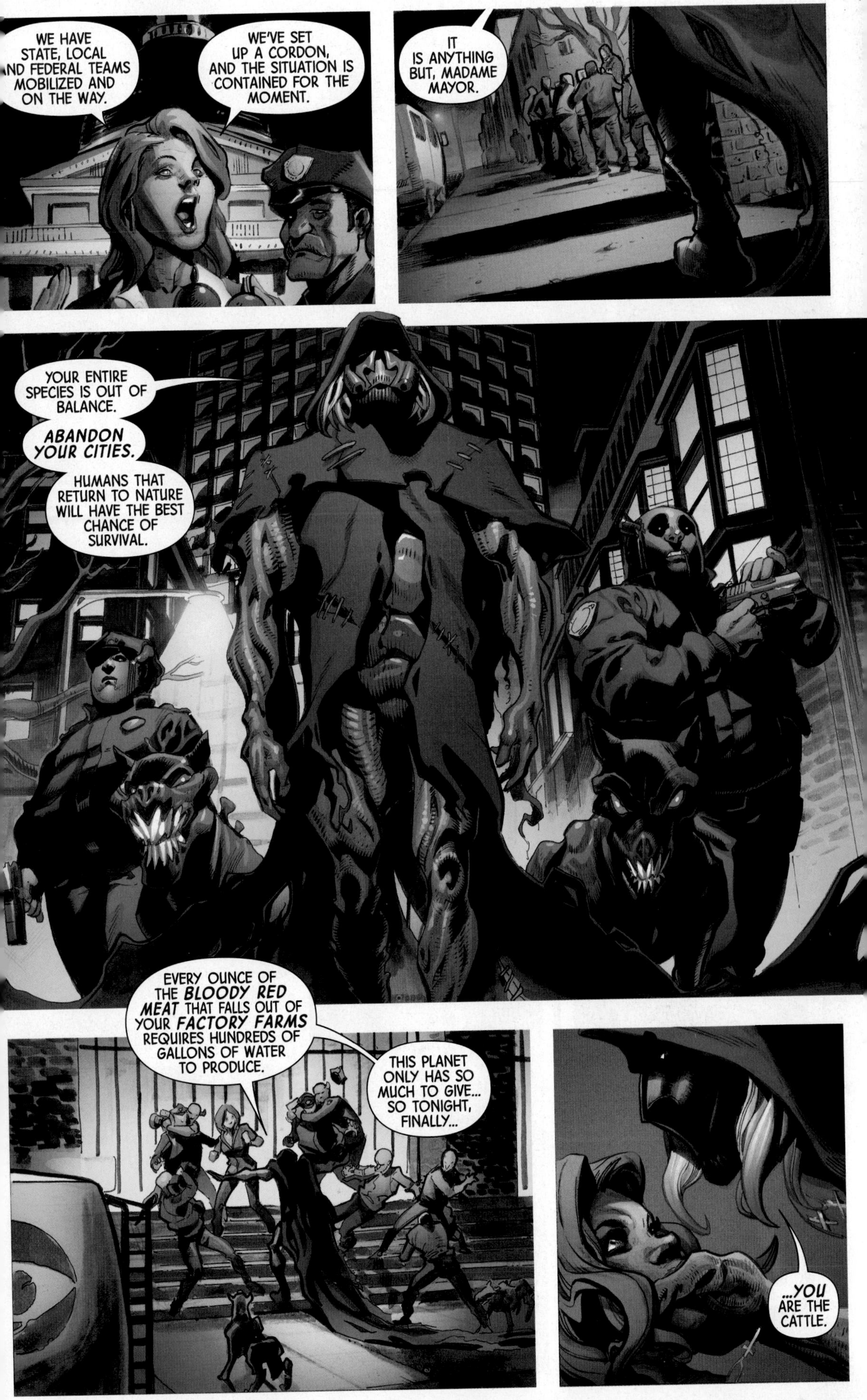
WE HAVE STATE, LOCAL AND FEDERAL TEAMS MOBILIZED AND ON THE WAY.
WE'VE SET UP A CORDON, AND THE SITUATION IS CONTAINED FOR THE MOMENT.
IT IS ANYTHING BUT, MADAME MAYOR.
YOUR ENTIRE SPECIES IS OUT OF BALANCE.
ABANDON YOUR CITIES.
HUMANS THAT RETURN TO NATURE WILL HAVE THE BEST CHANCE OF SURVIVAL.
EVERY OUNCE OF THE ***BLOODY RED MEAT*** THAT FALLS OUT OF YOUR ***FACTORY FARMS*** REQUIRES HUNDREDS OF GALLONS OF WATER TO PRODUCE.
THIS PLANET ONLY HAS SO MUCH TO GIVE... SO TONIGHT, FINALLY...
...***YOU*** ARE THE CATTLE.

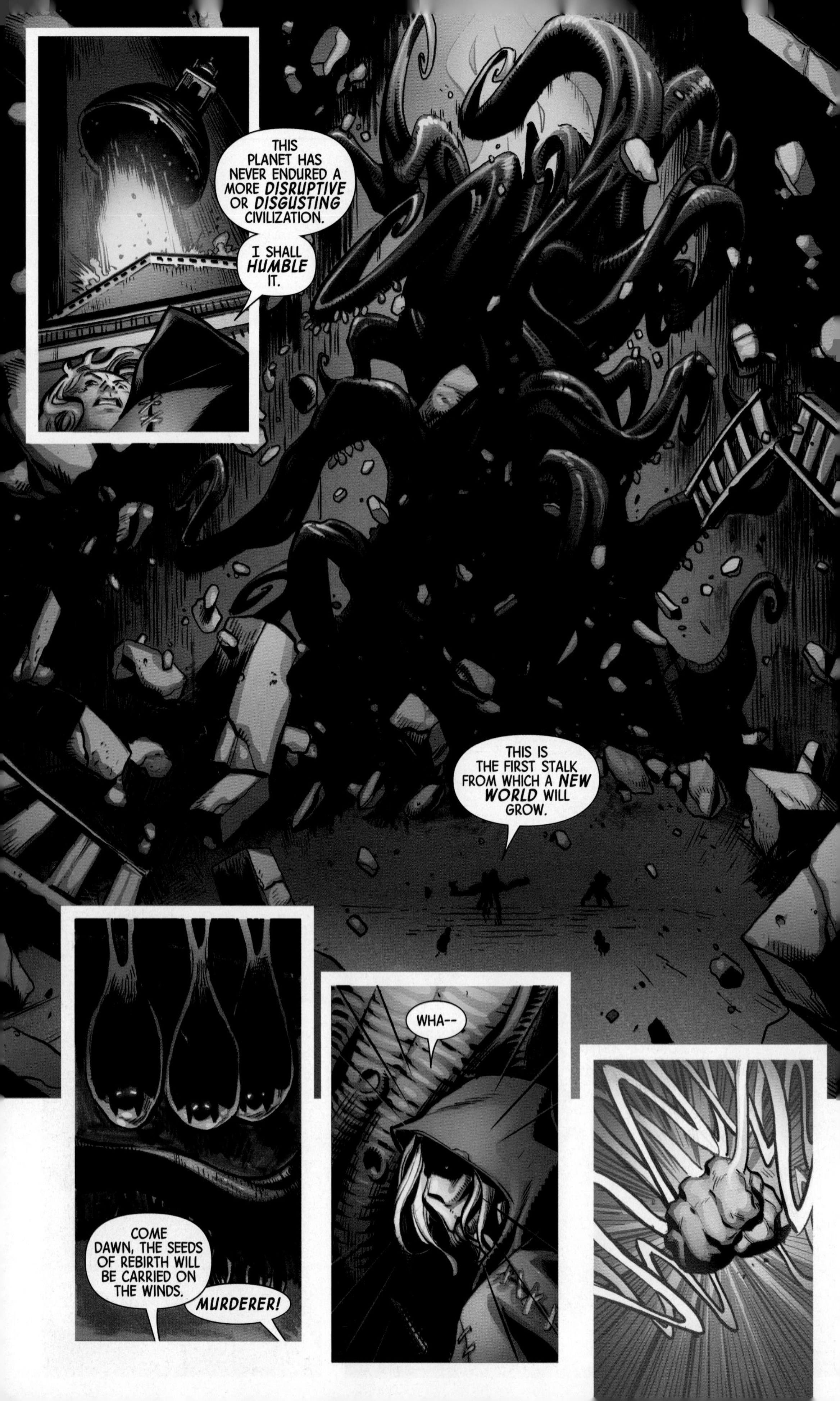
THIS PLANET HAS NEVER ENDURED A MORE DISRUPTIVE OR DISGUSTING CIVILIZATION.
I SHALL HUMBLE IT.
THIS IS THE FIRST STALK FROM WHICH A NEW WORLD WILL GROW.
COME DAWN, THE SEEDS OF REBIRTH WILL BE CARRIED ON THE WINDS.
MURDERER!
WHA--

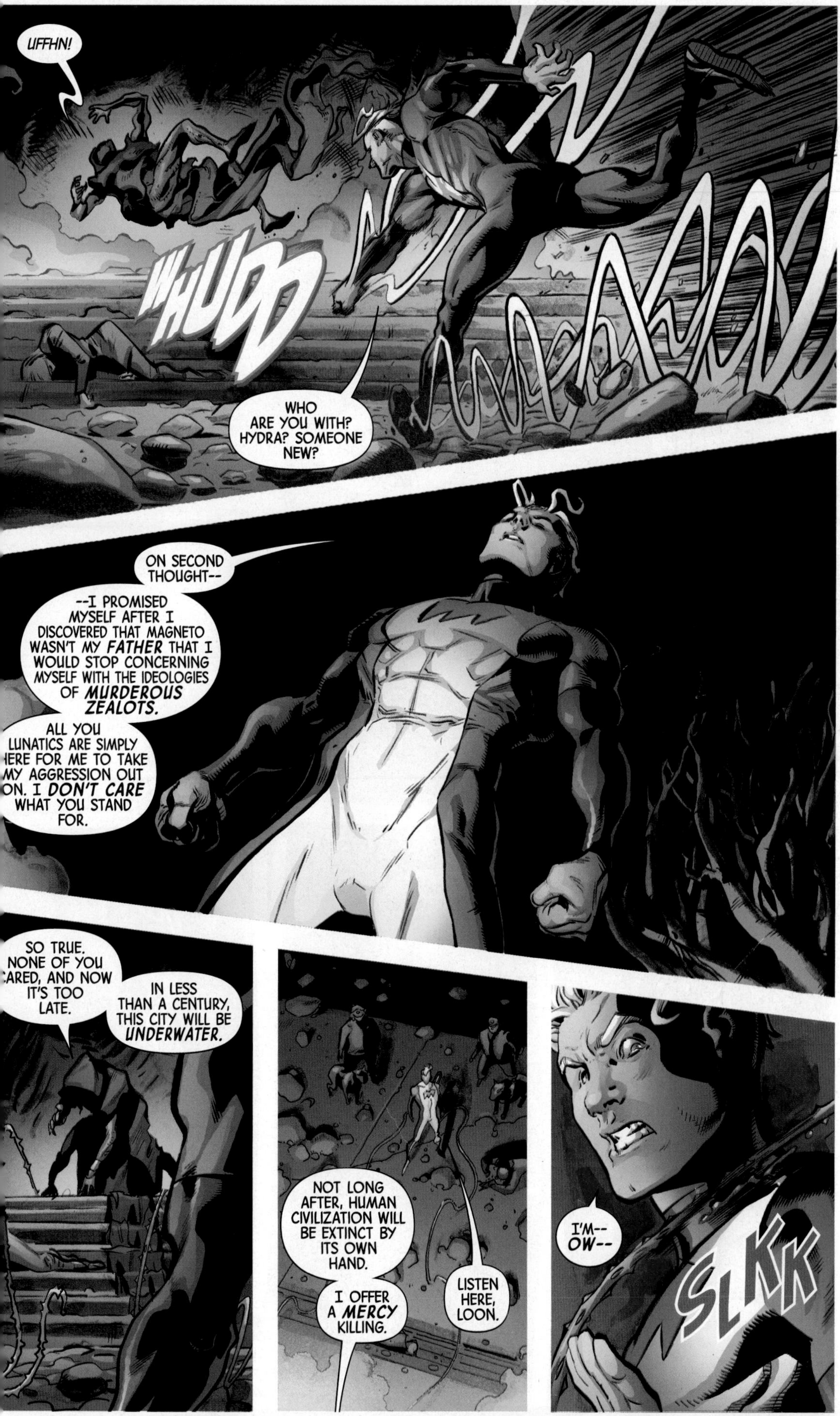
UFFHN!
WHUDD
WHO ARE YOU WITH? HYDRA? SOMEONE NEW?
ON SECOND THOUGHT--
--I PROMISED MYSELF AFTER I DISCOVERED THAT MAGNETO WASN'T MY FATHER THAT I WOULD STOP CONCERNING MYSELF WITH THE IDEOLOGIES OF MURDEROUS ZEALOTS.
ALL YOU LUNATICS ARE SIMPLY HERE FOR ME TO TAKE MY AGGRESSION OUT ON. I DON'T CARE WHAT YOU STAND FOR.
SO TRUE. NONE OF YOU CARED, AND NOW IT'S TOO LATE.
IN LESS THAN A CENTURY, THIS CITY WILL BE UNDERWATER.
NOT LONG AFTER, HUMAN CIVILIZATION WILL BE EXTINCT BY ITS OWN HAND.
I OFFER A MERCY KILLING.
LISTEN HERE, LOON.
I'M-- OW--
SLKK

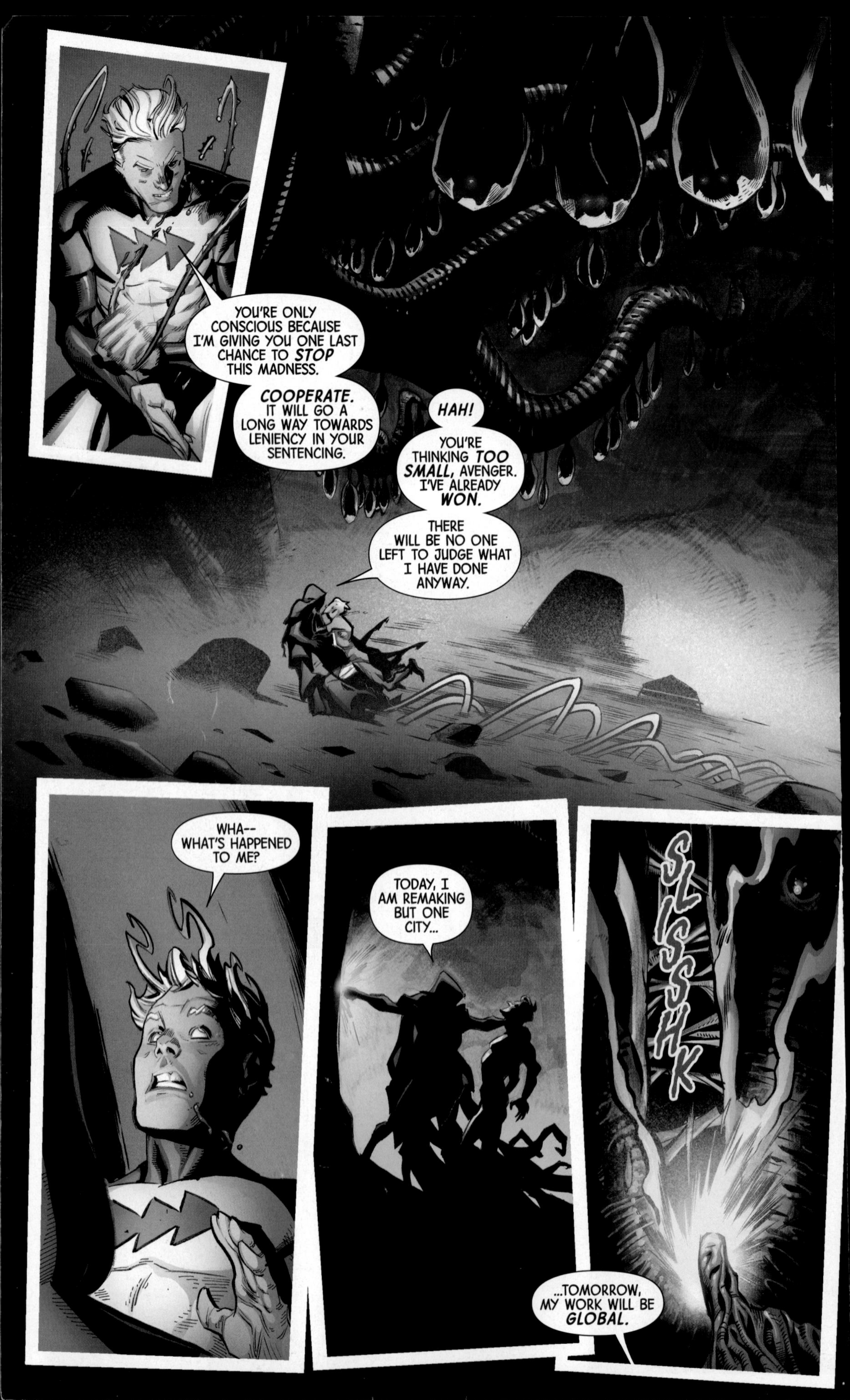
YOU'RE ONLY CONSCIOUS BECAUSE I'M GIVING YOU ONE LAST CHANCE TO *STOP* THIS MADNESS.
COOPERATE. IT WILL GO A LONG WAY TOWARDS LENIENCY IN YOUR SENTENCING.
HAH!
YOU'RE THINKING *TOO SMALL,* AVENGER. I'VE ALREADY *WON.*
THERE WILL BE NO ONE LEFT TO JUDGE WHAT I HAVE DONE ANYWAY.
WHA-- WHAT'S HAPPENED TO ME?
TODAY, I AM REMAKING BUT ONE CITY...
SLISSHK
...TOMORROW, MY WORK WILL BE *GLOBAL.*

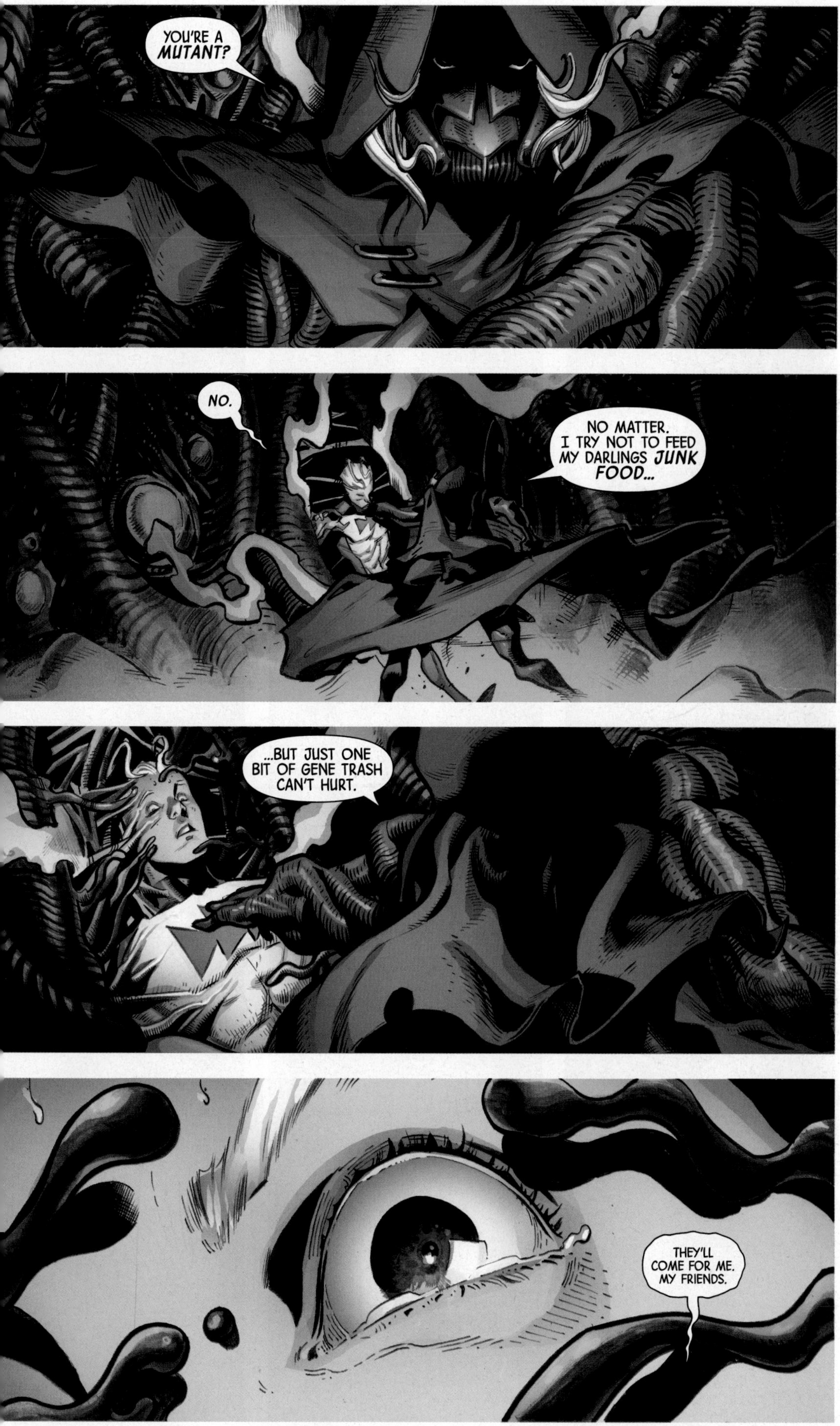
YOU'RE A MUTANT?
NO.
NO MATTER. I TRY NOT TO FEED MY DARLINGS JUNK FOOD...
...BUT JUST ONE BIT OF GENE TRASH CAN'T HURT.
THEY'LL COME FOR ME. MY FRIENDS.

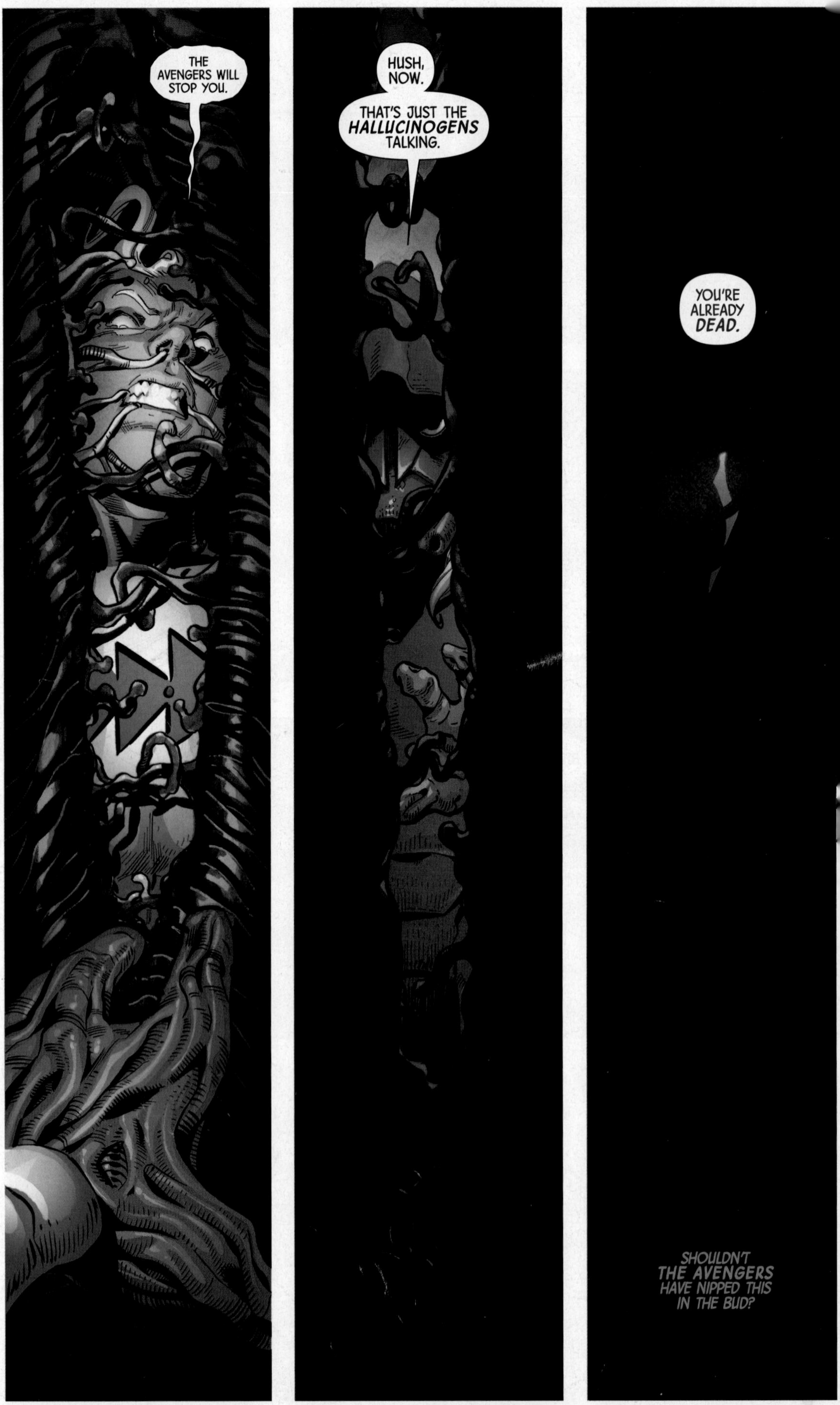
THE AVENGERS WILL STOP YOU.
HUSH, NOW.
THAT'S JUST THE HALLUCINOGENS TALKING.
YOU'RE ALREADY DEAD.
SHOULDN'T THE AVENGERS HAVE NIPPED THIS IN THE BUD?

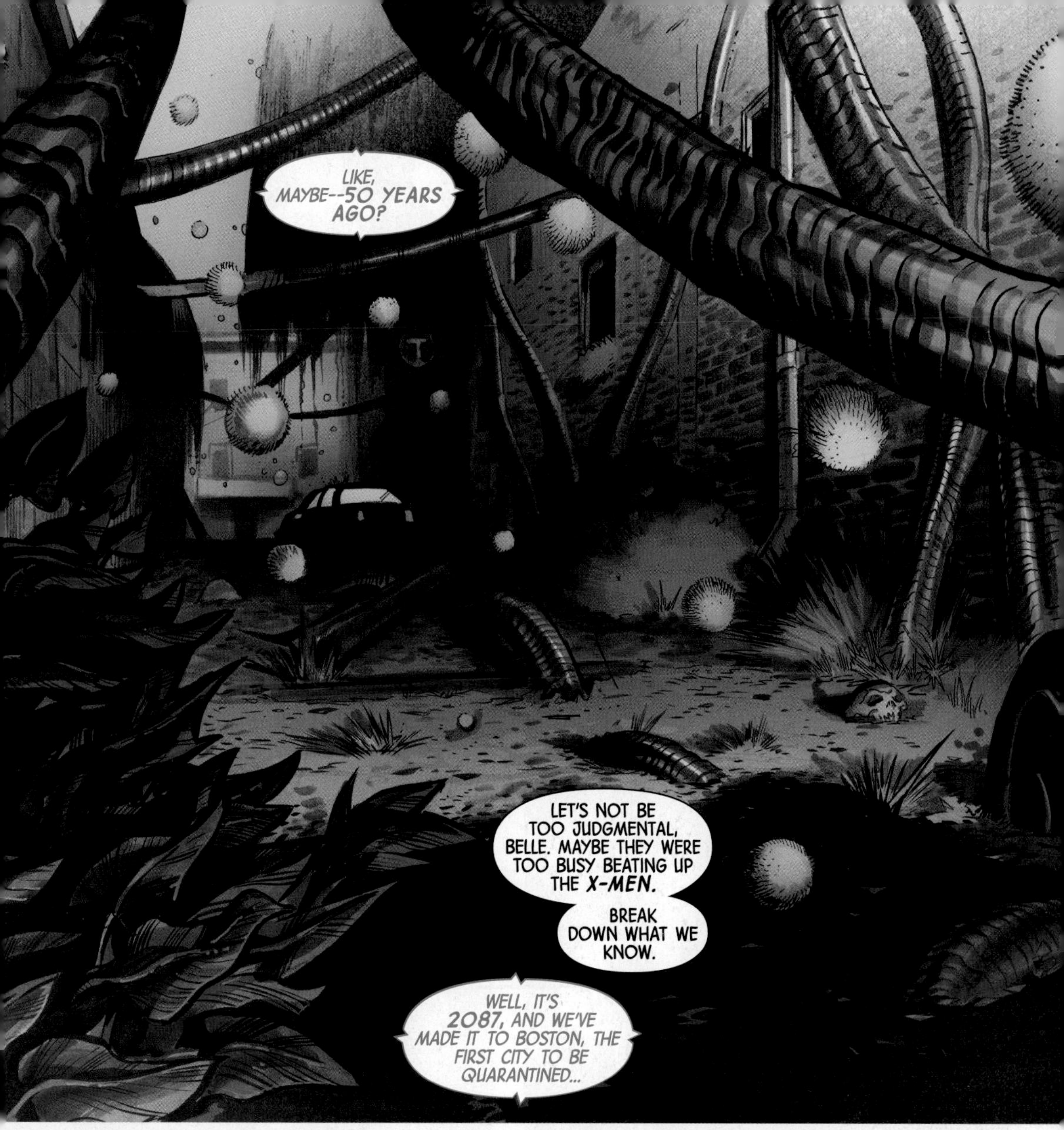
LIKE, MAYBE--50 YEARS AGO?
LET'S NOT BE TOO JUDGMENTAL, BELLE. MAYBE THEY WERE TOO BUSY BEATING UP THE X-MEN.
BREAK DOWN WHAT WE KNOW.
WELL, IT'S 2087, AND WE'VE MADE IT TO BOSTON, THE FIRST CITY TO BE QUARANTINED...

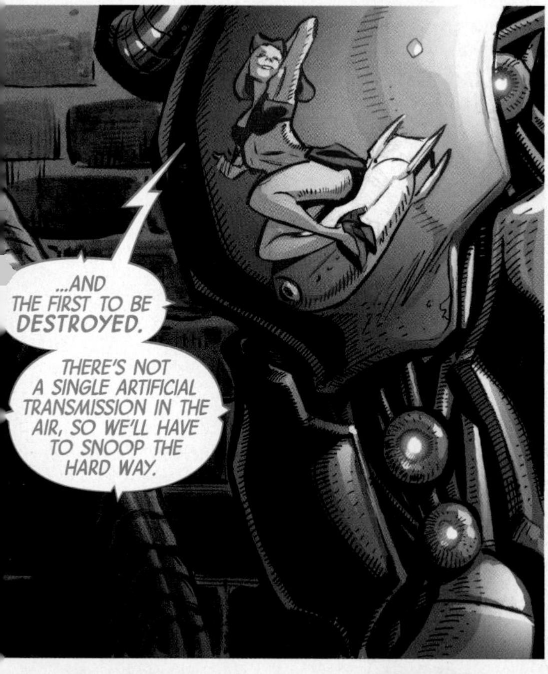
...AND THE FIRST TO BE DESTROYED.
THERE'S NOT A SINGLE ARTIFICIAL TRANSMISSION IN THE AIR, SO WE'LL HAVE TO SNOOP THE HARD WAY.

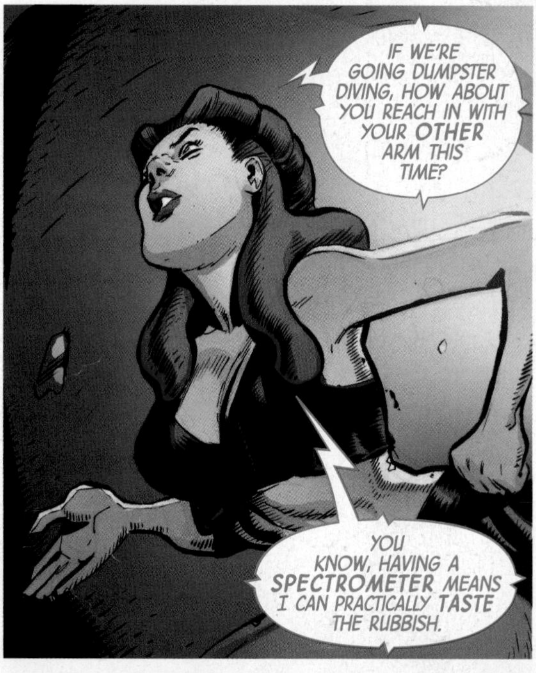
IF WE'RE GOING DUMPSTER DIVING, HOW ABOUT YOU REACH IN WITH YOUR OTHER ARM THIS TIME?
YOU KNOW, HAVING A SPECTROMETER MEANS I CAN PRACTICALLY TASTE THE RUBBISH.

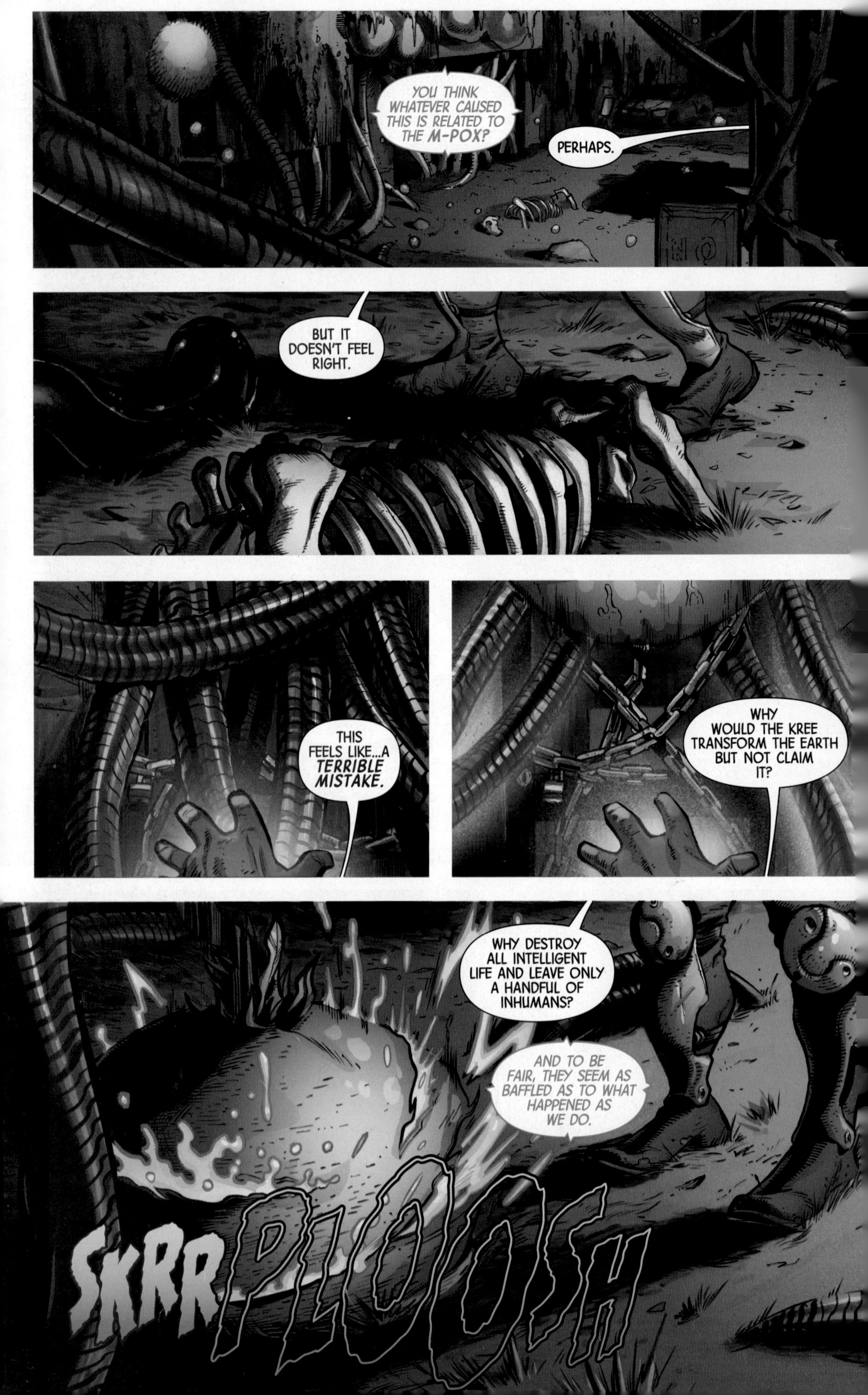
YOU THINK WHATEVER CAUSED THIS IS RELATED TO THE M-POX?
PERHAPS.
BUT IT DOESN'T FEEL RIGHT.
THIS FEELS LIKE...A TERRIBLE MISTAKE.
WHY WOULD THE KREE TRANSFORM THE EARTH BUT NOT CLAIM IT?
WHY DESTROY ALL INTELLIGENT LIFE AND LEAVE ONLY A HANDFUL OF INHUMANS?
AND TO BE FAIR, THEY SEEM AS BAFFLED AS TO WHAT HAPPENED AS WE DO.
SKRRPLOOSH

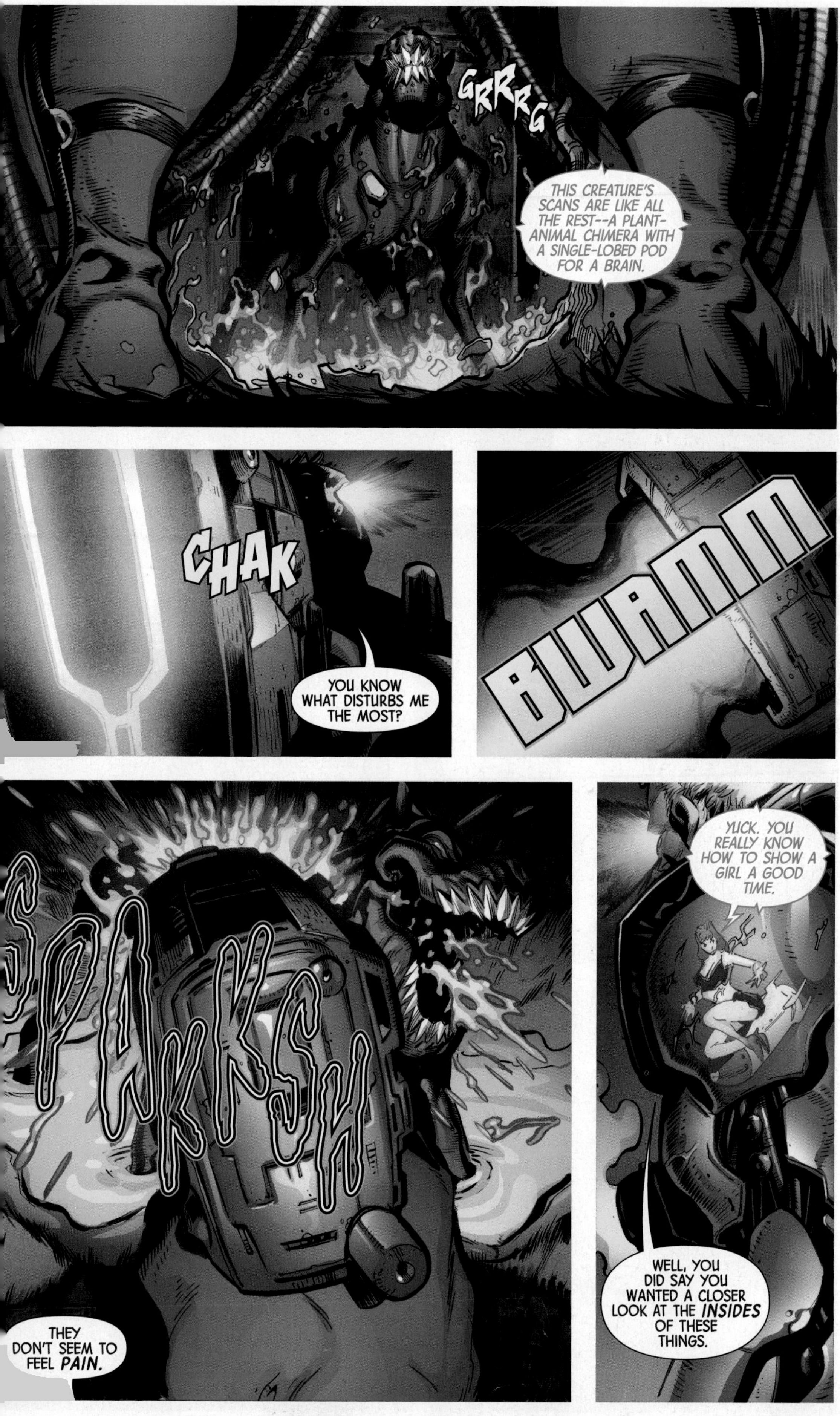
GRRRG
THIS CREATURE'S SCANS ARE LIKE ALL THE REST--A PLANT-ANIMAL CHIMERA WITH A SINGLE-LOBED POD FOR A BRAIN.
CHAK
YOU KNOW WHAT DISTURBS ME THE MOST?
BWAMM
SPLAKKSH
THEY DON'T SEEM TO FEEL PAIN.
YUCK. YOU REALLY KNOW HOW TO SHOW A GIRL A GOOD TIME.
WELL, YOU DID SAY YOU WANTED A CLOSER LOOK AT THE INSIDES OF THESE THINGS.

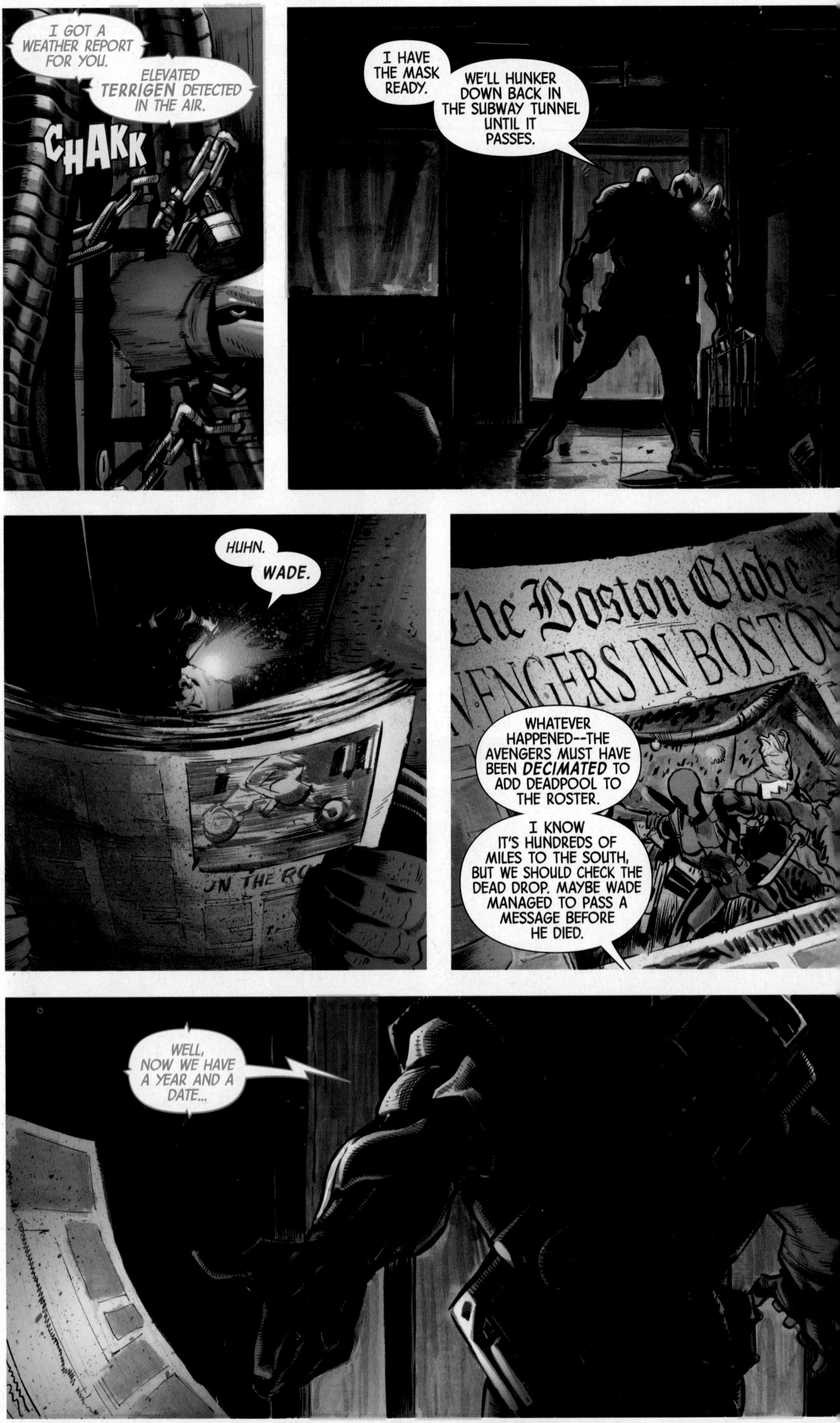
I GOT A WEATHER REPORT FOR YOU.
ELEVATED TERRIGEN DETECTED IN THE AIR.
CHAKK
I HAVE THE MASK READY.
WE'LL HUNKER DOWN BACK IN THE SUBWAY TUNNEL UNTIL IT PASSES.
HUHN.
WADE.
The Boston Globe
AVENGERS IN BOSTON
WHATEVER HAPPENED--THE AVENGERS MUST HAVE BEEN DECIMATED TO ADD DEADPOOL TO THE ROSTER.
I KNOW IT'S HUNDREDS OF MILES TO THE SOUTH, BUT WE SHOULD CHECK THE DEAD DROP. MAYBE WADE MANAGED TO PASS A MESSAGE BEFORE HE DIED.
WELL, NOW WE HAVE A YEAR AND A DATE...

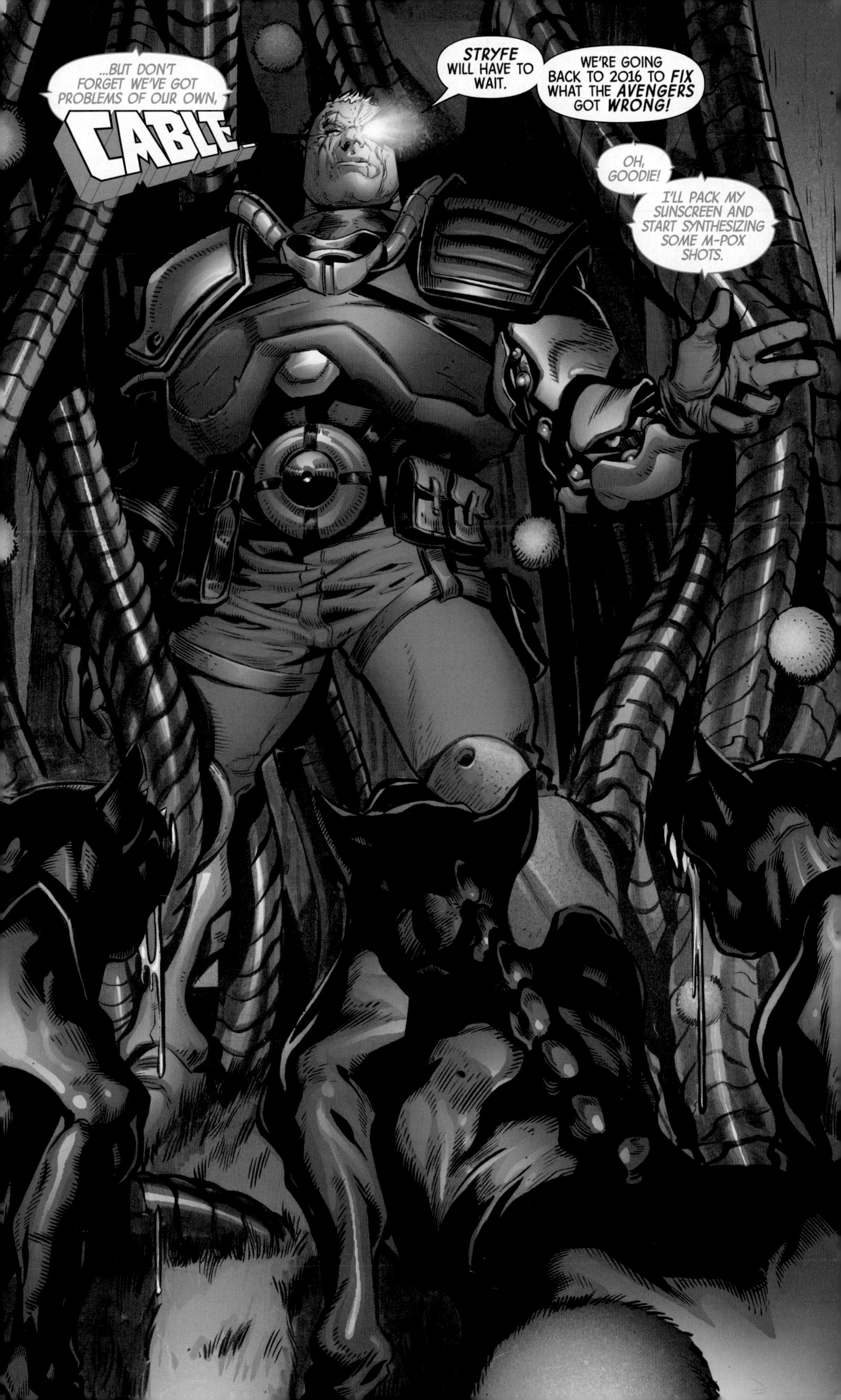

...BUT DON'T FORGET WE'VE GOT PROBLEMS OF OUR OWN,
CABLE.
STRYFE WILL HAVE TO WAIT.
WE'RE GOING BACK TO 2016 TO FIX WHAT THE AVENGERS GOT WRONG!
OH, GOODIE!
I'LL PACK MY SUNSCREEN AND START SYNTHESIZING SOME M-POX SHOTS.

3

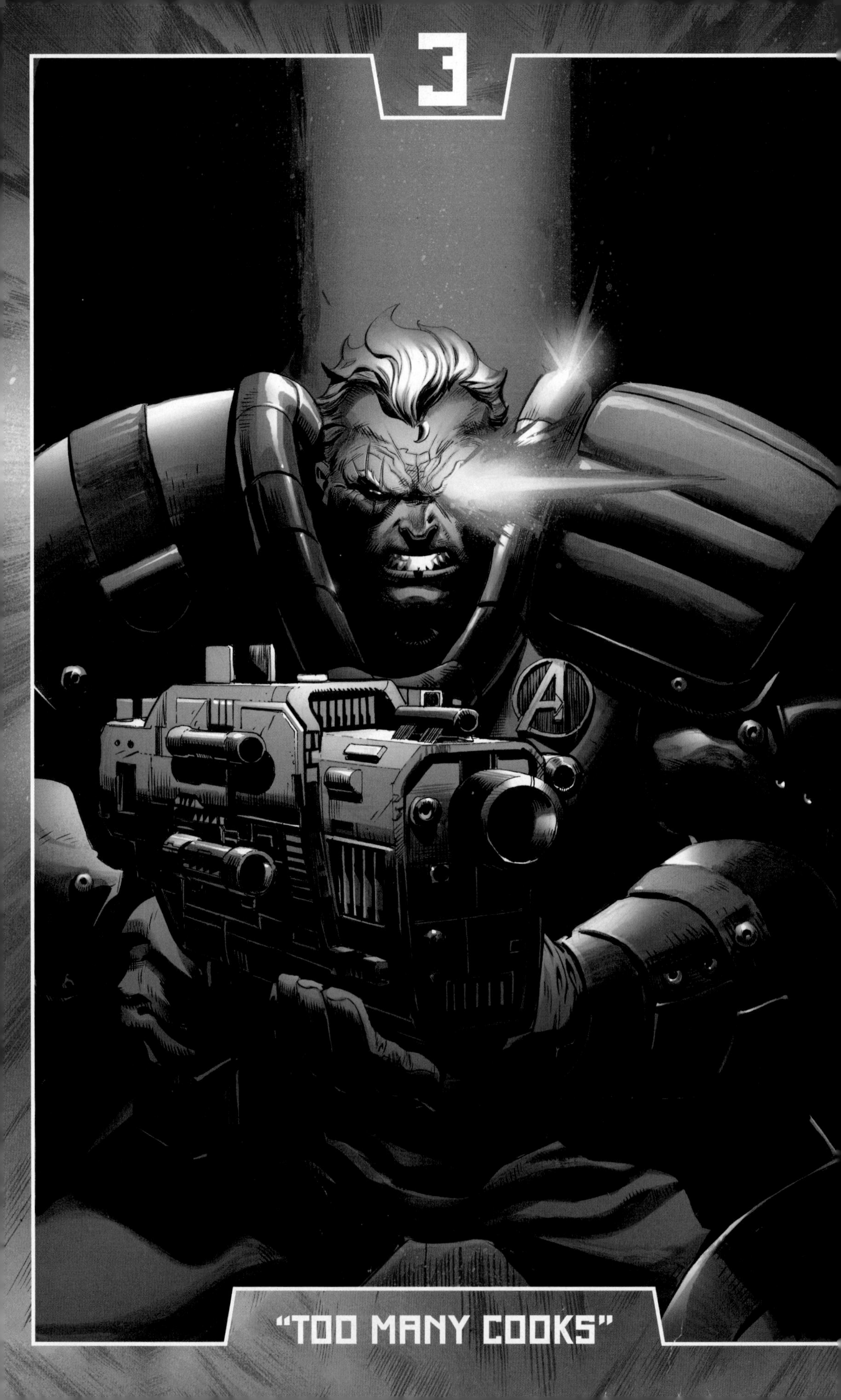

"TOO MANY COOKS"

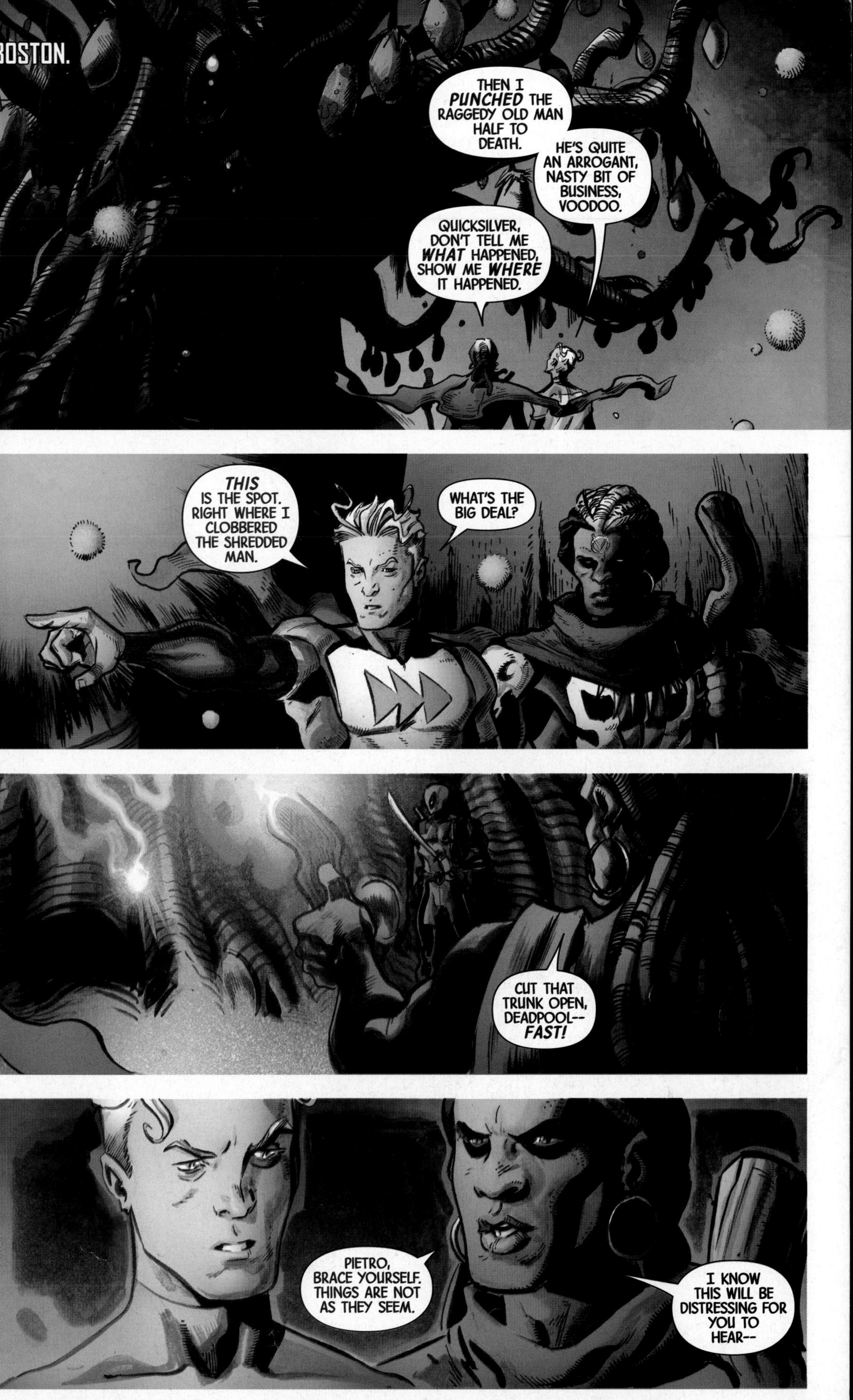

BOSTON.
THEN I PUNCHED THE RAGGEDY OLD MAN HALF TO DEATH.
HE'S QUITE AN ARROGANT, NASTY BIT OF BUSINESS, VOODOO.
QUICKSILVER, DON'T TELL ME WHAT HAPPENED, SHOW ME WHERE IT HAPPENED.
THIS IS THE SPOT. RIGHT WHERE I CLOBBERED THE SHREDDED MAN.
WHAT'S THE BIG DEAL?
CUT THAT TRUNK OPEN, DEADPOOL-- FAST!
PIETRO, BRACE YOURSELF. THINGS ARE NOT AS THEY SEEM.
I KNOW THIS WILL BE DISTRESSING FOR YOU TO HEAR--

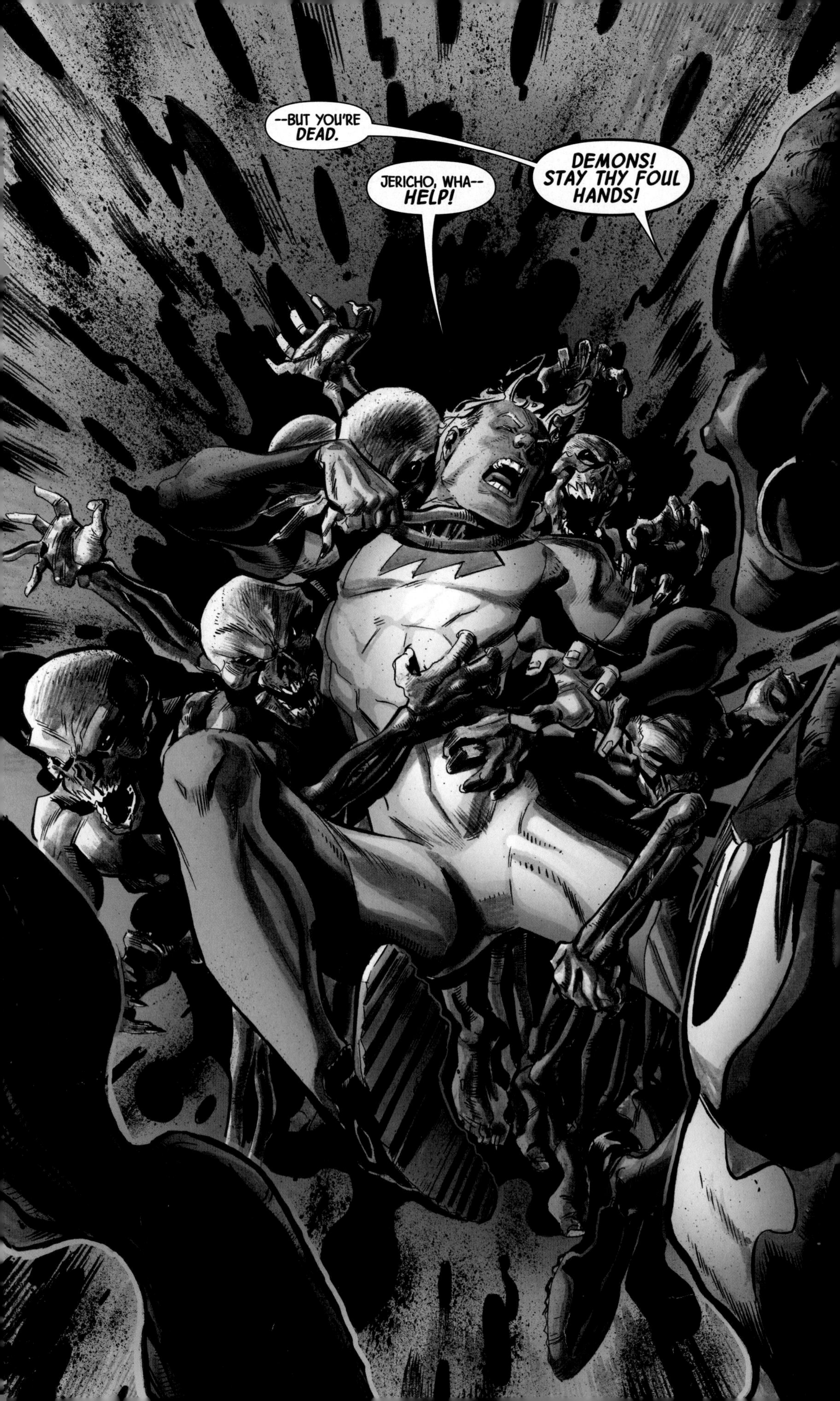
--BUT YOU'RE DEAD.
JERICHO, WHA-- HELP!
DEMONS! STAY THY FOUL HANDS!

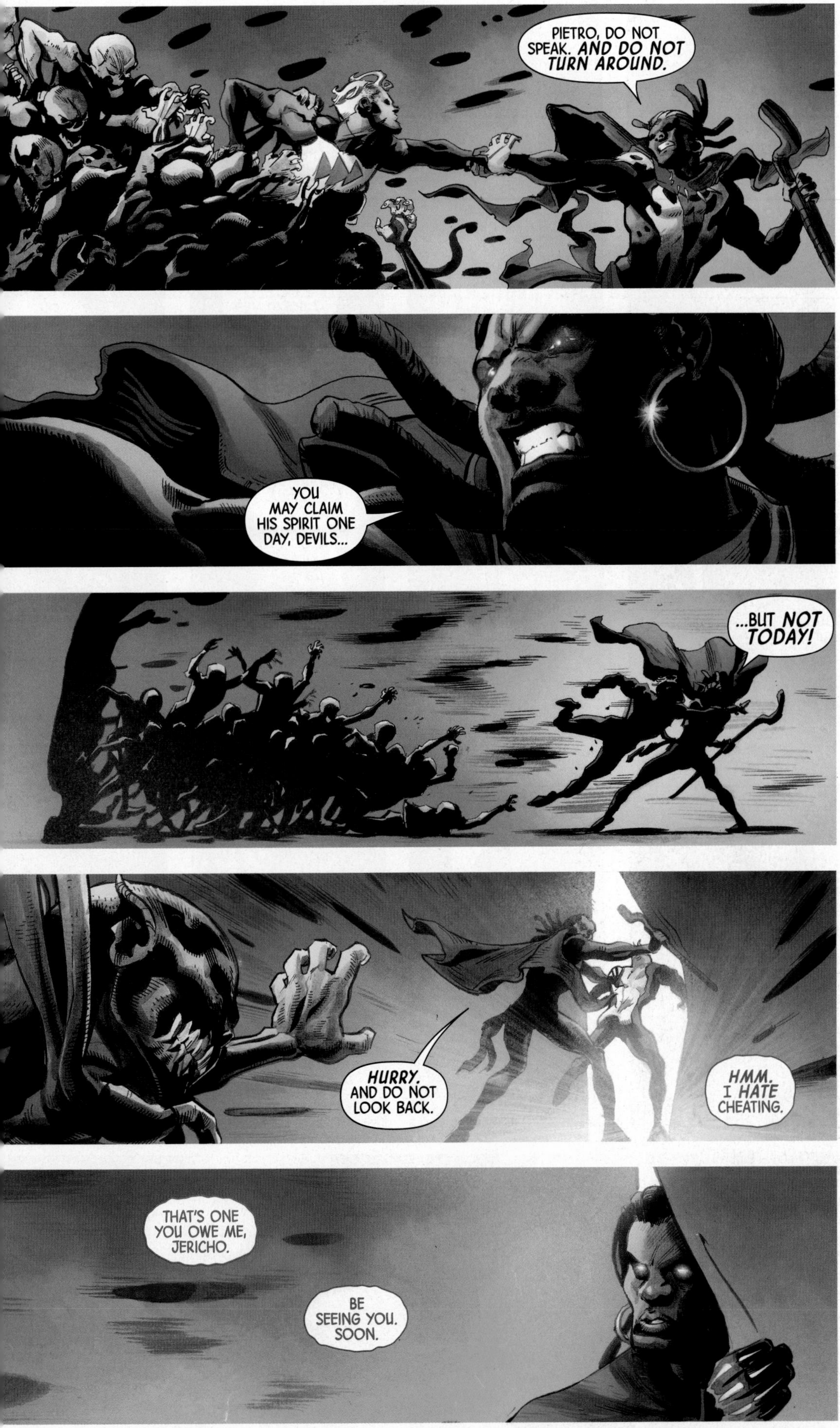
PIETRO, DO NOT SPEAK. AND DO NOT TURN AROUND.
YOU MAY CLAIM HIS SPIRIT ONE DAY, DEVILS...
...BUT NOT TODAY!
HURRY. AND DO NOT LOOK BACK.
HMM. I HATE CHEATING.
THAT'S ONE YOU OWE ME, JERICHO.
BE SEEING YOU. SOON.

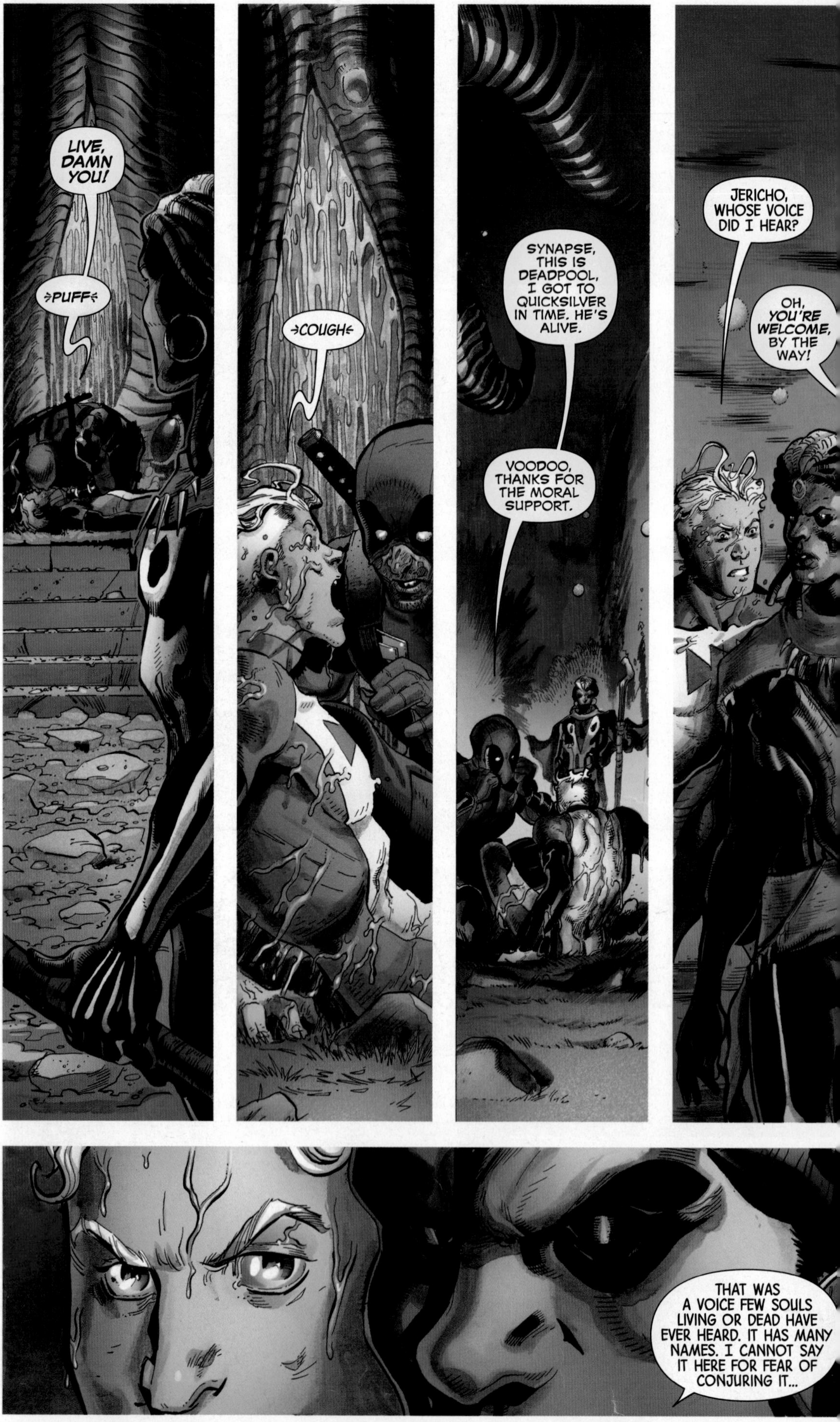
LIVE, DAMN YOU!
>PUFF<
>COUGH<
SYNAPSE, THIS IS DEADPOOL, I GOT TO QUICKSILVER IN TIME. HE'S ALIVE.
VOODOO, THANKS FOR THE MORAL SUPPORT.
JERICHO, WHOSE VOICE DID I HEAR?
OH, YOU'RE WELCOME, BY THE WAY!
THAT WAS A VOICE FEW SOULS LIVING OR DEAD HAVE EVER HEARD. IT HAS MANY NAMES. I CANNOT SAY IT HERE FOR FEAR OF CONJURING IT...

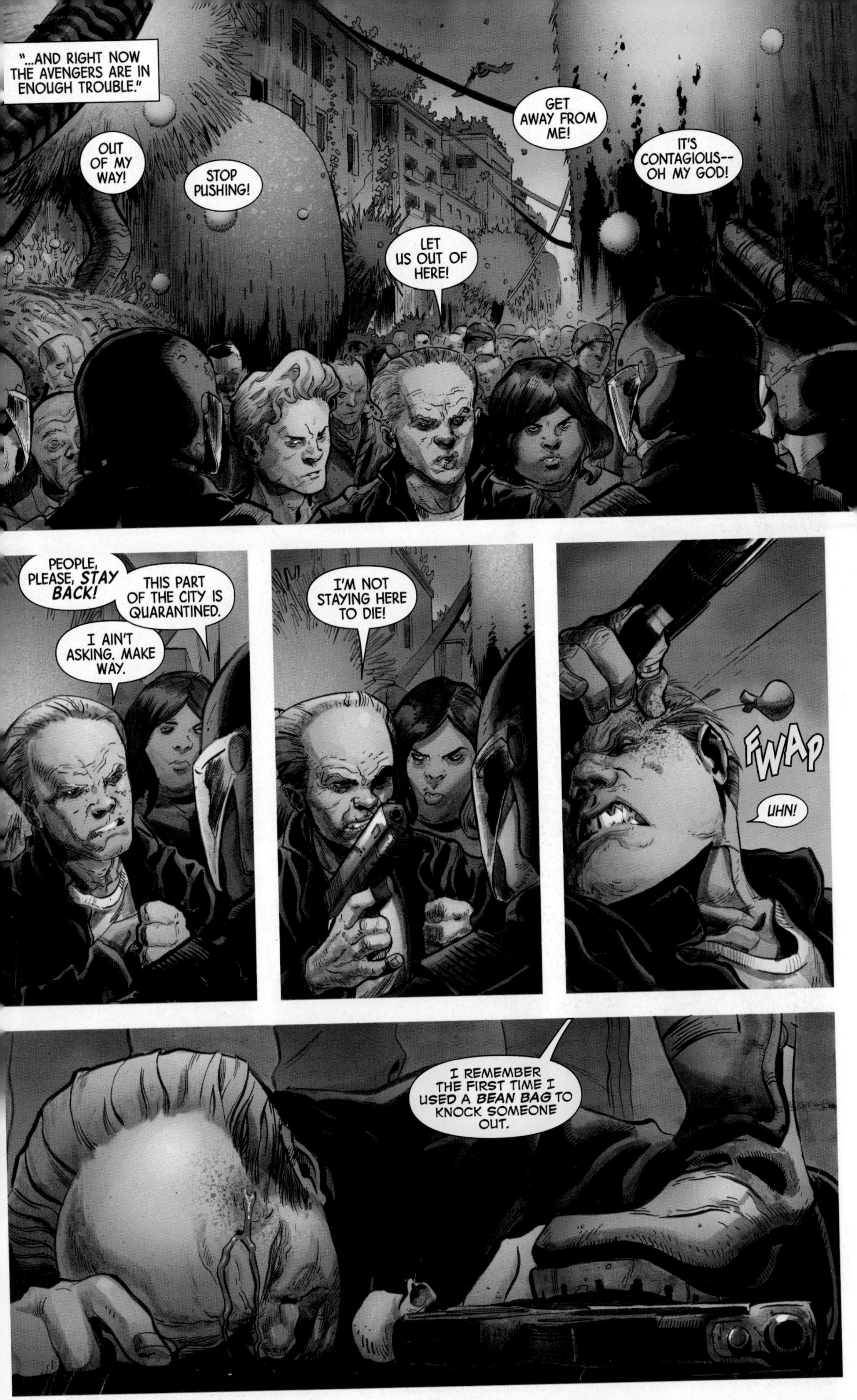
"...AND RIGHT NOW THE AVENGERS ARE IN ENOUGH TROUBLE."
OUT OF MY WAY!
STOP PUSHING!
GET AWAY FROM ME!
IT'S CONTAGIOUS-- OH MY GOD!
LET US OUT OF HERE!
PEOPLE, PLEASE, STAY BACK!
THIS PART OF THE CITY IS QUARANTINED.
I AIN'T ASKING. MAKE WAY.
I'M NOT STAYING HERE TO DIE!
FWAP
UHN!
I REMEMBER THE FIRST TIME I USED A BEAN BAG TO KNOCK SOMEONE OUT.

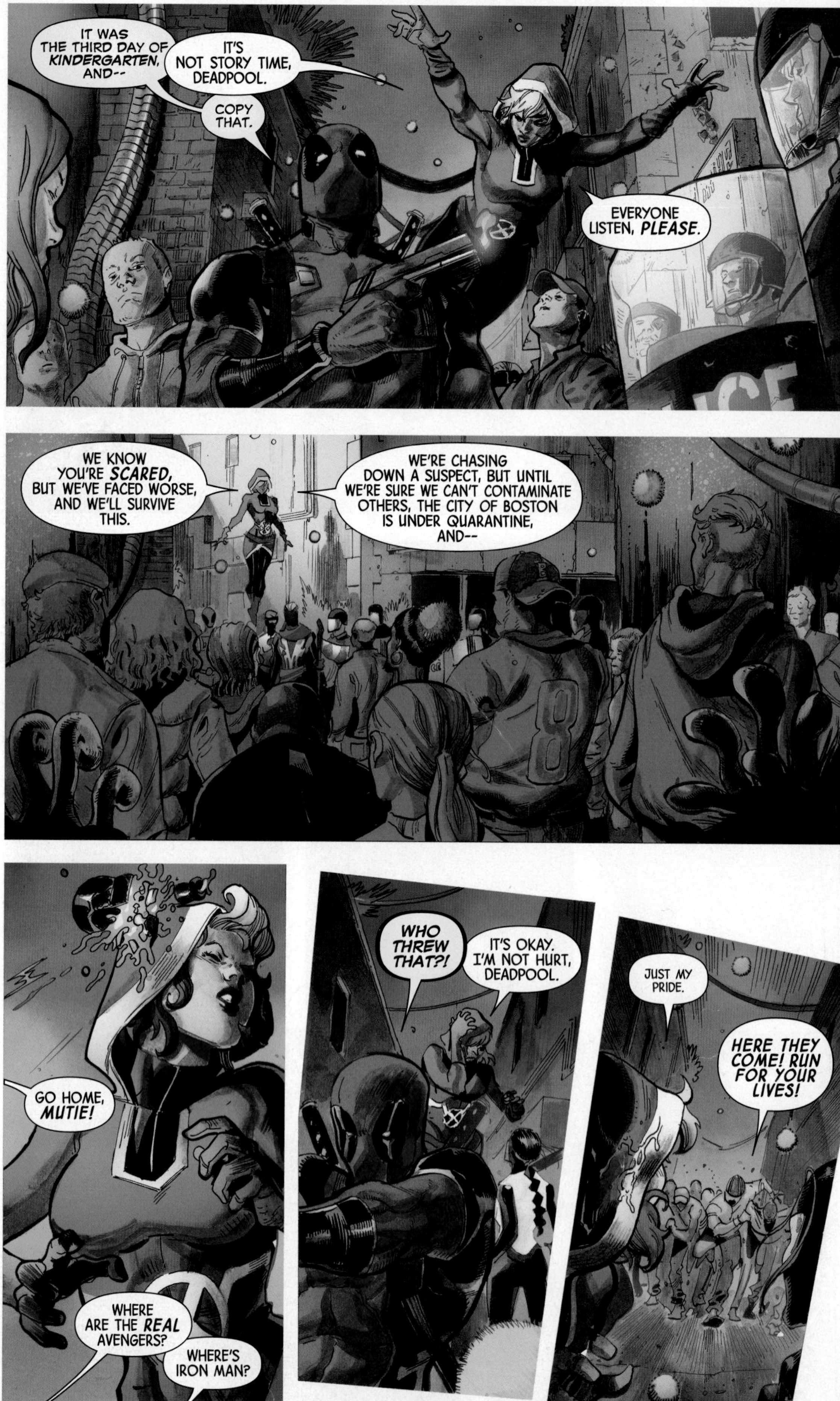

IT WAS THE THIRD DAY OF KINDERGARTEN, AND--
IT'S NOT STORY TIME, DEADPOOL.
COPY THAT.
EVERYONE LISTEN, PLEASE.
WE KNOW YOU'RE SCARED, BUT WE'VE FACED WORSE, AND WE'LL SURVIVE THIS.
WE'RE CHASING DOWN A SUSPECT, BUT UNTIL WE'RE SURE WE CAN'T CONTAMINATE OTHERS, THE CITY OF BOSTON IS UNDER QUARANTINE, AND--
GO HOME, MUTIE!
WHERE ARE THE REAL AVENGERS?
WHERE'S IRON MAN?
WHO THREW THAT?!
IT'S OKAY. I'M NOT HURT, DEADPOOL.
JUST MY PRIDE.
HERE THEY COME! RUN FOR YOUR LIVES!

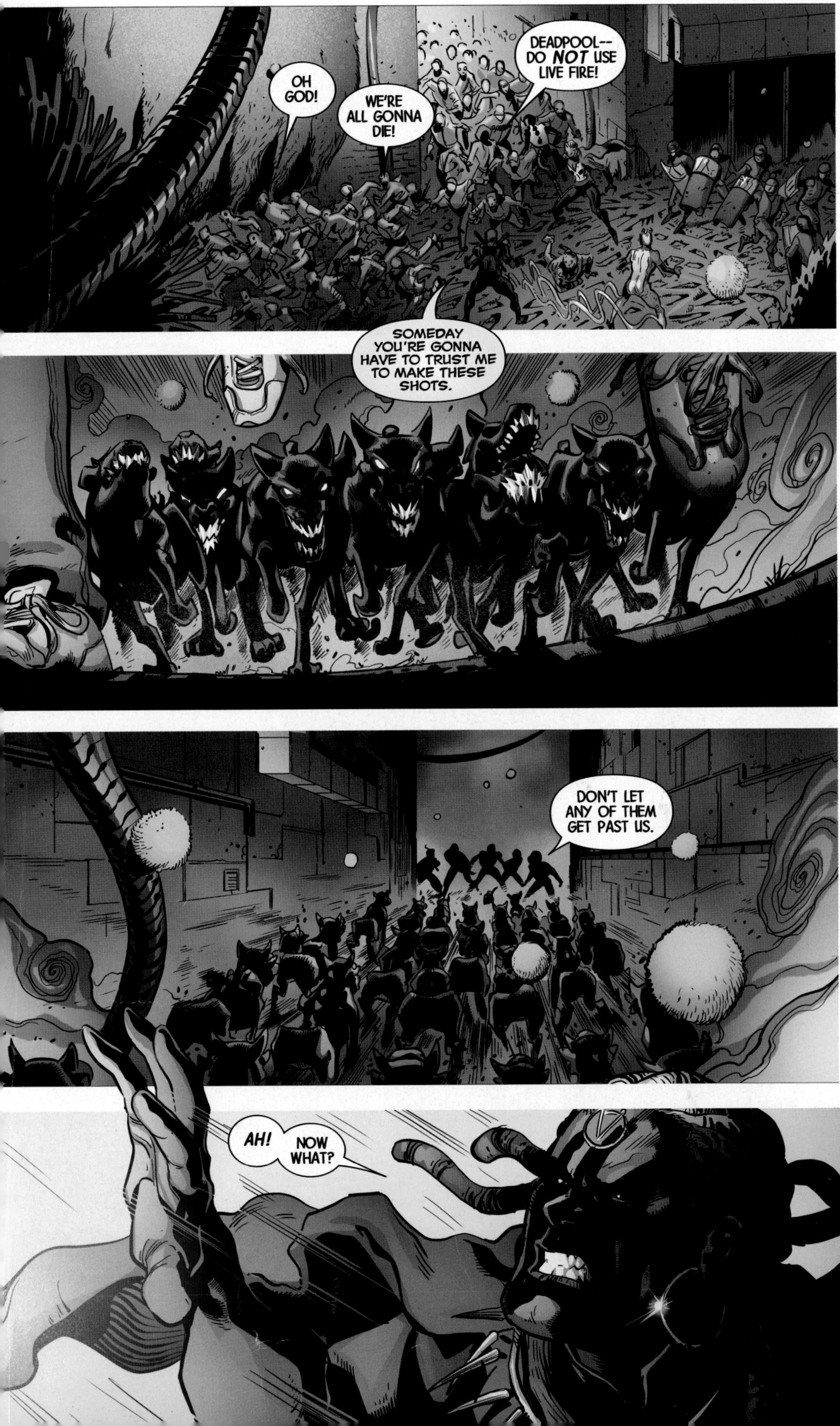

OH GOD!
WE'RE ALL GONNA DIE!
DEADPOOL-- DO NOT USE LIVE FIRE!
SOMEDAY YOU'RE GONNA HAVE TO TRUST ME TO MAKE THESE SHOTS.
DON'T LET ANY OF THEM GET PAST US.
AH!
NOW WHAT?

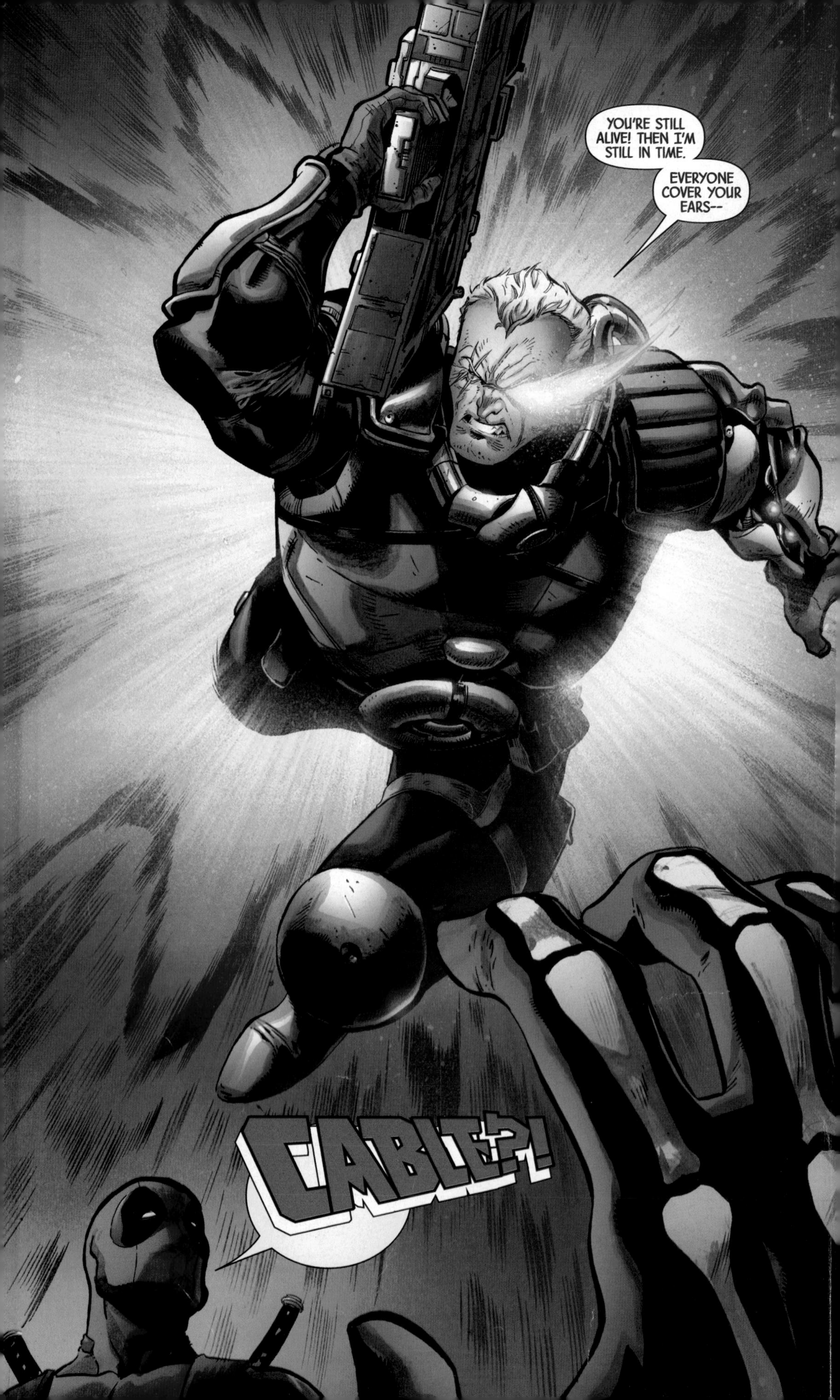
YOU'RE STILL ALIVE! THEN I'M STILL IN TIME.
EVERYONE COVER YOUR EARS--
CABLE?!

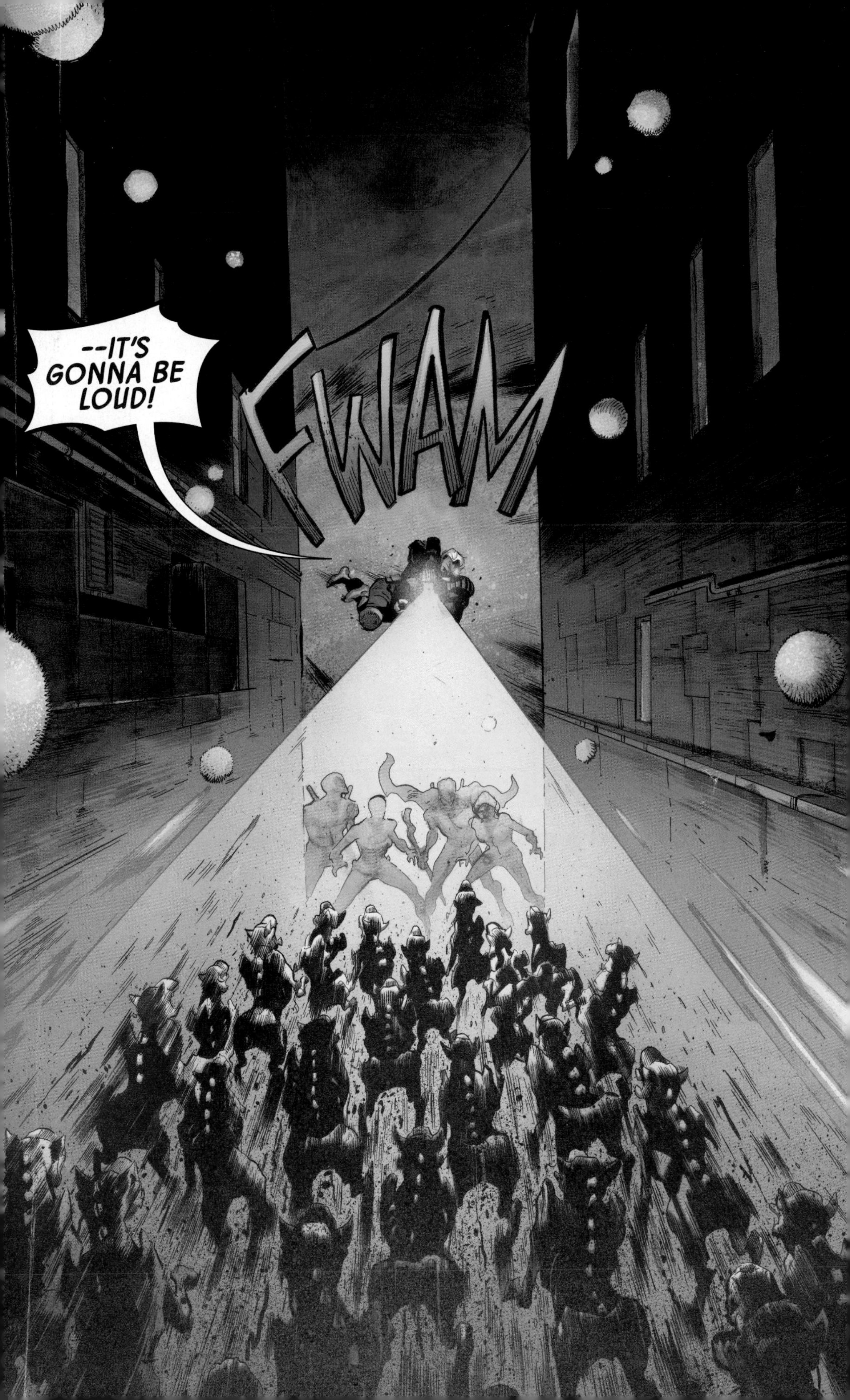
--IT'S GONNA BE LOUD!
FWAM

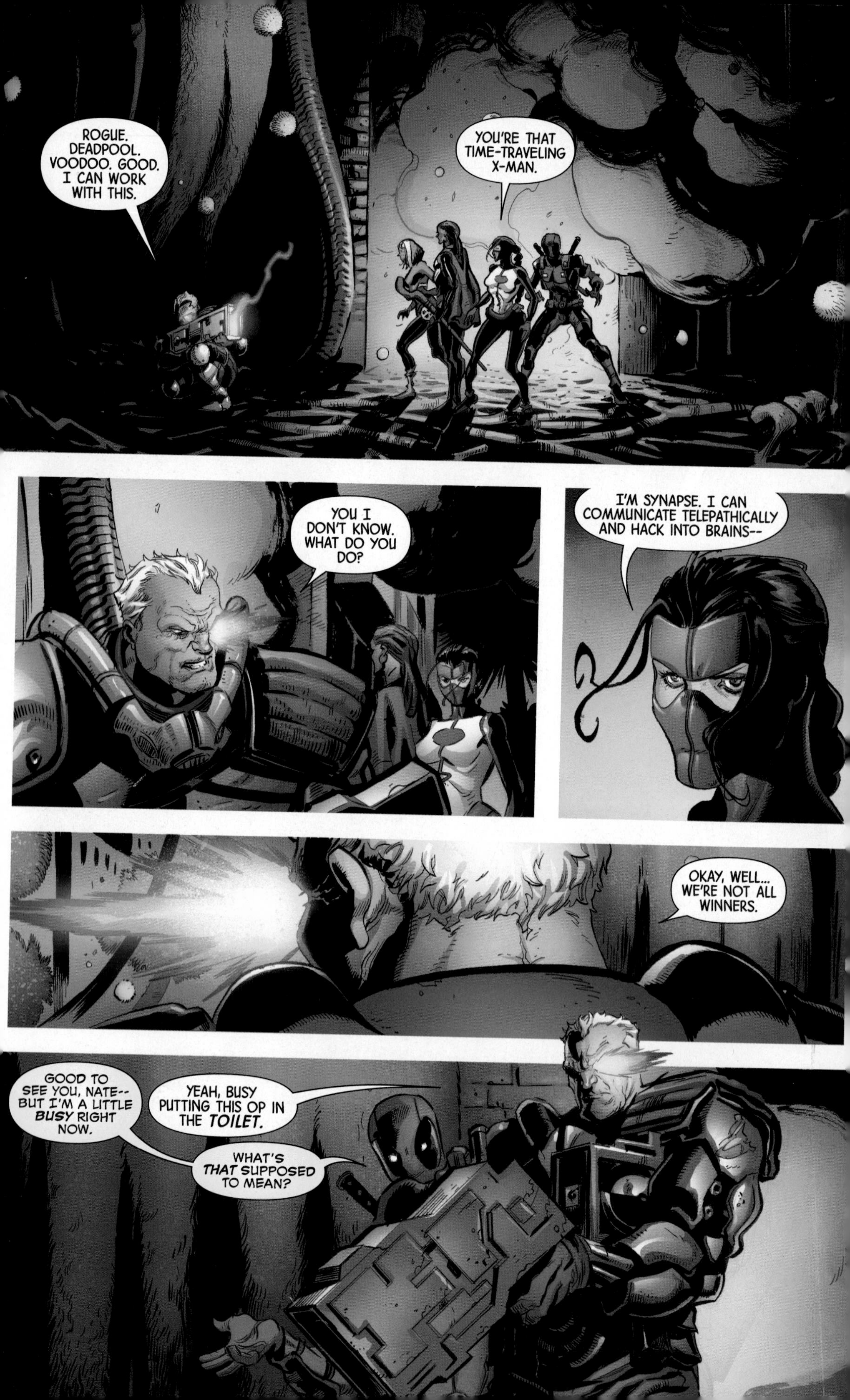
ROGUE. DEADPOOL. VOODOO. GOOD. I CAN WORK WITH THIS.
YOU'RE THAT TIME-TRAVELING X-MAN.
YOU I DON'T KNOW. WHAT DO YOU DO?
I'M SYNAPSE. I CAN COMMUNICATE TELEPATHICALLY AND HACK INTO BRAINS--
OKAY, WELL... WE'RE NOT ALL WINNERS.
GOOD TO SEE YOU, NATE-- BUT I'M A LITTLE BUSY RIGHT NOW.
YEAH, BUSY PUTTING THIS OP IN THE TOILET.
WHAT'S THAT SUPPOSED TO MEAN?

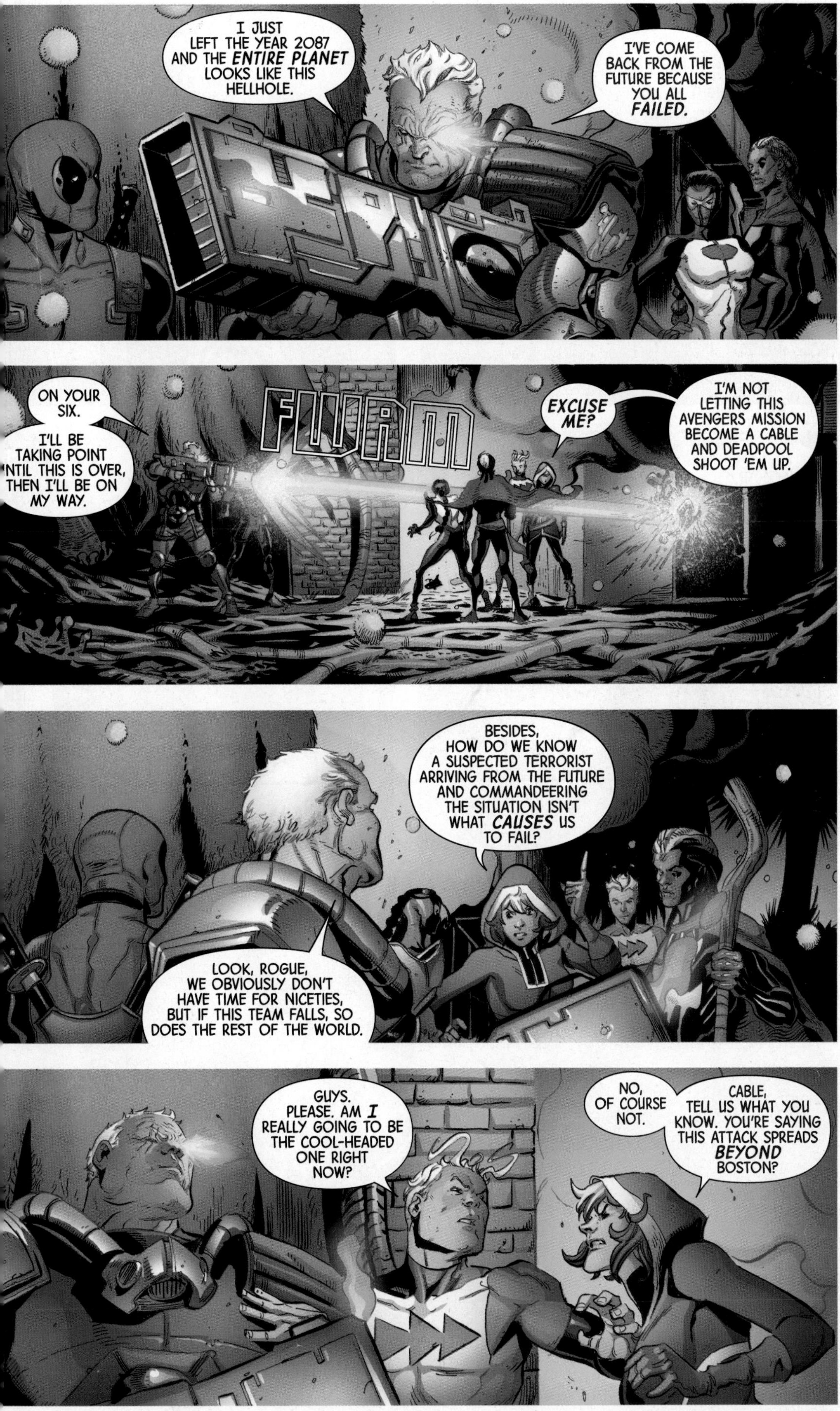
I JUST LEFT THE YEAR 2087 AND THE ENTIRE PLANET LOOKS LIKE THIS HELLHOLE.
I'VE COME BACK FROM THE FUTURE BECAUSE YOU ALL FAILED.
ON YOUR SIX.
I'LL BE TAKING POINT 'NTIL THIS IS OVER, THEN I'LL BE ON MY WAY.
FWRM
EXCUSE ME?
I'M NOT LETTING THIS AVENGERS MISSION BECOME A CABLE AND DEADPOOL SHOOT 'EM UP.
BESIDES, HOW DO WE KNOW A SUSPECTED TERRORIST ARRIVING FROM THE FUTURE AND COMMANDEERING THE SITUATION ISN'T WHAT CAUSES US TO FAIL?
LOOK, ROGUE, WE OBVIOUSLY DON'T HAVE TIME FOR NICETIES, BUT IF THIS TEAM FALLS, SO DOES THE REST OF THE WORLD.
GUYS. PLEASE. AM I REALLY GOING TO BE THE COOL-HEADED ONE RIGHT NOW?
NO, OF COURSE NOT.
CABLE, TELL US WHAT YOU KNOW. YOU'RE SAYING THIS ATTACK SPREADS BEYOND BOSTON?

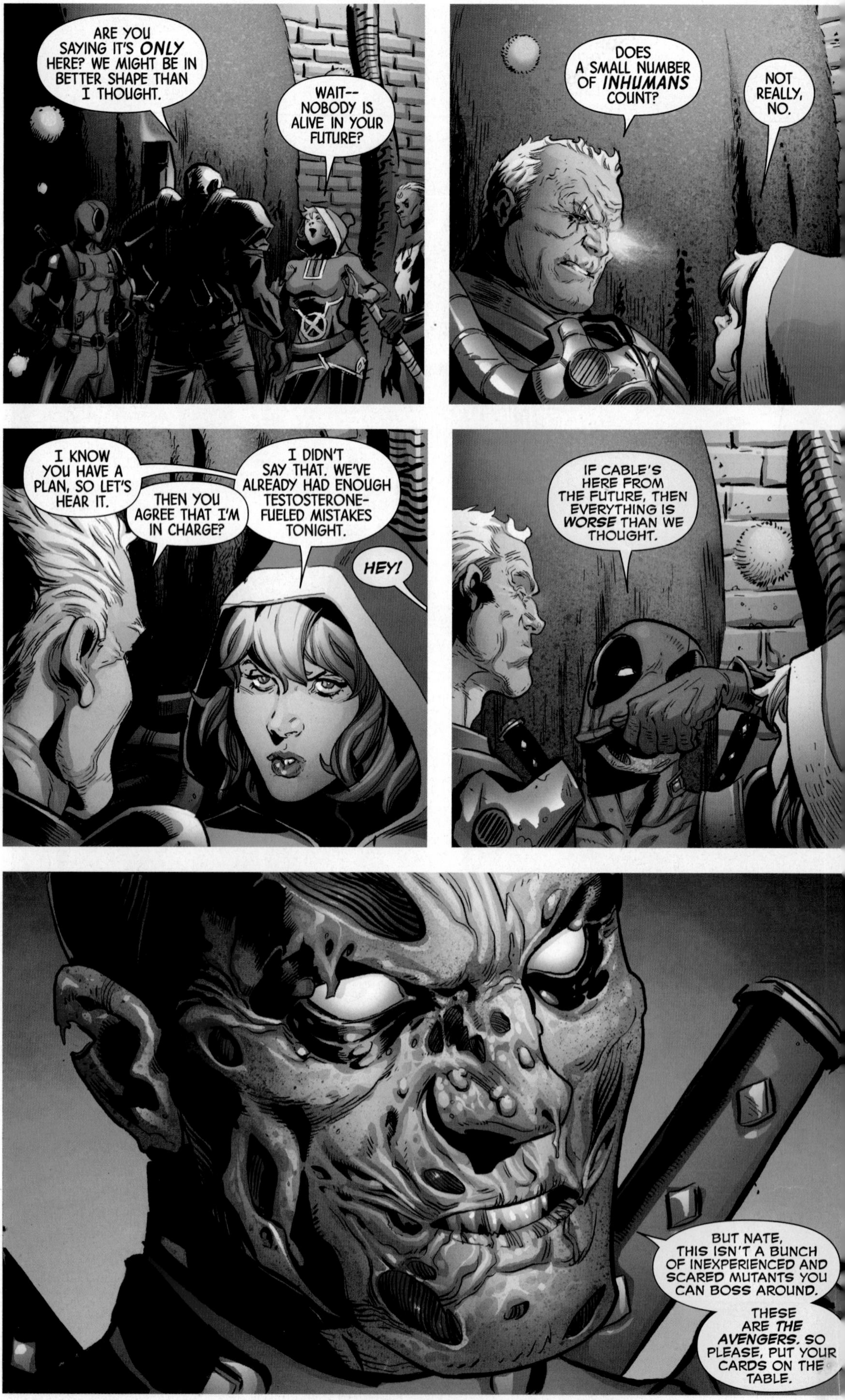
ARE YOU SAYING IT'S ONLY HERE? WE MIGHT BE IN BETTER SHAPE THAN I THOUGHT.
WAIT-- NOBODY IS ALIVE IN YOUR FUTURE?
DOES A SMALL NUMBER OF INHUMANS COUNT?
NOT REALLY, NO.
I KNOW YOU HAVE A PLAN, SO LET'S HEAR IT.
THEN YOU AGREE THAT I'M IN CHARGE?
I DIDN'T SAY THAT. WE'VE ALREADY HAD ENOUGH TESTOSTERONE-FUELED MISTAKES TONIGHT.
HEY!
IF CABLE'S HERE FROM THE FUTURE, THEN EVERYTHING IS WORSE THAN WE THOUGHT.
BUT NATE, THIS ISN'T A BUNCH OF INEXPERIENCED AND SCARED MUTANTS YOU CAN BOSS AROUND.
THESE ARE THE AVENGERS. SO PLEASE, PUT YOUR CARDS ON THE TABLE.

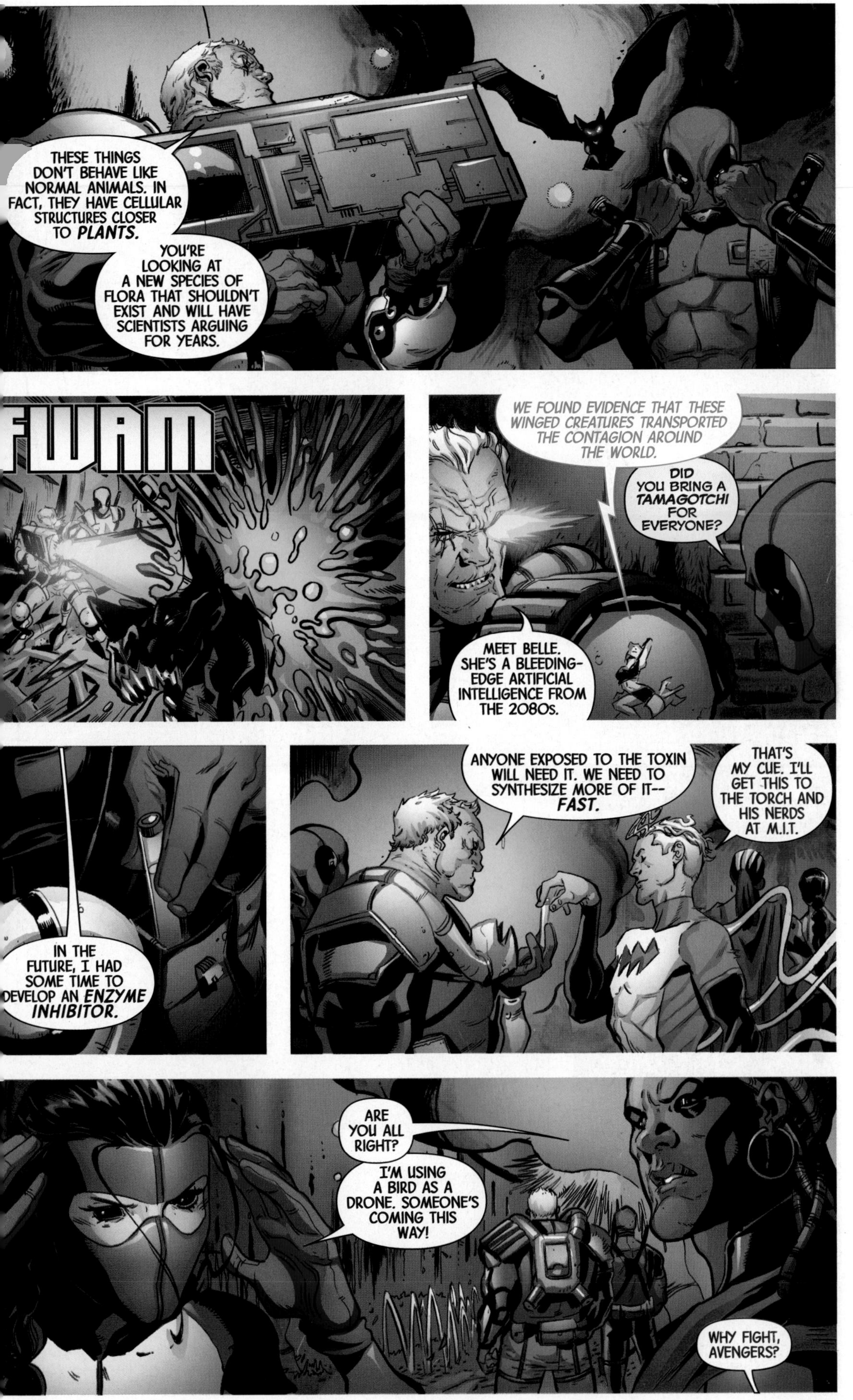
THESE THINGS DON'T BEHAVE LIKE NORMAL ANIMALS. IN FACT, THEY HAVE CELLULAR STRUCTURES CLOSER TO PLANTS.
YOU'RE LOOKING AT A NEW SPECIES OF FLORA THAT SHOULDN'T EXIST AND WILL HAVE SCIENTISTS ARGUING FOR YEARS.
FWAM
WE FOUND EVIDENCE THAT THESE WINGED CREATURES TRANSPORTED THE CONTAGION AROUND THE WORLD.
DID YOU BRING A TAMAGOTCHI FOR EVERYONE?
MEET BELLE. SHE'S A BLEEDING-EDGE ARTIFICIAL INTELLIGENCE FROM THE 2080s.
IN THE FUTURE, I HAD SOME TIME TO DEVELOP AN ENZYME INHIBITOR.
ANYONE EXPOSED TO THE TOXIN WILL NEED IT. WE NEED TO SYNTHESIZE MORE OF IT-- FAST.
THAT'S MY CUE. I'LL GET THIS TO THE TORCH AND HIS NERDS AT M.I.T.
ARE YOU ALL RIGHT?
I'M USING A BIRD AS A DRONE. SOMEONE'S COMING THIS WAY!
WHY FIGHT, AVENGERS?

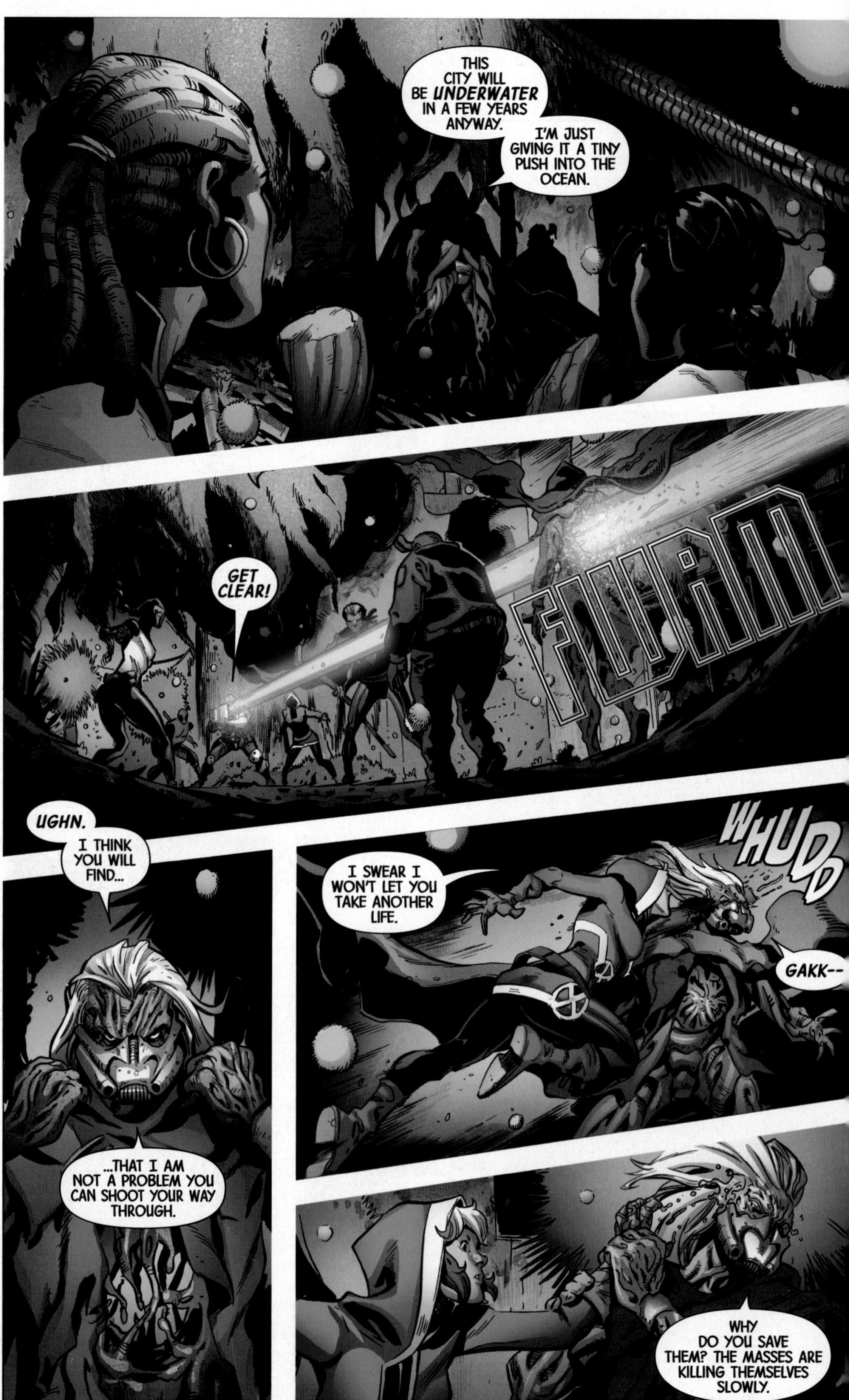
THIS CITY WILL BE UNDERWATER IN A FEW YEARS ANYWAY.
I'M JUST GIVING IT A TINY PUSH INTO THE OCEAN.
GET CLEAR!
FWRM
UGHN.
I THINK YOU WILL FIND...
...THAT I AM NOT A PROBLEM YOU CAN SHOOT YOUR WAY THROUGH.
WHUDD
I SWEAR I WON'T LET YOU TAKE ANOTHER LIFE.
GAKK--
WHY DO YOU SAVE THEM? THE MASSES ARE KILLING THEMSELVES SLOWLY.

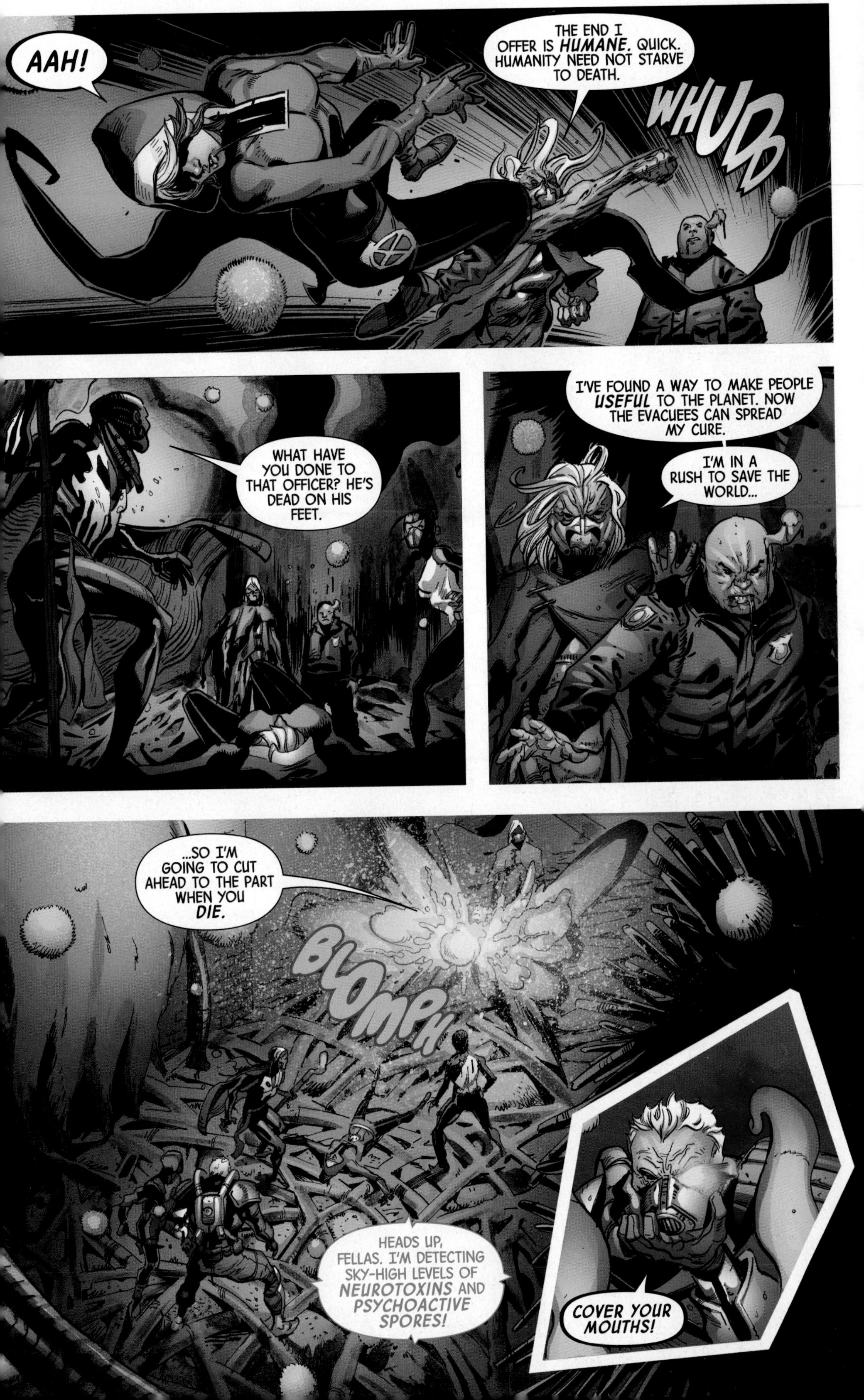
AAH!
THE END I OFFER IS HUMANE. QUICK. HUMANITY NEED NOT STARVE TO DEATH.
WHUDD
WHAT HAVE YOU DONE TO THAT OFFICER? HE'S DEAD ON HIS FEET.
I'VE FOUND A WAY TO MAKE PEOPLE USEFUL TO THE PLANET. NOW THE EVACUEES CAN SPREAD MY CURE.
I'M IN A RUSH TO SAVE THE WORLD...
...SO I'M GOING TO CUT AHEAD TO THE PART WHEN YOU DIE.
BLOMPH
HEADS UP, FELLAS. I'M DETECTING SKY-HIGH LEVELS OF NEUROTOXINS AND PSYCHOACTIVE SPORES!
COVER YOUR MOUTHS!

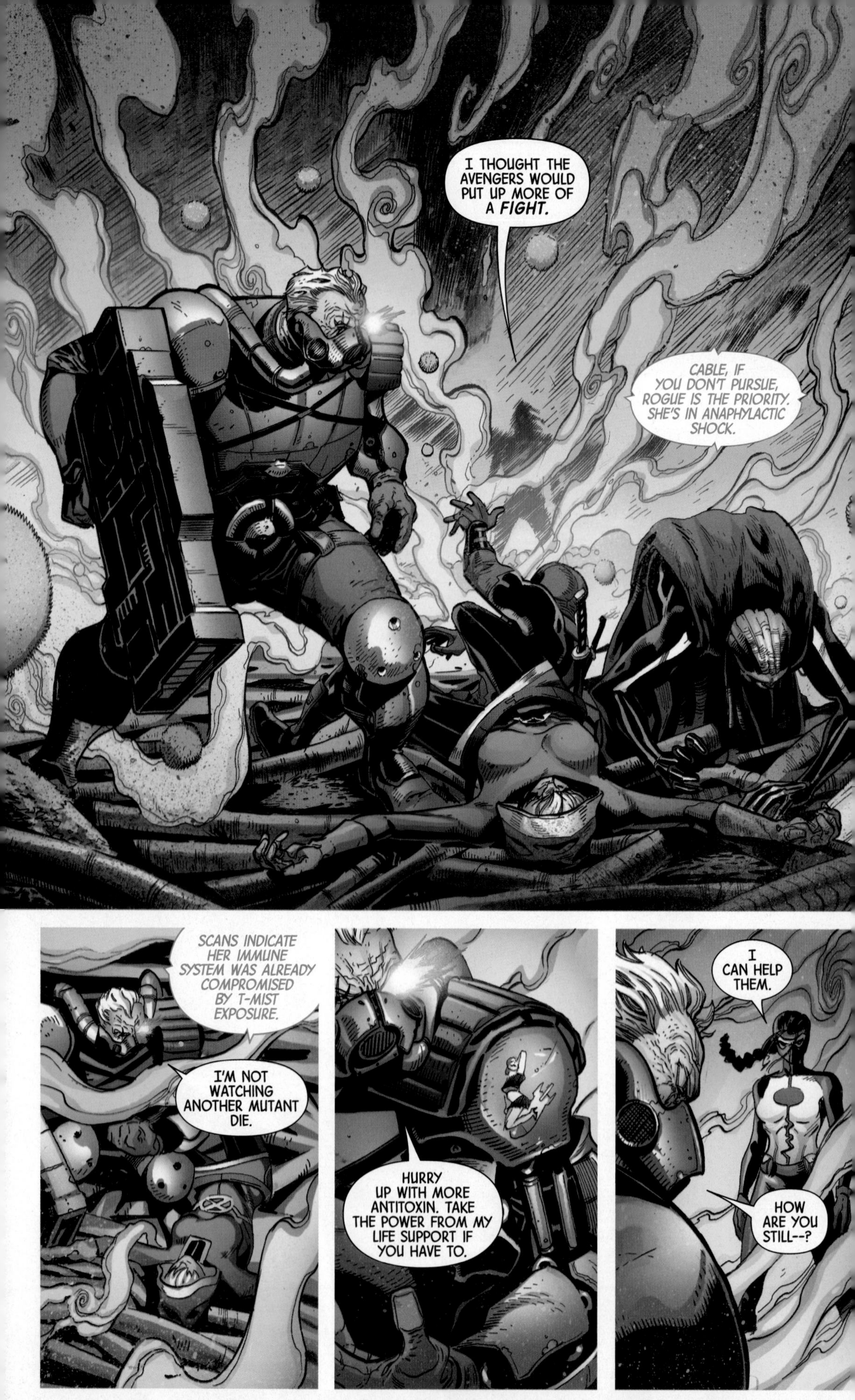

I THOUGHT THE AVENGERS WOULD PUT UP MORE OF A FIGHT.
CABLE, IF YOU DON'T PURSUE, ROGUE IS THE PRIORITY. SHE'S IN ANAPHYLACTIC SHOCK.
SCANS INDICATE HER IMMUNE SYSTEM WAS ALREADY COMPROMISED BY T-MIST EXPOSURE.
I'M NOT WATCHING ANOTHER MUTANT DIE.
HURRY UP WITH MORE ANTITOXIN. TAKE THE POWER FROM MY LIFE SUPPORT IF YOU HAVE TO.
I CAN HELP THEM.
HOW ARE YOU STILL--?

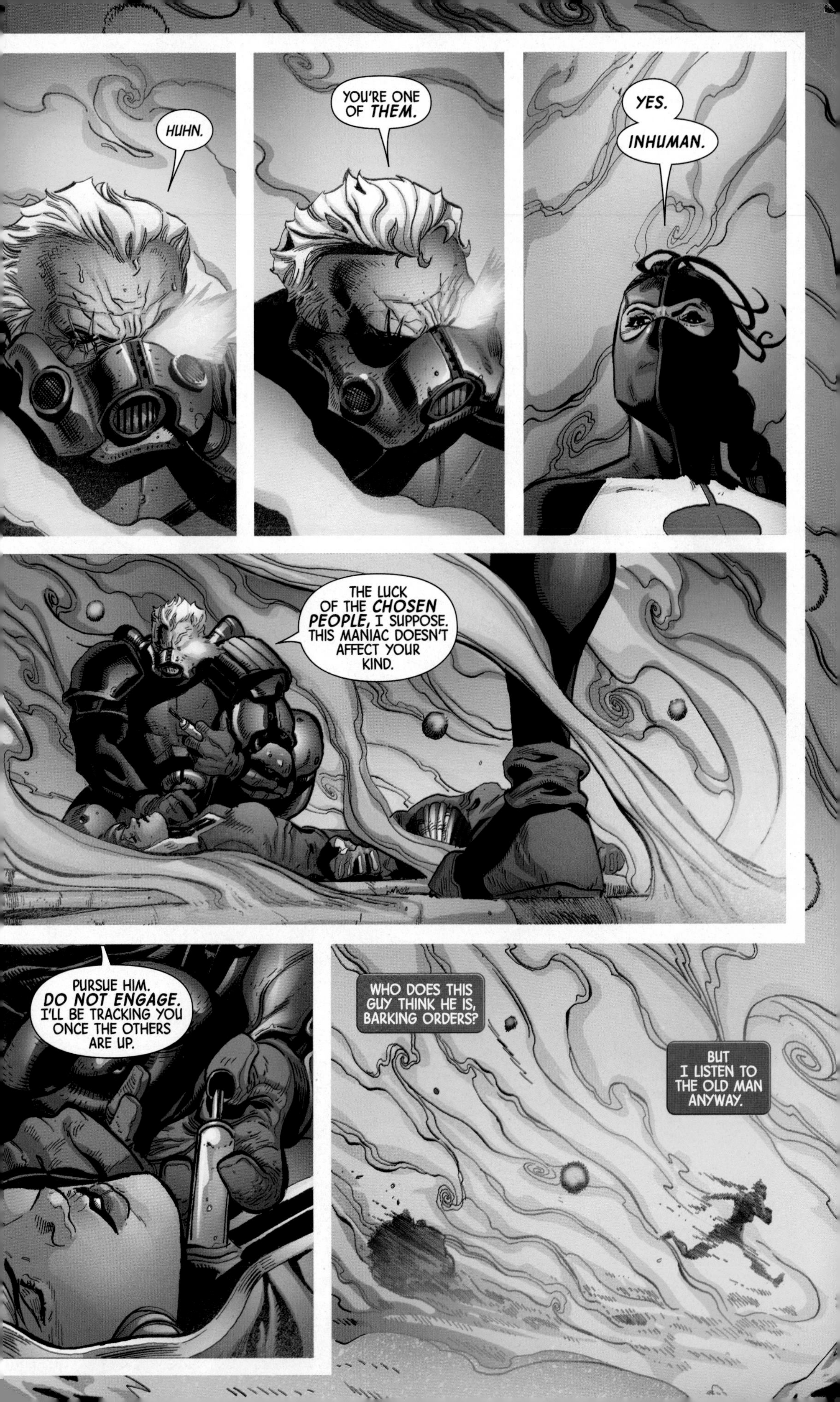
HUHN.
YOU'RE ONE OF *THEM.*
YES.
INHUMAN.
THE LUCK OF THE *CHOSEN PEOPLE,* I SUPPOSE. THIS MANIAC DOESN'T AFFECT YOUR KIND.
PURSUE HIM. *DO NOT ENGAGE.* I'LL BE TRACKING YOU ONCE THE OTHERS ARE UP.
WHO DOES THIS GUY THINK HE IS, BARKING ORDERS?
BUT I LISTEN TO THE OLD MAN ANYWAY.

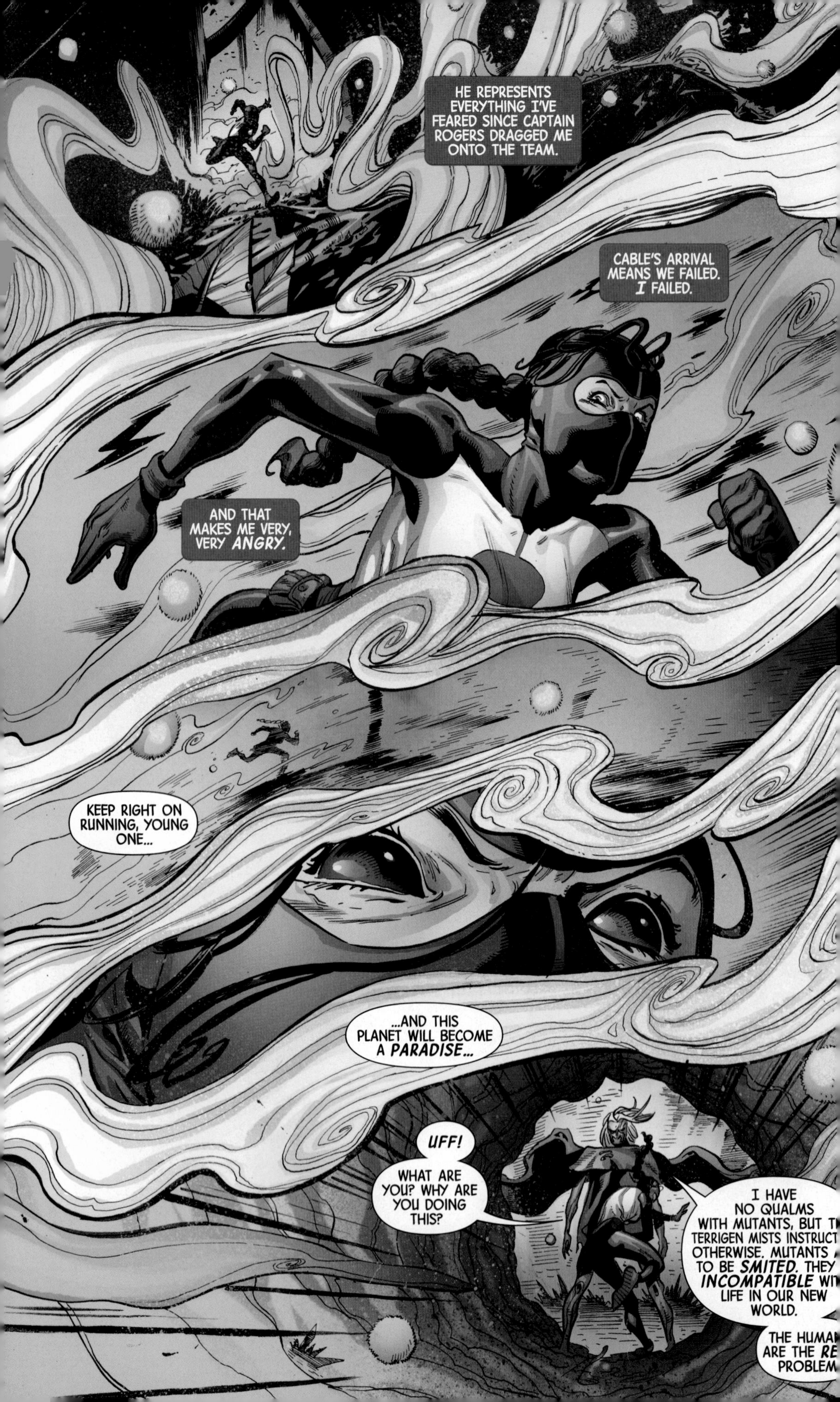

HE REPRESENTS EVERYTHING I'VE FEARED SINCE CAPTAIN ROGERS DRAGGED ME ONTO THE TEAM.
CABLE'S ARRIVAL MEANS WE FAILED. *I* FAILED.
AND THAT MAKES ME VERY, VERY *ANGRY.*
KEEP RIGHT ON RUNNING, YOUNG ONE...
...AND THIS PLANET WILL BECOME A *PARADISE*...
UFF!
WHAT ARE YOU? WHY ARE YOU DOING THIS?
I HAVE NO QUALMS WITH MUTANTS, BUT T TERRIGEN MISTS INSTRUCT OTHERWISE. MUTANTS TO BE *SMITED.* THEY *INCOMPATIBLE* WI LIFE IN OUR NEW WORLD.
THE HUMA ARE THE *RE* PROBLEM

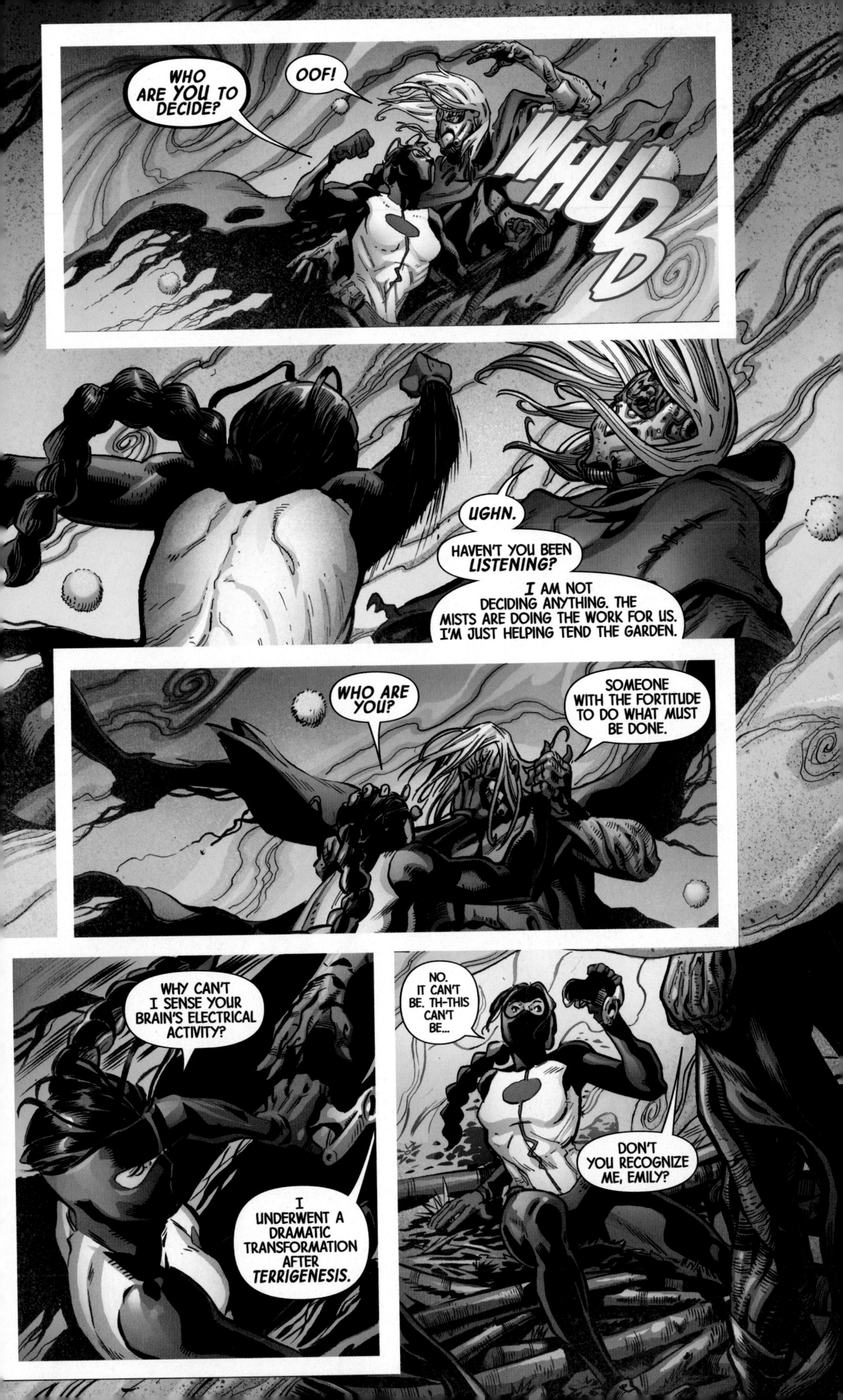

WHO ARE YOU TO DECIDE?
OOF!
WHUD
UGHN.
HAVEN'T YOU BEEN LISTENING?
I AM NOT DECIDING ANYTHING. THE MISTS ARE DOING THE WORK FOR US. I'M JUST HELPING TEND THE GARDEN.
WHO ARE YOU?
SOMEONE WITH THE FORTITUDE TO DO WHAT MUST BE DONE.
WHY CAN'T I SENSE YOUR BRAIN'S ELECTRICAL ACTIVITY?
I UNDERWENT A DRAMATIC TRANSFORMATION AFTER TERRIGENESIS.
NO. IT CAN'T BE. TH-THIS CAN'T BE...
DON'T YOU RECOGNIZE ME, EMILY?

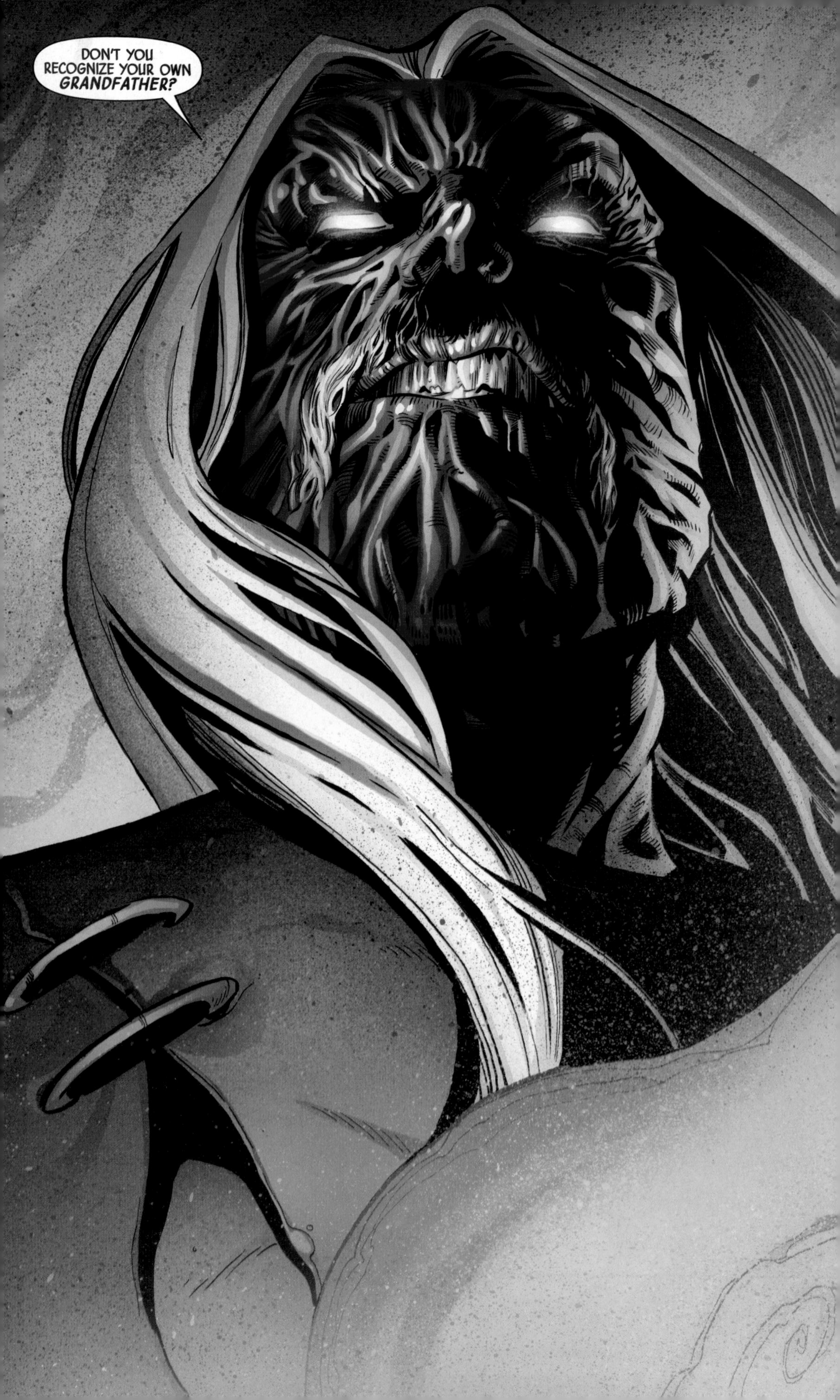
DON'T YOU RECOGNIZE YOUR OWN *GRANDFATHER?*

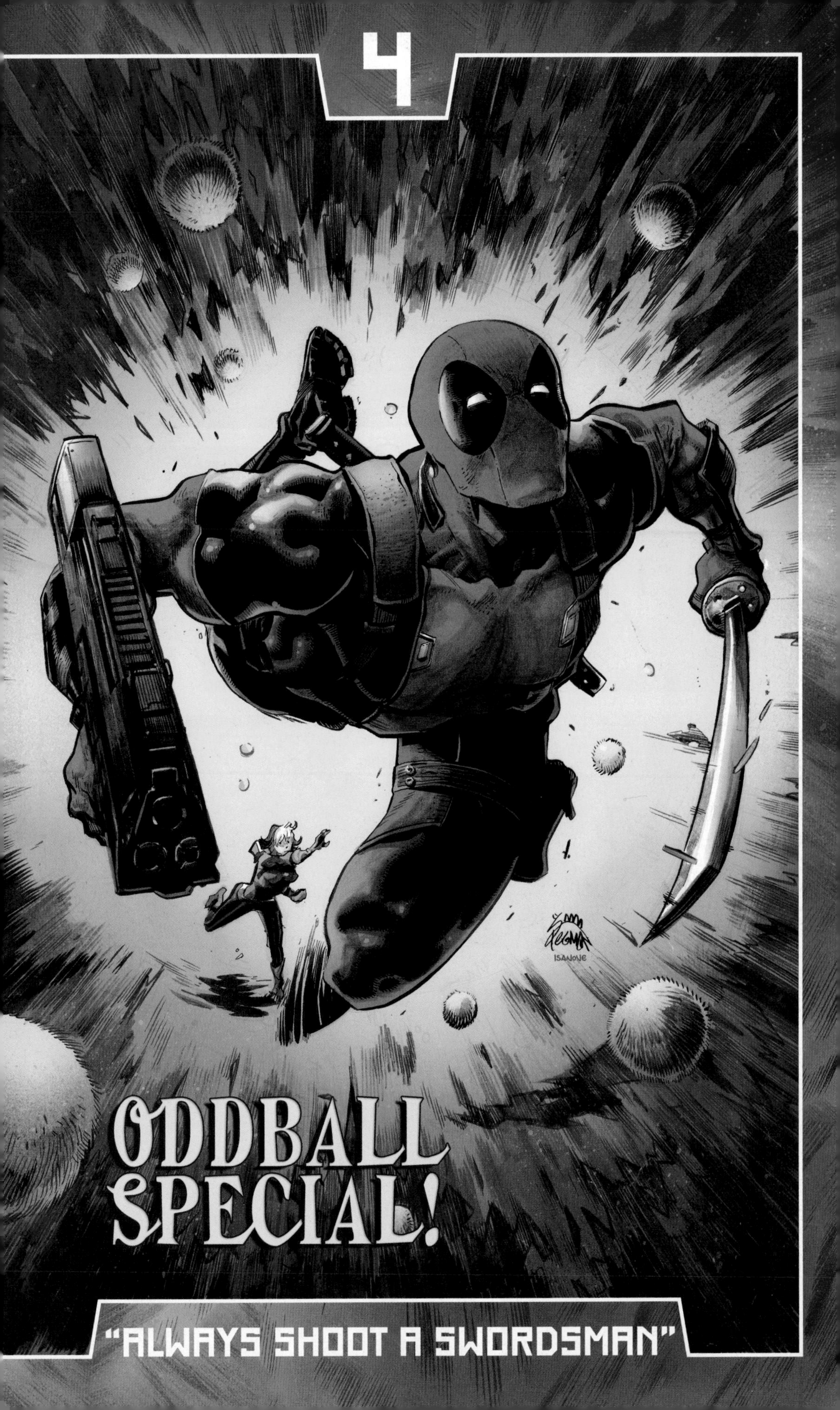
4
ODDBALL SPECIAL!
"ALWAYS SHOOT A SWORDSMAN"

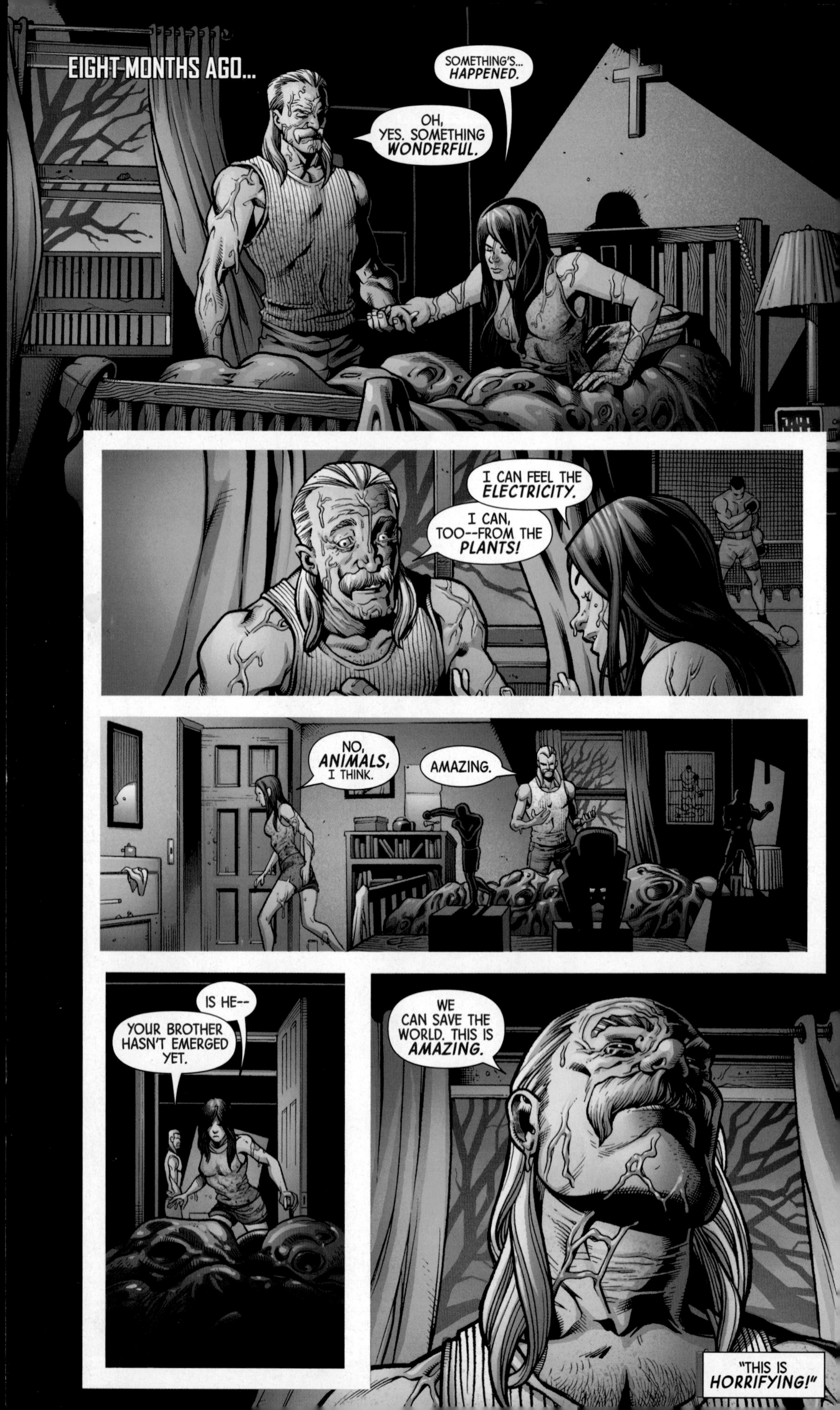
EIGHT MONTHS AGO...
SOMETHING'S... HAPPENED.
OH, YES. SOMETHING WONDERFUL.
I CAN FEEL THE ELECTRICITY.
I CAN, TOO--FROM THE PLANTS!
NO, ANIMALS, I THINK.
AMAZING.
IS HE--
YOUR BROTHER HASN'T EMERGED YET.
WE CAN SAVE THE WORLD. THIS IS AMAZING.
"THIS IS HORRIFYING!"

THIS IS ALL A MISTAKE, RIGHT?

PLEASE, I'M *BEGGING* YOU. THIS IS NOT YOU. YOU NEED *HELP*.

I'M SORRY, EMILY, TRULY. I KNOW HOW *SENSITIVE* YOU ARE. PERHAPS NOW EVEN MORE SO AFTER TERRIGENESIS, BUT...

...I AM NOT THE ONE IN NEED OF AID. DON'T YOU SEE? A MASS EXTINCTION IS THE ONLY WAY TO *SAVE THE PLANET*. IT CAN'T SUPPORT ALL THE *HUMAN* LIVES.

PLEASE, IF YOU EVER LOVED ME, YOU'LL *STOP* THIS RIGHT NOW.

I WILL *NOT* YIELD. NOT EVEN FOR MY OWN GRANDDAUGHTER.

NO ONE CAN STOP ME!

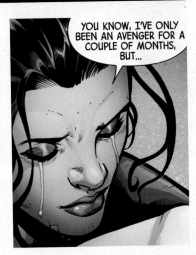

YOU KNOW, I'VE ONLY BEEN AN AVENGER FOR A COUPLE OF MONTHS, BUT...

...YOU'RE THE *FOURTH* PERSON TO YELL THAT AT ME.

AND IT HASN'T BEEN TRUE ONCE!

"I'M RELOADING, DEADPOOL."

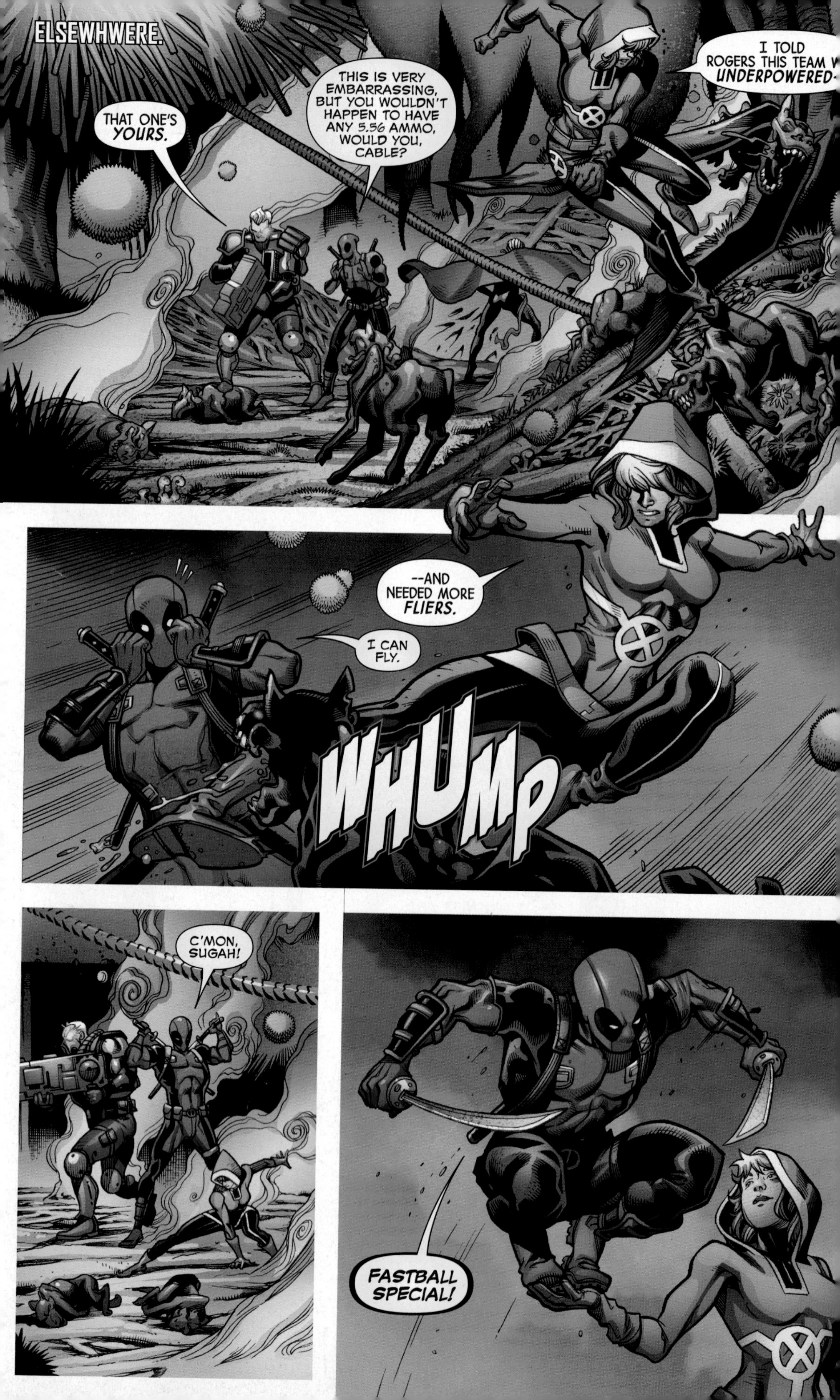
ELSEWHWERE.
THAT ONE'S YOURS.
THIS IS VERY EMBARRASSING, BUT YOU WOULDN'T HAPPEN TO HAVE ANY 5.56 AMMO, WOULD YOU, CABLE?
I TOLD ROGERS THIS TEAM W UNDERPOWERED--
--AND NEEDED MORE FLIERS.
I CAN FLY.
WHUMP
C'MON, SUGAH!
FASTBALL SPECIAL!

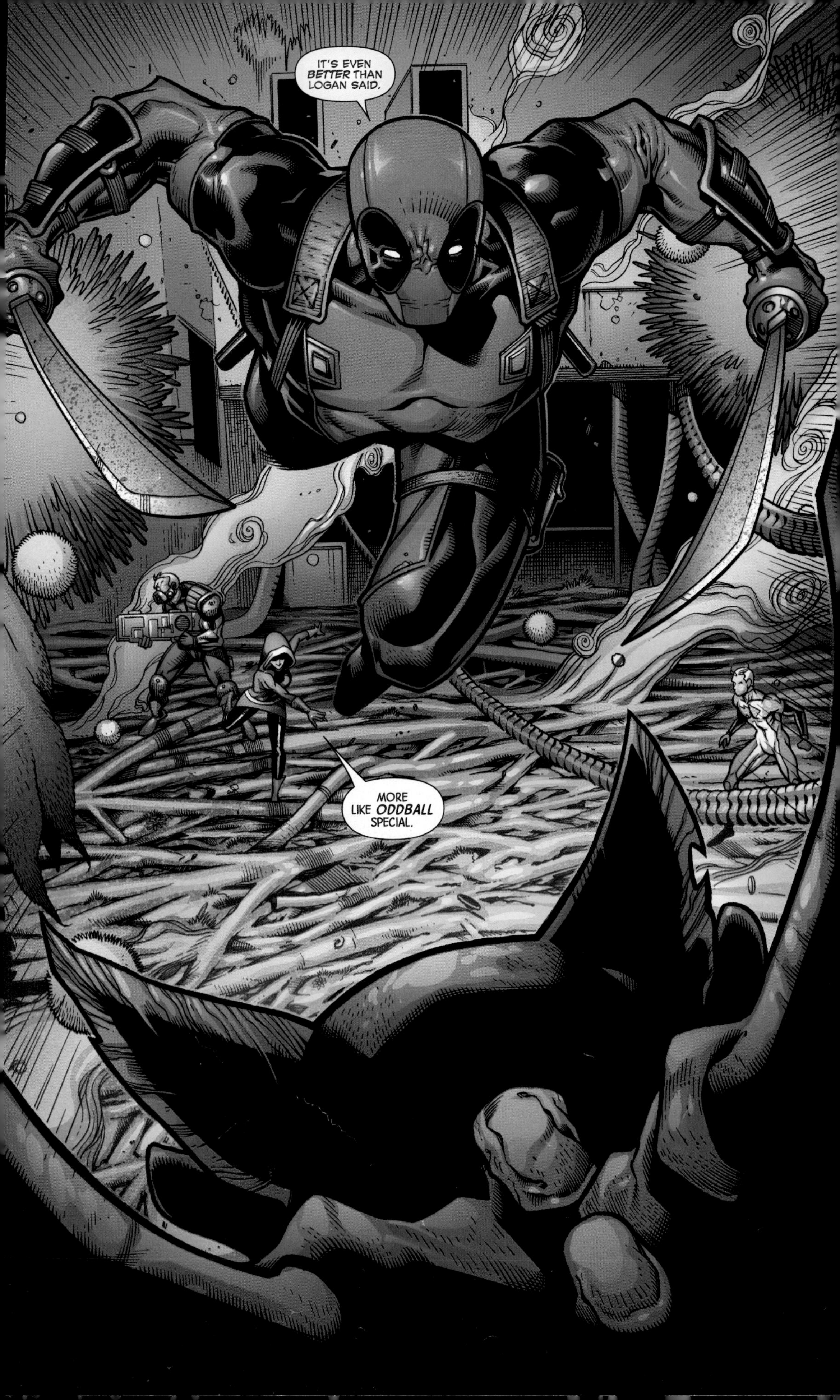
IT'S EVEN BETTER THAN LOGAN SAID.
MORE LIKE ODDBALL SPECIAL.

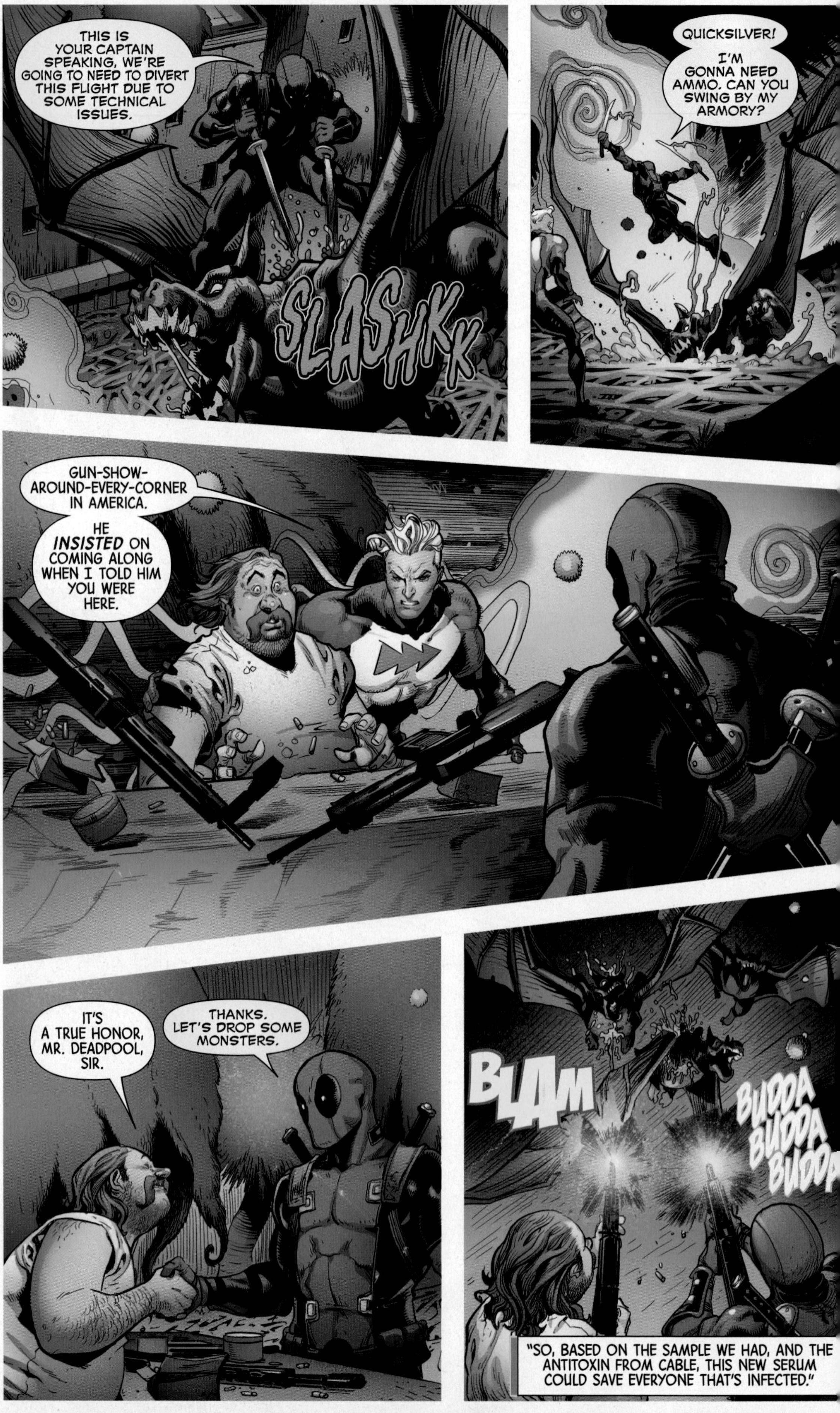
THIS IS YOUR CAPTAIN SPEAKING, WE'RE GOING TO NEED TO DIVERT THIS FLIGHT DUE TO SOME TECHNICAL ISSUES.
SLASHKK
QUICKSILVER!
I'M GONNA NEED AMMO. CAN YOU SWING BY MY ARMORY?
GUN-SHOW-AROUND-EVERY-CORNER IN AMERICA.
HE *INSISTED* ON COMING ALONG WHEN I TOLD HIM YOU WERE HERE.
IT'S A TRUE HONOR, MR. DEADPOOL, SIR.
THANKS. LET'S DROP SOME MONSTERS.
BLAM
BUDDA BUDDA BUDDA
"SO, BASED ON THE SAMPLE WE HAD, AND THE ANTITOXIN FROM CABLE, THIS NEW SERUM COULD SAVE EVERYONE THAT'S INFECTED."

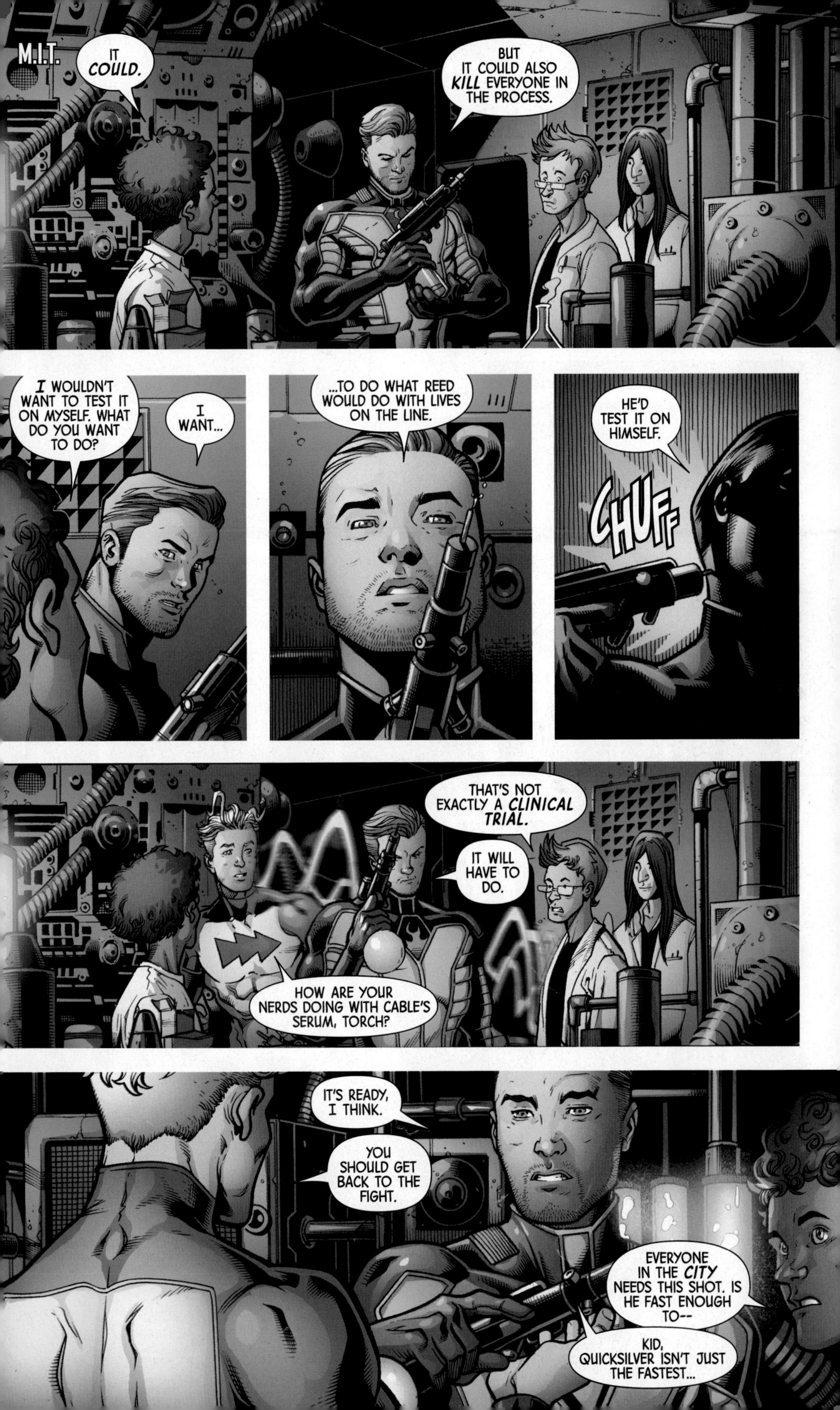
M.I.T.
IT COULD.
BUT IT COULD ALSO KILL EVERYONE IN THE PROCESS.
I WOULDN'T WANT TO TEST IT ON MYSELF. WHAT DO YOU WANT TO DO?
I WANT...
...TO DO WHAT REED WOULD DO WITH LIVES ON THE LINE.
HE'D TEST IT ON HIMSELF.
CHUFF
THAT'S NOT EXACTLY A CLINICAL TRIAL.
IT WILL HAVE TO DO.
HOW ARE YOUR NERDS DOING WITH CABLE'S SERUM, TORCH?
IT'S READY, I THINK.
YOU SHOULD GET BACK TO THE FIGHT.
EVERYONE IN THE CITY NEEDS THIS SHOT. IS HE FAST ENOUGH TO--
KID, QUICKSILVER ISN'T JUST THE FASTEST...

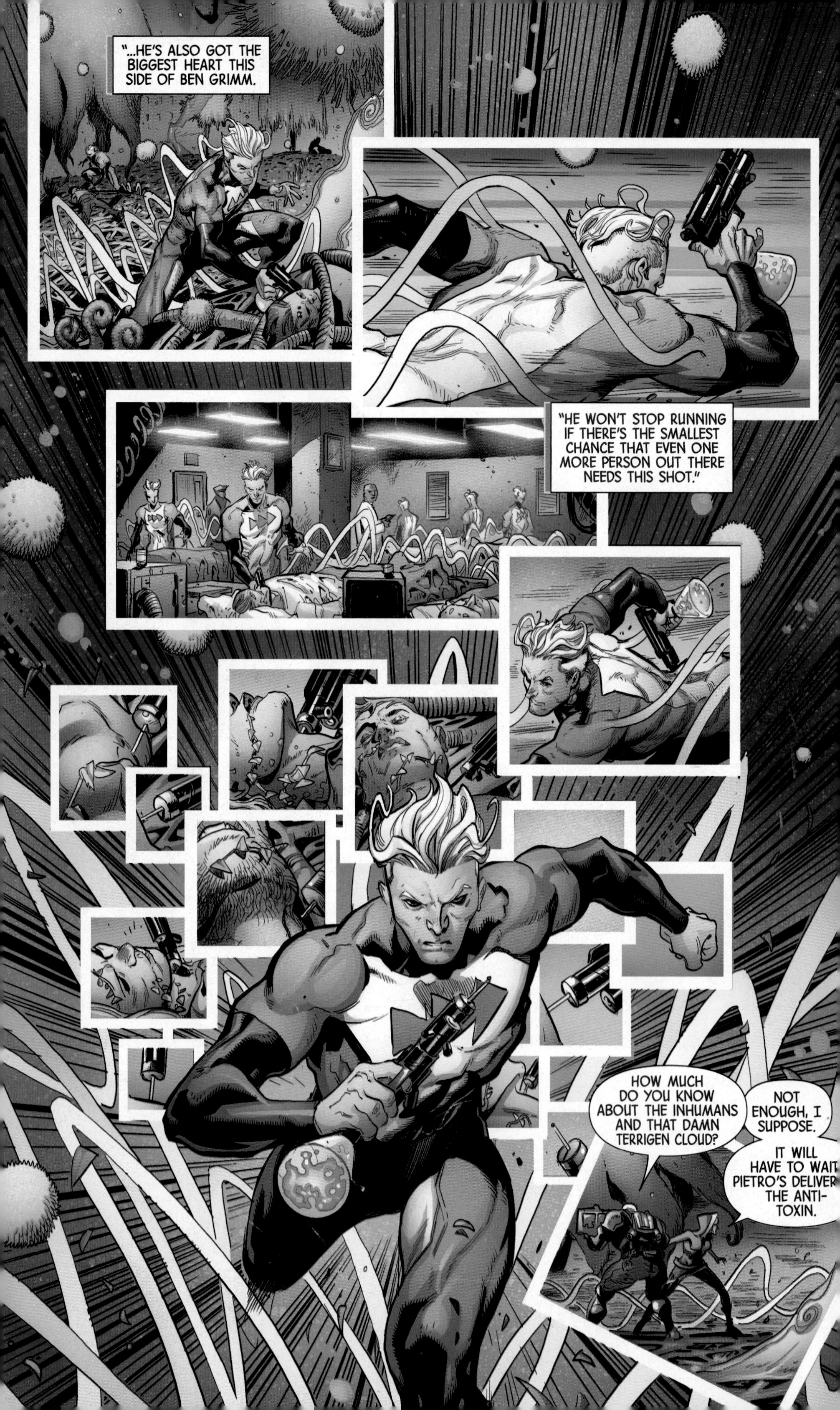
"...HE'S ALSO GOT THE BIGGEST HEART THIS SIDE OF BEN GRIMM.
"HE WON'T STOP RUNNING IF THERE'S THE SMALLEST CHANCE THAT EVEN ONE MORE PERSON OUT THERE NEEDS THIS SHOT."
HOW MUCH DO YOU KNOW ABOUT THE INHUMANS AND THAT DAMN TERRIGEN CLOUD?
NOT ENOUGH, I SUPPOSE.
IT WILL HAVE TO WAIT PIETRO'S DELIVER THE ANTI-TOXIN.

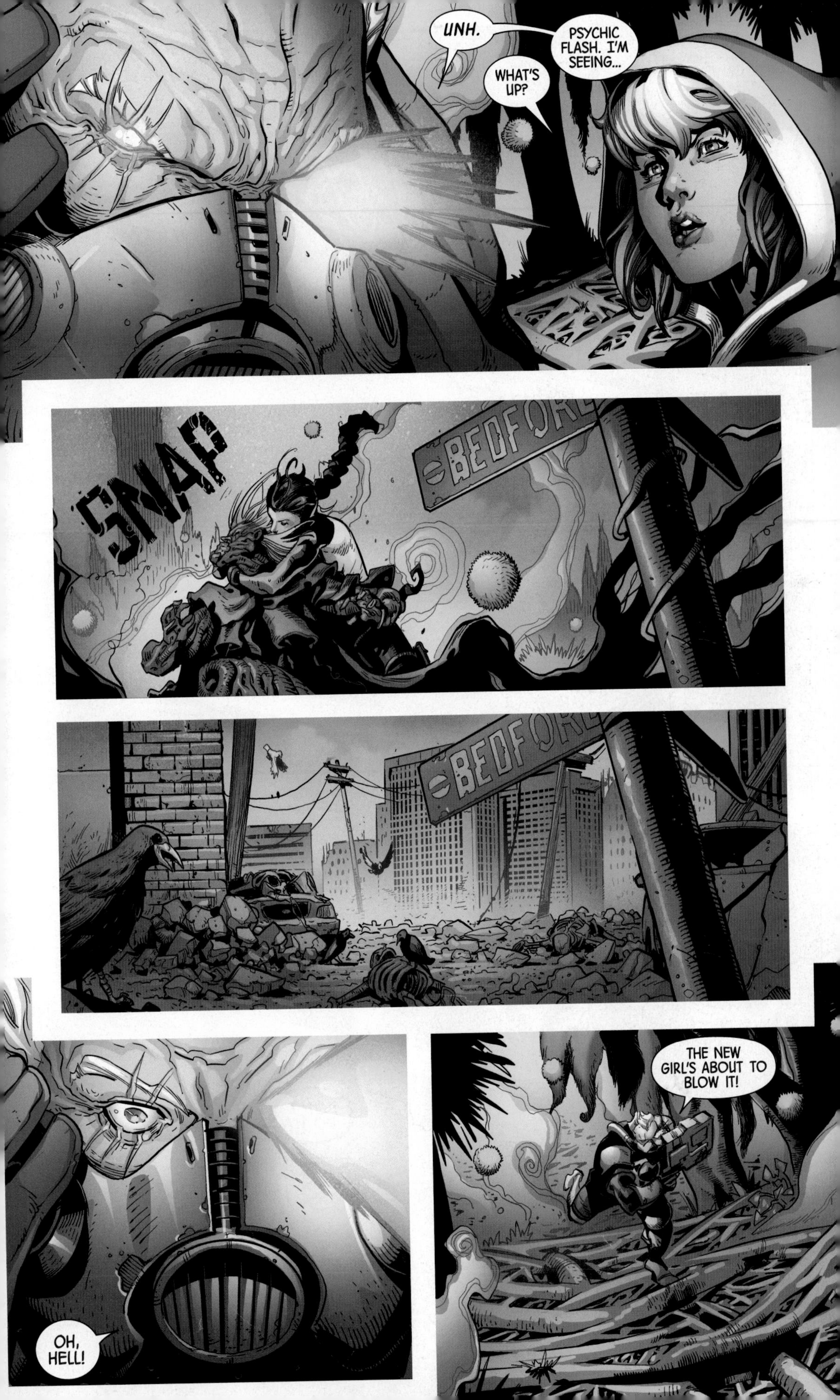
UNH.
PSYCHIC FLASH. I'M SEEING...
WHAT'S UP?
SNAP
BEDFORD
BEDFORD
THE NEW GIRL'S ABOUT TO BLOW IT!
OH, HELL!

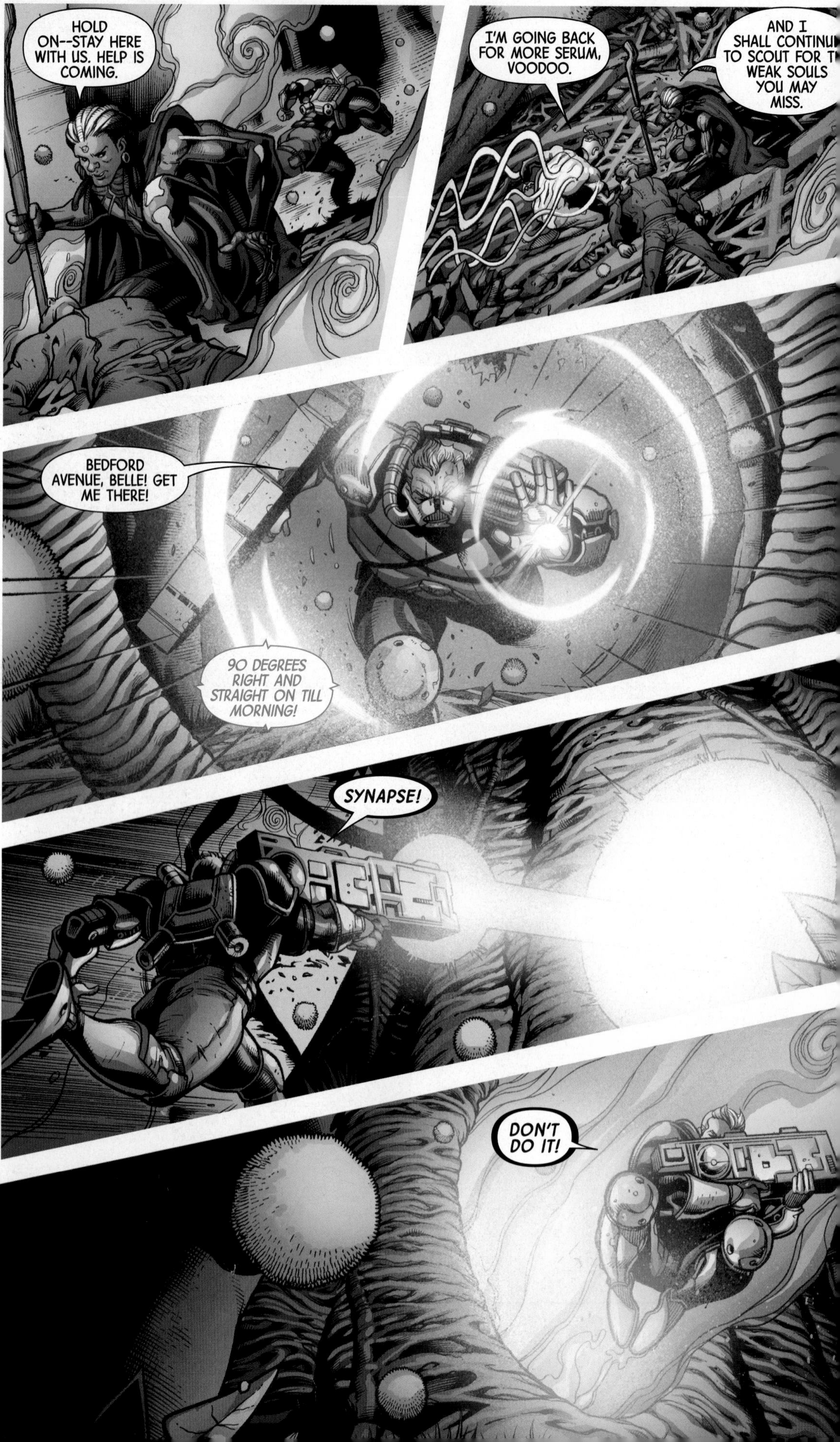
HOLD ON--STAY HERE WITH US. HELP IS COMING.
I'M GOING BACK FOR MORE SERUM, VOODOO.
AND I SHALL CONTINU TO SCOUT FOR T WEAK SOULS YOU MAY MISS.
BEDFORD AVENUE, BELLE! GET ME THERE!
90 DEGREES RIGHT AND STRAIGHT ON TILL MORNING!
SYNAPSE!
DON'T DO IT!

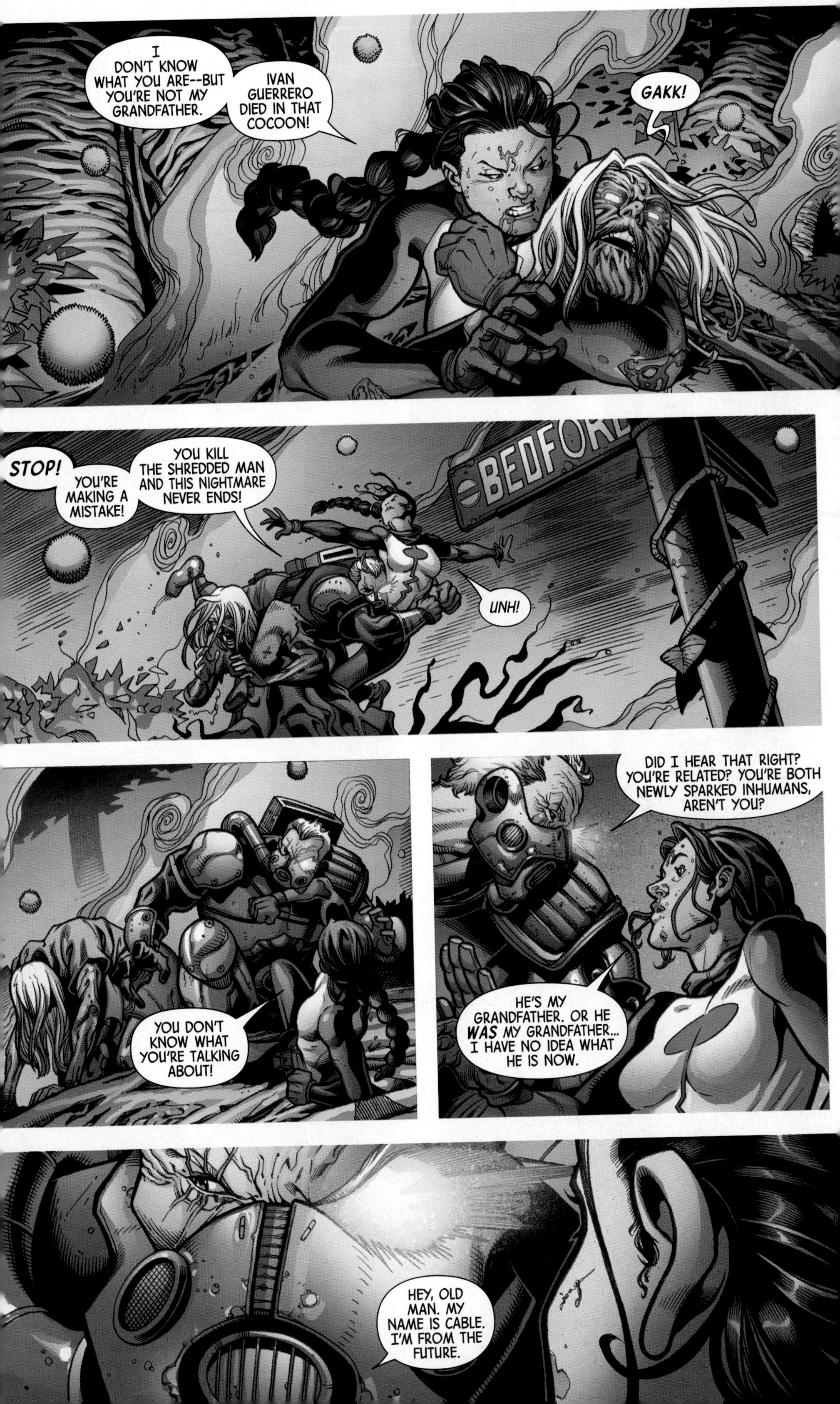
I DON'T KNOW WHAT YOU ARE--BUT YOU'RE NOT MY GRANDFATHER.
IVAN GUERRERO DIED IN THAT COCOON!
GAKK!
STOP!
YOU'RE MAKING A MISTAKE!
YOU KILL THE SHREDDED MAN AND THIS NIGHTMARE NEVER ENDS!
BEDFORD
UNH!
YOU DON'T KNOW WHAT YOU'RE TALKING ABOUT!
DID I HEAR THAT RIGHT? YOU'RE RELATED? YOU'RE BOTH NEWLY SPARKED INHUMANS, AREN'T YOU?
HE'S MY GRANDFATHER. OR HE *WAS* MY GRANDFATHER... I HAVE NO IDEA WHAT HE IS NOW.
HEY, OLD MAN. MY NAME IS CABLE. I'M FROM THE FUTURE.

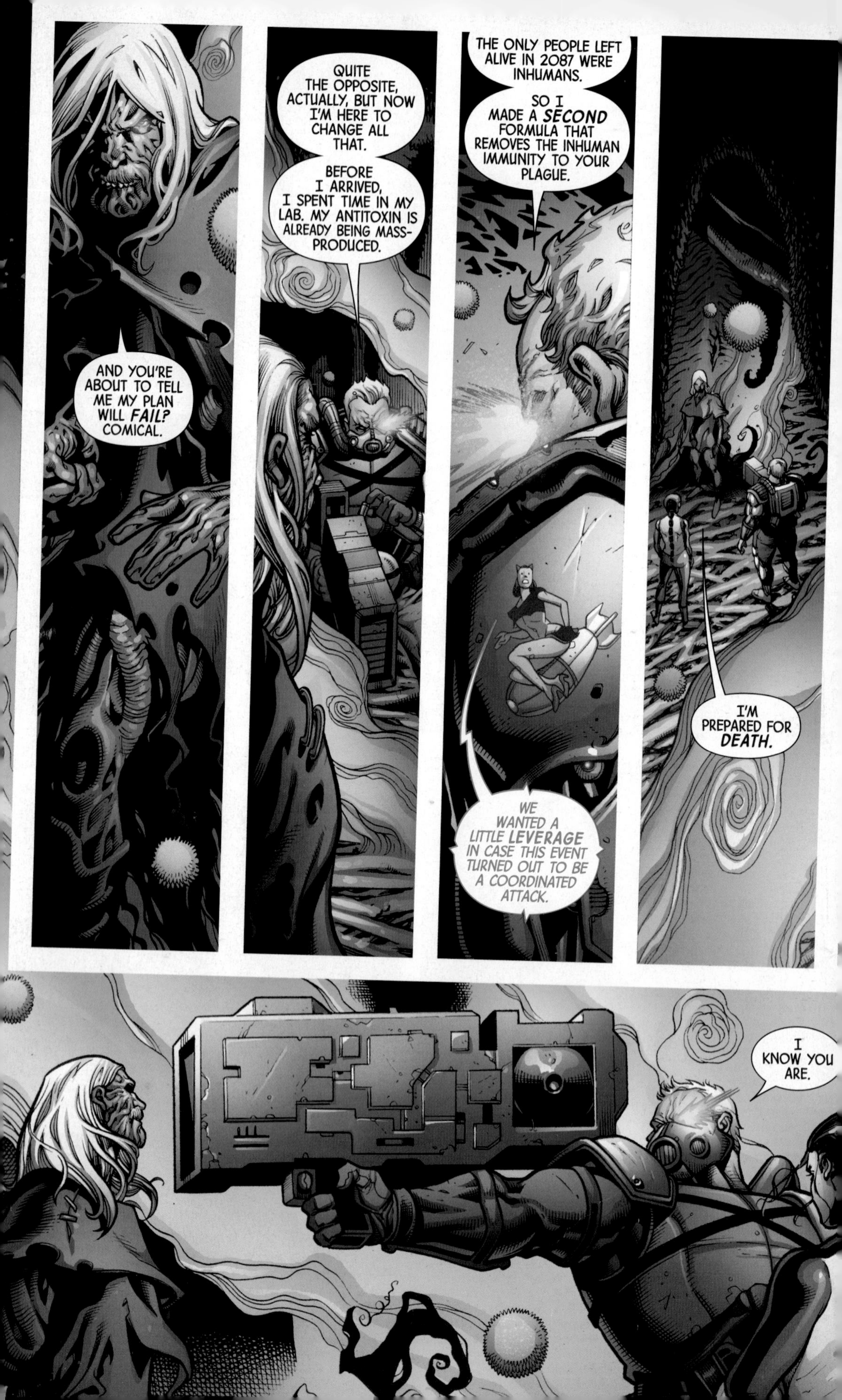
AND YOU'RE ABOUT TO TELL ME MY PLAN WILL FAIL? COMICAL.
QUITE THE OPPOSITE, ACTUALLY, BUT NOW I'M HERE TO CHANGE ALL THAT.
BEFORE I ARRIVED, I SPENT TIME IN MY LAB. MY ANTITOXIN IS ALREADY BEING MASS-PRODUCED.
THE ONLY PEOPLE LEFT ALIVE IN 2087 WERE INHUMANS.
SO I MADE A SECOND FORMULA THAT REMOVES THE INHUMAN IMMUNITY TO YOUR PLAGUE.
WE WANTED A LITTLE LEVERAGE IN CASE THIS EVENT TURNED OUT TO BE A COORDINATED ATTACK.
I'M PREPARED FOR DEATH.
I KNOW YOU ARE.

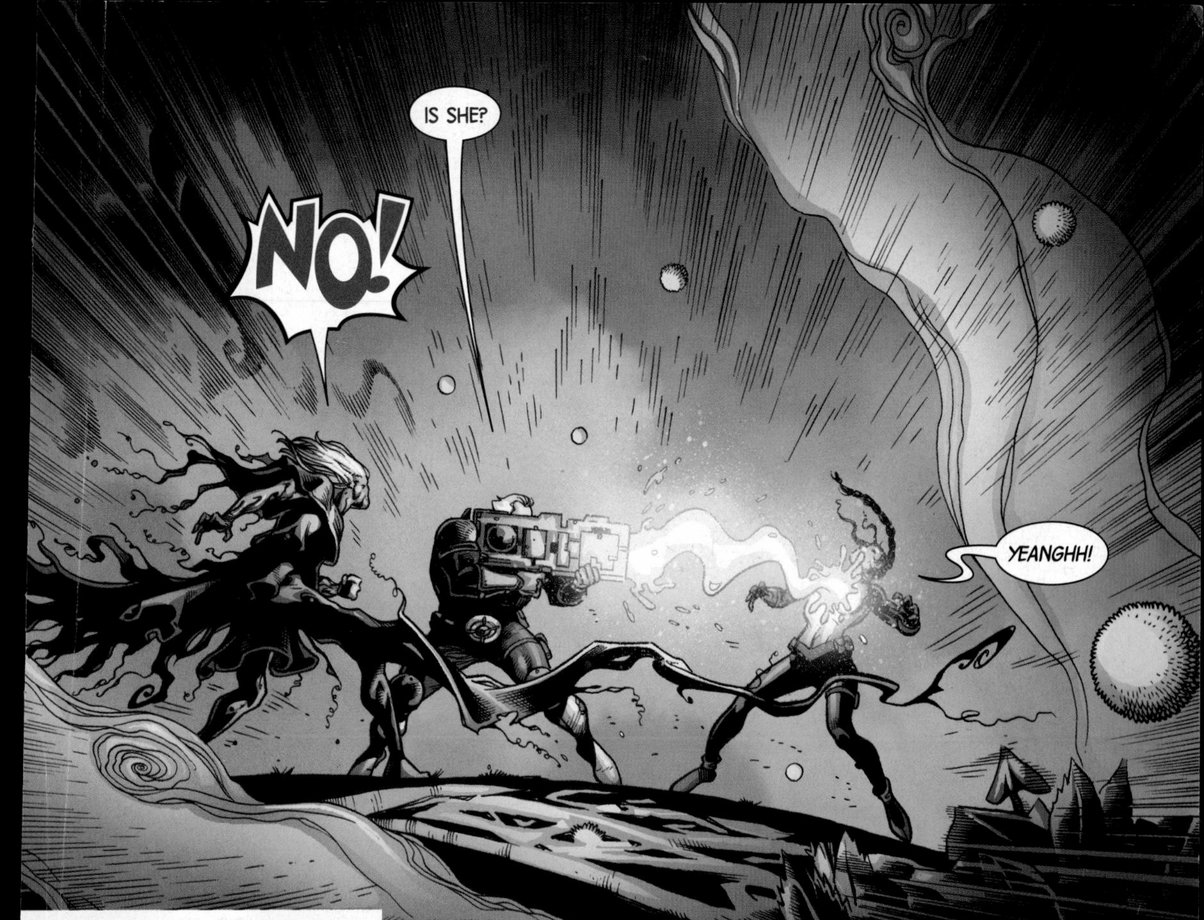
NO!
IS SHE?
YEANGHH!

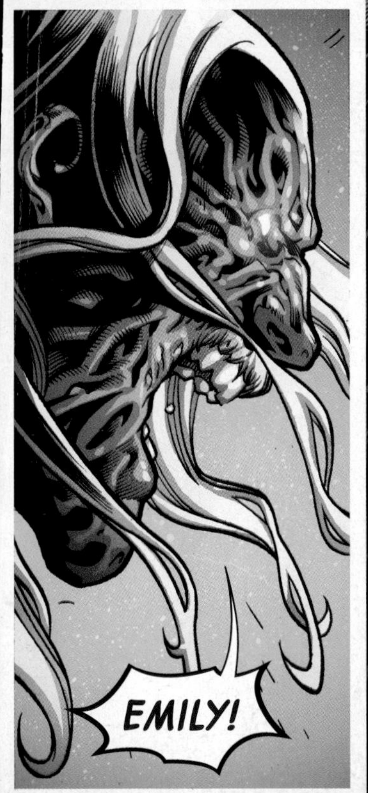
EMILY!

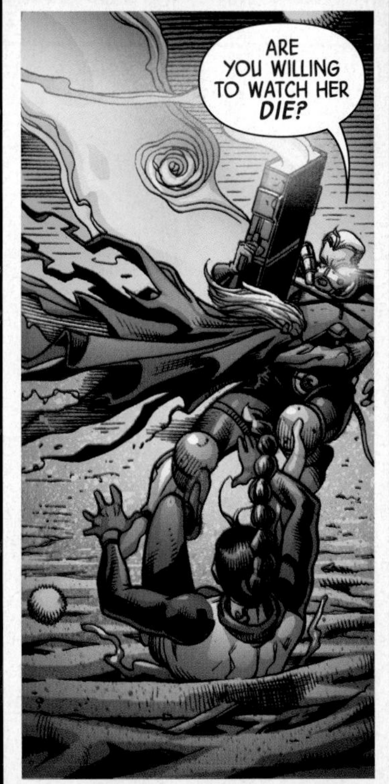
ARE YOU WILLING TO WATCH HER DIE?

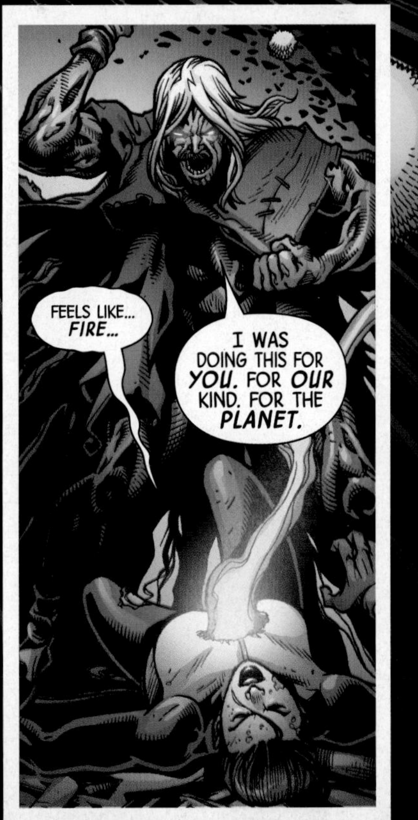
I WAS DOING THIS FOR YOU. FOR OUR KIND. FOR THE PLANET.
FEELS LIKE... FIRE...

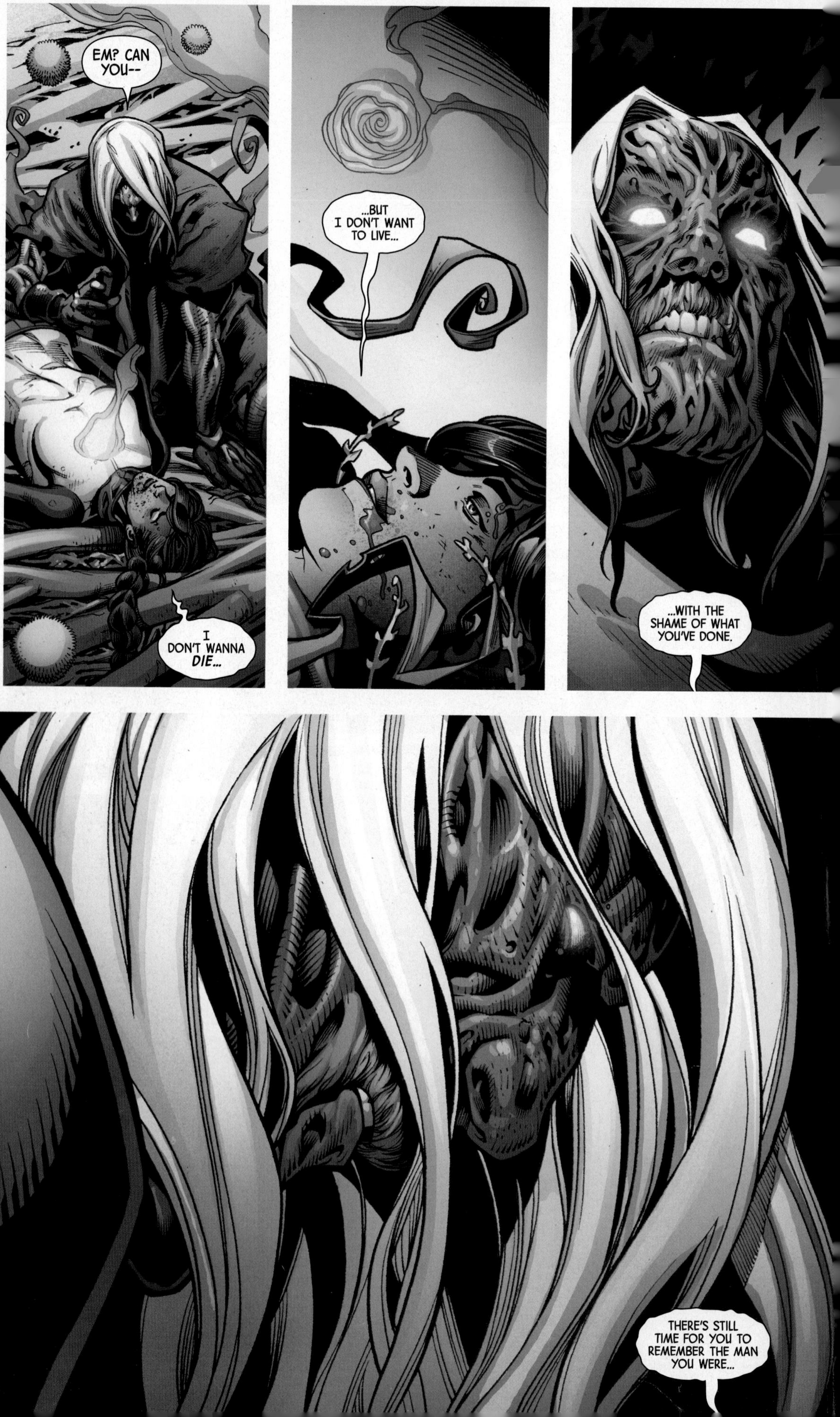
EM? CAN YOU--
I DON'T WANNA *DIE*...
...BUT I DON'T WANT TO LIVE...
...WITH THE SHAME OF WHAT YOU'VE DONE.
THERE'S STILL TIME FOR YOU TO REMEMBER THE MAN YOU WERE...

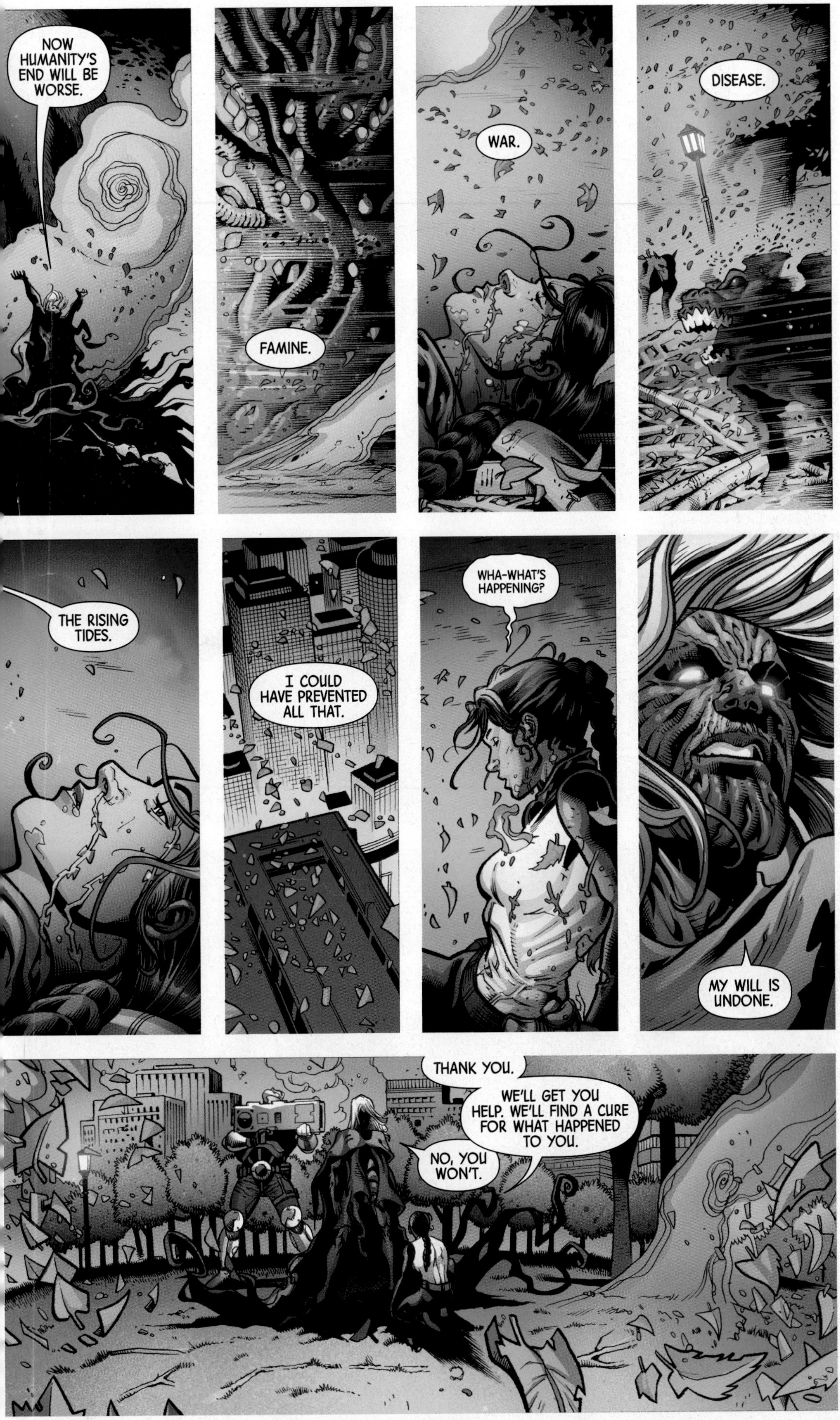
NOW HUMANITY'S END WILL BE WORSE.
FAMINE.
WAR.
DISEASE.
THE RISING TIDES.
I COULD HAVE PREVENTED ALL THAT.
WHA-WHAT'S HAPPENING?
MY WILL IS UNDONE.
THANK YOU.
WE'LL GET YOU HELP. WE'LL FIND A CURE FOR WHAT HAPPENED TO YOU.
NO, YOU WON'T.

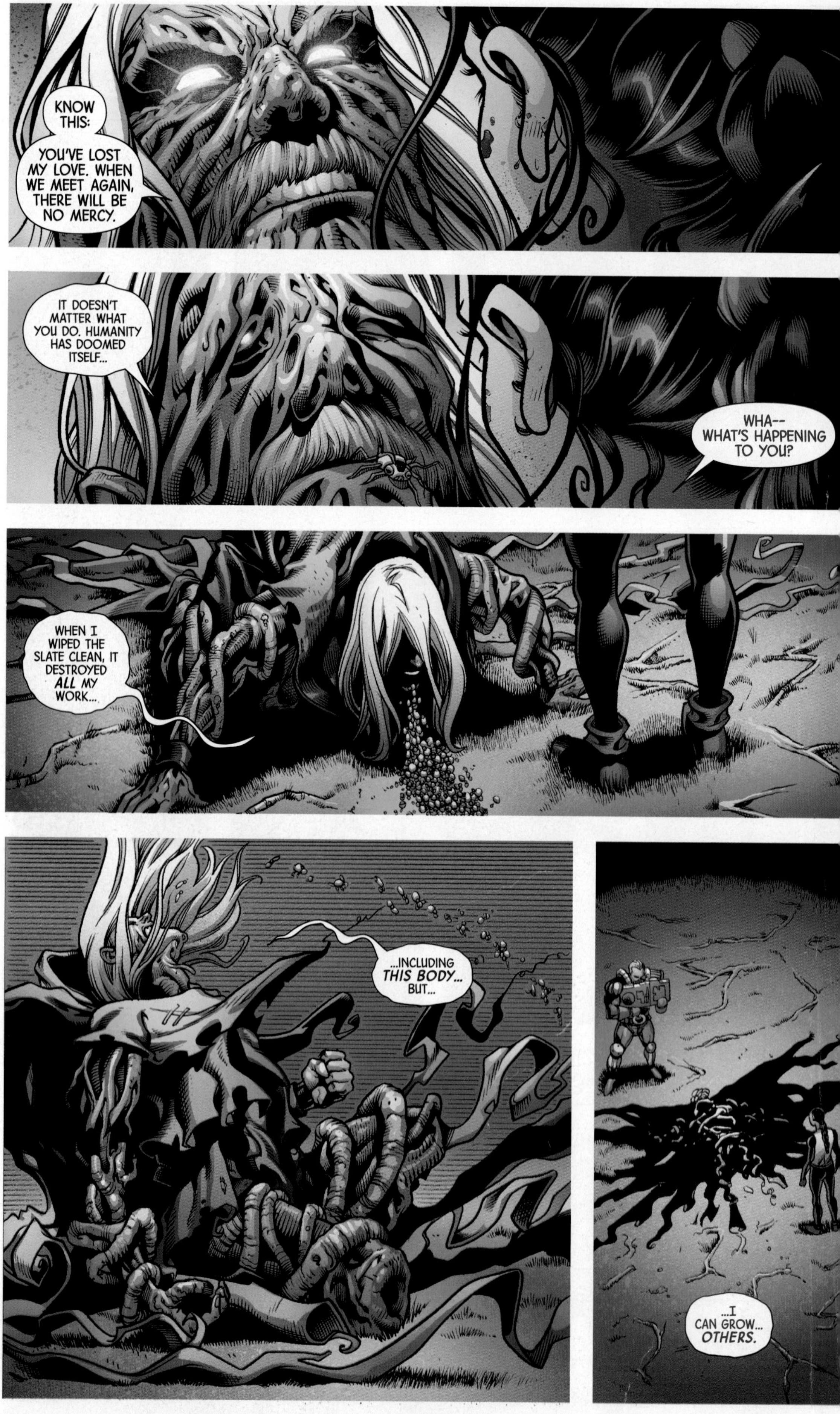
KNOW THIS:
YOU'VE LOST MY LOVE. WHEN WE MEET AGAIN, THERE WILL BE NO MERCY.
IT DOESN'T MATTER WHAT YOU DO. HUMANITY HAS DOOMED ITSELF...
WHA-- WHAT'S HAPPENING TO YOU?
WHEN I WIPED THE SLATE CLEAN, IT DESTROYED *ALL* MY WORK...
...INCLUDING *THIS BODY*... BUT...
...I CAN GROW... *OTHERS.*

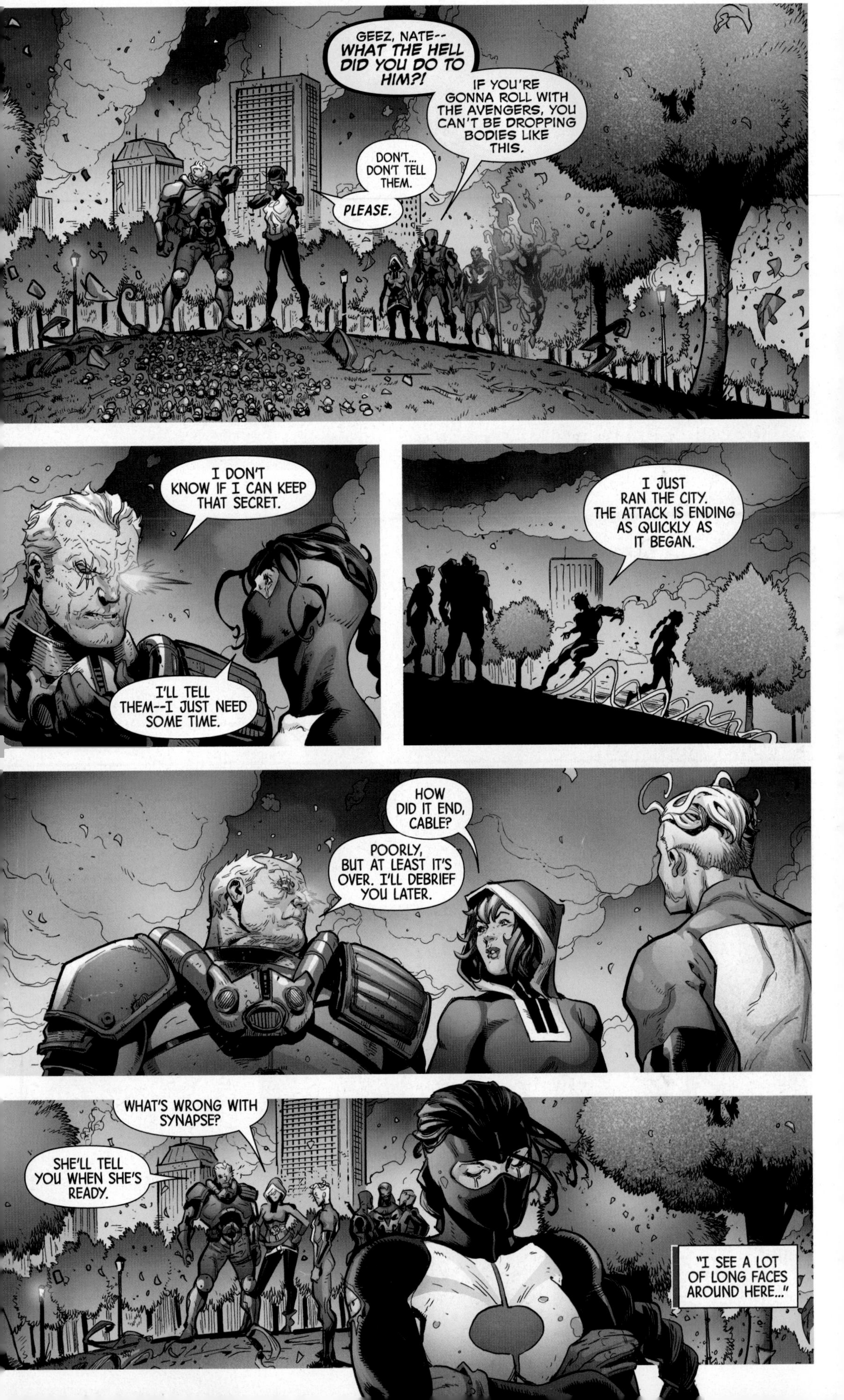
GEEZ, NATE-- WHAT THE HELL DID YOU DO TO HIM?!
IF YOU'RE GONNA ROLL WITH THE AVENGERS, YOU CAN'T BE DROPPING BODIES LIKE THIS.
DON'T... DON'T TELL THEM.
PLEASE.
I DON'T KNOW IF I CAN KEEP THAT SECRET.
I'LL TELL THEM--I JUST NEED SOME TIME.
I JUST RAN THE CITY. THE ATTACK IS ENDING AS QUICKLY AS IT BEGAN.
HOW DID IT END, CABLE?
POORLY, BUT AT LEAST IT'S OVER. I'LL DEBRIEF YOU LATER.
WHAT'S WRONG WITH SYNAPSE?
SHE'LL TELL YOU WHEN SHE'S READY.
"I SEE A LOT OF LONG FACES AROUND HERE..."

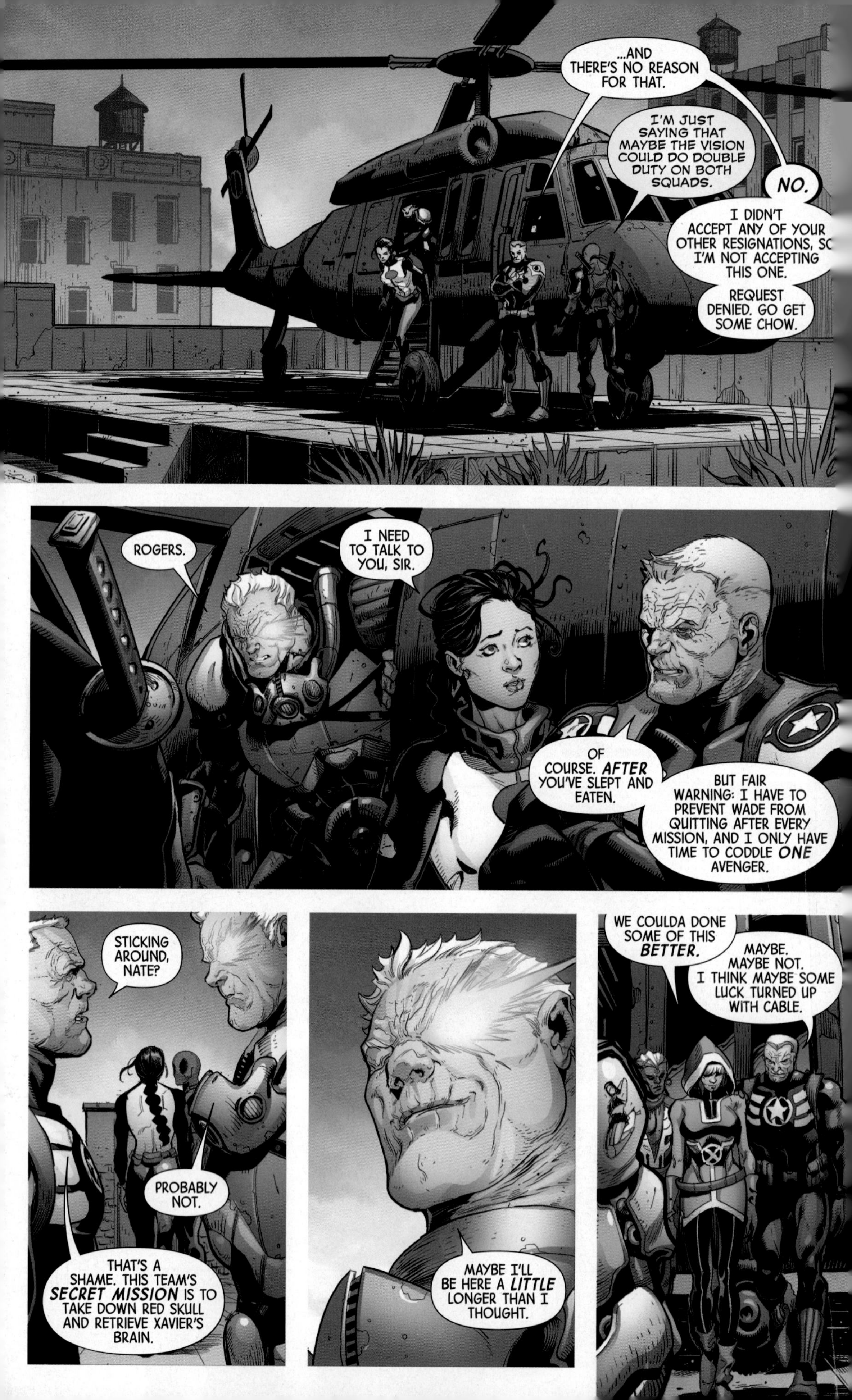
I'M JUST SAYING THAT MAYBE THE VISION COULD DO DOUBLE DUTY ON BOTH SQUADS.
...AND THERE'S NO REASON FOR THAT.
NO.
I DIDN'T ACCEPT ANY OF YOUR OTHER RESIGNATIONS, SO I'M NOT ACCEPTING THIS ONE.
REQUEST DENIED. GO GET SOME CHOW.
ROGERS.
I NEED TO TALK TO YOU, SIR.
OF COURSE. AFTER YOU'VE SLEPT AND EATEN.
BUT FAIR WARNING: I HAVE TO PREVENT WADE FROM QUITTING AFTER EVERY MISSION, AND I ONLY HAVE TIME TO CODDLE ONE AVENGER.
STICKING AROUND, NATE?
PROBABLY NOT.
THAT'S A SHAME. THIS TEAM'S SECRET MISSION IS TO TAKE DOWN RED SKULL AND RETRIEVE XAVIER'S BRAIN.
MAYBE I'LL BE HERE A LITTLE LONGER THAN I THOUGHT.
WE COULDA DONE SOME OF THIS BETTER.
MAYBE. MAYBE NOT. I THINK MAYBE SOME LUCK TURNED UP WITH CABLE.

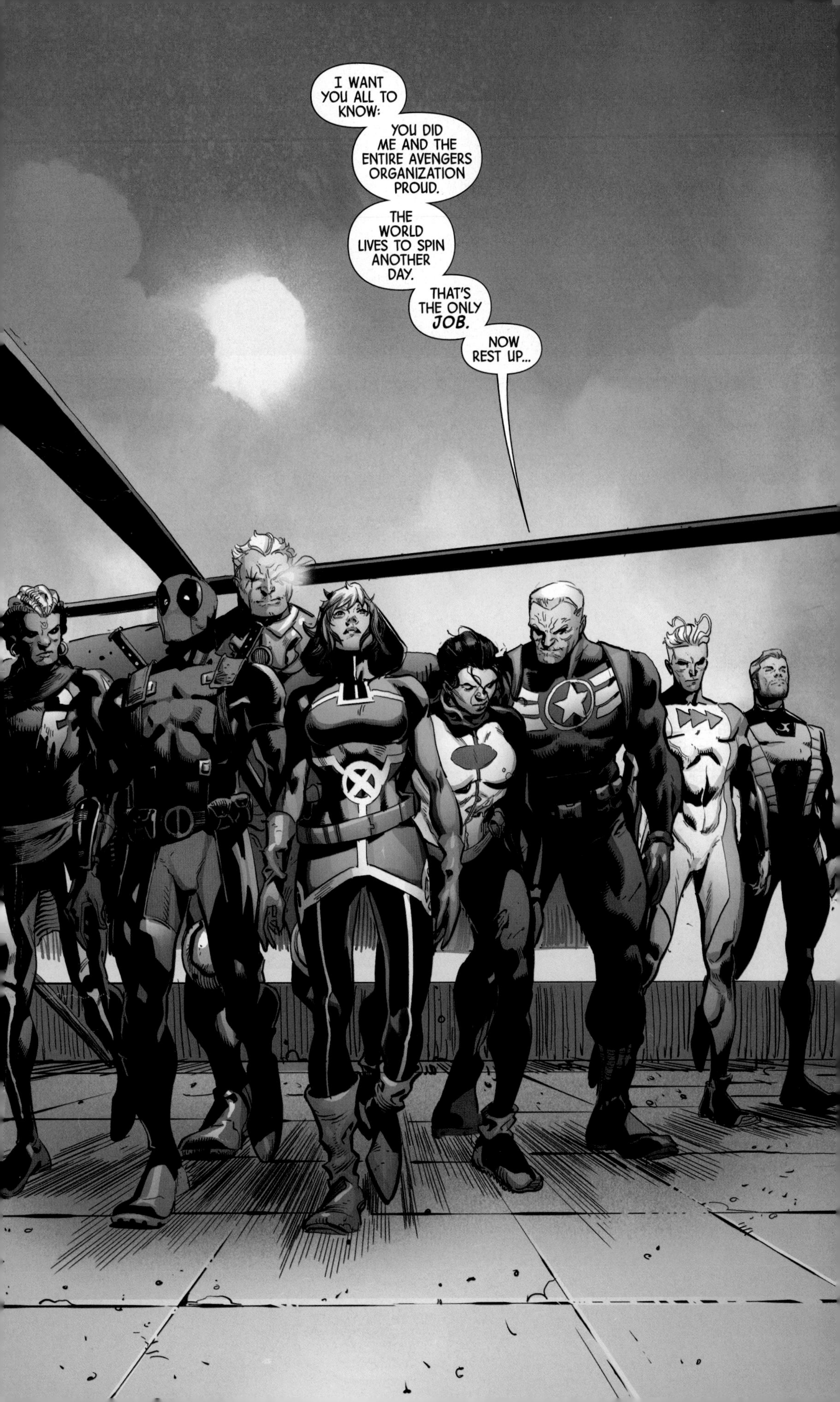
I WANT YOU ALL TO KNOW:
YOU DID ME AND THE ENTIRE AVENGERS ORGANIZATION PROUD.
THE WORLD LIVES TO SPIN ANOTHER DAY.
THAT'S THE ONLY JOB.
NOW REST UP...

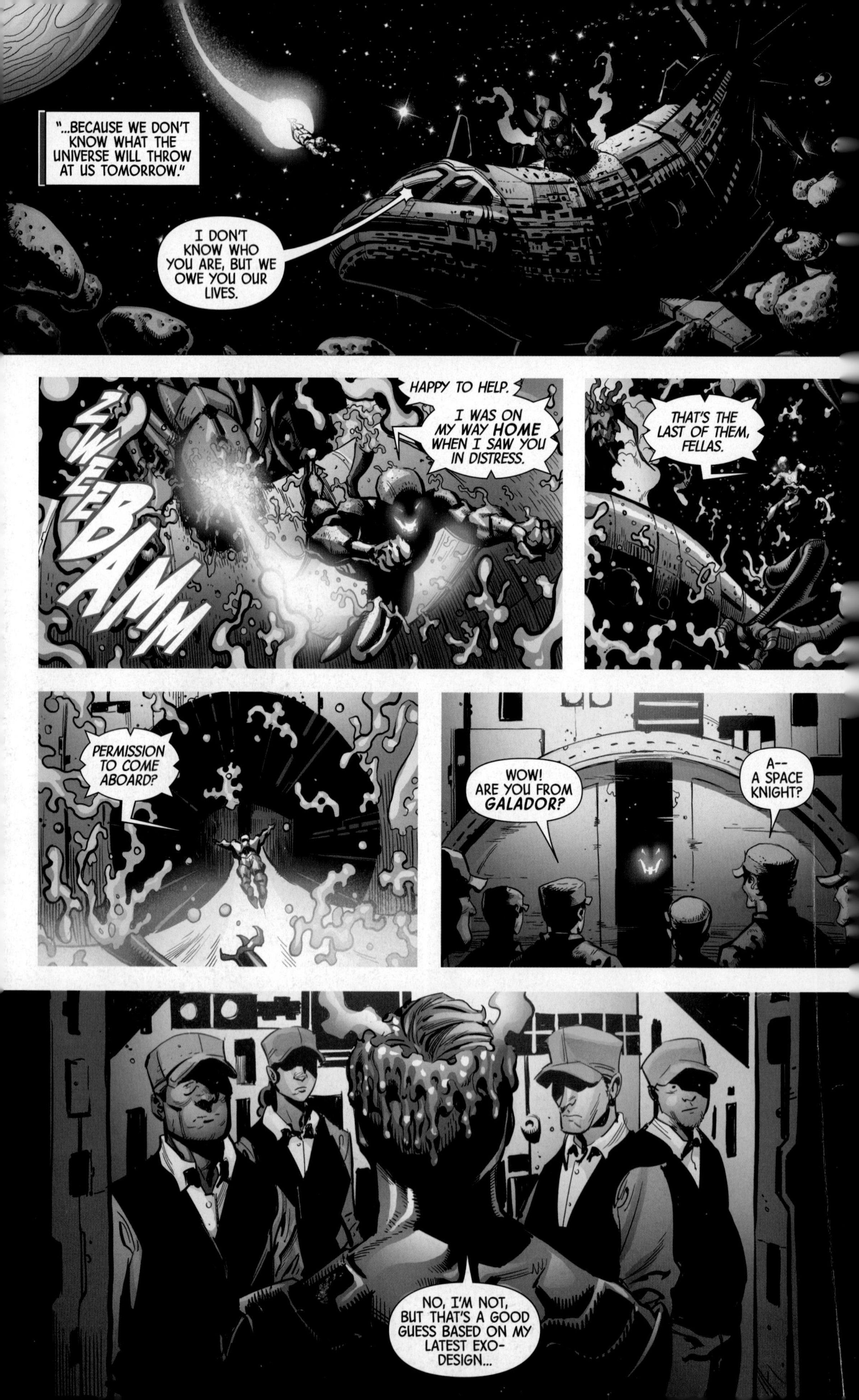
"...BECAUSE WE DON'T KNOW WHAT THE UNIVERSE WILL THROW AT US TOMORROW."
I DON'T KNOW WHO YOU ARE, BUT WE OWE YOU OUR LIVES.
ZWEEBDAMM
HAPPY TO HELP.
I WAS ON MY WAY HOME WHEN I SAW YOU IN DISTRESS.
THAT'S THE LAST OF THEM, FELLAS.
PERMISSION TO COME ABOARD?
WOW! ARE YOU FROM GALADOR?
A-- A SPACE KNIGHT?
NO, I'M NOT, BUT THAT'S A GOOD GUESS BASED ON MY LATEST EXO-DESIGN...

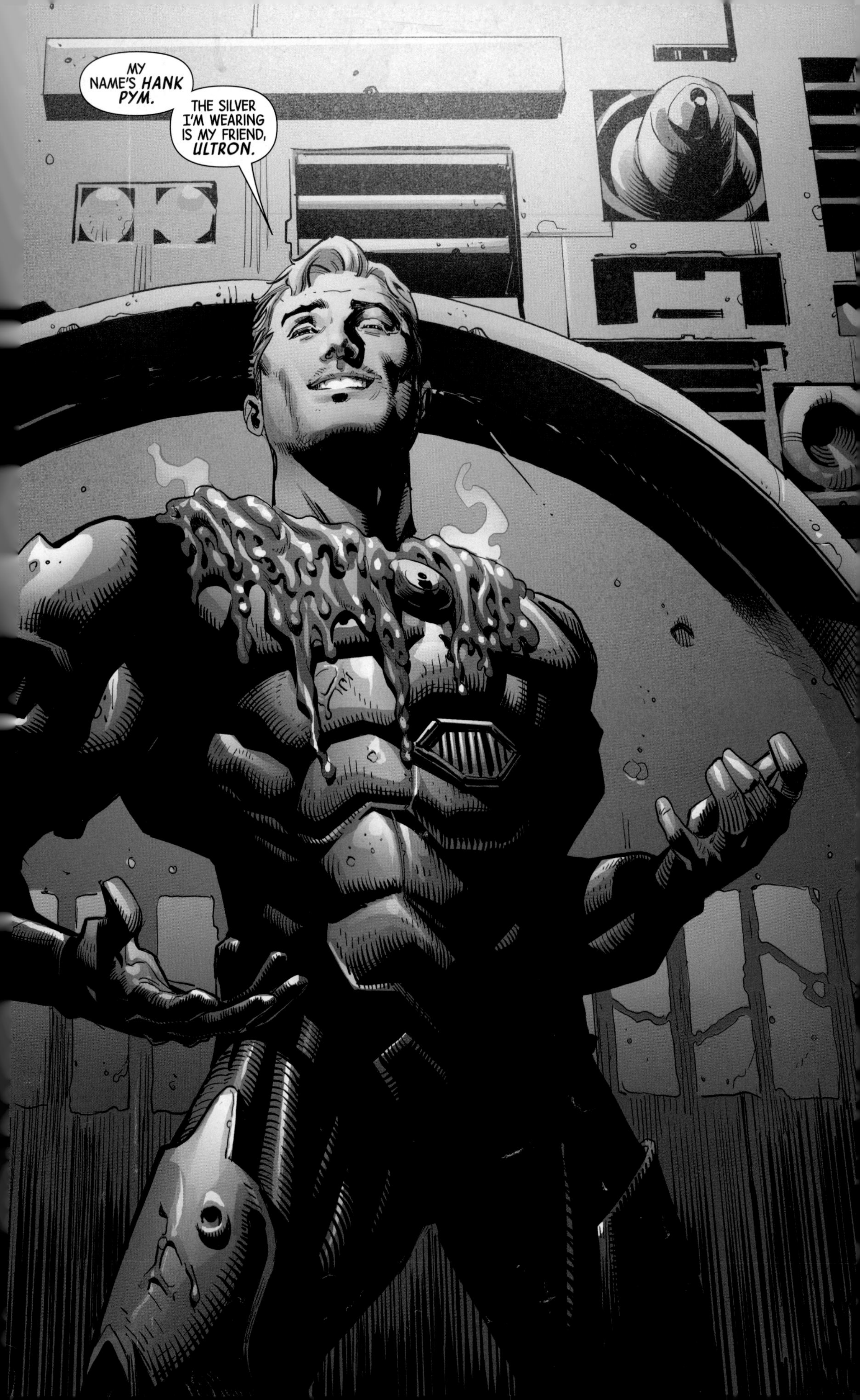
MY NAME'S HANK PYM.
THE SILVER I'M WEARING IS MY FRIEND, ULTRON.

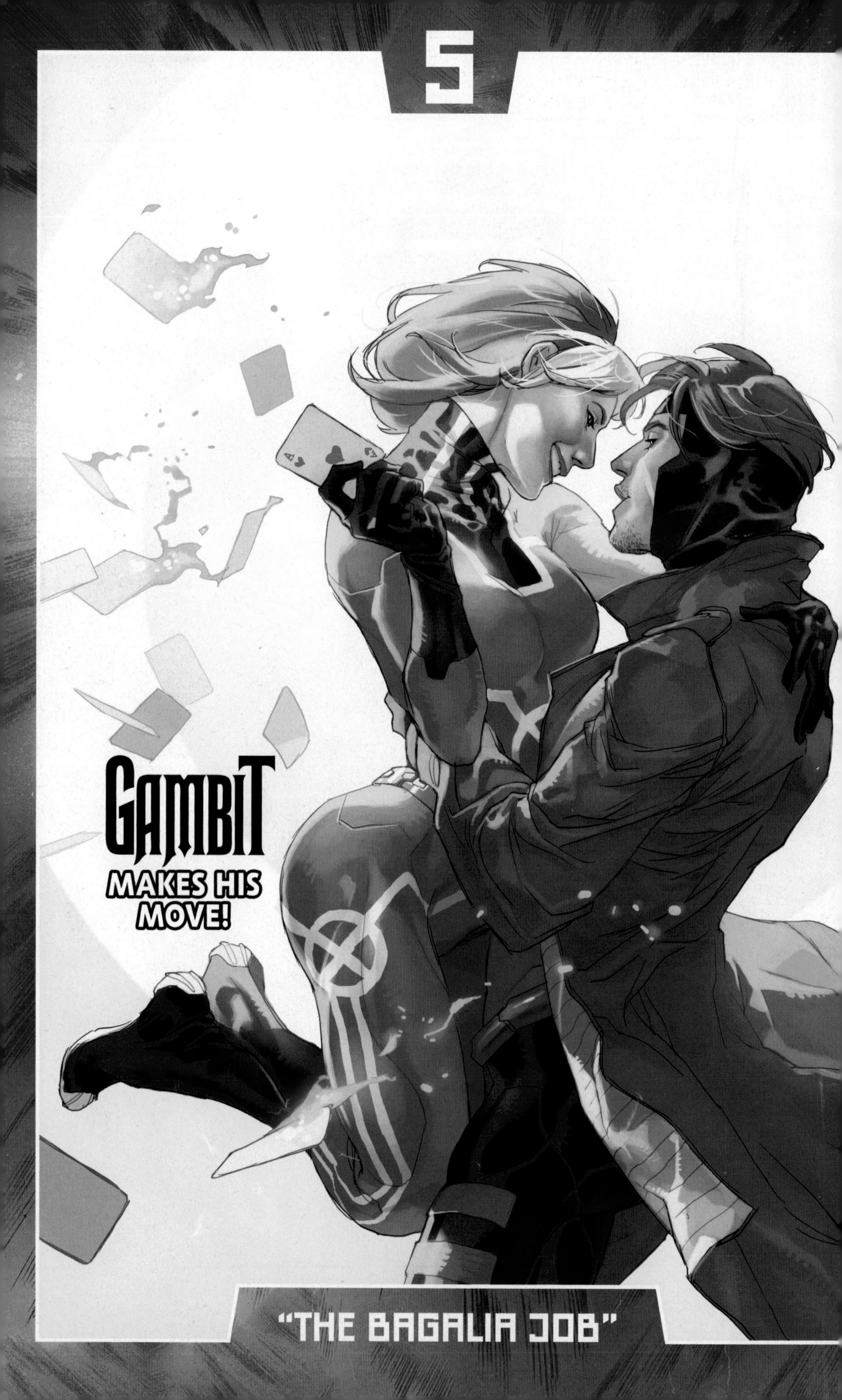
5
GAMBIT
MAKES HIS MOVE!
"THE BAGALIA JOB"

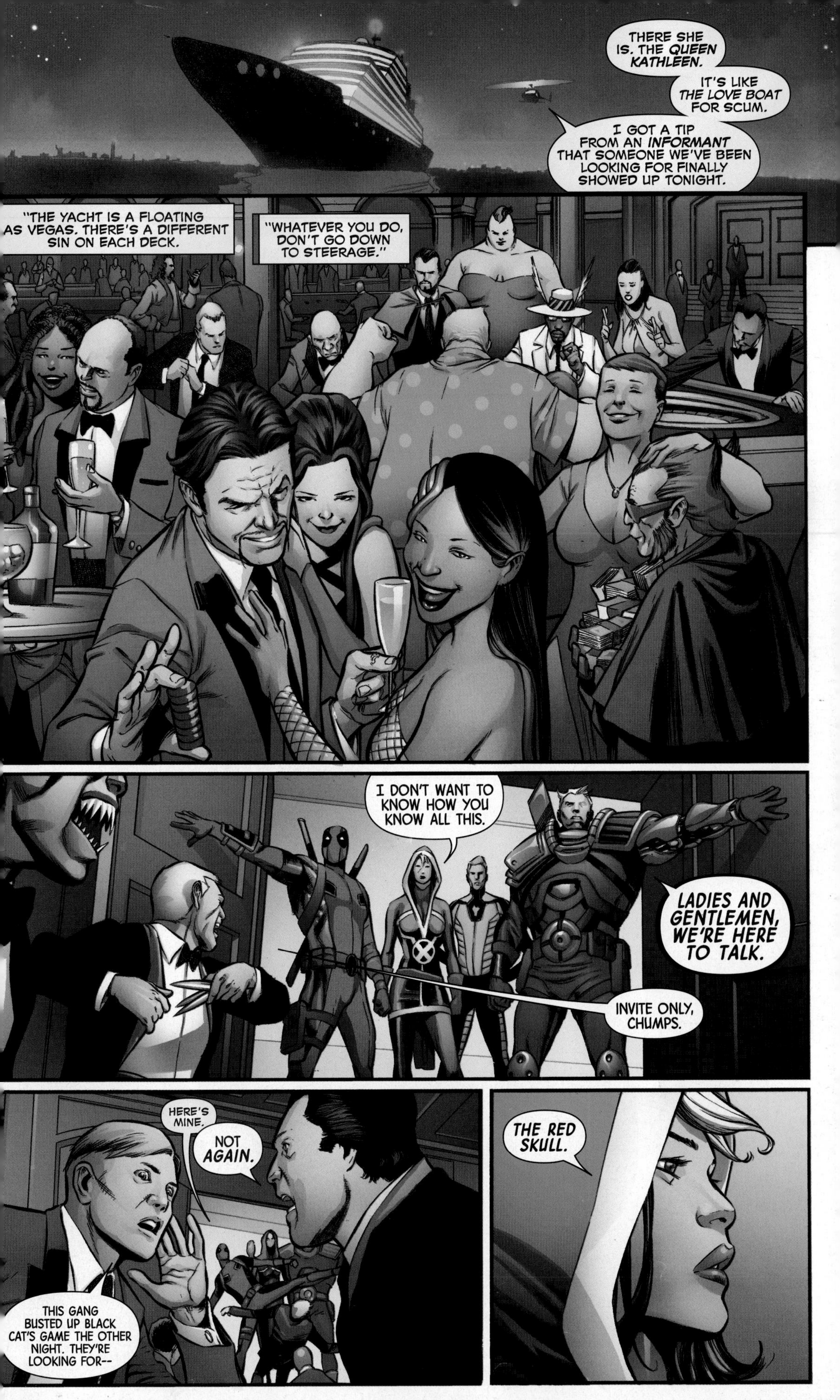

THERE SHE IS. THE QUEEN KATHLEEN.
IT'S LIKE THE LOVE BOAT FOR SCUM.
I GOT A TIP FROM AN INFORMANT THAT SOMEONE WE'VE BEEN LOOKING FOR FINALLY SHOWED UP TONIGHT.
"THE YACHT IS A FLOATING AS VEGAS. THERE'S A DIFFERENT SIN ON EACH DECK.
"WHATEVER YOU DO, DON'T GO DOWN TO STEERAGE."
I DON'T WANT TO KNOW HOW YOU KNOW ALL THIS.
LADIES AND GENTLEMEN, WE'RE HERE TO TALK.
INVITE ONLY, CHUMPS.
HERE'S MINE.
NOT AGAIN.
THIS GANG BUSTED UP BLACK CAT'S GAME THE OTHER NIGHT. THEY'RE LOOKING FOR--
THE RED SKULL.

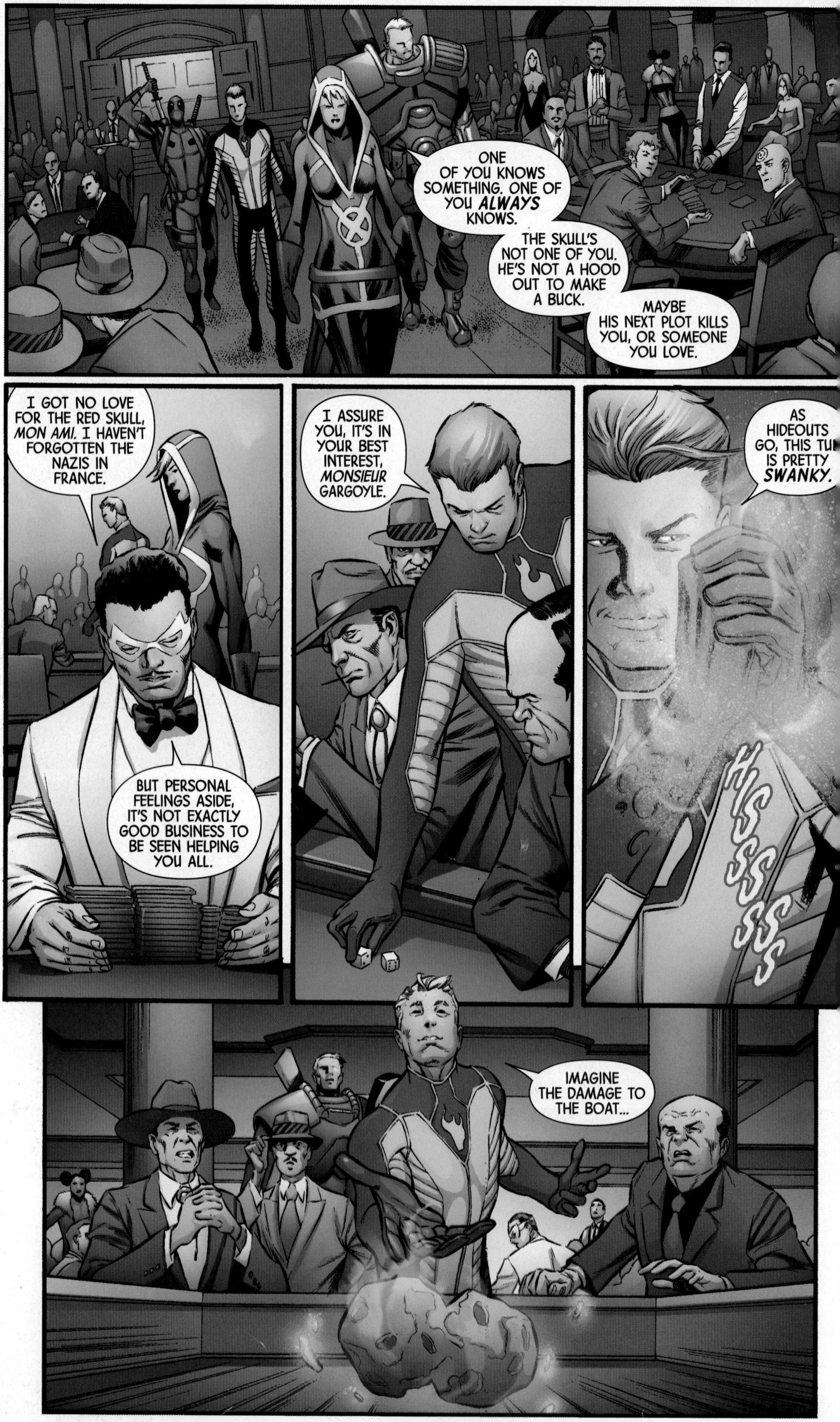

ONE OF YOU KNOWS SOMETHING. ONE OF YOU *ALWAYS* KNOWS.
THE SKULL'S NOT ONE OF YOU. HE'S NOT A HOOD OUT TO MAKE A BUCK.
MAYBE HIS NEXT PLOT KILLS YOU, OR SOMEONE YOU LOVE.
I GOT NO LOVE FOR THE RED SKULL, *MON AMI*. I HAVEN'T FORGOTTEN THE NAZIS IN FRANCE.
BUT PERSONAL FEELINGS ASIDE, IT'S NOT EXACTLY GOOD BUSINESS TO BE SEEN HELPING YOU ALL.
I ASSURE YOU, IT'S IN YOUR BEST INTEREST, *MONSIEUR* GARGOYLE.
AS HIDEOUTS GO, THIS TU
IS PRETTY *SWANKY*.
HISSSSSS
IMAGINE THE DAMAGE TO THE BOAT...

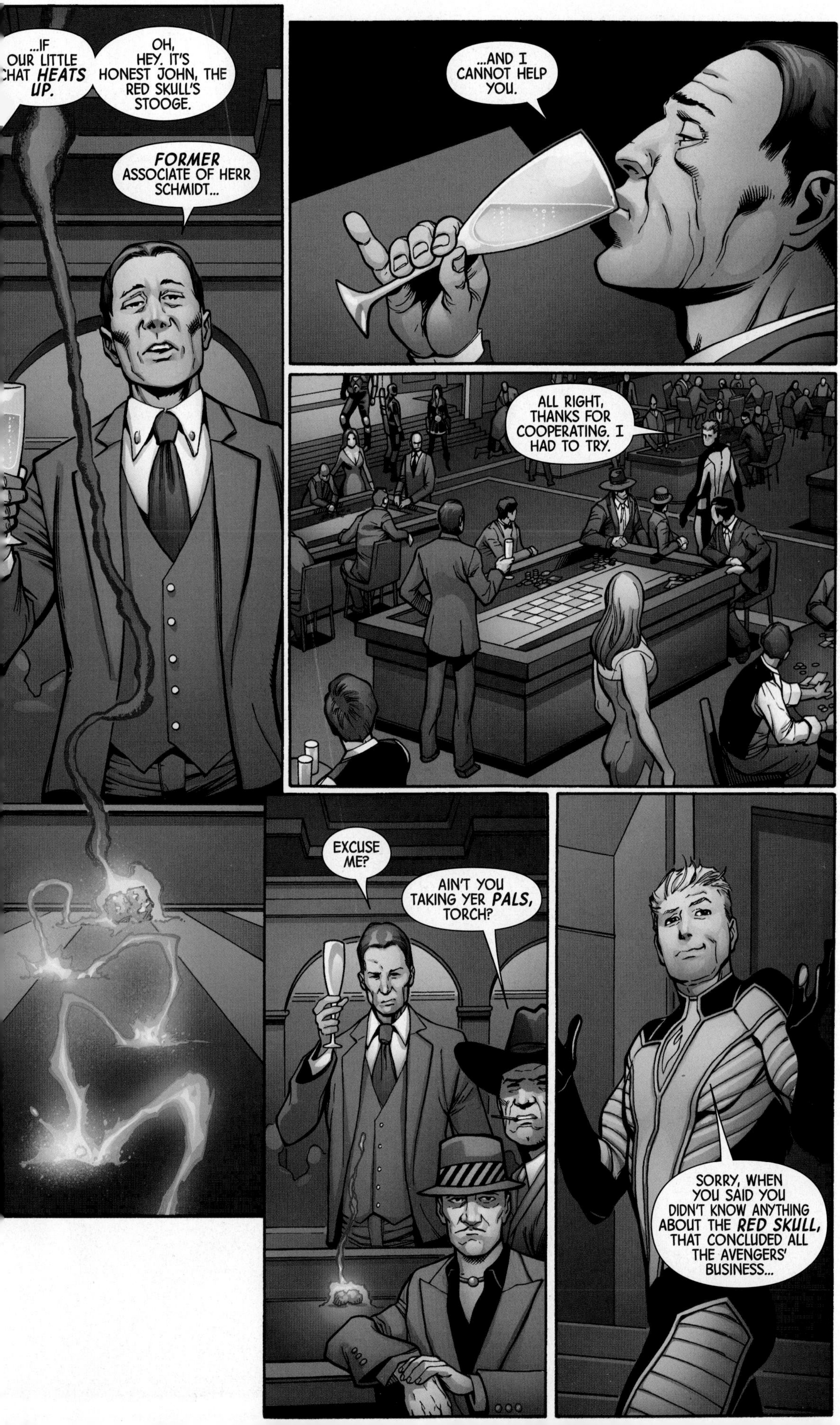
...IF OUR LITTLE CHAT HEATS UP.
OH, HEY. IT'S HONEST JOHN, THE RED SKULL'S STOOGE.
FORMER ASSOCIATE OF HERR SCHMIDT...
...AND I CANNOT HELP YOU.
ALL RIGHT, THANKS FOR COOPERATING. I HAD TO TRY.
EXCUSE ME?
AIN'T YOU TAKING YER PALS, TORCH?
SORRY, WHEN YOU SAID YOU DIDN'T KNOW ANYTHING ABOUT THE RED SKULL, THAT CONCLUDED ALL THE AVENGERS' BUSINESS...

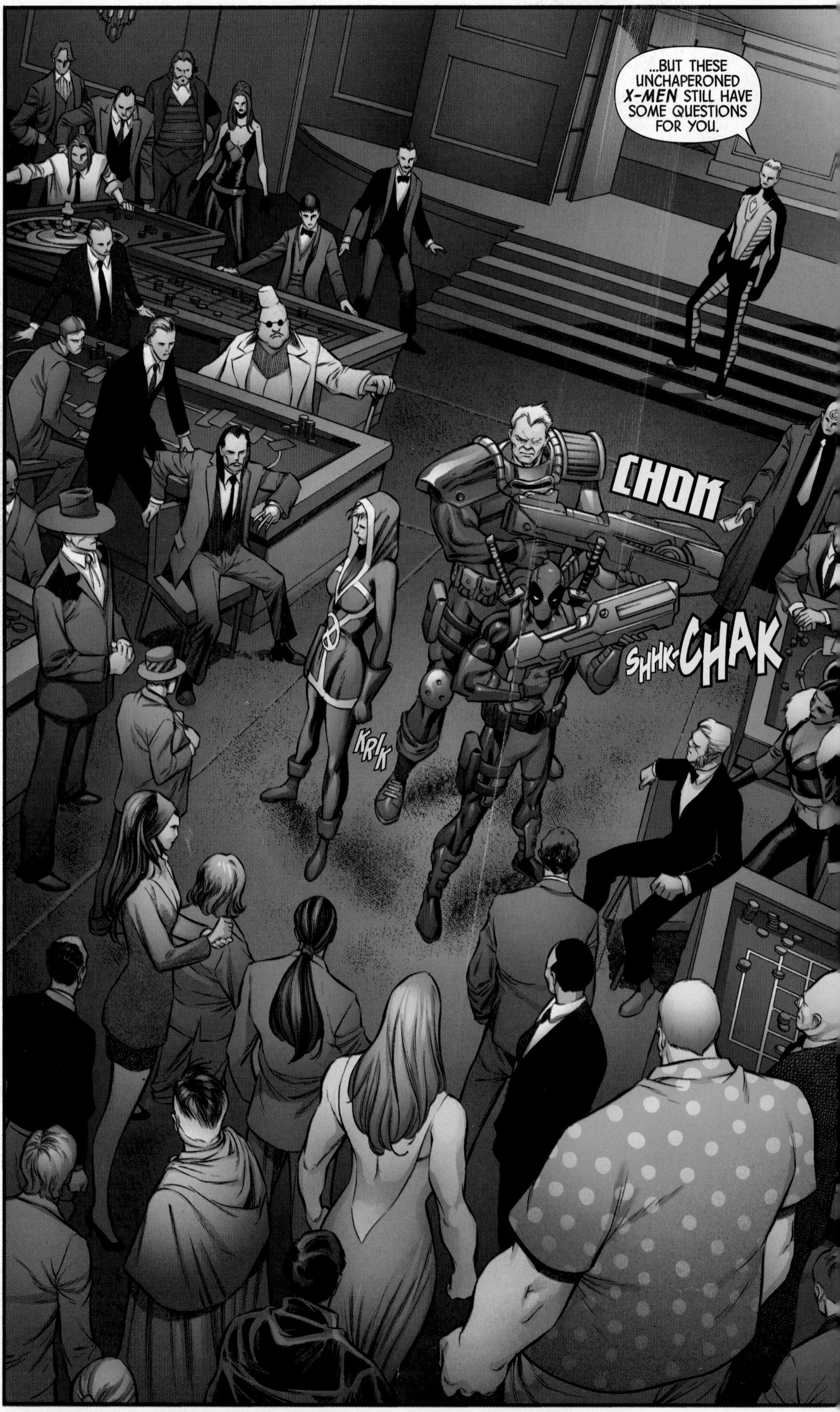
...BUT THESE UNCHAPERONED X-MEN STILL HAVE SOME QUESTIONS FOR YOU.
CHOK
SHHK-CHAK
KRIK

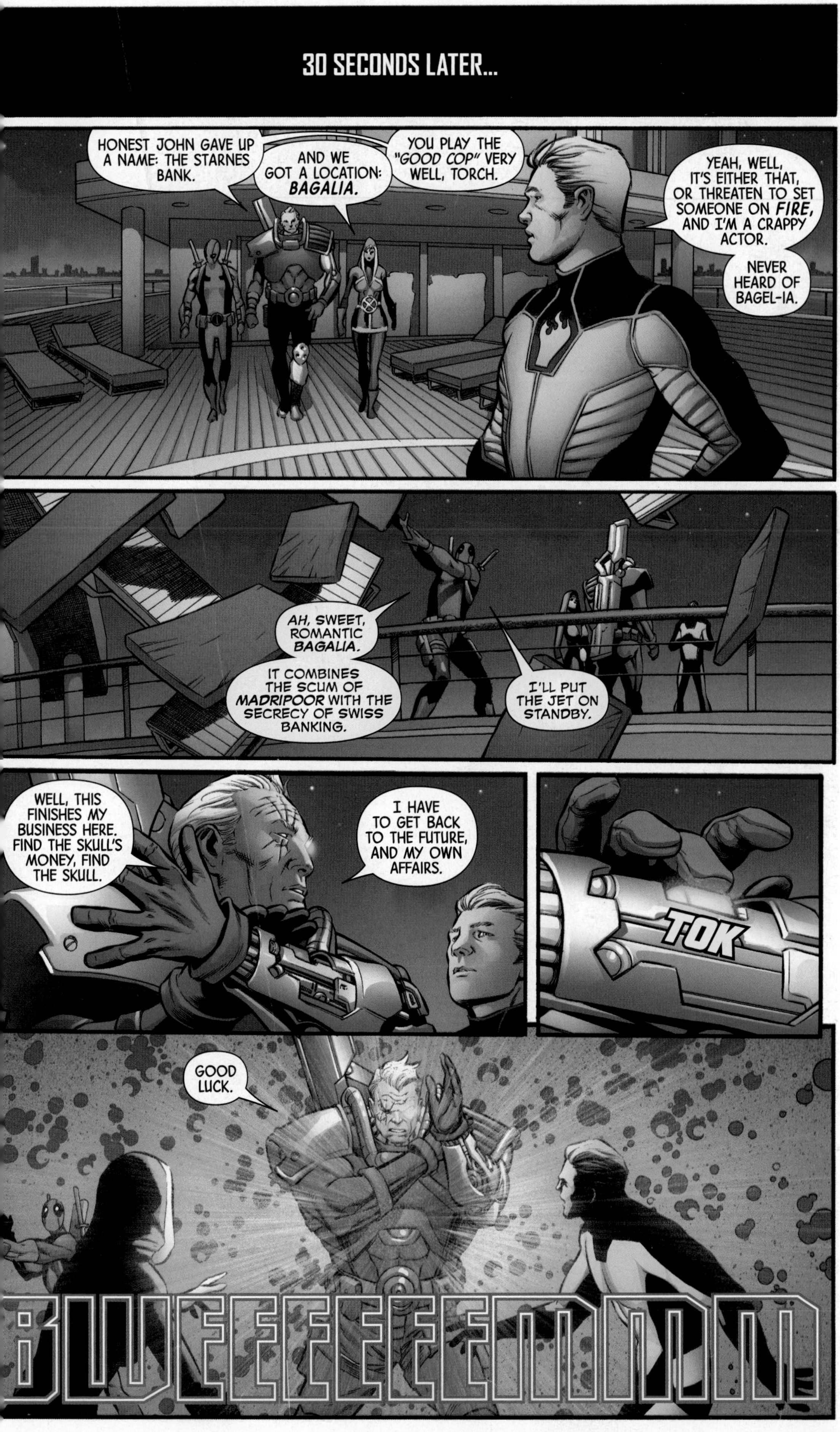
30 SECONDS LATER...
HONEST JOHN GAVE UP A NAME: THE STARNES BANK.
AND WE GOT A LOCATION: *BAGALIA.*
YOU PLAY THE *"GOOD COP"* VERY WELL, TORCH.
YEAH, WELL, IT'S EITHER THAT, OR THREATEN TO SET SOMEONE ON *FIRE,* AND I'M A CRAPPY ACTOR.
NEVER HEARD OF BAGEL-IA.
AH, SWEET, ROMANTIC *BAGALIA.*
IT COMBINES THE SCUM OF *MADRIPOOR* WITH THE SECRECY OF SWISS BANKING.
I'LL PUT THE JET ON STANDBY.
WELL, THIS FINISHES MY BUSINESS HERE. FIND THE SKULL'S MONEY, FIND THE SKULL.
I HAVE TO GET BACK TO THE FUTURE, AND MY OWN AFFAIRS.
TOK
GOOD LUCK.
BWEEEEEEMMMM

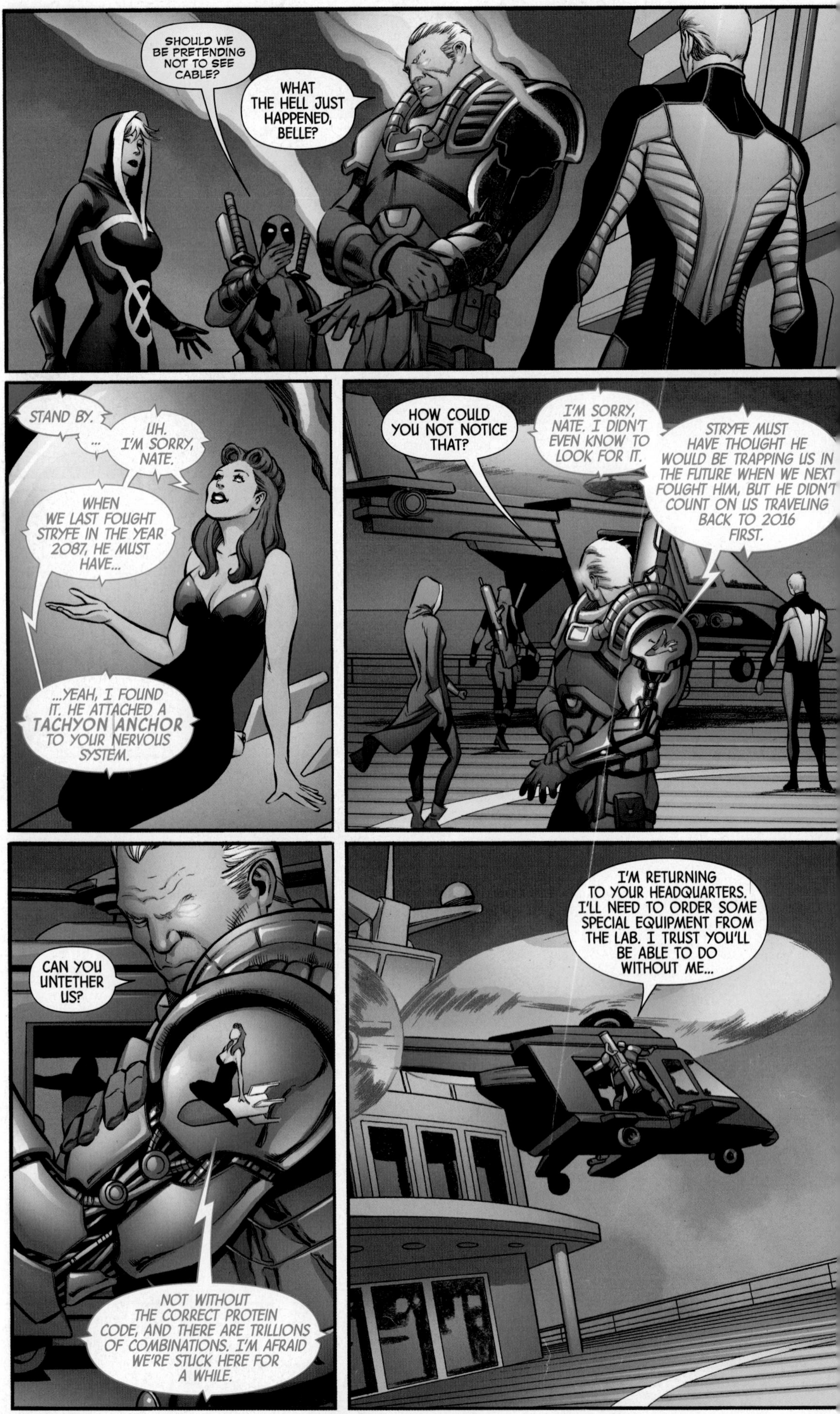
SHOULD WE BE PRETENDING NOT TO SEE CABLE?
WHAT THE HELL JUST HAPPENED, BELLE?
STAND BY.
...
UH. I'M SORRY, NATE.
WHEN WE LAST FOUGHT STRYFE IN THE YEAR 2087, HE MUST HAVE...
...YEAH, I FOUND IT. HE ATTACHED A TACHYON ANCHOR TO YOUR NERVOUS SYSTEM.
HOW COULD YOU NOT NOTICE THAT?
I'M SORRY, NATE. I DIDN'T EVEN KNOW TO LOOK FOR IT.
STRYFE MUST HAVE THOUGHT HE WOULD BE TRAPPING US IN THE FUTURE WHEN WE NEXT FOUGHT HIM, BUT HE DIDN'T COUNT ON US TRAVELING BACK TO 2016 FIRST.
CAN YOU UNTETHER US?
NOT WITHOUT THE CORRECT PROTEIN CODE, AND THERE ARE TRILLIONS OF COMBINATIONS. I'M AFRAID WE'RE STUCK HERE FOR A WHILE.
I'M RETURNING TO YOUR HEADQUARTERS. I'LL NEED TO ORDER SOME SPECIAL EQUIPMENT FROM THE LAB. I TRUST YOU'LL BE ABLE TO DO WITHOUT ME...

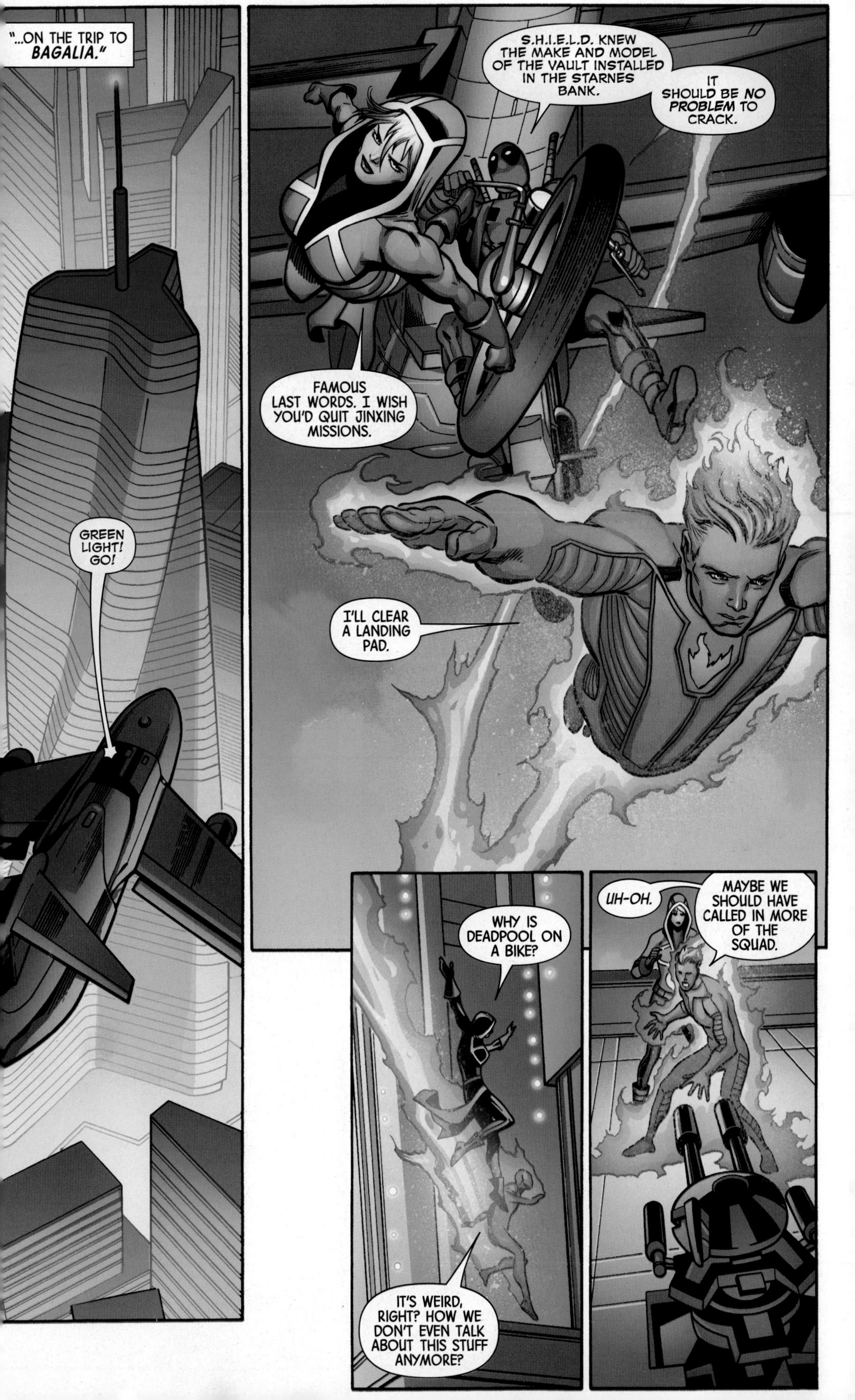
"...ON THE TRIP TO BAGALIA."
GREEN LIGHT! GO!
S.H.I.E.L.D. KNEW THE MAKE AND MODEL OF THE VAULT INSTALLED IN THE STARNES BANK.
IT SHOULD BE NO PROBLEM TO CRACK.
FAMOUS LAST WORDS. I WISH YOU'D QUIT JINXING MISSIONS.
I'LL CLEAR A LANDING PAD.
WHY IS DEADPOOL ON A BIKE?
IT'S WEIRD, RIGHT? HOW WE DON'T EVEN TALK ABOUT THIS STUFF ANYMORE?
UH-OH.
MAYBE WE SHOULD HAVE CALLED IN MORE OF THE SQUAD.

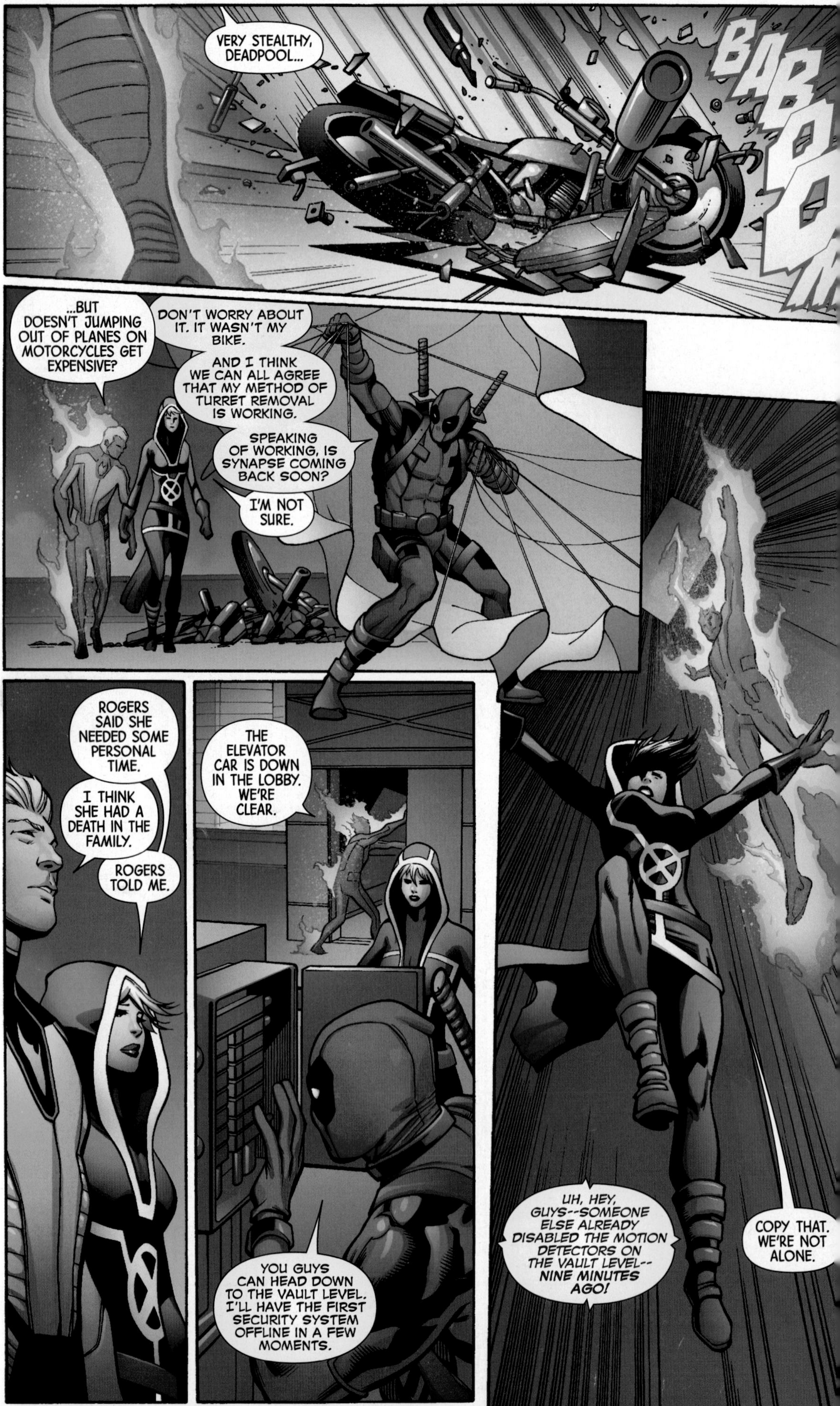

VERY STEALTHY, DEADPOOL...
BABOOM
...BUT DOESN'T JUMPING OUT OF PLANES ON MOTORCYCLES GET EXPENSIVE?
DON'T WORRY ABOUT IT. IT WASN'T MY BIKE.
AND I THINK WE CAN ALL AGREE THAT MY METHOD OF TURRET REMOVAL IS WORKING.
SPEAKING OF WORKING, IS SYNAPSE COMING BACK SOON?
I'M NOT SURE.
ROGERS SAID SHE NEEDED SOME PERSONAL TIME.
I THINK SHE HAD A DEATH IN THE FAMILY.
ROGERS TOLD ME.
THE ELEVATOR CAR IS DOWN IN THE LOBBY. WE'RE CLEAR.
YOU GUYS CAN HEAD DOWN TO THE VAULT LEVEL. I'LL HAVE THE FIRST SECURITY SYSTEM OFFLINE IN A FEW MOMENTS.
UH, HEY, GUYS--SOMEONE ELSE ALREADY DISABLED THE MOTION DETECTORS ON THE VAULT LEVEL--NINE MINUTES AGO!
COPY THAT. WE'RE NOT ALONE.

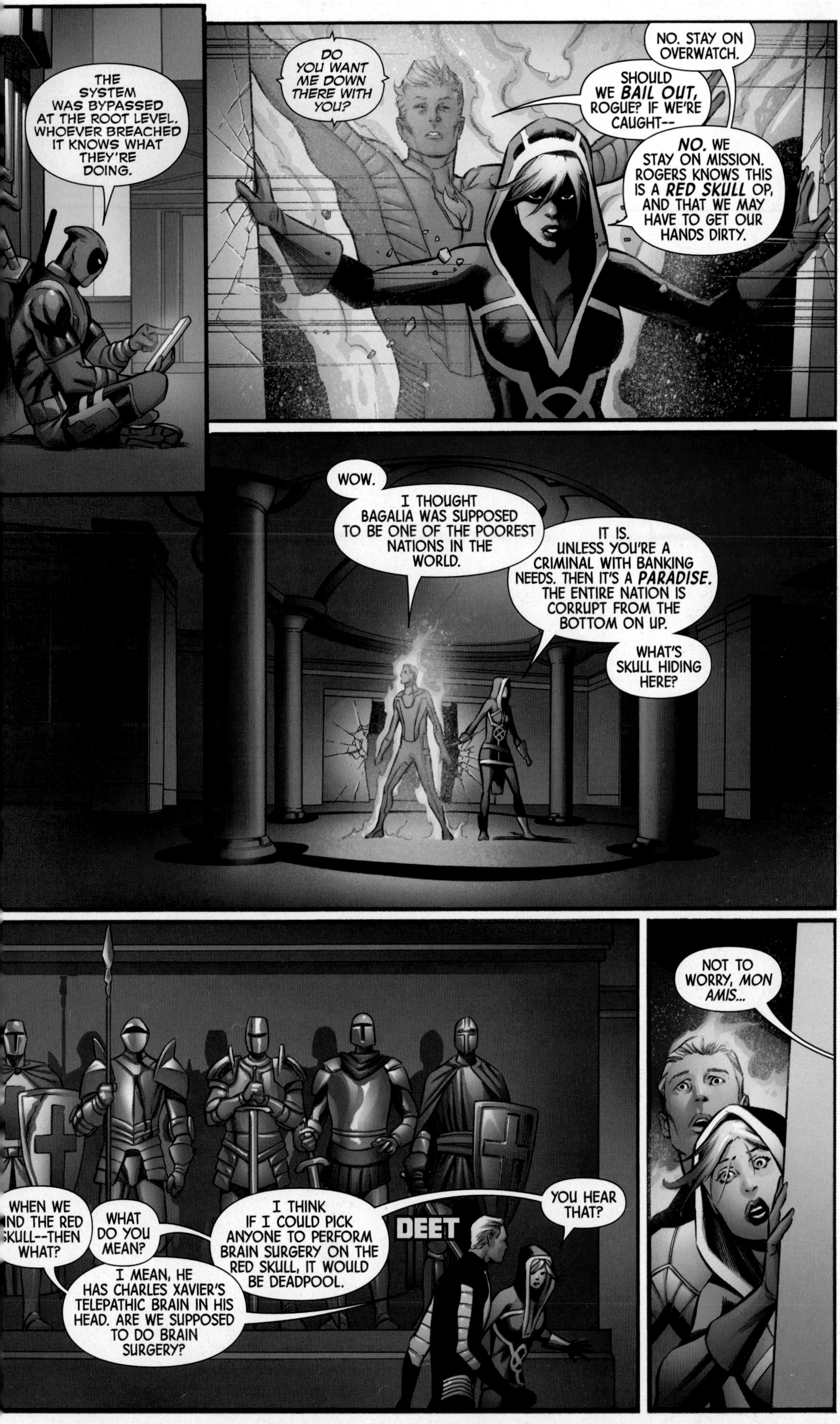
THE SYSTEM WAS BYPASSED AT THE ROOT LEVEL. WHOEVER BREACHED IT KNOWS WHAT THEY'RE DOING.
DO YOU WANT ME DOWN THERE WITH YOU?
NO. STAY ON OVERWATCH.
SHOULD WE BAIL OUT, ROGUE? IF WE'RE CAUGHT--
NO. WE STAY ON MISSION. ROGERS KNOWS THIS IS A RED SKULL OP, AND THAT WE MAY HAVE TO GET OUR HANDS DIRTY.
WOW.
I THOUGHT BAGALIA WAS SUPPOSED TO BE ONE OF THE POOREST NATIONS IN THE WORLD.
IT IS. UNLESS YOU'RE A CRIMINAL WITH BANKING NEEDS. THEN IT'S A PARADISE. THE ENTIRE NATION IS CORRUPT FROM THE BOTTOM ON UP.
WHAT'S SKULL HIDING HERE?
WHEN WE ND THE RED SKULL--THEN WHAT?
WHAT DO YOU MEAN?
I MEAN, HE HAS CHARLES XAVIER'S TELEPATHIC BRAIN IN HIS HEAD. ARE WE SUPPOSED TO DO BRAIN SURGERY?
I THINK IF I COULD PICK ANYONE TO PERFORM BRAIN SURGERY ON THE RED SKULL, IT WOULD BE DEADPOOL.
DEET
YOU HEAR THAT?
NOT TO WORRY, MON AMIS...

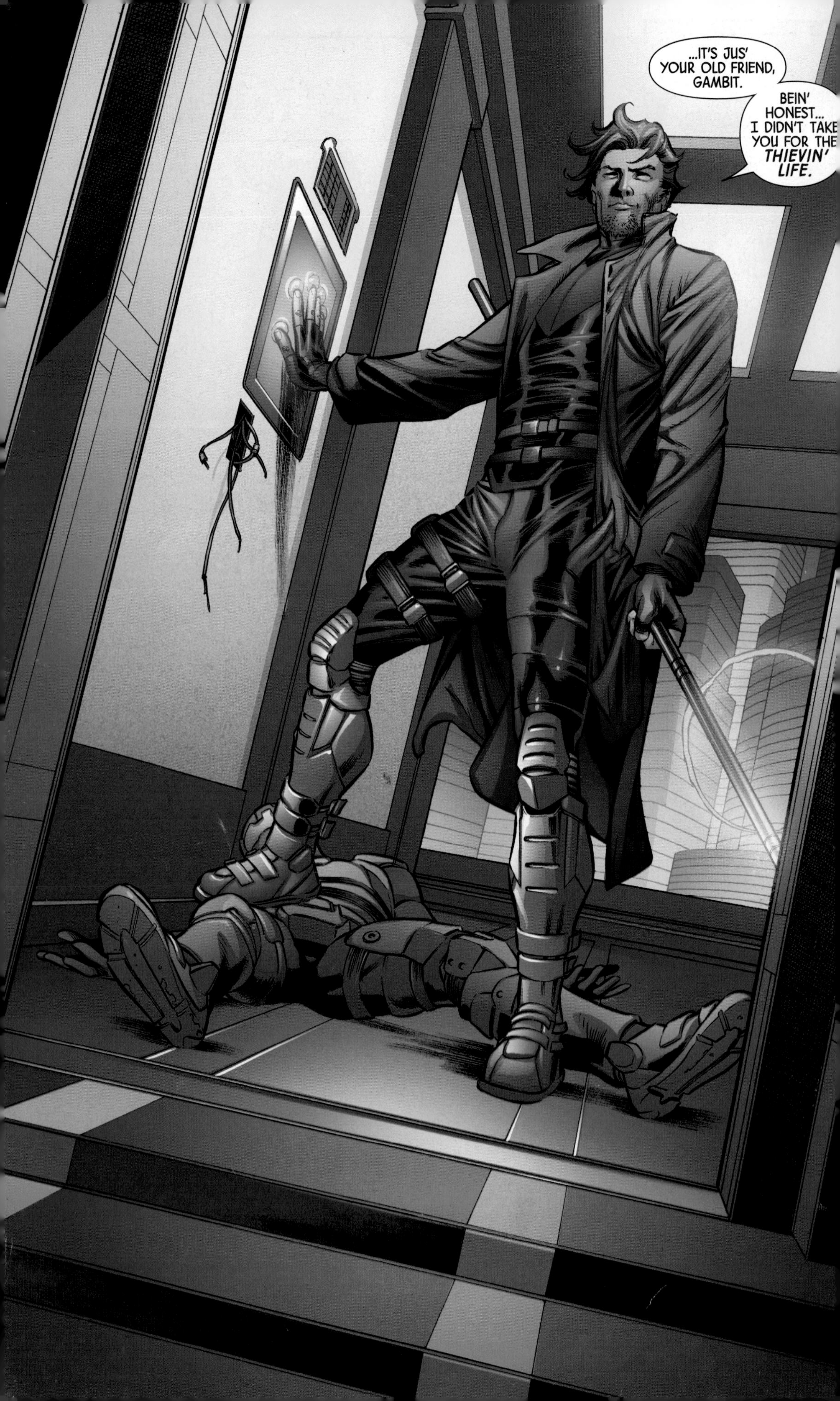
...IT'S JUS' YOUR OLD FRIEND, GAMBIT.
BEIN' HONEST... I DIDN'T TAKE YOU FOR THE *THIEVIN' LIFE.*

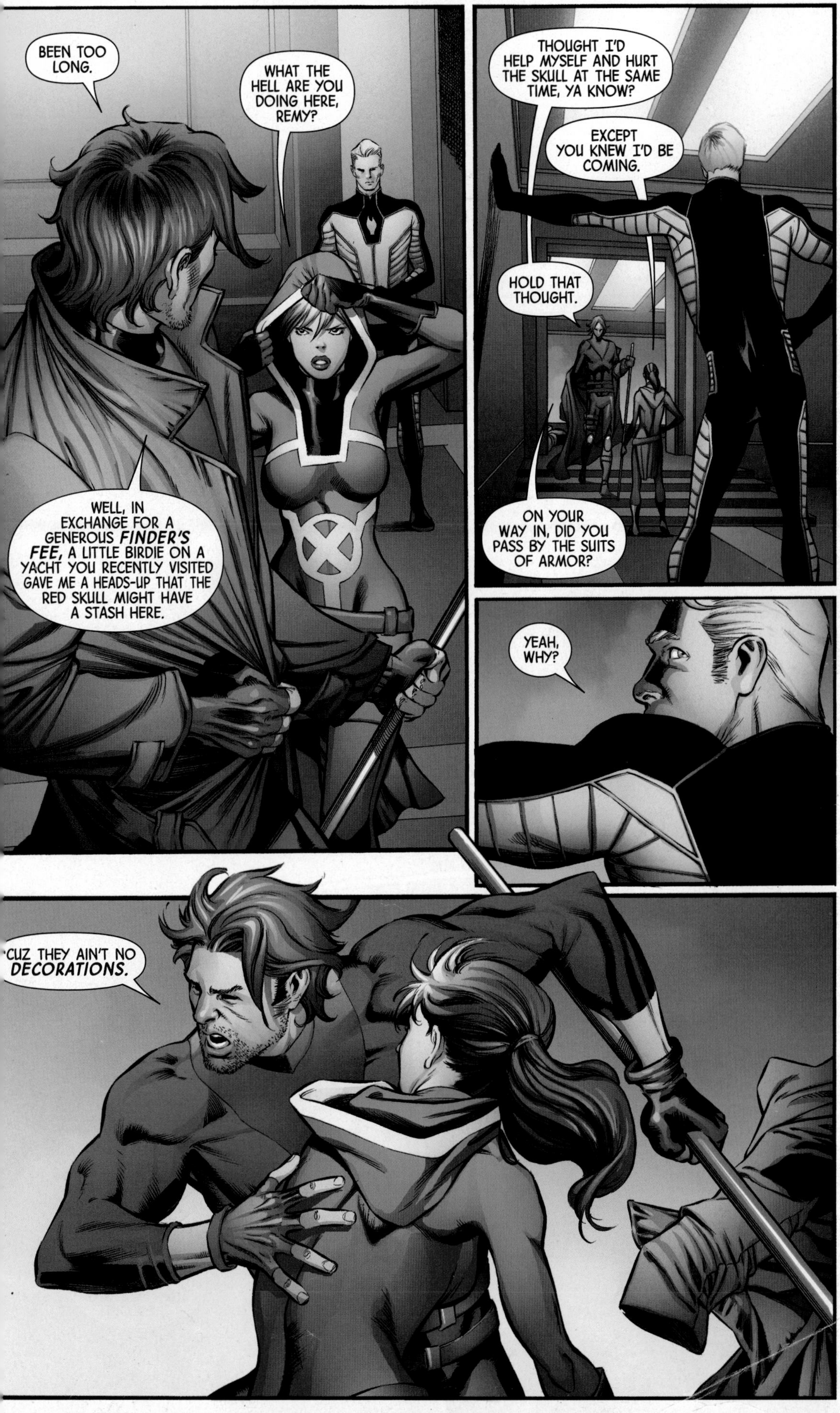
BEEN TOO LONG.
WHAT THE HELL ARE YOU DOING HERE, REMY?
WELL, IN EXCHANGE FOR A GENEROUS FINDER'S FEE, A LITTLE BIRDIE ON A YACHT YOU RECENTLY VISITED GAVE ME A HEADS-UP THAT THE RED SKULL MIGHT HAVE A STASH HERE.
THOUGHT I'D HELP MYSELF AND HURT THE SKULL AT THE SAME TIME, YA KNOW?
EXCEPT YOU KNEW I'D BE COMING.
HOLD THAT THOUGHT.
ON YOUR WAY IN, DID YOU PASS BY THE SUITS OF ARMOR?
YEAH, WHY?
'CUZ THEY AIN'T NO DECORATIONS.

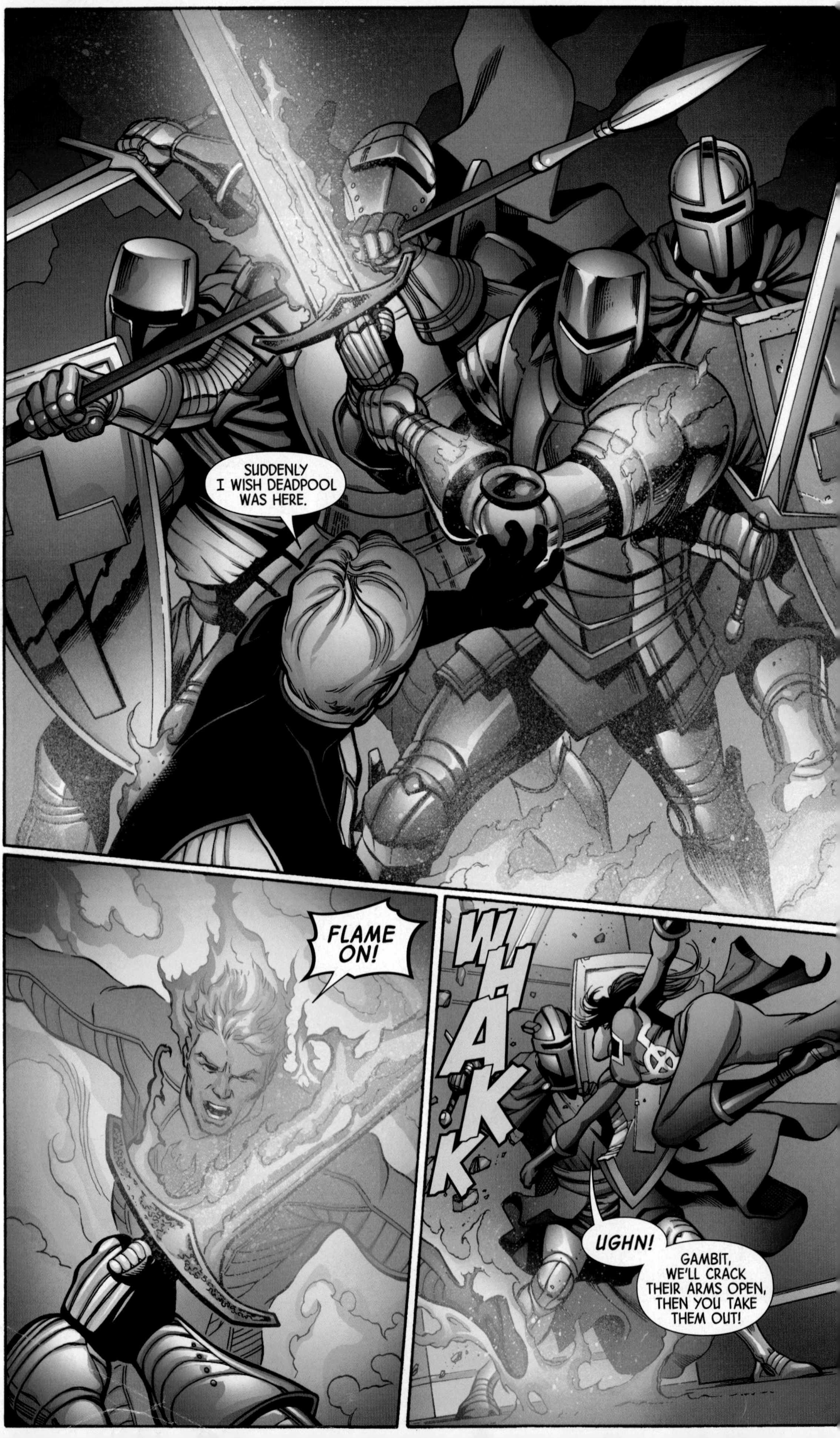
SUDDENLY I WISH DEADPOOL WAS HERE.
FLAME ON!
WHAK
UGHN!
GAMBIT, WE'LL CRACK THEIR ARMS OPEN, THEN YOU TAKE THEM OUT!

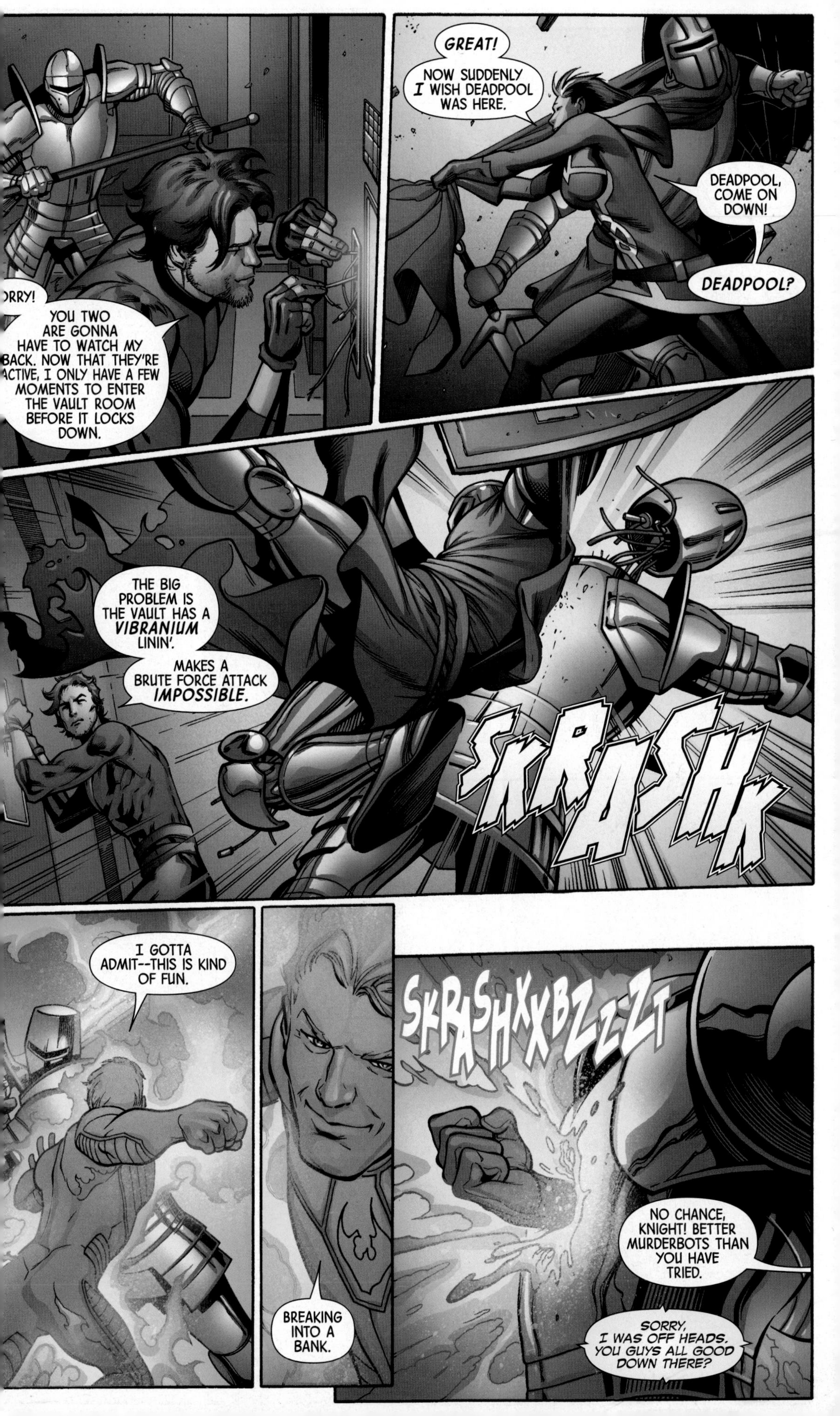
ORRY!
YOU TWO ARE GONNA HAVE TO WATCH MY BACK. NOW THAT THEY'RE ACTIVE, I ONLY HAVE A FEW MOMENTS TO ENTER THE VAULT ROOM BEFORE IT LOCKS DOWN.
GREAT!
NOW SUDDENLY I WISH DEADPOOL WAS HERE.
DEADPOOL, COME ON DOWN!
DEADPOOL?
THE BIG PROBLEM IS THE VAULT HAS A VIBRANIUM LININ'.
MAKES A BRUTE FORCE ATTACK IMPOSSIBLE.
SKRASHK
I GOTTA ADMIT--THIS IS KIND OF FUN.
BREAKING INTO A BANK.
SKRASHXXBZZZT
NO CHANCE, KNIGHT! BETTER MURDERBOTS THAN YOU HAVE TRIED.
SORRY, I WAS OFF HEADS. YOU GUYS ALL GOOD DOWN THERE?

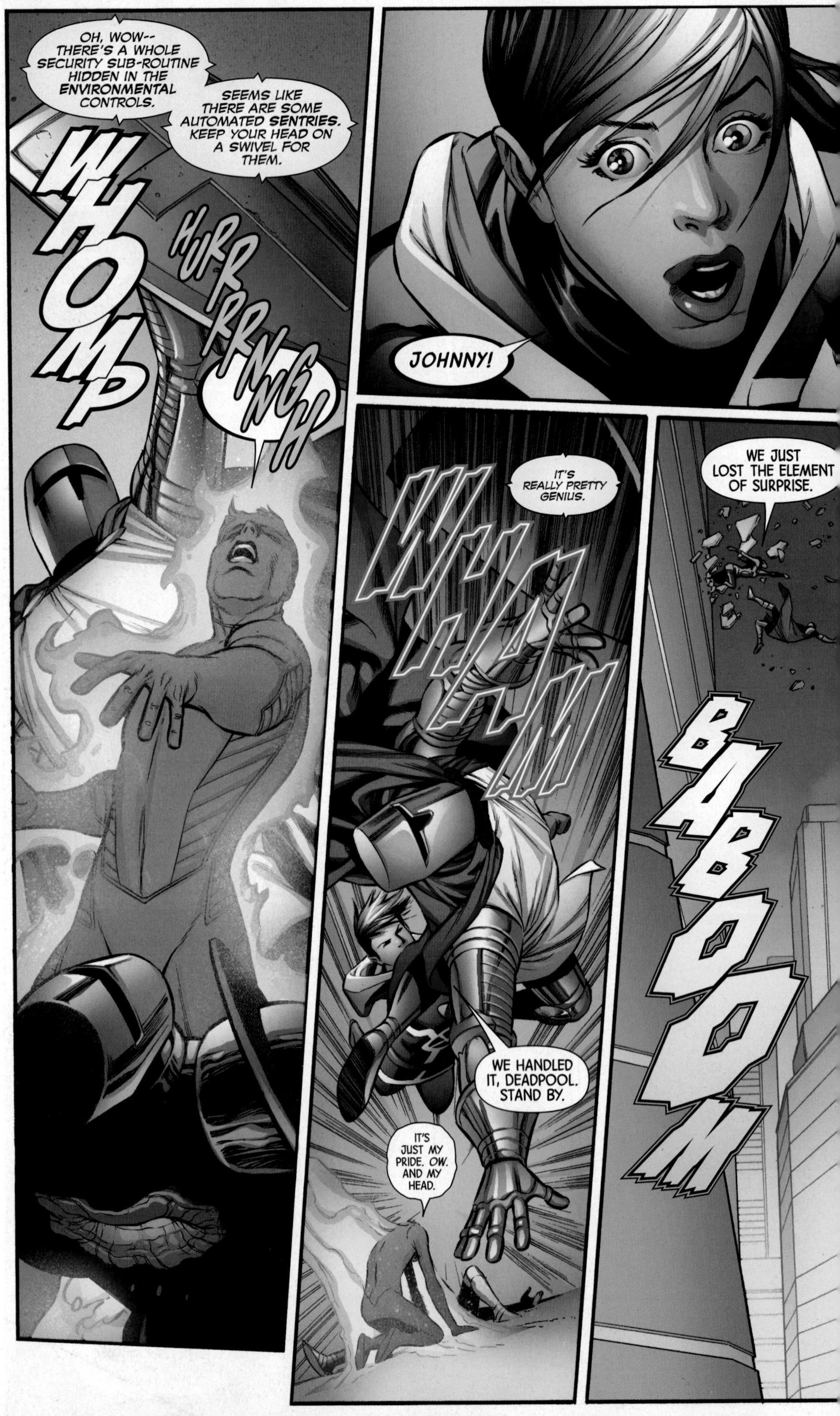

OH, WOW-- THERE'S A WHOLE SECURITY SUB-ROUTINE HIDDEN IN THE ENVIRONMENTAL CONTROLS.
SEEMS LIKE THERE ARE SOME AUTOMATED SENTRIES. KEEP YOUR HEAD ON A SWIVEL FOR THEM.
WHOMP
HURRRNGH
JOHNNY!
WHAM
IT'S REALLY PRETTY GENIUS.
WE HANDLED IT, DEADPOOL. STAND BY.
IT'S JUST MY PRIDE. OW. AND MY HEAD.
WE JUST LOST THE ELEMENT OF SURPRISE.
BABOOM

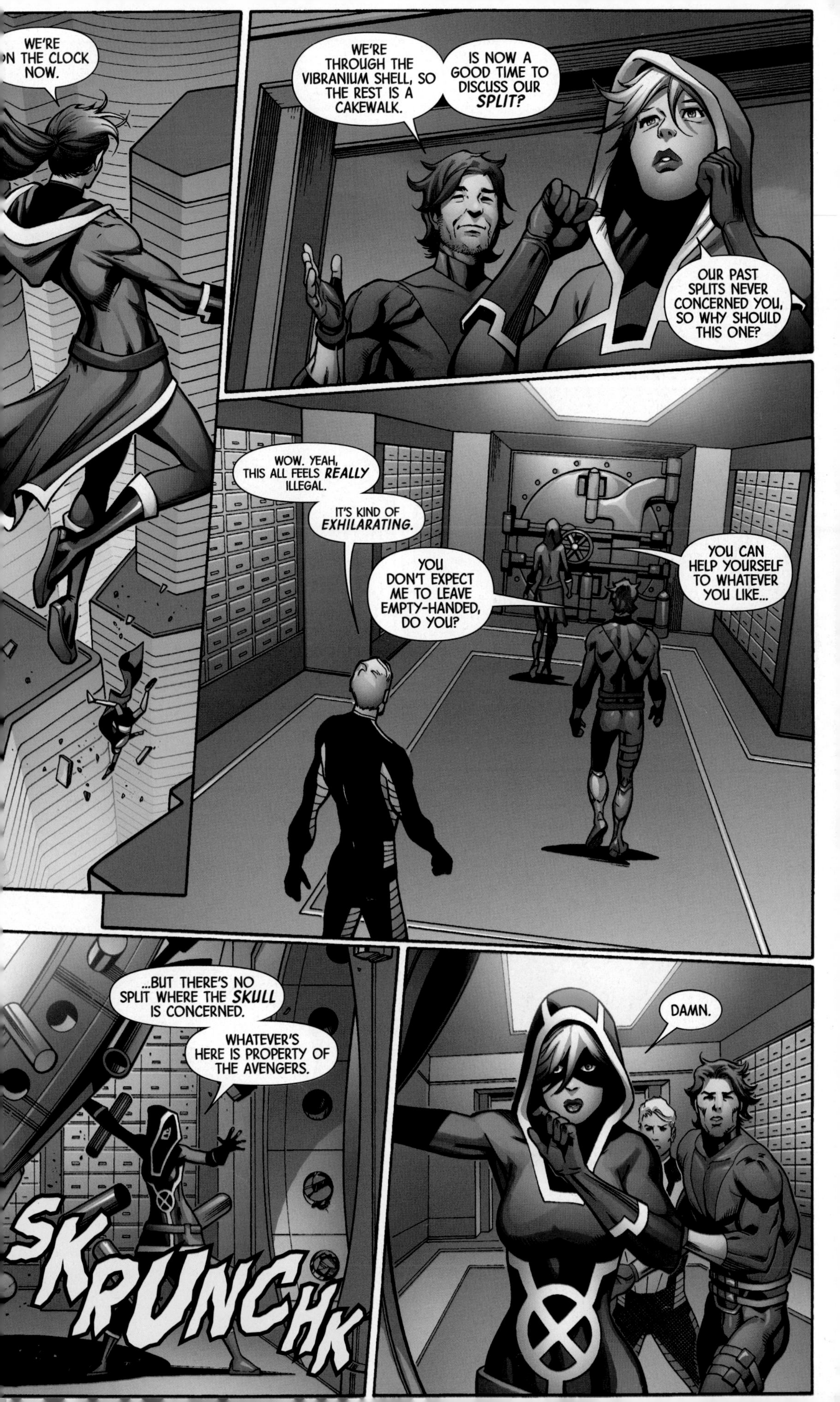
WE'RE ON THE CLOCK NOW.
WE'RE THROUGH THE VIBRANIUM SHELL, SO THE REST IS A CAKEWALK.
IS NOW A GOOD TIME TO DISCUSS OUR SPLIT?
OUR PAST SPLITS NEVER CONCERNED YOU, SO WHY SHOULD THIS ONE?
WOW. YEAH, THIS ALL FEELS REALLY ILLEGAL.
IT'S KIND OF EXHILARATING.
YOU DON'T EXPECT ME TO LEAVE EMPTY-HANDED, DO YOU?
YOU CAN HELP YOURSELF TO WHATEVER YOU LIKE...
...BUT THERE'S NO SPLIT WHERE THE SKULL IS CONCERNED.
WHATEVER'S HERE IS PROPERTY OF THE AVENGERS.
SKRUNCHK
DAMN.

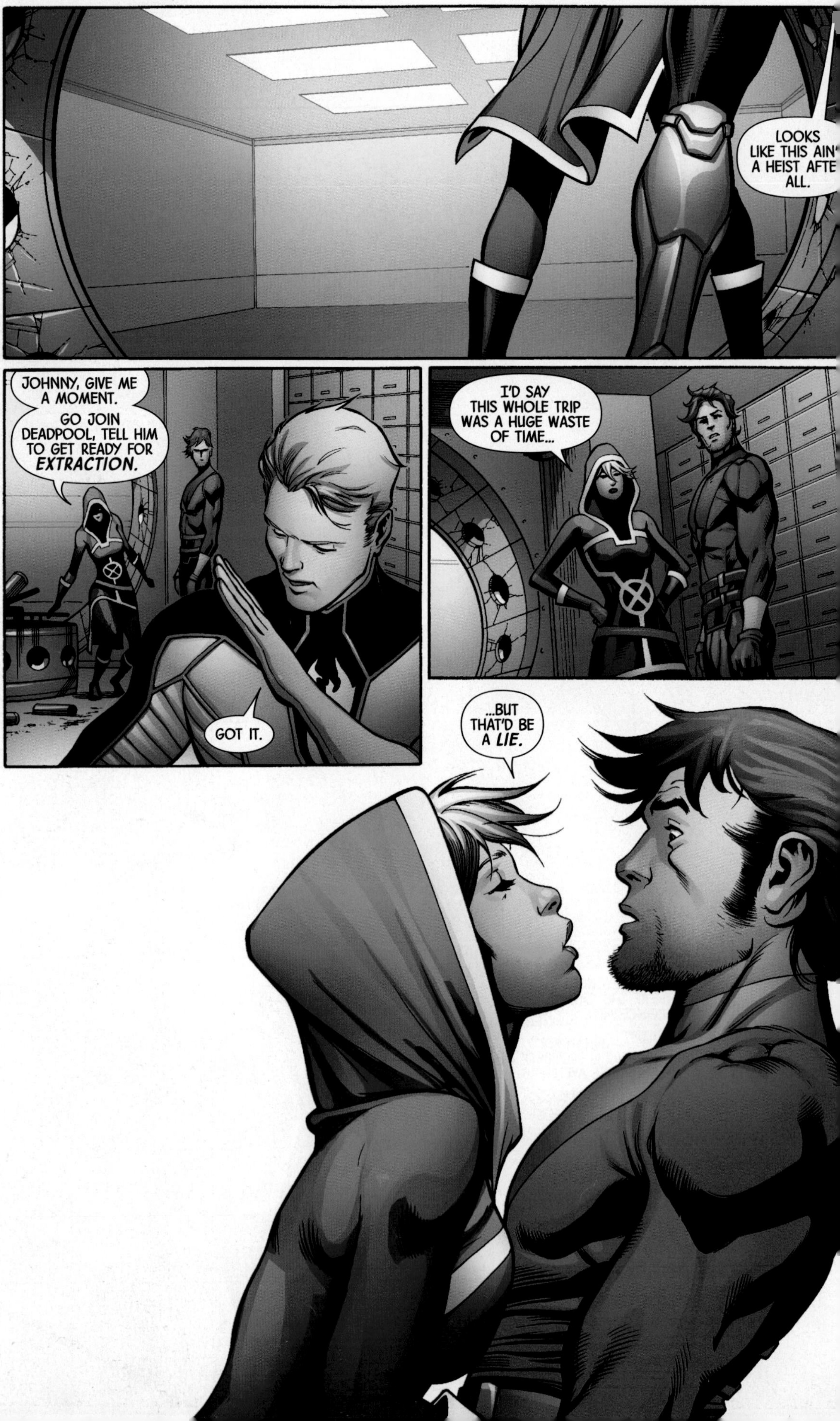

LOOKS LIKE THIS AIN' A HEIST AFTE ALL.
JOHNNY, GIVE ME A MOMENT.
GO JOIN DEADPOOL, TELL HIM TO GET READY FOR EXTRACTION.
GOT IT.
I'D SAY THIS WHOLE TRIP WAS A HUGE WASTE OF TIME...
...BUT THAT'D BE A LIE.

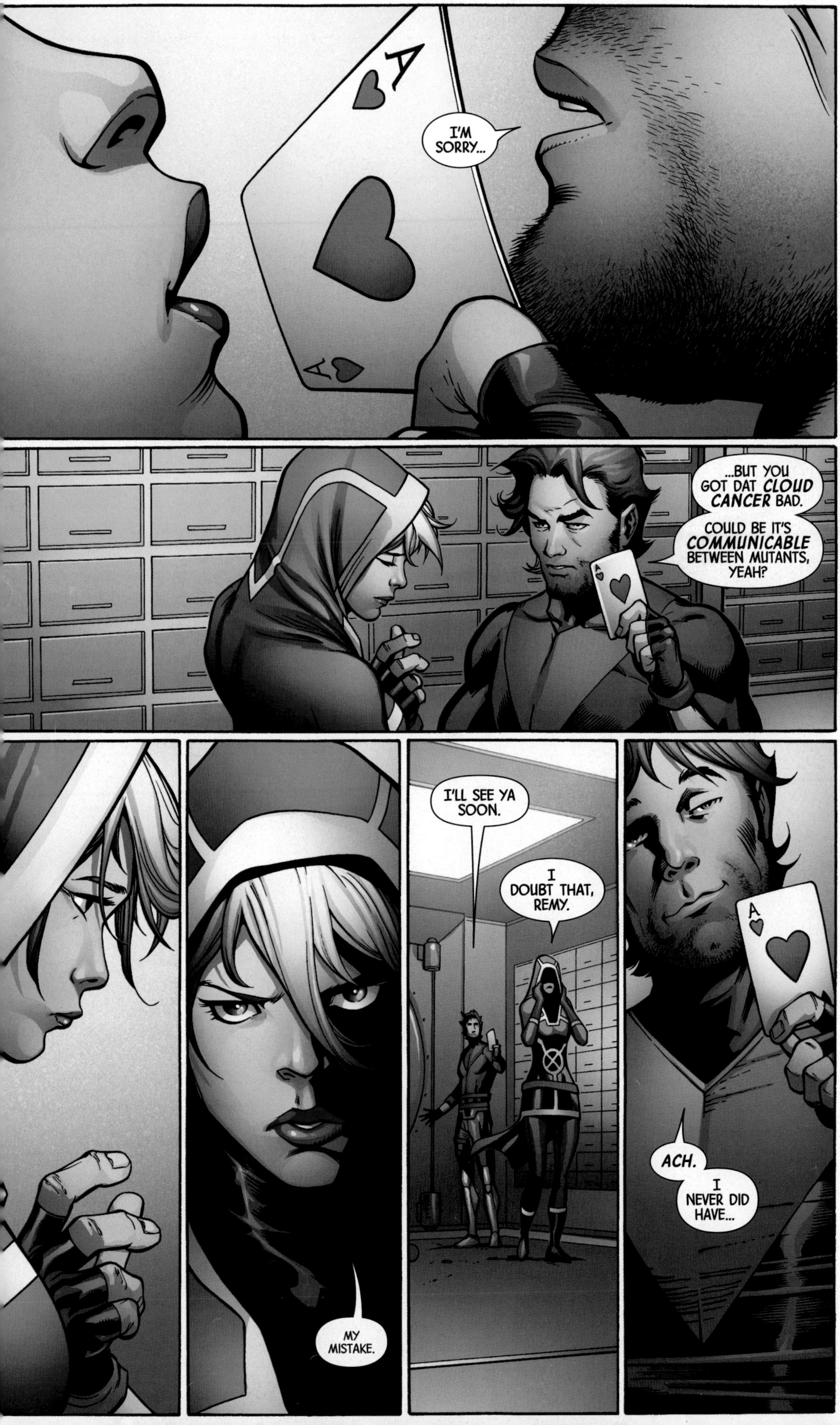
I'M SORRY...
...BUT YOU GOT DAT *CLOUD CANCER* BAD.
COULD BE IT'S *COMMUNICABLE* BETWEEN MUTANTS, YEAH?
MY MISTAKE.
I'LL SEE YA SOON.
I DOUBT THAT, REMY.
ACH.
I NEVER DID HAVE...

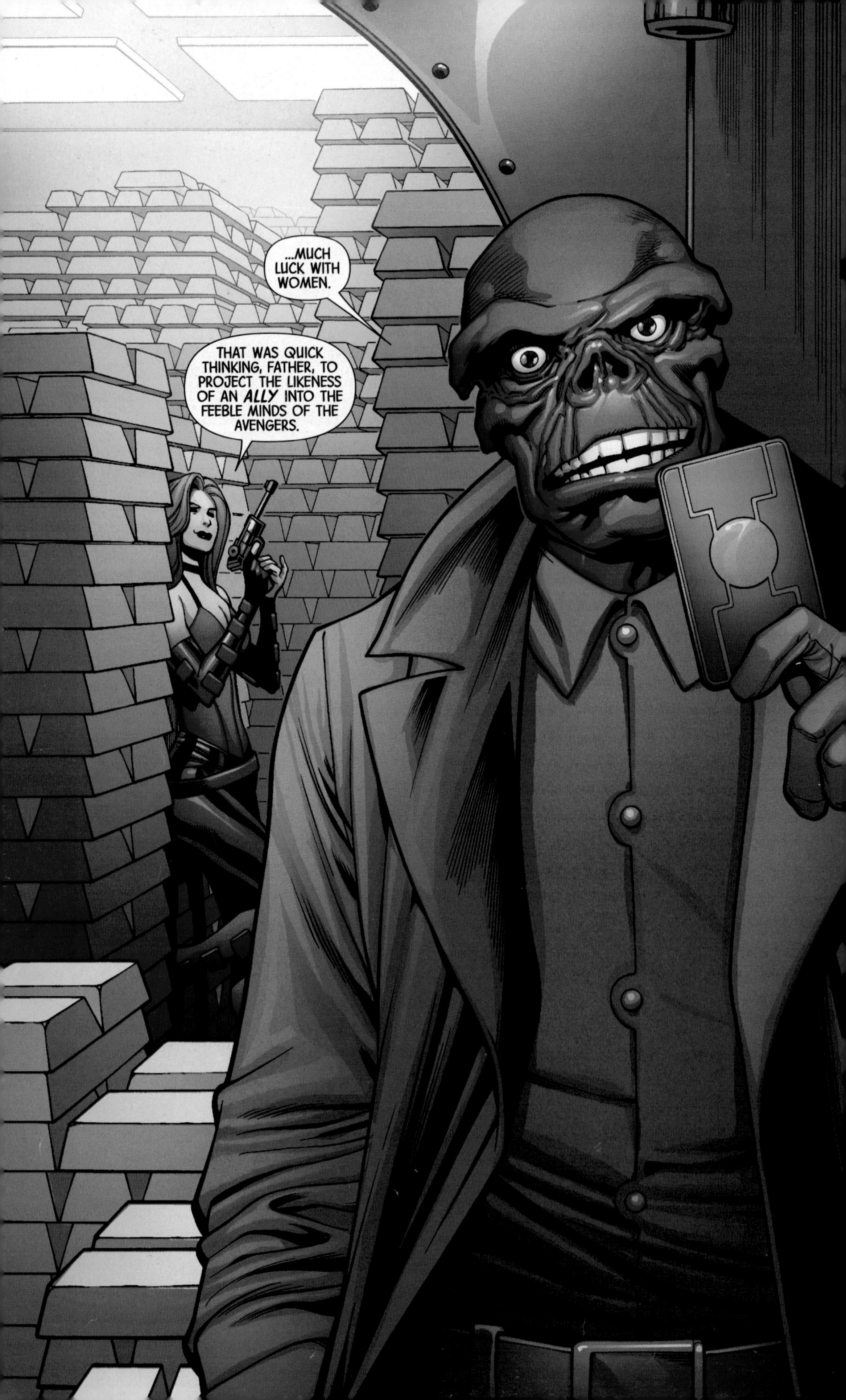
THAT WAS QUICK THINKING, FATHER, TO PROJECT THE LIKENESS OF AN *ALLY* INTO THE FEEBLE MINDS OF THE AVENGERS.
...MUCH LUCK WITH WOMEN.

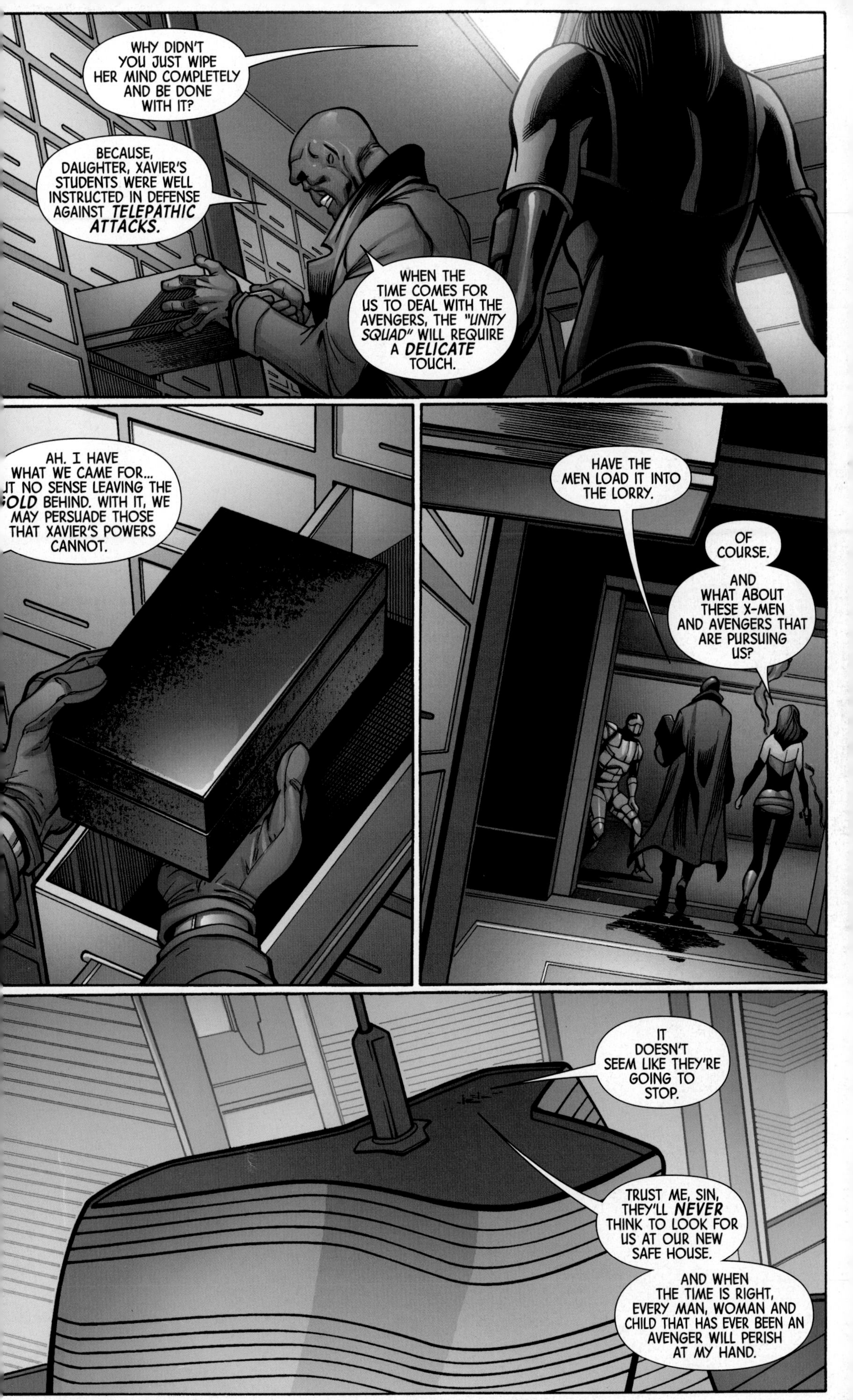
WHY DIDN'T YOU JUST WIPE HER MIND COMPLETELY AND BE DONE WITH IT?
BECAUSE, DAUGHTER, XAVIER'S STUDENTS WERE WELL INSTRUCTED IN DEFENSE AGAINST TELEPATHIC ATTACKS.
WHEN THE TIME COMES FOR US TO DEAL WITH THE AVENGERS, THE "UNITY SQUAD" WILL REQUIRE A DELICATE TOUCH.
AH. I HAVE WHAT WE CAME FOR... IT NO SENSE LEAVING THE GOLD BEHIND. WITH IT, WE MAY PERSUADE THOSE THAT XAVIER'S POWERS CANNOT.
HAVE THE MEN LOAD IT INTO THE LORRY.
OF COURSE.
AND WHAT ABOUT THESE X-MEN AND AVENGERS THAT ARE PURSUING US?
IT DOESN'T SEEM LIKE THEY'RE GOING TO STOP.
TRUST ME, SIN, THEY'LL NEVER THINK TO LOOK FOR US AT OUR NEW SAFE HOUSE.
AND WHEN THE TIME IS RIGHT, EVERY MAN, WOMAN AND CHILD THAT HAS EVER BEEN AN AVENGER WILL PERISH AT MY HAND.

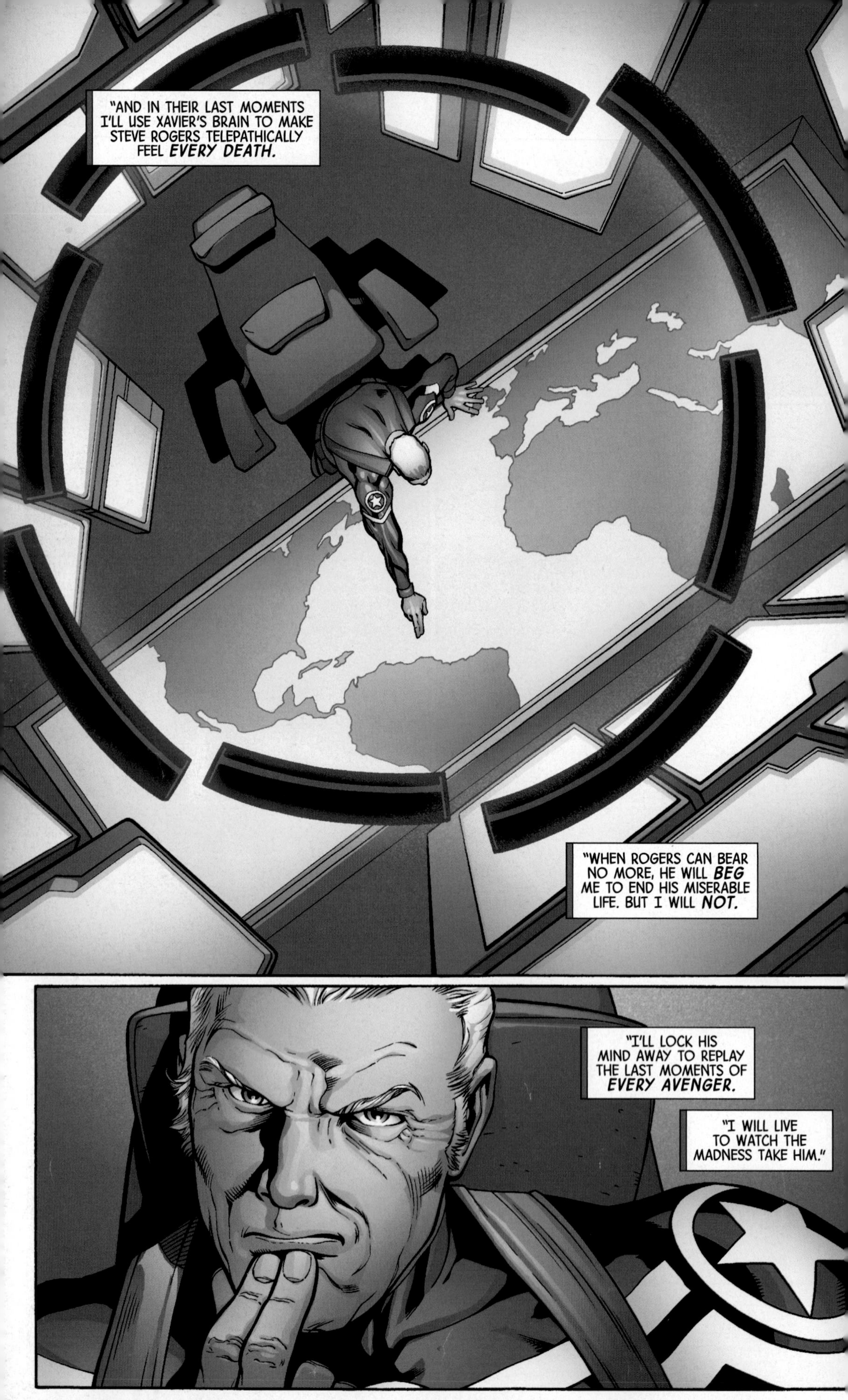
"AND IN THEIR LAST MOMENTS I'LL USE XAVIER'S BRAIN TO MAKE STEVE ROGERS TELEPATHICALLY FEEL *EVERY DEATH.*
"WHEN ROGERS CAN BEAR NO MORE, HE WILL *BEG* ME TO END HIS MISERABLE LIFE. BUT I WILL *NOT.*
"I'LL LOCK HIS MIND AWAY TO REPLAY THE LAST MOMENTS OF *EVERY AVENGER.*
"I WILL LIVE TO WATCH THE MADNESS TAKE HIM."

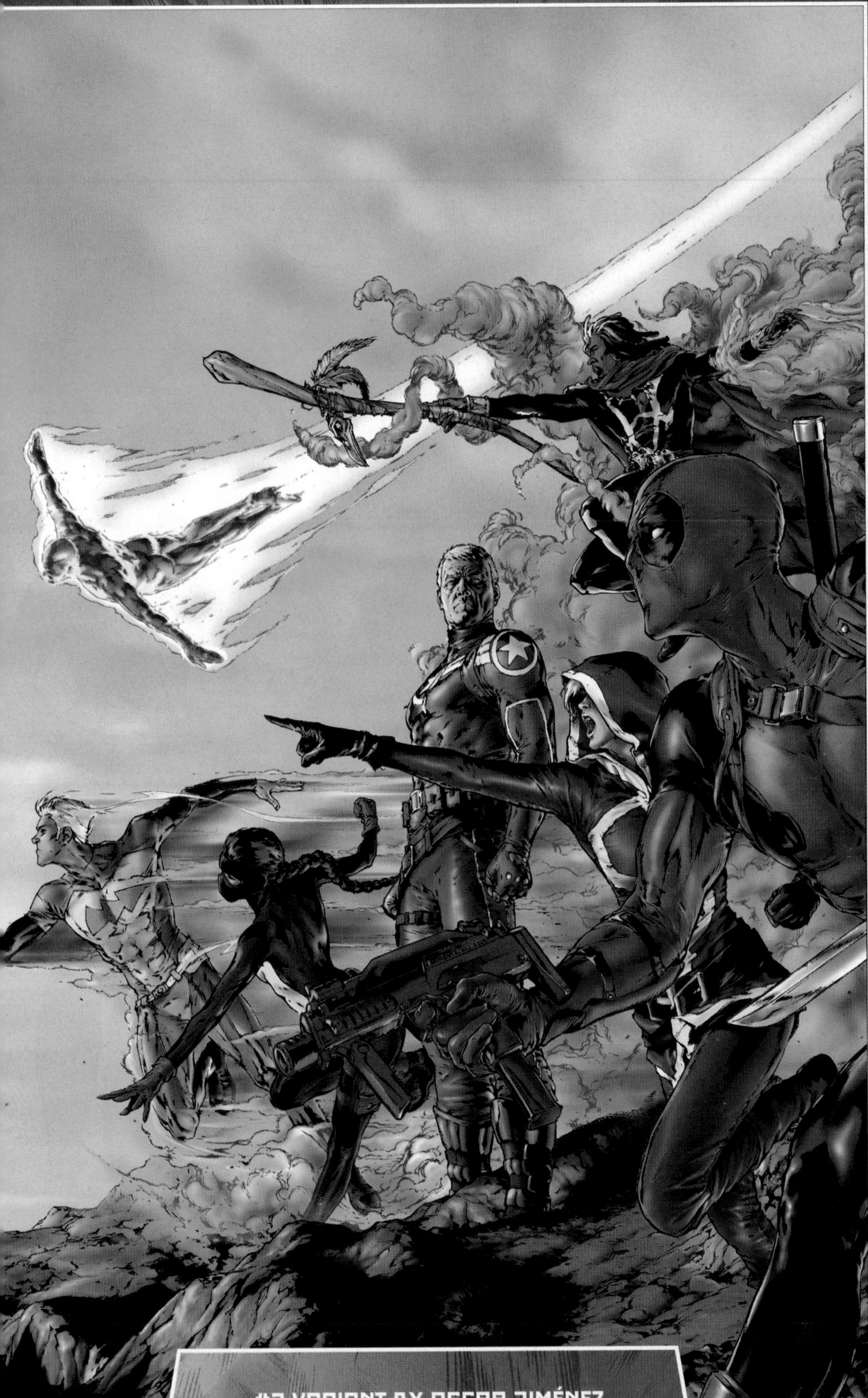

#2 VARIANT BY OSCAR JIMÉNEZ

6

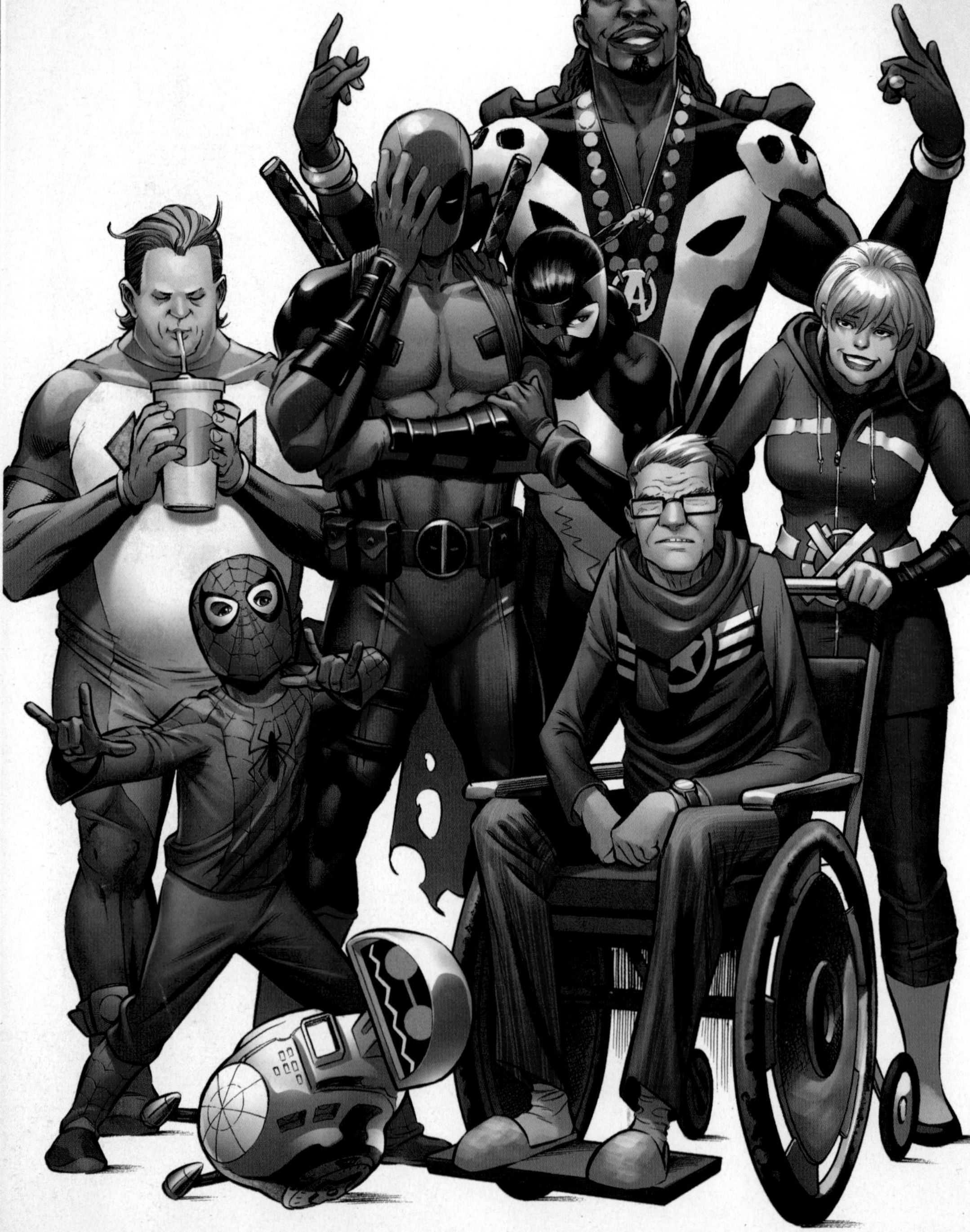

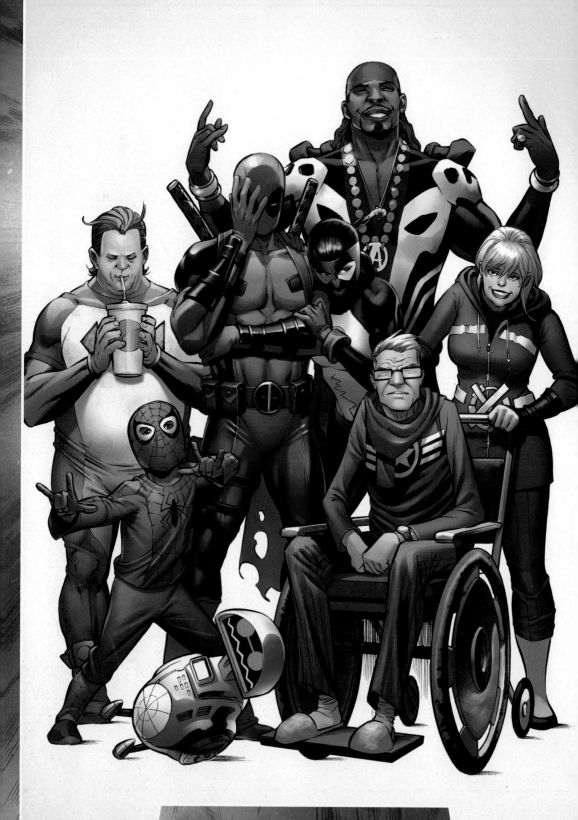

"THE UNINVITED"

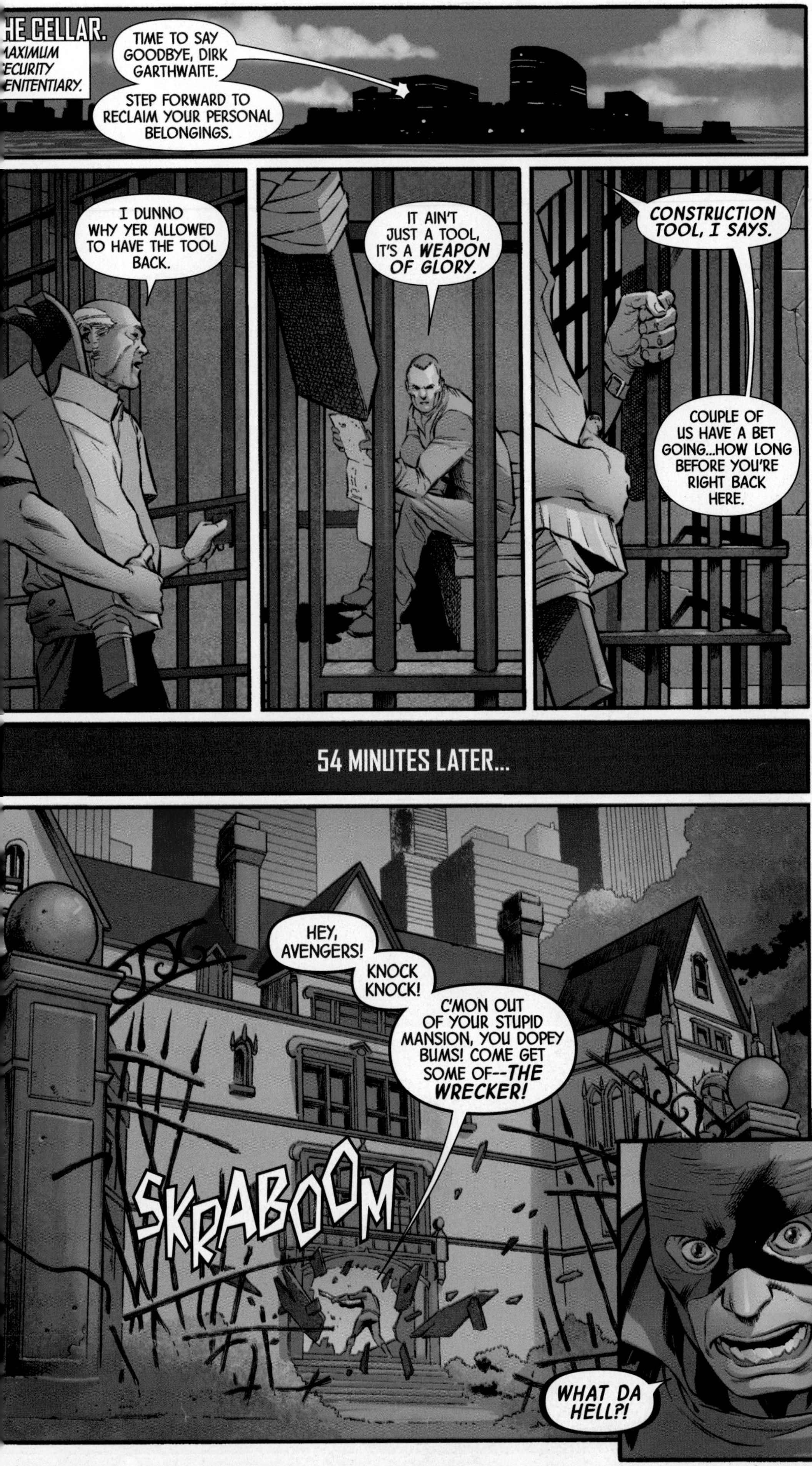
HE CELLAR.
AXIMUM ECURITY ENITENTIARY.
TIME TO SAY GOODBYE, DIRK GARTHWAITE.
STEP FORWARD TO RECLAIM YOUR PERSONAL BELONGINGS.
I DUNNO WHY YER ALLOWED TO HAVE THE TOOL BACK.
IT AIN'T JUST A TOOL, IT'S A WEAPON OF GLORY.
CONSTRUCTION TOOL, I SAYS.
COUPLE OF US HAVE A BET GOING...HOW LONG BEFORE YOU'RE RIGHT BACK HERE.
54 MINUTES LATER...
HEY, AVENGERS!
KNOCK KNOCK!
C'MON OUT OF YOUR STUPID MANSION, YOU DOPEY BUMS! COME GET SOME OF--THE WRECKER!
SKRABOOM
WHAT DA HELL?!

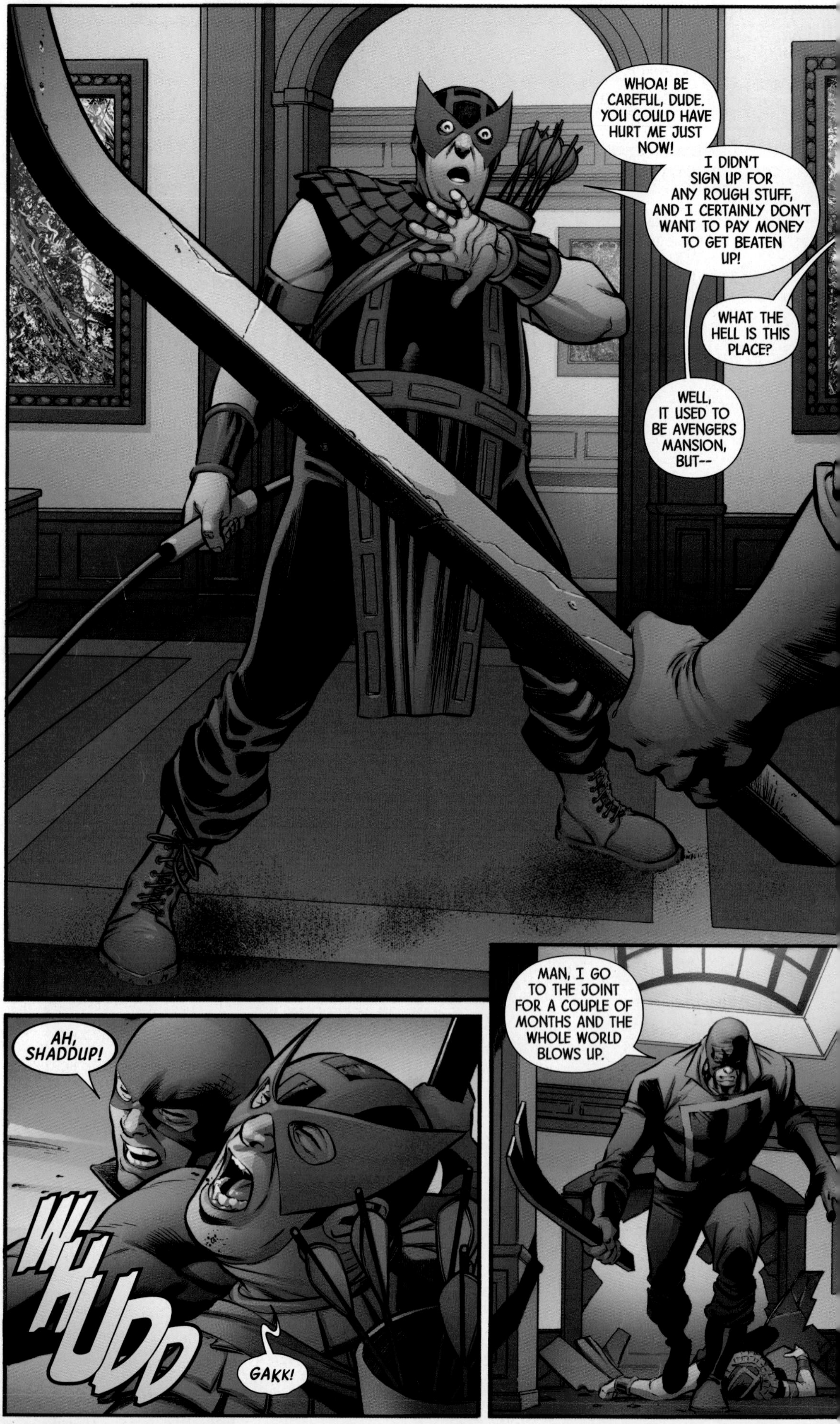

WHOA! BE CAREFUL, DUDE. YOU COULD HAVE HURT ME JUST NOW!
I DIDN'T SIGN UP FOR ANY ROUGH STUFF, AND I CERTAINLY DON'T WANT TO PAY MONEY TO GET BEATEN UP!
WHAT THE HELL IS THIS PLACE?
WELL, IT USED TO BE AVENGERS MANSION, BUT--
AH, SHADDUP!
WHUDD
GAKK!
MAN, I GO TO THE JOINT FOR A COUPLE OF MONTHS AND THE WHOLE WORLD BLOWS UP.

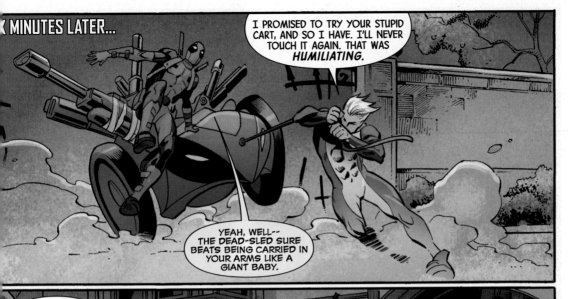

I PROMISED TO TRY YOUR STUPID CART, AND SO I HAVE. I'LL NEVER TOUCH IT AGAIN. THAT WAS *HUMILIATING.*

YEAH, WELL-- THE DEAD-SLED SURE BEATS BEING CARRIED IN YOUR ARMS LIKE A GIANT BABY.

CARTING YOU AROUND IS ALMOST AS DREADFUL AS BEING BACK AT AVENGERS MANSION.

I SWORE I WOULDN'T RETURN AFTER IT BECAME A *THEME HOTEL.*

HEY, MAN, I'D RATHER BE OUT LOOKING FOR THE *RED SKULL,* TOO--BUT WE GOTTA PUT OUT THE FIRES AS THEY COME.

TH-THANK YOU FOR COMING SO FAST.

WHAT DO *YOU* CARE ABOUT THE RED SKULL USING XAVIER'S BRAIN?

LOOK, I'M TRYING TO LIVE UP TO LOGAN'S LEGACY-- BY KILLING EVERYONE *HE* WOULD IF HE STILL POSSESSED THE GIFT OF LIFE.

PLUS, WHATEVER'S WRONG WITH MY HEAD MAKES IT IMPOSSIBLE FOR TELEPATHS TO PUT A *WHAMMY* ON ME.

I'M THE NATURAL TIP OF THE SPEAR AGAINST THE RED SKULL WHILE HE HAS CHUCK'S BRAIN.

HOW COMFORTING.

THE VANDAL IS *UPSTAIRS.* HANDLE IT. I'LL SWEEP THE REST OF THE MANSION.

KRABOOMSHK

HEY!

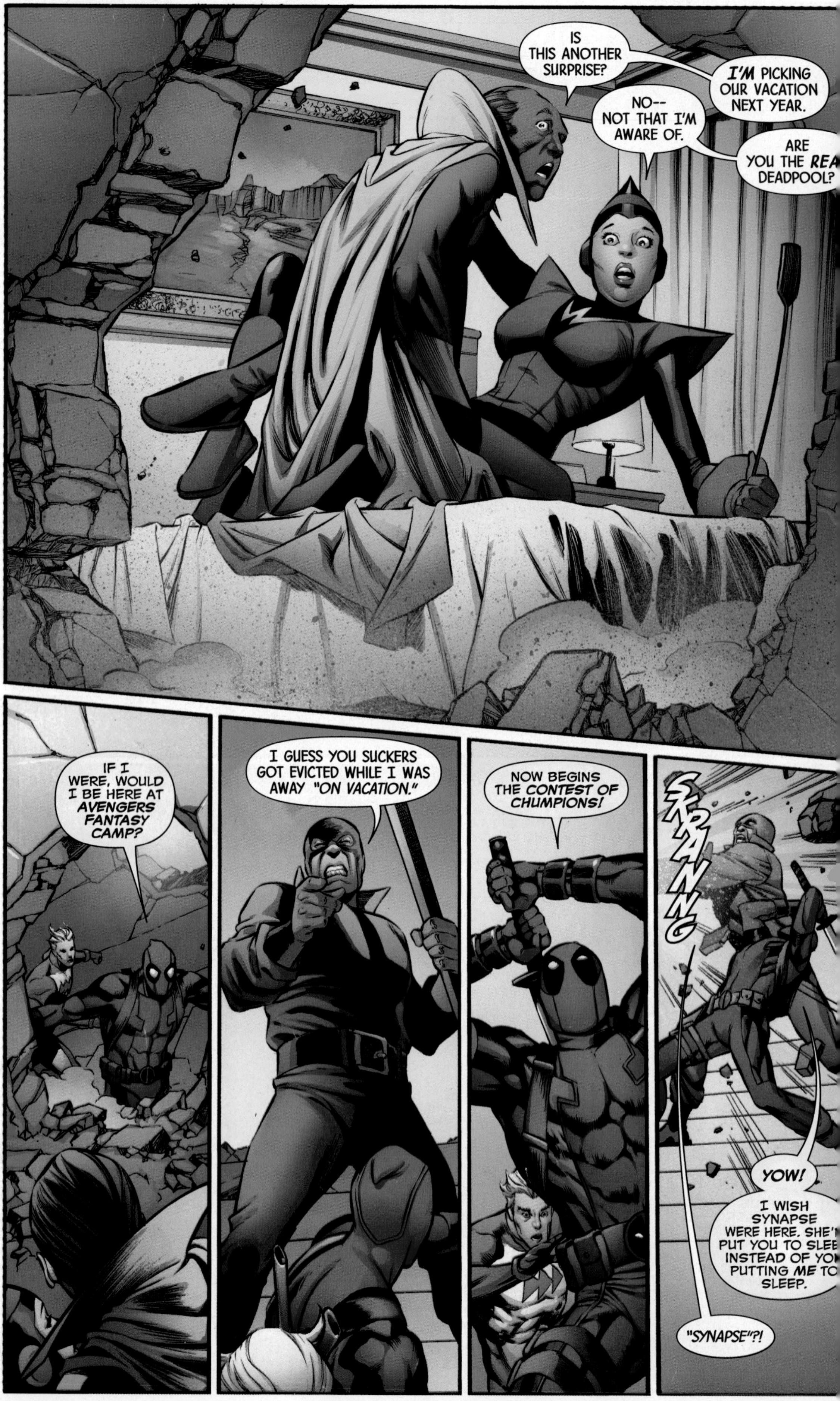
IS THIS ANOTHER SURPRISE?
I'M PICKING OUR VACATION NEXT YEAR.
NO-- NOT THAT I'M AWARE OF.
ARE YOU THE REA DEADPOOL?
IF I WERE, WOULD I BE HERE AT AVENGERS FANTASY CAMP?
I GUESS YOU SUCKERS GOT EVICTED WHILE I WAS AWAY "ON VACATION."
NOW BEGINS THE CONTEST OF CHUMPIONS!
SKRANNG
YOW!
I WISH SYNAPSE WERE HERE. SHE' PUT YOU TO SLEE INSTEAD OF YO PUTTING ME TO SLEEP.
"SYNAPSE"?!

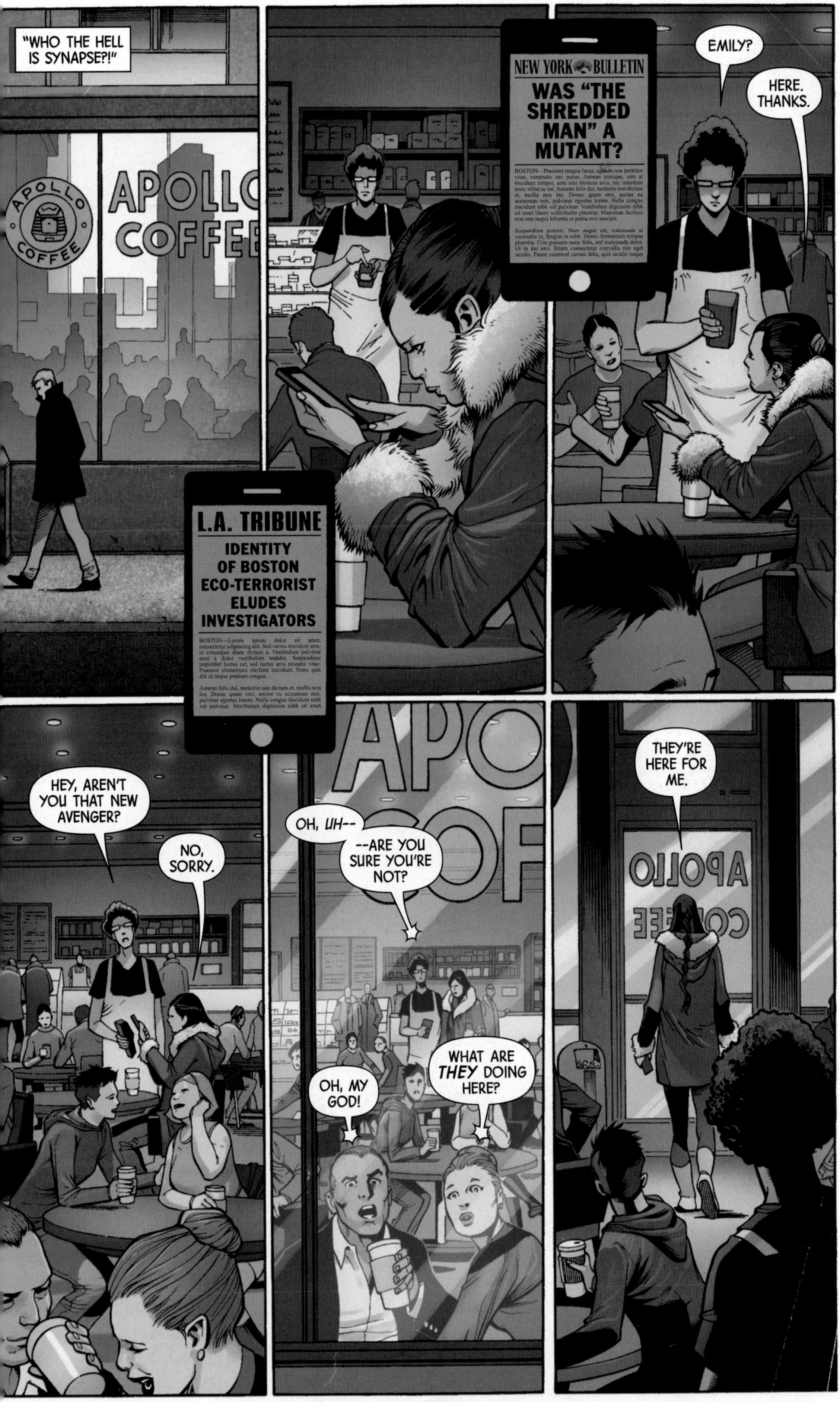
"WHO THE HELL IS SYNAPSE?!"
APOLLO COFFEE
APOLLO COFFEE
NEW YORK BULLETIN
WAS "THE SHREDDED MAN" A MUTANT?
EMILY?
HERE. THANKS.
L.A. TRIBUNE
IDENTITY OF BOSTON ECO-TERRORIST ELUDES INVESTIGATORS
HEY, AREN'T YOU THAT NEW AVENGER?
NO, SORRY.
APO COF
OH, UH--
--ARE YOU SURE YOU'RE NOT?
OH, MY GOD!
WHAT ARE *THEY* DOING HERE?
THEY'RE HERE FOR ME.
APOLLO COFFEE

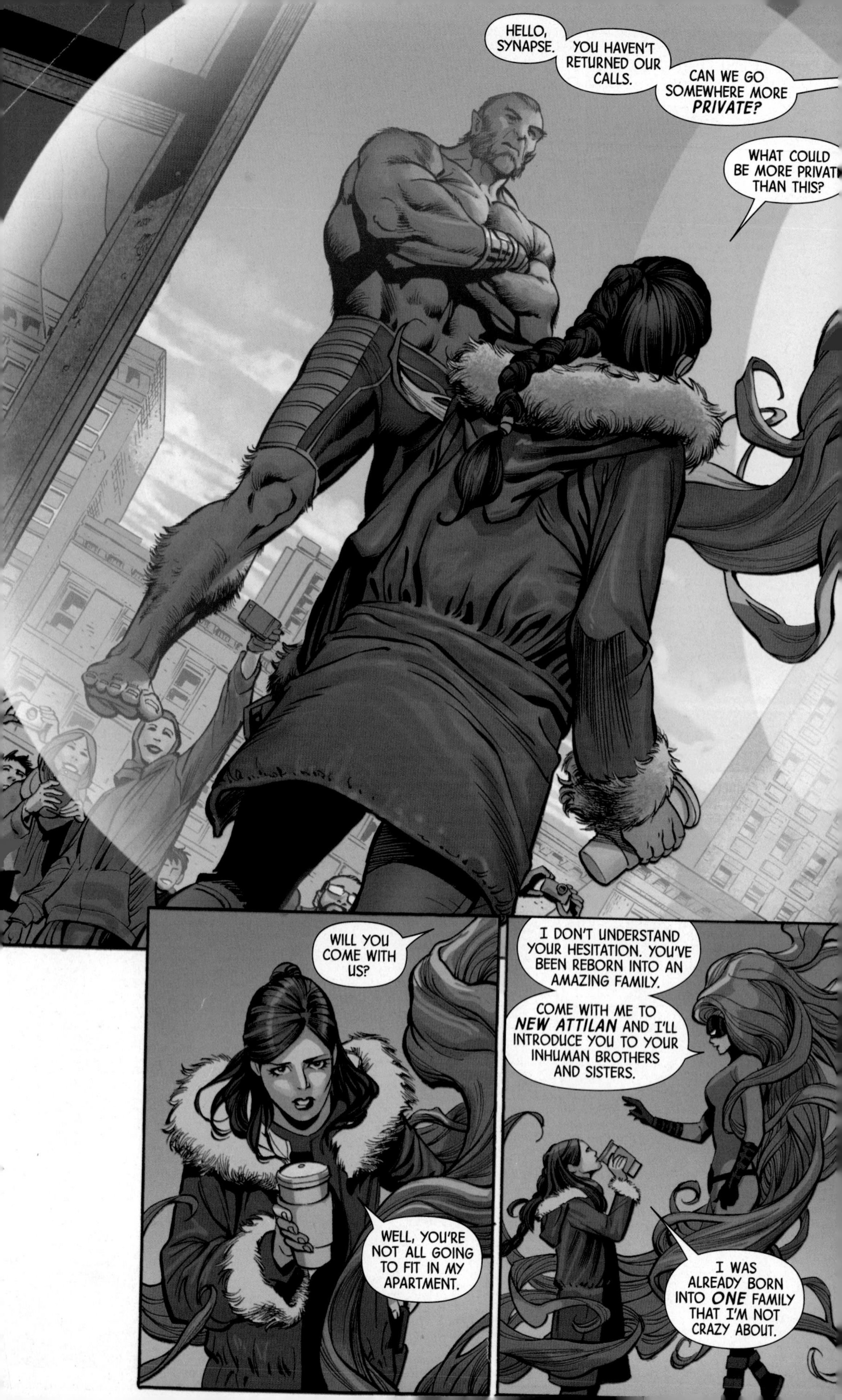
HELLO, SYNAPSE.
YOU HAVEN'T RETURNED OUR CALLS.
CAN WE GO SOMEWHERE MORE *PRIVATE?*
WHAT COULD BE MORE PRIVAT THAN THIS?
WILL YOU COME WITH US?
WELL, YOU'RE NOT ALL GOING TO FIT IN MY APARTMENT.
I DON'T UNDERSTAND YOUR HESITATION. YOU'VE BEEN REBORN INTO AN AMAZING FAMILY.
COME WITH ME TO *NEW ATTILAN* AND I'LL INTRODUCE YOU TO YOUR INHUMAN BROTHERS AND SISTERS.
I WAS ALREADY BORN INTO *ONE* FAMILY THAT I'M NOT CRAZY ABOUT.

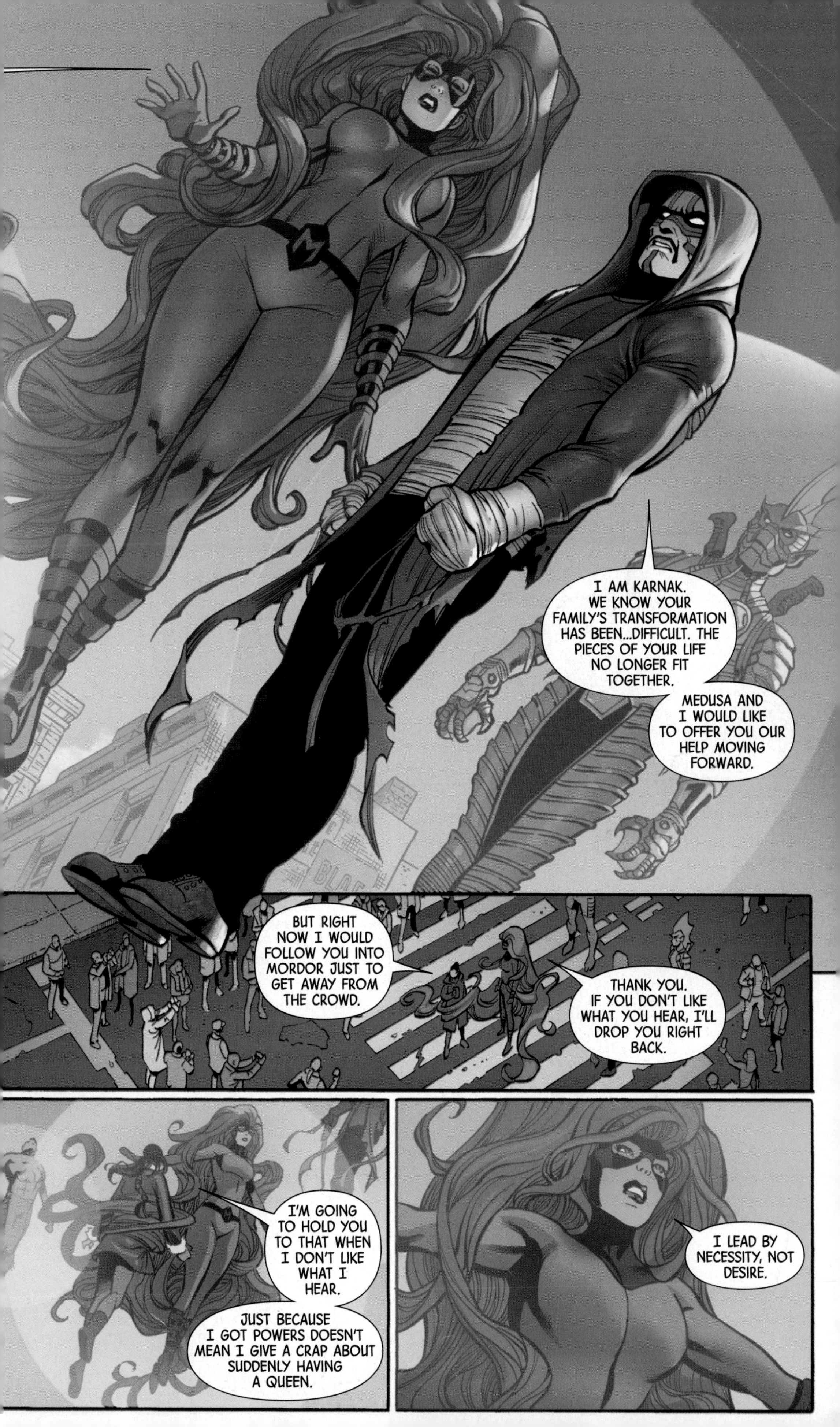
I AM KARNAK. WE KNOW YOUR FAMILY'S TRANSFORMATION HAS BEEN...DIFFICULT. THE PIECES OF YOUR LIFE NO LONGER FIT TOGETHER.
MEDUSA AND I WOULD LIKE TO OFFER YOU OUR HELP MOVING FORWARD.
BUT RIGHT NOW I WOULD FOLLOW YOU INTO MORDOR JUST TO GET AWAY FROM THE CROWD.
THANK YOU. IF YOU DON'T LIKE WHAT YOU HEAR, I'LL DROP YOU RIGHT BACK.
I'M GOING TO HOLD YOU TO THAT WHEN I DON'T LIKE WHAT I HEAR.
JUST BECAUSE I GOT POWERS DOESN'T MEAN I GIVE A CRAP ABOUT SUDDENLY HAVING A QUEEN.
I LEAD BY NECESSITY, NOT DESIRE.

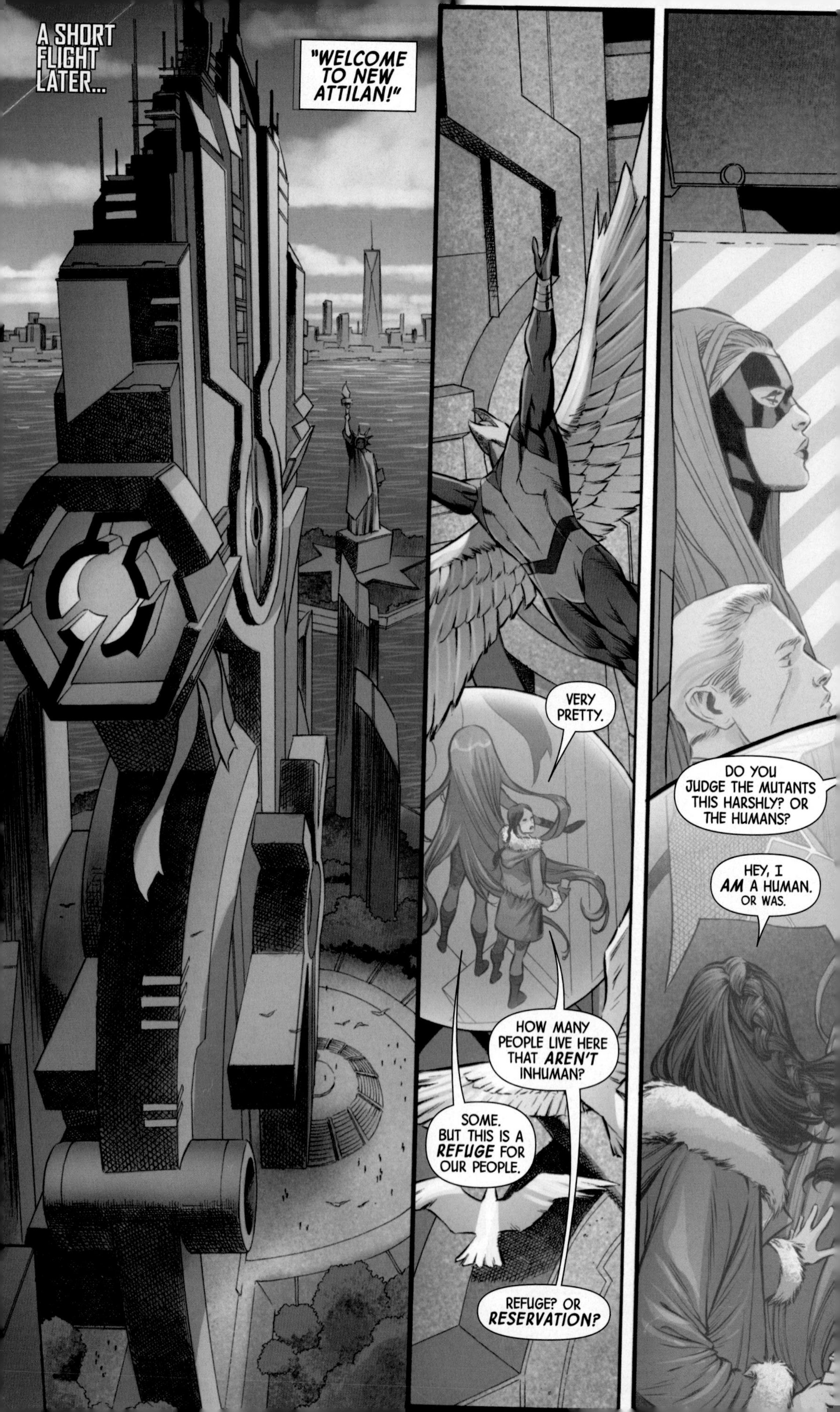
A SHORT FLIGHT LATER...
"WELCOME TO NEW ATTILAN!"
VERY PRETTY.
HOW MANY PEOPLE LIVE HERE THAT AREN'T INHUMAN?
SOME. BUT THIS IS A REFUGE FOR OUR PEOPLE.
REFUGE? OR RESERVATION?
DO YOU JUDGE THE MUTANTS THIS HARSHLY? OR THE HUMANS?
HEY, I AM A HUMAN. OR WAS.

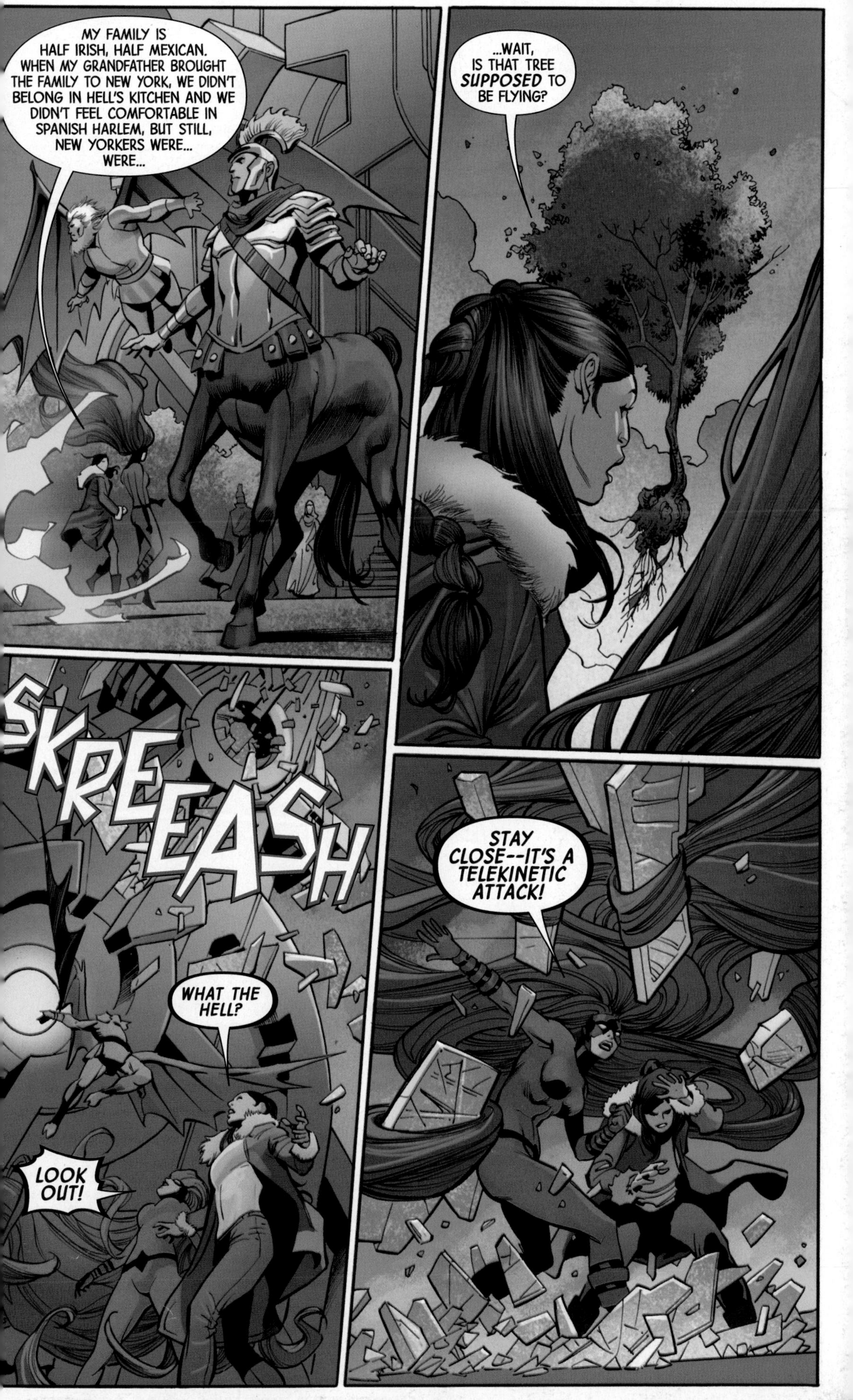
MY FAMILY IS HALF IRISH, HALF MEXICAN. WHEN MY GRANDFATHER BROUGHT THE FAMILY TO NEW YORK, WE DIDN'T BELONG IN HELL'S KITCHEN AND WE DIDN'T FEEL COMFORTABLE IN SPANISH HARLEM, BUT STILL, NEW YORKERS WERE... WERE...
...WAIT, IS THAT TREE *SUPPOSED* TO BE FLYING?
SKREEASH
WHAT THE HELL?
LOOK OUT!
STAY CLOSE--IT'S A TELEKINETIC ATTACK!

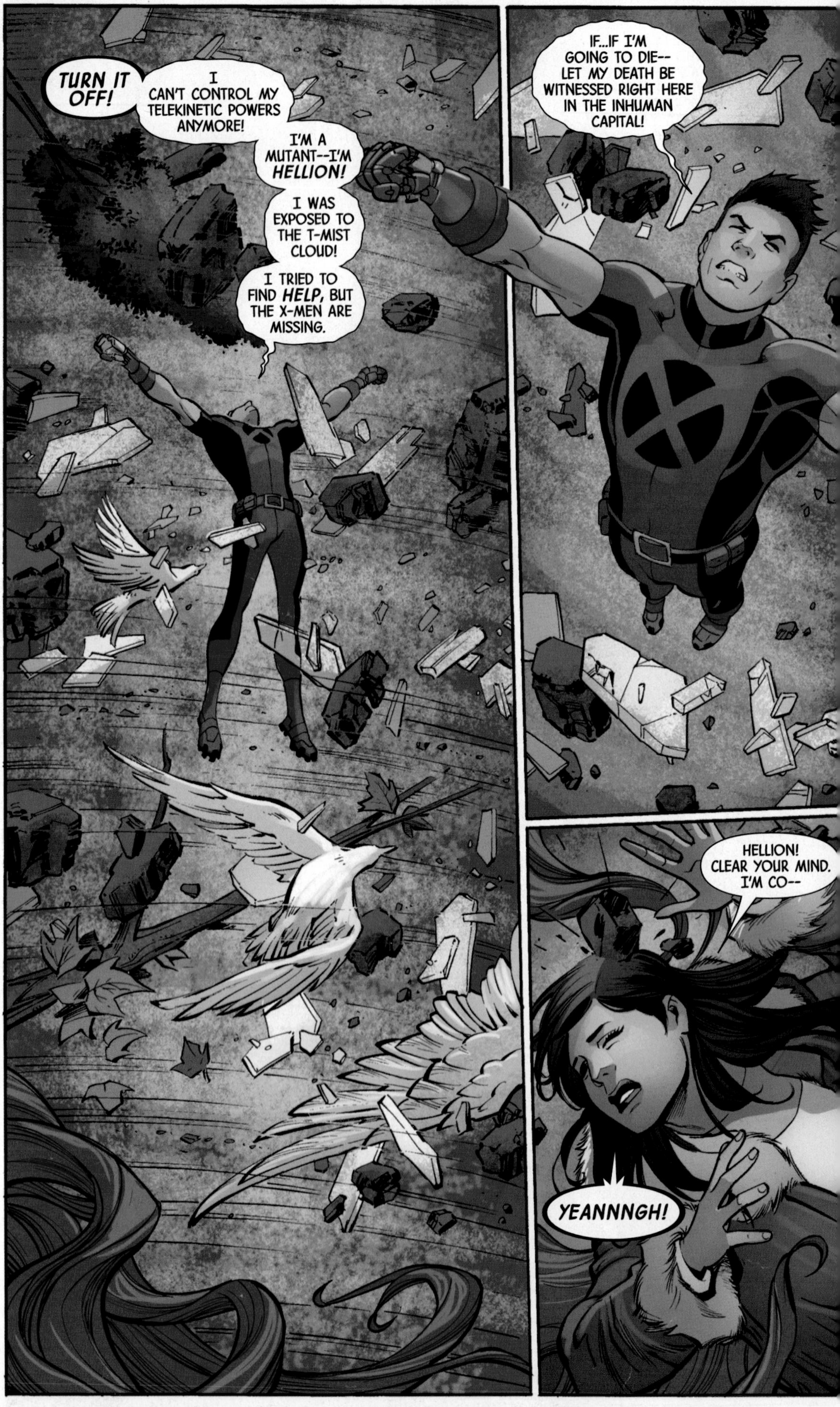
TURN IT OFF!
I CAN'T CONTROL MY TELEKINETIC POWERS ANYMORE!
I'M A MUTANT--I'M HELLION!
I WAS EXPOSED TO THE T-MIST CLOUD!
I TRIED TO FIND HELP, BUT THE X-MEN ARE MISSING.
IF...IF I'M GOING TO DIE-- LET MY DEATH BE WITNESSED RIGHT HERE IN THE INHUMAN CAPITAL!
HELLION! CLEAR YOUR MIND. I'M CO--
YEANNNGH!

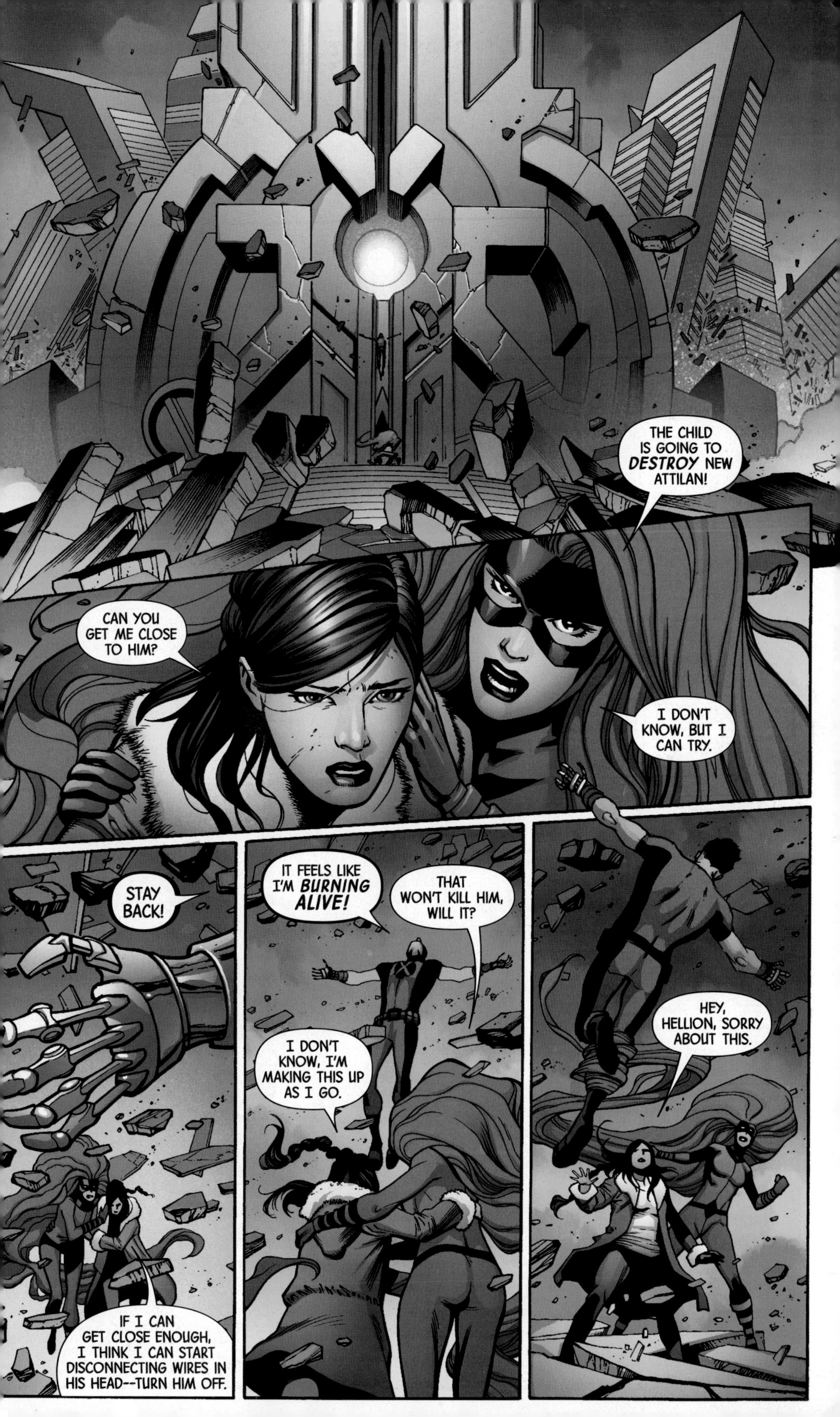
THE CHILD IS GOING TO DESTROY NEW ATTILAN!
CAN YOU GET ME CLOSE TO HIM?
I DON'T KNOW, BUT I CAN TRY.
STAY BACK!
IF I CAN GET CLOSE ENOUGH, I THINK I CAN START DISCONNECTING WIRES IN HIS HEAD--TURN HIM OFF.
IT FEELS LIKE I'M BURNING ALIVE!
THAT WON'T KILL HIM, WILL IT?
I DON'T KNOW, I'M MAKING THIS UP AS I GO.
HEY, HELLION, SORRY ABOUT THIS.

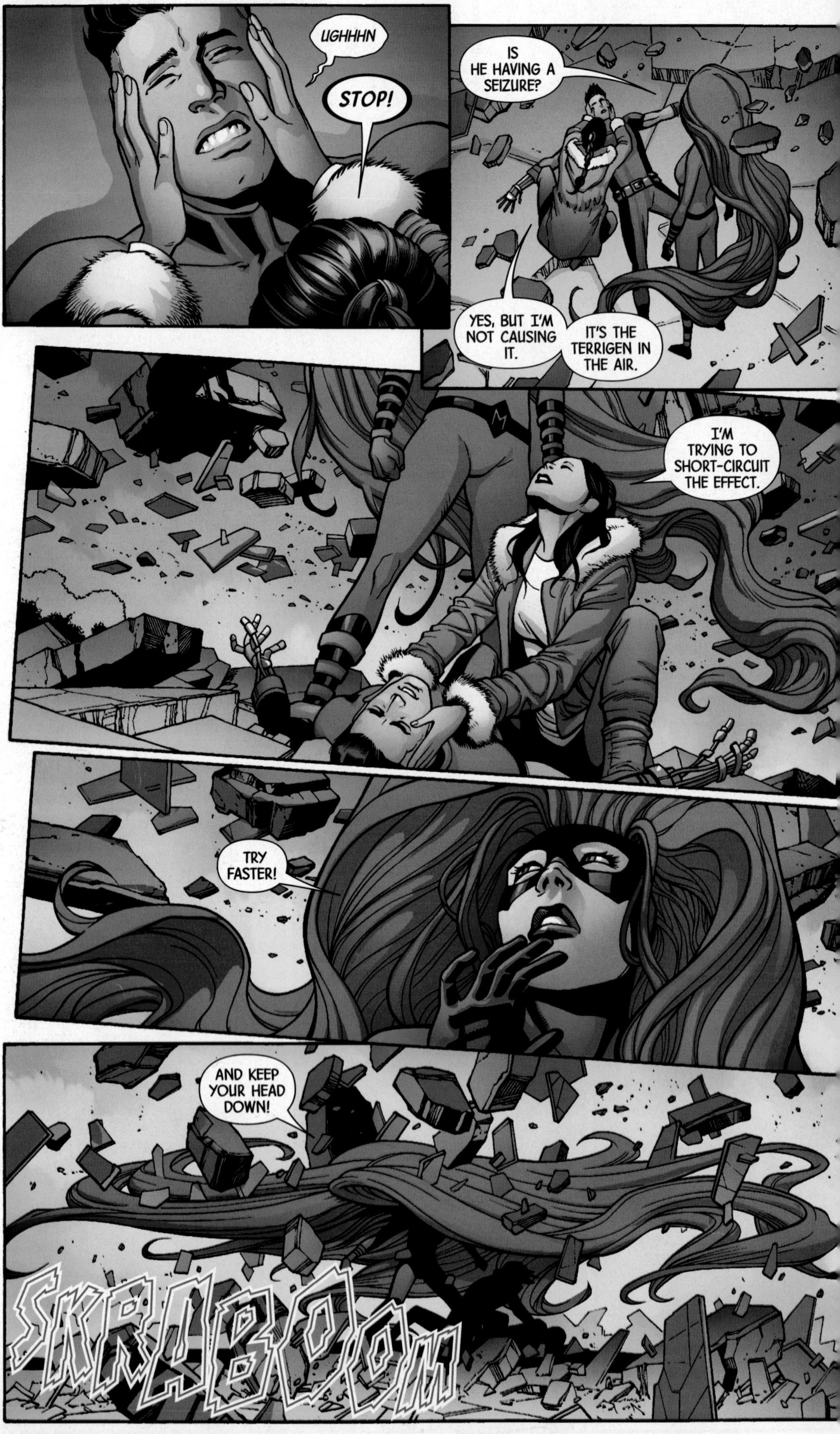
UGHHHN
STOP!
IS HE HAVING A SEIZURE?
YES, BUT I'M NOT CAUSING IT.
IT'S THE TERRIGEN IN THE AIR.
I'M TRYING TO SHORT-CIRCUIT THE EFFECT.
TRY FASTER!
AND KEEP YOUR HEAD DOWN!
SKRABOOM

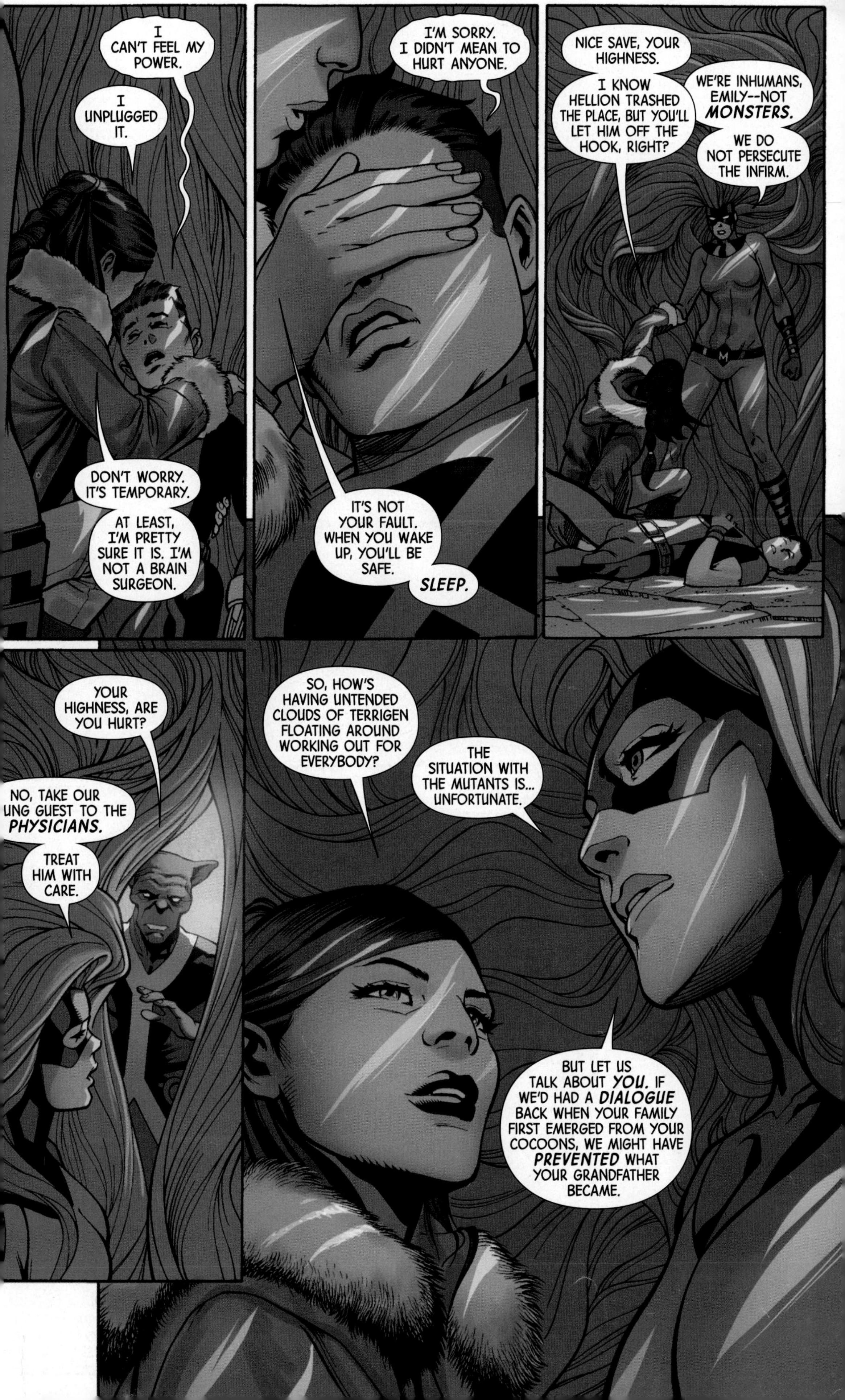
I CAN'T FEEL MY POWER.
I UNPLUGGED IT.
DON'T WORRY. IT'S TEMPORARY.
AT LEAST, I'M PRETTY SURE IT IS. I'M NOT A BRAIN SURGEON.
I'M SORRY. I DIDN'T MEAN TO HURT ANYONE.
IT'S NOT YOUR FAULT. WHEN YOU WAKE UP, YOU'LL BE SAFE.
SLEEP.
NICE SAVE, YOUR HIGHNESS.
I KNOW HELLION TRASHED THE PLACE, BUT YOU'LL LET HIM OFF THE HOOK, RIGHT?
WE'RE INHUMANS, EMILY--NOT MONSTERS.
WE DO NOT PERSECUTE THE INFIRM.
YOUR HIGHNESS, ARE YOU HURT?
NO, TAKE OUR UNG GUEST TO THE PHYSICIANS.
TREAT HIM WITH CARE.
SO, HOW'S HAVING UNTENDED CLOUDS OF TERRIGEN FLOATING AROUND WORKING OUT FOR EVERYBODY?
THE SITUATION WITH THE MUTANTS IS... UNFORTUNATE.
BUT LET US TALK ABOUT YOU. IF WE'D HAD A DIALOGUE BACK WHEN YOUR FAMILY FIRST EMERGED FROM YOUR COCOONS, WE MIGHT HAVE PREVENTED WHAT YOUR GRANDFATHER BECAME.

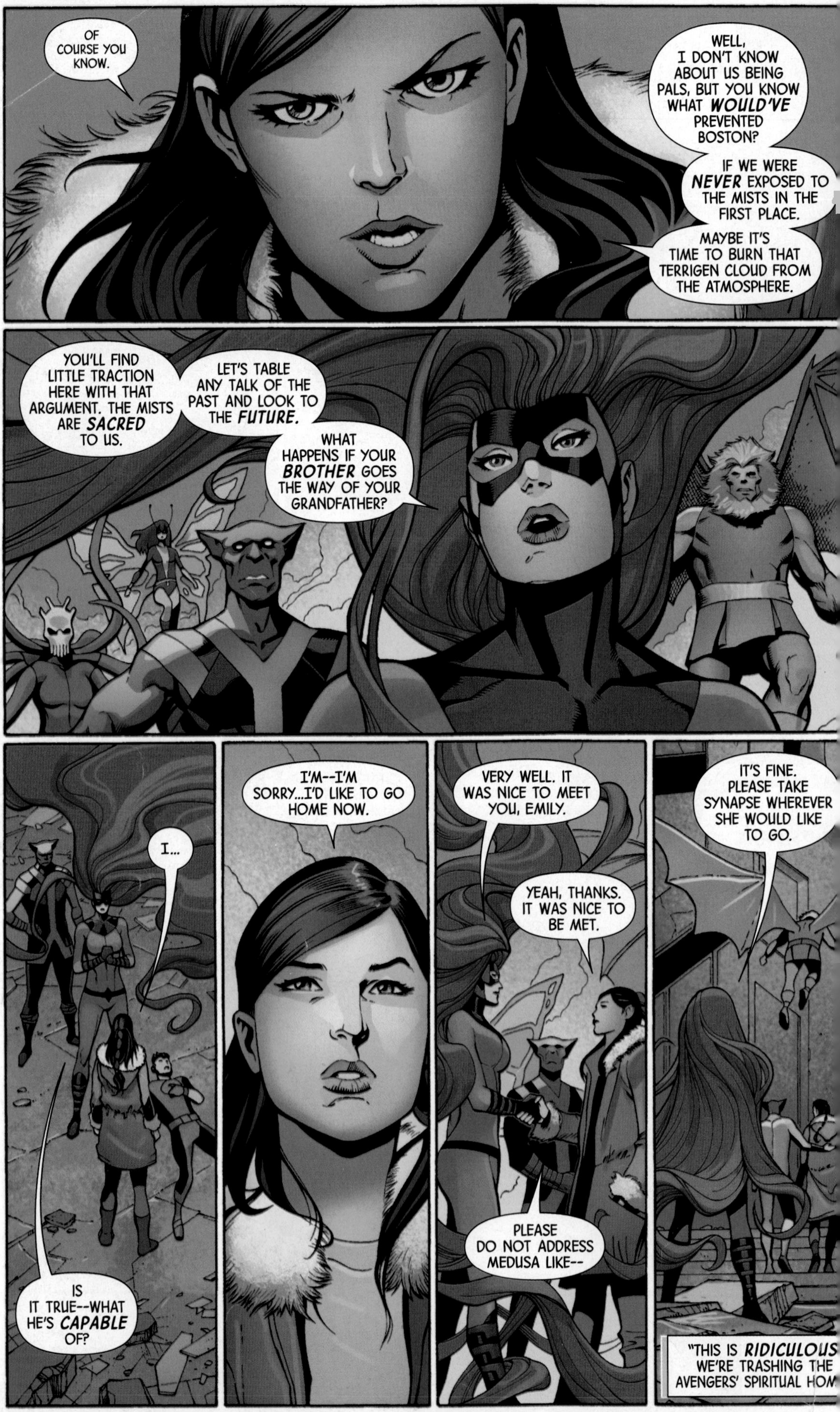

OF COURSE YOU KNOW.
WELL, I DON'T KNOW ABOUT US BEING PALS, BUT YOU KNOW WHAT *WOULD'VE* PREVENTED BOSTON?
IF WE WERE *NEVER* EXPOSED TO THE MISTS IN THE FIRST PLACE.
MAYBE IT'S TIME TO BURN THAT TERRIGEN CLOUD FROM THE ATMOSPHERE.
YOU'LL FIND LITTLE TRACTION HERE WITH THAT ARGUMENT. THE MISTS ARE *SACRED* TO US.
LET'S TABLE ANY TALK OF THE PAST AND LOOK TO THE *FUTURE.*
WHAT HAPPENS IF YOUR *BROTHER* GOES THE WAY OF YOUR GRANDFATHER?
I...
IS IT TRUE--WHAT HE'S *CAPABLE* OF?
I'M--I'M SORRY...I'D LIKE TO GO HOME NOW.
VERY WELL. IT WAS NICE TO MEET YOU, EMILY.
YEAH, THANKS. IT WAS NICE TO BE MET.
PLEASE DO NOT ADDRESS MEDUSA LIKE--
IT'S FINE. PLEASE TAKE SYNAPSE WHEREVER SHE WOULD LIKE TO GO.
"THIS IS *RIDICULOUS* WE'RE TRASHING THE AVENGERS' SPIRITUAL HOM

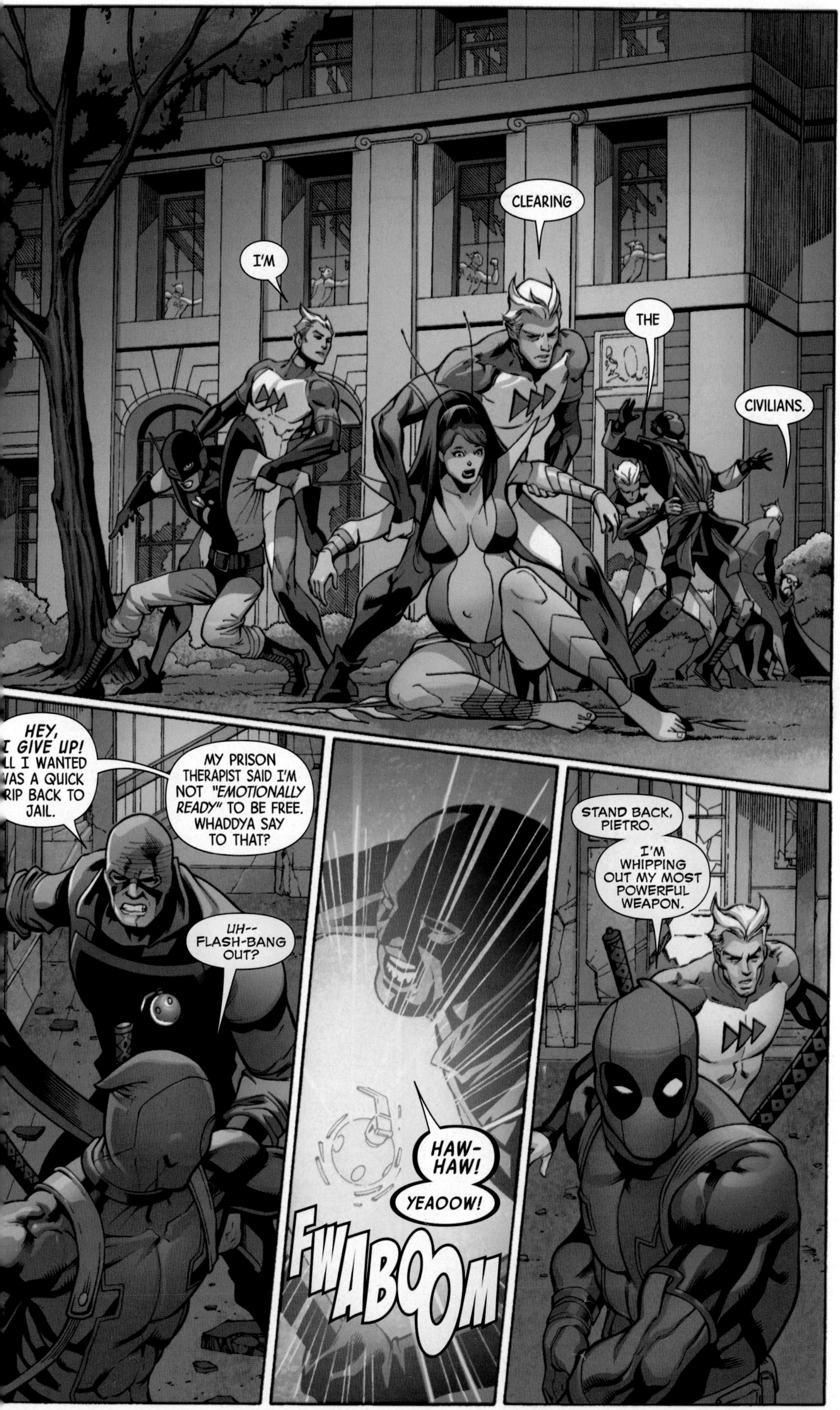

I'M
CLEARING
THE
CIVILIANS.
HEY, I GIVE UP! ALL I WANTED WAS A QUICK TRIP BACK TO JAIL.
MY PRISON THERAPIST SAID I'M NOT "EMOTIONALLY READY" TO BE FREE. WHADDYA SAY TO THAT?
UH-- FLASH-BANG OUT?
HAW-HAW!
YEAOOW!
FWABOOM
STAND BACK, PIETRO.
I'M WHIPPING OUT MY MOST POWERFUL WEAPON.

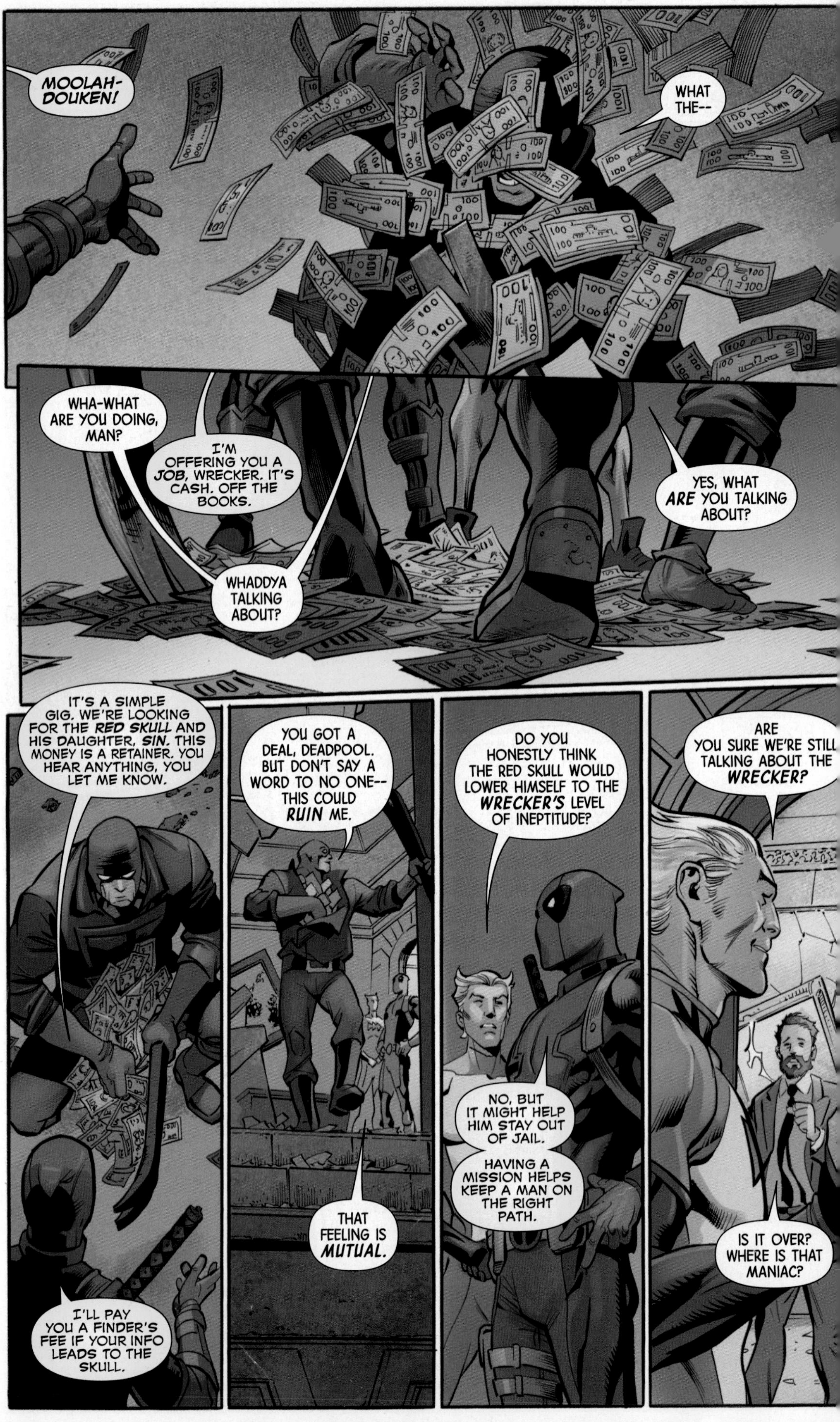
MOOLAH-DOUKEN!
WHAT THE--
WHA-WHAT ARE YOU DOING, MAN?
I'M OFFERING YOU A JOB, WRECKER. IT'S CASH. OFF THE BOOKS.
WHADDYA TALKING ABOUT?
YES, WHAT ARE YOU TALKING ABOUT?
IT'S A SIMPLE GIG. WE'RE LOOKING FOR THE RED SKULL AND HIS DAUGHTER, SIN. THIS MONEY IS A RETAINER. YOU HEAR ANYTHING, YOU LET ME KNOW.
I'LL PAY YOU A FINDER'S FEE IF YOUR INFO LEADS TO THE SKULL.
YOU GOT A DEAL, DEADPOOL. BUT DON'T SAY A WORD TO NO ONE-- THIS COULD RUIN ME.
THAT FEELING IS MUTUAL.
DO YOU HONESTLY THINK THE RED SKULL WOULD LOWER HIMSELF TO THE WRECKER'S LEVEL OF INEPTITUDE?
NO, BUT IT MIGHT HELP HIM STAY OUT OF JAIL.
HAVING A MISSION HELPS KEEP A MAN ON THE RIGHT PATH.
ARE YOU SURE WE'RE STILL TALKING ABOUT THE WRECKER?
IS IT OVER? WHERE IS THAT MANIAC?

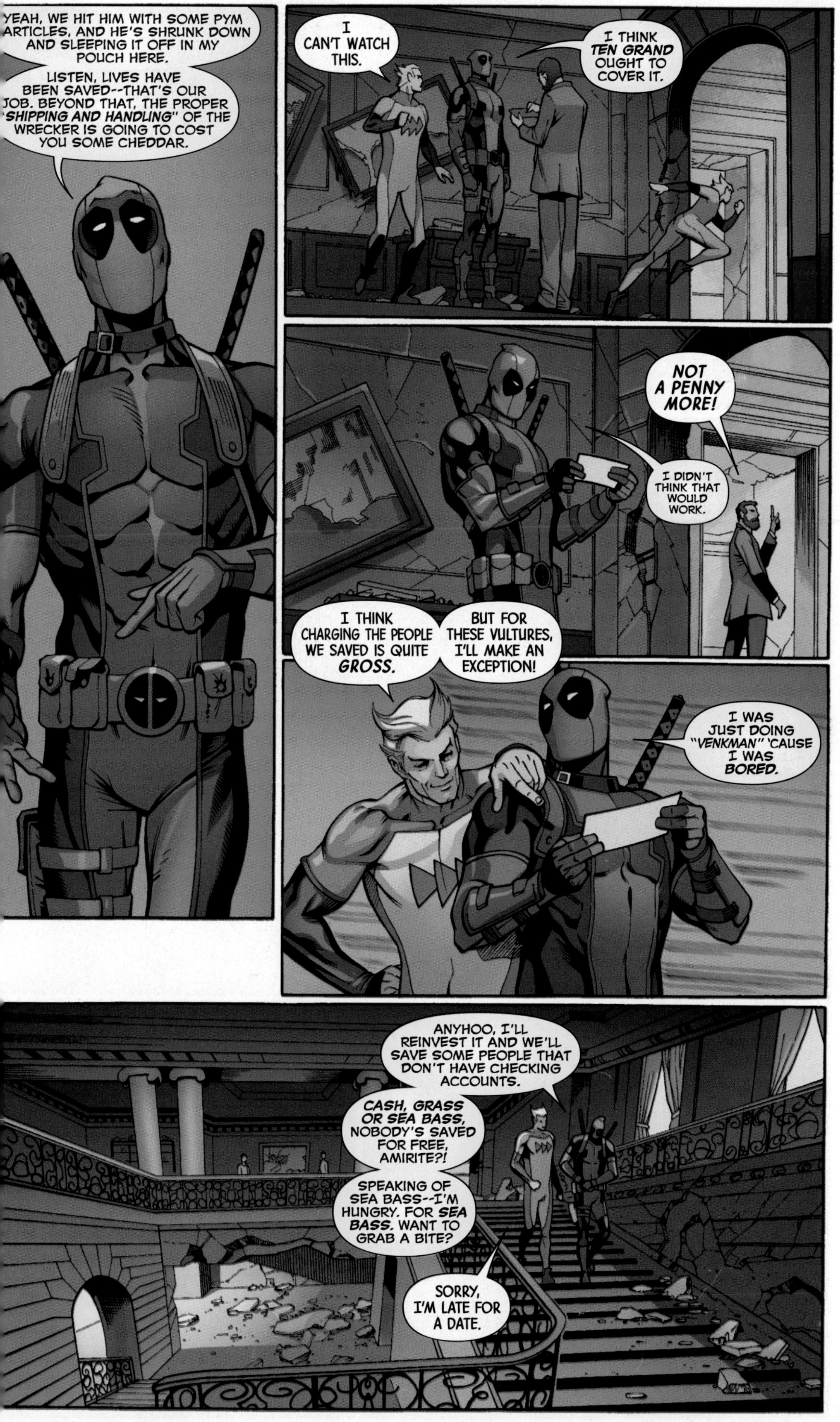
YEAH, WE HIT HIM WITH SOME PYM PARTICLES, AND HE'S SHRUNK DOWN AND SLEEPING IT OFF IN MY POUCH HERE.
LISTEN, LIVES HAVE BEEN SAVED--THAT'S OUR JOB. BEYOND THAT, THE PROPER "SHIPPING AND HANDLING" OF THE WRECKER IS GOING TO COST YOU SOME CHEDDAR.
I CAN'T WATCH THIS.
I THINK TEN GRAND OUGHT TO COVER IT.
NOT A PENNY MORE!
I DIDN'T THINK THAT WOULD WORK.
I THINK CHARGING THE PEOPLE WE SAVED IS QUITE GROSS.
BUT FOR THESE VULTURES, I'LL MAKE AN EXCEPTION!
I WAS JUST DOING "VENKMAN" 'CAUSE I WAS BORED.
ANYHOO, I'LL REINVEST IT AND WE'LL SAVE SOME PEOPLE THAT DON'T HAVE CHECKING ACCOUNTS.
CASH, GRASS OR SEA BASS, NOBODY'S SAVED FOR FREE, AMIRITE?!
SPEAKING OF SEA BASS--I'M HUNGRY. FOR SEA BASS. WANT TO GRAB A BITE?
SORRY, I'M LATE FOR A DATE.

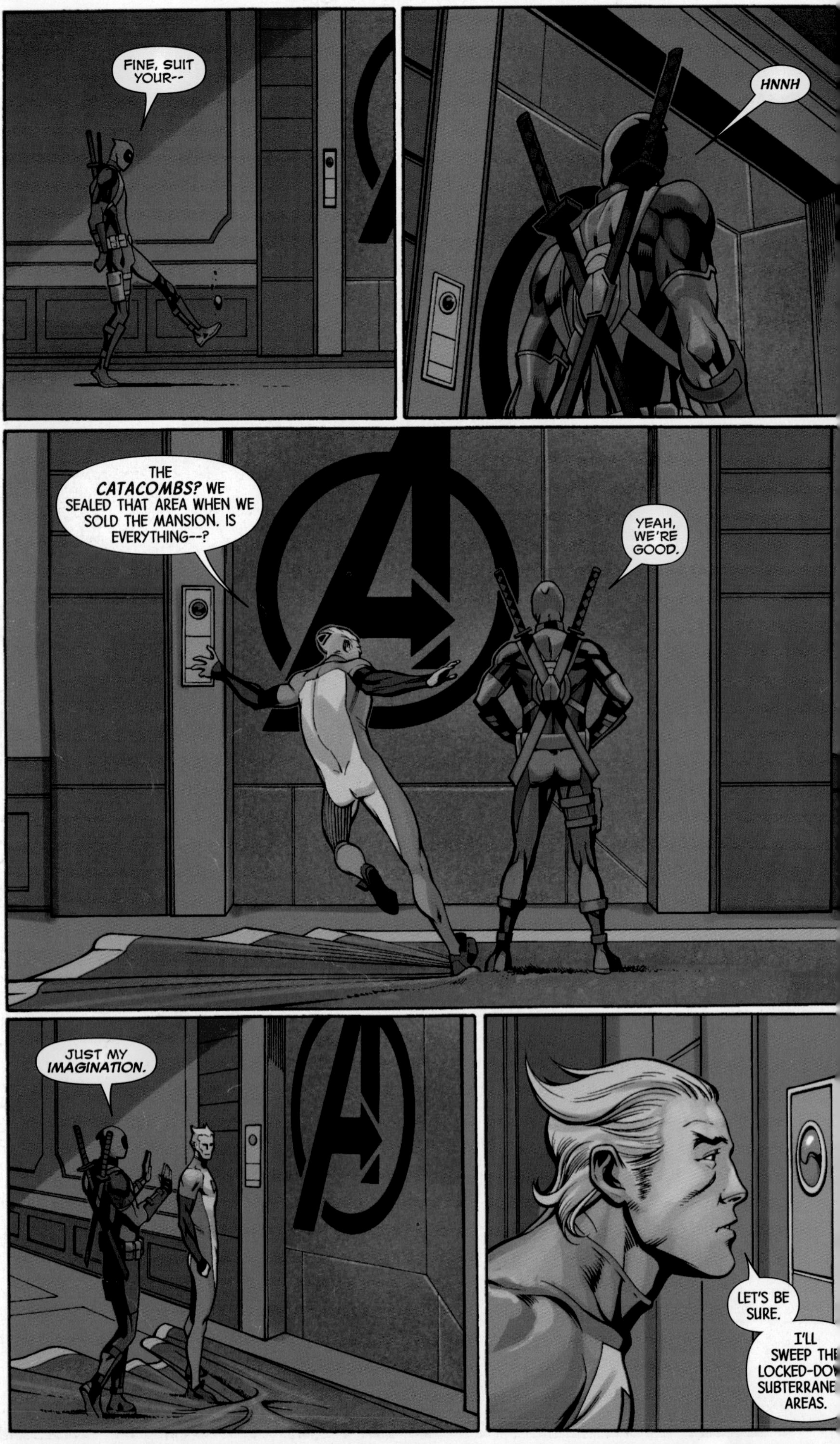
FINE, SUIT YOUR--
HNNH
THE CATACOMBS? WE SEALED THAT AREA WHEN WE SOLD THE MANSION. IS EVERYTHING--?
YEAH, WE'RE GOOD.
JUST MY IMAGINATION.
LET'S BE SURE.
I'LL SWEEP THE LOCKED-DOW SUBTERRANE AREAS.

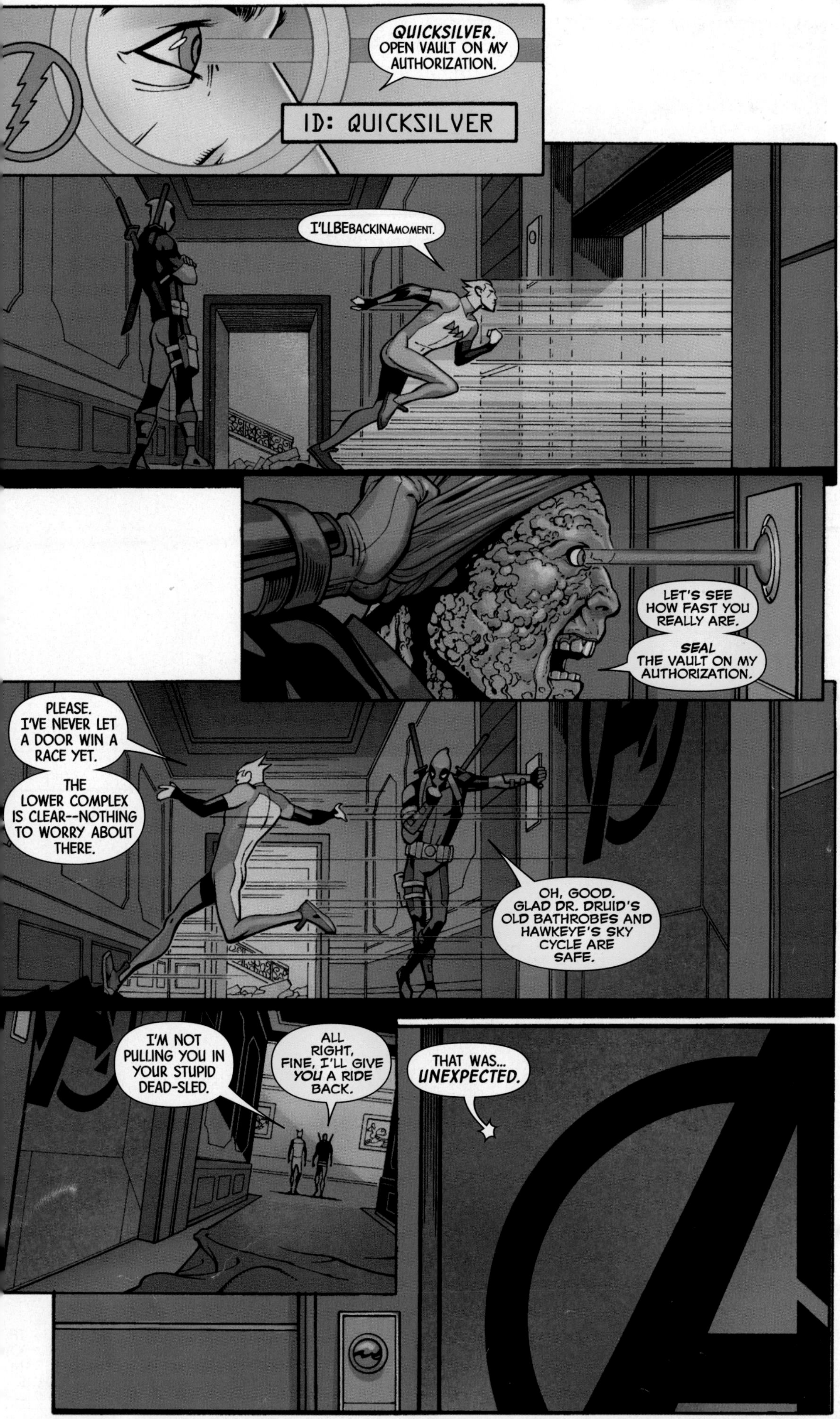
QUICKSILVER. OPEN VAULT ON MY AUTHORIZATION.
ID: QUICKSILVER
I'LLBEBACKINAMOMENT.
LET'S SEE HOW FAST YOU REALLY ARE.
SEAL THE VAULT ON MY AUTHORIZATION.
PLEASE. I'VE NEVER LET A DOOR WIN A RACE YET.
THE LOWER COMPLEX IS CLEAR--NOTHING TO WORRY ABOUT THERE.
OH, GOOD. GLAD DR. DRUID'S OLD BATHROBES AND HAWKEYE'S SKY CYCLE ARE SAFE.
I'M NOT PULLING YOU IN YOUR STUPID DEAD-SLED.
ALL RIGHT, FINE, I'LL GIVE YOU A RIDE BACK.
THAT WAS... UNEXPECTED.

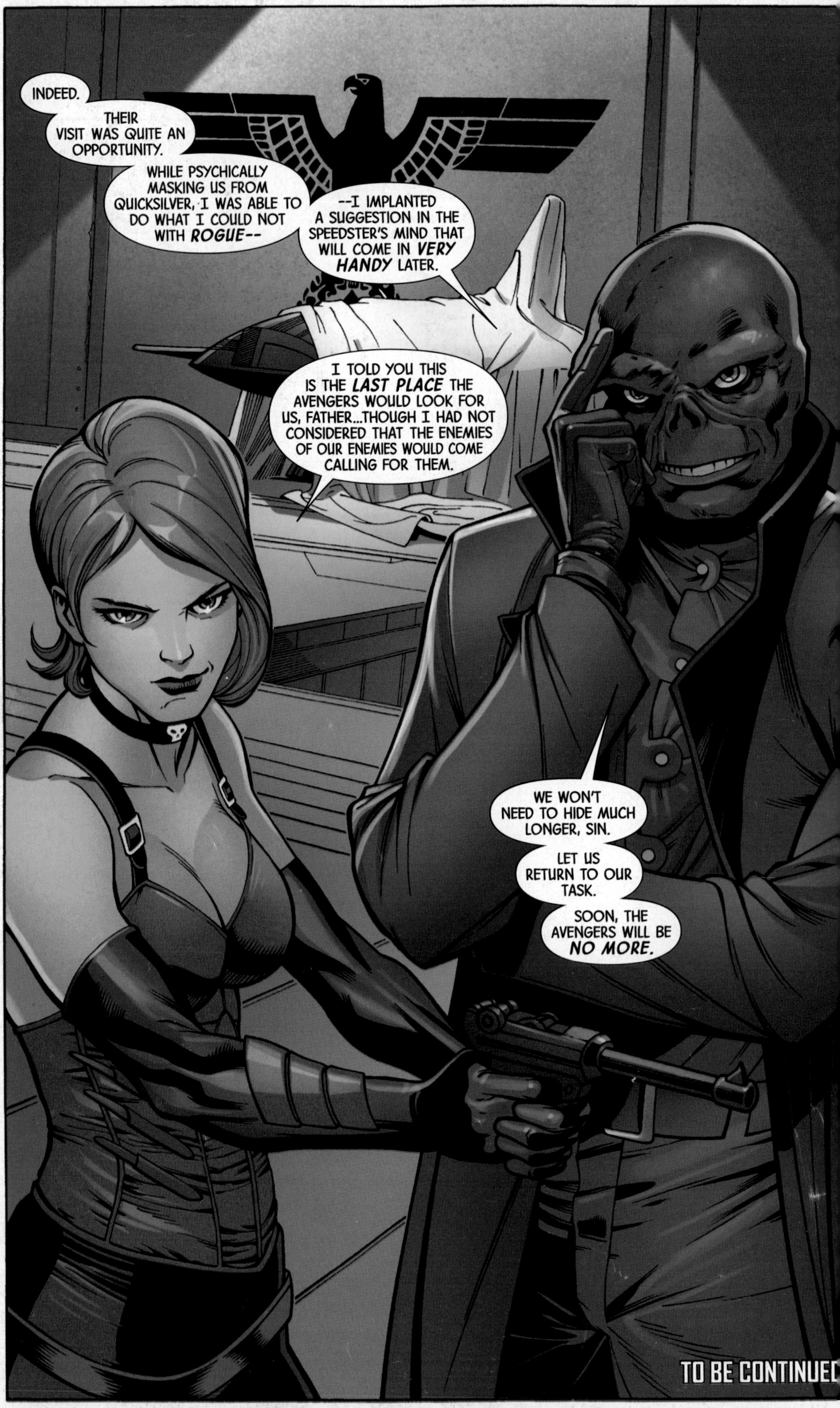
INDEED.
THEIR VISIT WAS QUITE AN OPPORTUNITY.
WHILE PSYCHICALLY MASKING US FROM QUICKSILVER, I WAS ABLE TO DO WHAT I COULD NOT WITH ROGUE--
--I IMPLANTED A SUGGESTION IN THE SPEEDSTER'S MIND THAT WILL COME IN VERY HANDY LATER.
I TOLD YOU THIS IS THE LAST PLACE THE AVENGERS WOULD LOOK FOR US, FATHER...THOUGH I HAD NOT CONSIDERED THAT THE ENEMIES OF OUR ENEMIES WOULD COME CALLING FOR THEM.
WE WON'T NEED TO HIDE MUCH LONGER, SIN.
LET US RETURN TO OUR TASK.
SOON, THE AVENGERS WILL BE NO MORE.
TO BE CONTINUED

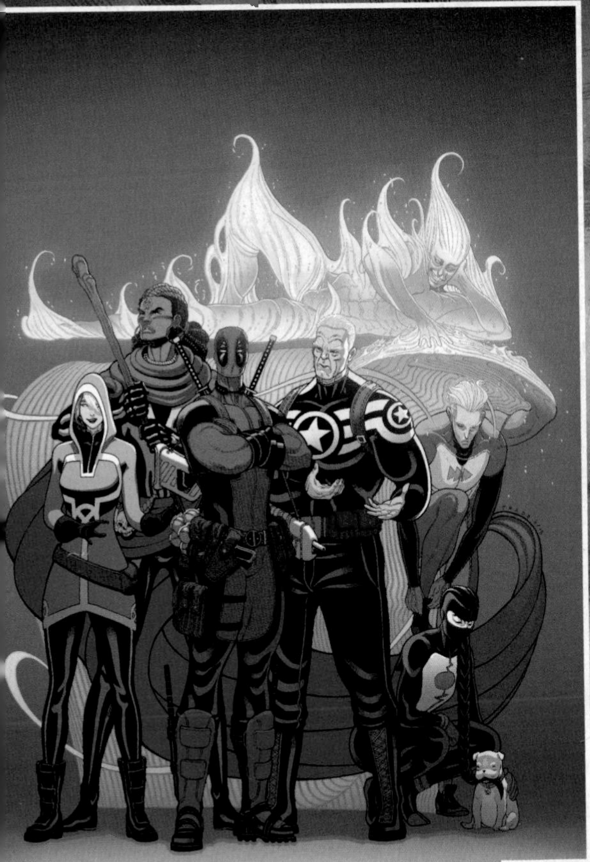

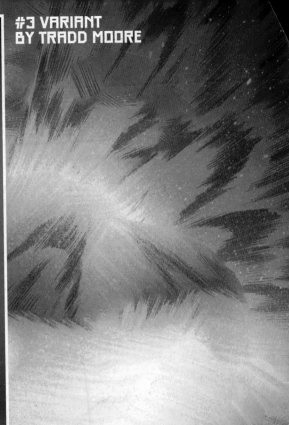

#3 VARIANT
BY TRADD MOORE

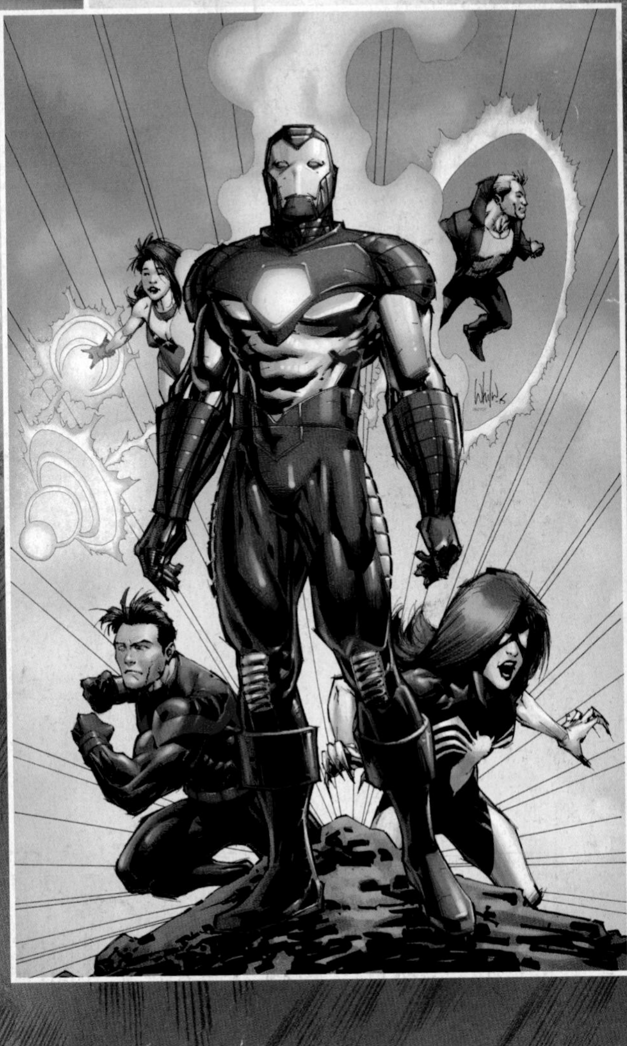

#3 MARVEL '92 VARIANT BY
WHILCE PORTACIO
& CHRIS SOTOMAYOR

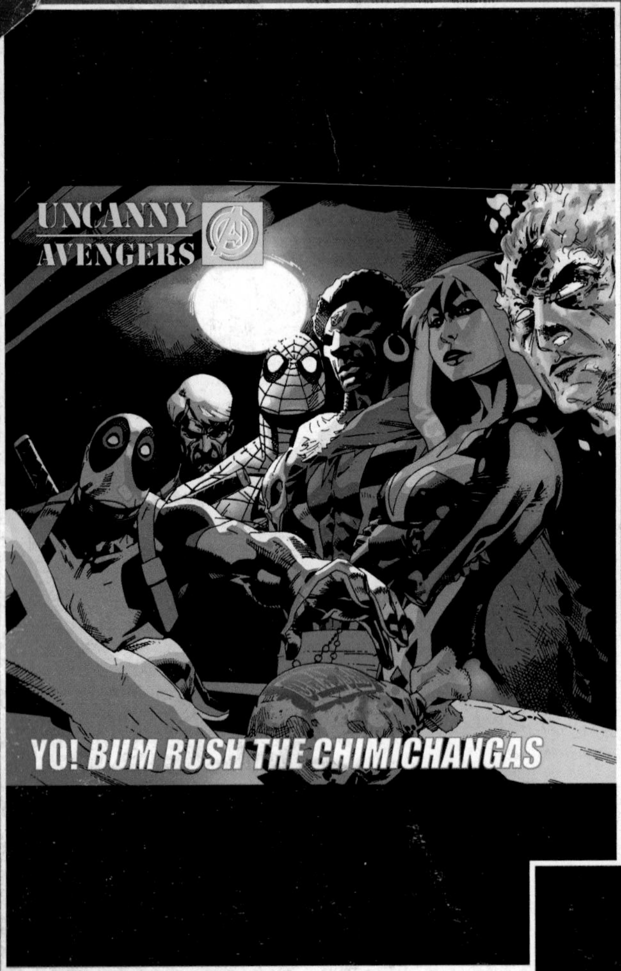
UNCANNY AVENGERS
YO! BUM RUSH THE CHIMICHANGAS

#1 HIP-HOP VARIANT BY JASON PEARSON

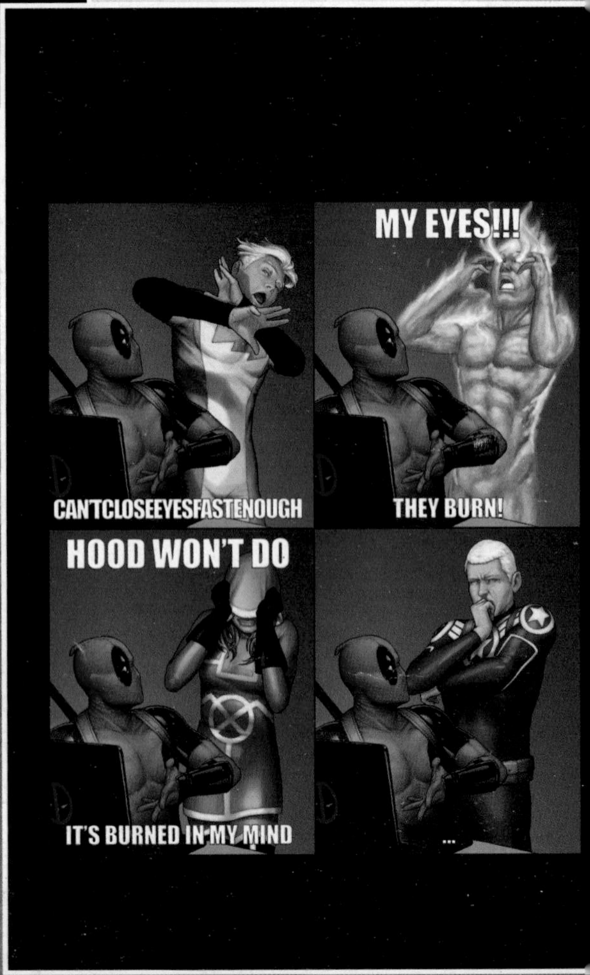
MY EYES!!!
CAN'TCLOSEEYESFASTENOUGH
THEY BURN!
HOOD WON'T DO
IT'S BURNED IN MY MIND
...

#4 DEADPOOL VARIANT BY JOHN TYLER CHRISTOPHER